The Spirit of Resistance in Music and Spoken Word of South Africa's Eastern Cape

The Spirit of Resistance in Music and Spoken Word of South Africa's Eastern Cape

Lindsay Michie

LEXINGTON BOOKS
Lanham • Boulder • New York • London

Published by Lexington Books
An imprint of The Rowman & Littlefield Publishing Group, Inc.
4501 Forbes Boulevard, Suite 200, Lanham, Maryland 20706
www.rowman.com

86-90 Paul Street, London EC2A 4NE

Copyright © 2021 by The Rowman & Littlefield Publishing Group, Inc.

All rights reserved. No part of this book may be reproduced in any form or by any electronic or mechanical means, including information storage and retrieval systems, without written permission from the publisher, except by a reviewer who may quote passages in a review.

British Library Cataloguing in Publication Information Available

Library of Congress Cataloging-in-Publication Data

Names: Eades, Lindsay Michie, 1962– author.
Title: The spirit of resistance in music and spoken word of South Africa's Eastern Cape / Lindsay Michie.
Description: Lanham : Lexington Books, 2021. | Includes bibliographical references and index.
Identifiers: LCCN 2021030822 (print) | LCCN 2021030823 (ebook) | ISBN 9781498576208 (cloth) | ISBN 9781498576215 (epub) | ISBN 9781498576222 (paper)
Subjects: LCSH: Music—Social aspects—South Africa—Eastern Cape—History. | Oral tradition—Social aspects—South Africa—Eastern Cape—History. | Government, Resistance to—South Africa—Eastern Cape—History. | Xhosa (African people)—South Africa—Eastern Cape—Social conditions. | Eastern Cape (South Africa)—Social conditions—History. | Eastern Cape (South Africa)—Race relations—History.
Classification: LCC DT2060 .E34 2021 (print) | LCC DT2060 (ebook) | DDC 968.75004963985—dc23
LC record available at https://lccn.loc.gov/2021030822
LC ebook record available at https://lccn.loc.gov/2021030823

For Audrey

Contents

Preface	ix
Acknowledgments	xi
Chapter 1: "We Create Our Own Language"	1
Chapter 2: "Unite Like a Ball of Scrapings": Early History to the 1850s	15
Chapter 3: "Turn Phalo's Land on Its Head": Late Nineteenth and Early Twentieth Centuries	45
Chapter 4: "You Sent Us the Light, We Sit in the Dark": 1920s–1940s	91
Chapter 5: "A Spirit That Could Not Be Broken": 1950s–1960s	125
Chapter 6: "A Land in Calamity's Shadow": 1970s–1980s	167
Chapter 7: "Our Bull Has Escaped from the Pound": 1990s to the Present	219
Bibliography	253
Index	267
About the Author	283

Preface

The primary aim of this volume is to act as a synthesis of much of the valuable work already carried out by numerous scholars and researchers on the intersection between music and spoken word and resistance in South Africa, and narrow the focus to the Eastern Cape. This region plays a unique role in the history of South African protest politics at the same time that its inhabitants have often suffered disproportionately in relation to the rest of the country, from the tragedy of the Cattle Killing Movement in the nineteenth century to the persistent poverty, spread of HIV-AIDS, and the outbreak of COVID-19 in the twentieth and twenty-first centuries. The intention of this study, consequently, is to introduce the general public to Eastern Cape performance artists, activists, organizations, and movements that used inventive and historical means to raise awareness of their plight and brought pressure to bear on the authorities and systems that caused it, all the while exhibiting the depth, originality, and inspiration of their culture. By including this region's contribution to the larger narrative of the connection between creativity, mass movements, and the forging of a modern African identity, and by concentrating to a large degree on the amaXhosa population, my hope is that more particular attention will be paid to those involved in this history and that future research will add to the story. Out of respect for the language and culture of the amaXhosa, I have as much as possible included the original isiXhosa versions of excerpts of spoken word and lyrics in each chapter as they are central to the true meaning and revolutionary message expressed in their history.

Acknowledgments

I owe a great debt of gratitude to the people of the Eastern Cape for inspiring this project. Many times, when I lived in Mthatha, I was asked by those I met there to please take their story back to my country and tell it as often as possible. Even as I continue to return to South Africa, I am still asked to do this and now feel it as a responsibility. I obviously cannot tell it exactly right. My perspective, however hard I strive to learn the languages of this region and attempt to be not only objective but sensitive to a people who have undergone four hundred years of serious oppression while responding in resolute and creative ways, is bound to be skewed by my own background, and by details and nuances I have failed to catch. The people of the Eastern Cape—the descendants of many of the historical figures in this book—will always know this history in a way that I will not. It is in their landscape, their experiences, and their personal stories passed down for generations. My telling the story is merely one attempt to keep it alive, share it with those outside of South Africa, and contribute to a rich collection of histories of this region that can and should be told in a myriad of ways.

With regard to the individuals who aided me in this project, many thanks go to Professor Russell Kaschula of the Languages Department at Rhodes University for assisting me in the initial stages of this research, and to African Music activist Dr. Boudina McConnachie, of Rhodes University, who also helped get me started and continued to provide encouragement and valuable resources and information throughout its evolution. I also received helpful advice from the director of the International Library of African Music Lee Watkins and former director Diane Thram and a great deal of assistance from the staff at ILAM. A very special thanks to Jeff Peires for giving me a job at UNITRA (Walter Sisulu University) all those years ago when I was fresh out of graduate school, for providing me more recently with insights and information on the early history of the AmaXhosa, particularly music associated with the Battle of Cacadu, for connecting me with Professor Jeff Opland, and for encouraging me in this project. Thanks also go to Zakes Mda for taking the time to reply to my emails and for his kind words and suggestions. I am always grateful to Dr. Gamede Vangeli who has supplied important information and been such a good friend and supporter of all these projects going all the way back to our early days together in the former Transkei, and to Kogie Thangavelu who was my traveling companion and cheered me along during much of my research in South Africa. Further thanks to Dumisa Mpupha for taking the time to share information and insights into the art of *izibongo*, as well as demonstrating his craft along with fellow *iimbongi* in memorable performances. Thanks also to Sylvia Bruinders of the South African College of Music for providing me with guidance and information on resistance music in general in South Africa, and to Lestie Hughes for finding me a copy of her Master's thesis, sharing her insights on music and the jazz scene in the Eastern Cape, and introducing me and my students to Patrick Pasha and Dudley Tito. I also owe a real debt of gratitude for all the previous research done on the Eastern Cape with regard to music, spoken word, and resistance, most especially that of Professor Jeff Opland whose monumental studies on oral poetry of the region contributed in no small degree to the sections on *izibongo* in this book and who also very kindly gave me valuable assistance in the use and translation of the work of prominent Eastern Cape *iimbongi*. Many thanks, also, to the family of *imbongi* David Yali-Manisi for playing an important role in the preservation of his work.

I would also like to thank the University of Lynchburg for providing me with the travel and research grants that helped to fund much of my work in South Africa, and Nelson Mandela University for all the help, support, information, hospitality and accommodation provided in recent years while I carried out research in the Eastern Cape, noting especially Francky and Aubrey Herbst, Peter Cunningham, Savo Heleta, Ongama Mtimka, Thandolwethu Nomarwayi, Ruby Xoliswa Zauka, Nuala Jansen, Divinia Pillay, Claire Raga, Tohiera Moodien, Kate Du Toit and Johannes van Rensburg. Thanks also to Logamurthie Athiemoolam and Ron Endley for connecting me with the Xhosa language program, as well as artist and activist Lionel Davis and Heather Mac for their insights on music and resistance in South Africa. I would also like to thank Sandile Zikalala and all the staff at the Steve Biko Heritage Site for providing important information, sources and assistance in this work, especially regarding Black Consciousness, and Charles Allen, Donzella Maupin, and Andreese Scott and the staff at Hampton University Archives for their valuable help in my research on musical connections between Lovedale and Hampton. Special thanks also to the staff at the Knight-Capron Library at the University of Lynchburg, particularly Jefferson

Harbin, Angela Arthur, Jennifer Horton, and Belinda Carroll, for helping me locate obscure references and sources, along with the staff at the University of Cape Town Archives, the staff at the Cory Library at Rhodes University, the staff at Fort Hare University, the staff at the University of Witwatersrand, and Leolyn Jackson at the University of the Western Cape. I am also very grateful to my editors Shelby Russell and Trevor Crowell for their guidance, flexibility, and patience, to production editor Jehanne Schweitzer, to my colleagues in the history department for their encouragement and support, and to Dan Eades and my siblings Forsyth Alexander, Emily Birch, and Ian Michie for their editorial advice.

None of this research would have been possible without the support and encouragement of the McConnachie family, especially Jenny McConnachie, who has hosted me on numerous occasions in my work, provided contacts, and listened to and encouraged me throughout, giving special insight gathered from her own experience of living and working in the Eastern Cape; I feel very lucky to have known Jenny and the McConnachies for all these years as they in no small way represent a significant part of my relationship with the Eastern Cape and they are a big part of the reason I initially came to South Africa. I would also like to give special recognition to "philosopher of the streets" Bradley Levack, Judy and Simon Oliver, and my good friends Shaddly and Ruwaidah Rajaal for their unending kindness, as well as all the women (and Zolani Ganya) at the Emmanuel Advice Care Centre in Kwa Noxolo—especially NoPinkie—and the "Mamas" at Red Location Backpackers for sharing their culture and history. Many thanks to Deirdre and Troy Fredericks for providing memories of the Eastern Cape and, as always, to family members Marcus Sandidge, Trina Sandidge, and Audrey Michie for their great help and encouragement.

Finally, I would like to acknowledge all the formal and informal musical and poetic "happenings" I was so fortunate to experience during my years in and subsequent visits to the Eastern Cape, and give a special appreciation for the creative spirit of this region and the infectious warmth of its population.

Chapter 1

"We Create Our Own Language"

The history of South Africa since the arrival of the Europeans in 1652 has been one marked by conquest, oppression and segregation based on the Western concept of race. As exercise of control passed from the mercantile policies of the Dutch East India Company in the seventeenth and eighteenth centuries, to the industrial and imperial policies of the British in the nineteenth and early twentieth centuries, to the "separate development" policies of the apartheid era; violence, restrictive legislation, and cultural repression have defined the unfolding relationship between white authorities and black populations in that region. Along with that history has been one of steady resistance on the part of those conquered and segregated by the colonial and apartheid systems, and the powerful tools of music and spoken word repeatedly served as weapons used to fight back against physical, psychological, and cultural invasion. The fluid relationship between song, rhythm, and spoken word that marks the long history and culture of the people of the Eastern Cape of South Africa has acted consistently in the service of protest from the colonial period through the apartheid and post-apartheid years, and illustrates the strong combination of creativity and militancy as defining characteristics of the amaXhosa and the related groups of people occupying the different areas that make up this region. The Eastern Cape, from early on, formed a fundamental component of the story of strong resistance to systematic subjugation and separation in South Africa.

    Although it has a geographic definition, because of its people and its history, the "Eastern Cape" as a social, cultural, and political concept is arguably borderless and spreads out across regions of South Africa. It has its African roots in the societies of the Khoi and the San people stretching across the southern Cape and in the migrating Nguni people that came south from other parts of sub-Saharan Africa. The Africans of this region of South Africa are historically grouped under the heading amaXhosa, although there are Xhosa-speaking people who do not strictly fall into this category. As a result of colonial and apartheid resettlement, dislocation, and the labor demands and restrictive policies of the nineteenth and twentieth centuries, however, many Xhosa people who were not born in the Eastern Cape were forced to live there, and many who were born there were forced to migrate elsewhere. This history means that much of the development of music and spoken word of the Eastern Cape is not just concentrated in its defined borders, but reaches into the cities in other parts of South Africa and mixes with a multitude of influences while still maintaining its own flavor. It has also spread to other parts of the world, particularly through the era of exile of many poets and musicians during apartheid. Miriam Makeba, whose father was Xhosa, wrote of the importance of holding on to her culture in performances: "If I sang my music from home, if I sang the music of my roots, only then could I be someone . . . although I was physically away, mentally I stayed at home."[1]

Similar to the role of music in resistance movements in other parts of the world, songs and oral performance in the service of protest and revolution in the Eastern Cape tend to come in three connected forms: those that tell stories of oppression, those that share coded messages among the oppressed, and those that unite a population in public and community gatherings in a shared expression of resistance and defiance. All three of these forms usually act as a critique of authority and often as a call to action. A fourth form of protest that is equally powerful, although more subtle, is resistance to and criticism of authority through songs and spoken word that work to preserve identity and culture. This latter form of music and oral poetry represents a current that runs through the other three types, making the statement to outside influences (whether viewed as positive or negative): we might adapt, we might resist, but we will find a way to hold on to our fundamental core.

The beauty and power of both music and spoken word as expressions of resistance lie in the simplicity of expression and economy of words that often propel a movement forward or provide a more dynamic and motivating message than a pamphlet, book, or political speech. In music and spoken word of the Eastern Cape of South Africa, the long and rich tradition of protest and criticism defies strict categorization and moves among different forms, messages, and double meanings with a flexibility that has stymied the West from the time that Europeans first encountered the San, Khoi-khoi, and Nguni people of southern Africa. The types of protest as expressed in the music and spoken word (often "praise-singing" or *izibongo*) of the Eastern Cape, despite this fluidity, can still be recognized even as they overlap, with songs and oral poetry criticizing authorities and systems in multi-faceted ways. In many instances, a song may start out as the fundamental expression of a situation, feeling, or ritual, and then be modified to fit the changing times or circumstances that have caused hardship and injustice. In the early history of European settlement in the Eastern Cape, for example, the mission stations that worked to convert Africans to Christianity suppressed musical activity to the point where the hymn was the only choice of outlet. Different groups of Xhosa people would then express a form of cultural resistance by adapting the hymn to other topics; it would become a work song, a love song, a wedding song, or merely a way to perform for pleasure. Since Western missionaries usually could not understand the tonal subtleties of African languages, secular messages could be grafted onto Western texts, such as using traditional proverbs or alluding to pre-colonial customs. One famous example that played a key role initially within the context of the Eastern Cape Frontier Wars and colonization is *"Intsimbi ka Ntsikana"* ("Nstikana's bells and Ntsikana's song") which is a call to worship. Set to a Xhosa tune, this piece served as a freedom song dating back to the War of Mlanjeni of 1850 during the period of conflict between the British and the Xhosa people, and the spirit of Ntsikana Gaba (the song's composer and an early Christian convert) was revived in the 1920s by the Industrial and Commercial Workers Union as a way to combine Xhosa nationalism and Christian separatism. Ntsikana appears in many discussions of the intersection of European and Xhosa culture, particularly music, during the late eighteenth and early nineteenth centuries, and his spirit is continually revived in music and oral poetry of the twentieth and twenty-first centuries.

The division between accepted canons of culture and absorption of outside influences among the amaXhosa is one that became prominent during the Frontier Wars, particularly the years of the Great Cattle Killing of 1856–57, an event that devastated Africans of the Eastern Cape and led to the ultimate defeat of the Xhosa-speaking people of that region. The division that emerged was later defined as two groups of people: the "school people" who were those converted by European missionaries, and the "red people" who were those who held on to indigenous beliefs and practices that were developing before the arrival of the Europeans. This divide continued to play out in the history of Eastern Cape music in the twentieth century and became further complicated by the ideology of "separate development" central to the policies of colonialism and apartheid. The approach of the "school people," who were often uneasy allies with the British missionaries and colonizers in the nineteenth century, became a threatening component of the African population in the twentieth century as they were more open to outside Western musical influences such as American jazz, the blues, and Western hymns, and they used these musical styles to communicate their struggles against oppression. The "red people" who strove to maintain the indigenous aspects of their culture in the face of European encroachment also present a contradiction, as their "traditions" were observed and defined through colonial and apartheid interpretations in the twentieth century and upheld as a means to maintain division within South Africa by claiming to preserve the "true culture" of

Africans. This policy included encouraging "Bantu songs" and praise-singing in opposition to the "corrupting influence" of jazz and modern music.

The period of the Frontier Wars and colonization also revealed the amaXhosa's fundamental suspicion of and resistance to the books and the written word brought by the European missionaries and officials. Initial exposure to writing came through the Bible and with that Bible, more often than not, came the gun. Descriptions of books or letters working hand-in-hand with a rifle to conquer communities and take their land appeared in Xhosa spoken words and songs during the nineteenth century. These descriptions carried into twentieth-century music and praise-singing where written words damaged and restricted the people of the Eastern Cape through treaties, legislation, and pass books. The spoken word and song were consistently viewed as more honest forms of expression, whereas the written word, like the white population, was often seen as untrustworthy.

The art of the *imbongi* or praise singer has remained an important element of Xhosa history. Nelson Mandela, for example, had his own personal *imbongi* when he was elected president of South Africa and *iimbongi* have served as a standard part of the Xhosa chief's entourage from early times. One of the necessary requirements of this art from the early history of the amaXhosa was a kind of patriotism that required critical thinking and true awareness of the circumstances of the times; a loyalty not to the chief, but to the beliefs and principles that he and his community stood for. An *imbongi* would, therefore, serve as a conduit between the chief and his people; a political commentator who did not merely praise the chief but communicated what was right and what needed to change or be fixed. This meant he had to compose his own poems or songs—often spontaneously. In the early twentieth century three prominent Xhosa poets of the Eastern Cape continued the culture of *iimbongi* through spoken and written word: Samuel Edward Drune Mqhayi, Nontsizi Mgqwetho, and John Solilo produced poems and praise songs that addressed colonization in their region and the hardship and confusion it caused among their people.

The role of the *imbongi* has often placed emphasis on impromptu performance as opposed to one that is rehearsed, and criticism plays an important part. An *imbongi* could criticize his people and even swear directly at a leader. In the periods of colonialism and apartheid, however, the role of mediator between chief and people could not be conducted as it had been in the past and the *iimbongi* were faced with two stark choices: conform to the system and offer only praise for the leaders that were usually installed and supported by white authorities; or continue to speak truth to power. With the first choice, the *imbongi* would lose credibility and be reduced to a mere entertainer. With the second choice, the *imbongi* would likely be arrested and detained or would go into exile—the same choices made by many singer-songwriters of the apartheid era. There was another possibility, though, connected to the tradition of preserving identity and speaking in allegory that acted as code. The *iimbongi* often found ways to criticize oppression during colonialism and apartheid without the authorities understanding what was being sung or spoken. Praise poems would be performed with beautiful lyrics and nuanced meaning so that even those who spoke isiXhosa would not immediately understand and would have to ask what the message was. "In a way," contemporary *imbongi* Dumisa Mpupha states, "we create our own language, our own words." Mpupha's description of this type of performance is a perfect example of the reinvention of past identity and practice to suit the present, and he finishes this explanation with the simple declaration, "You can't kill our spirit."[2]

The history of the territory of the Eastern Cape of South Africa informs much of the history of the culture of its people. The region encompasses the two former "homelands" of Transkei and Ciskei, and the Eastern Cape Province of the former Republic of South Africa. After the defeat of the amaXhosa and related peoples at the end of the nineteenth century, their absorption into the British Cape Colony came largely through the Glen Grey Act of 1894 which basically forced Xhosa men into work on the farms and mines of the Eastern Cape through a labor tax. The Natives Land Act of 1913 created "Native Reserves," as part of the formation of regional segregation that began with colonization and became entrenched with apartheid, and different areas in the Eastern Cape (usually the poorest) were carved out to represent "black spots" for Xhosa-speaking people. Large sections of the Eastern Cape, therefore, acted as labor reserves for the mines, factories, and farms of white South Africa. In the mines and urban areas where black labor was required yet severely restricted, there grew up a mishmash of cultural influences, especially musical, that the Xhosa migrant workers strongly influenced, having already fused Western influences with indigenous practices in the Cape Colony mission stations and towns established during the previous century. As David B. Coplan points out in his definitive work on black South African city music and theater *In Township Tonight!*, urban performing arts represent not the diluting or destruction of a tradition, but the creation of a culture: "part of a search for autonomy in an environment in which people have little control over anything except a culturally guided sense of collective humanity and individual self."[3] The emerging forms of performance and music of the first part of the nineteenth century in the cities and towns of the Eastern Cape, such as vaudeville, jazz, *marabi*, and *kwela*, and the mingling of Xhosa spoken word, dance, and music with other African plus Western influences (particularly American) in the large labor-concentrated areas of Johannesburg and Cape Town fed a new type of cultural resistance to oppression and segregation that became the heartbeat of the struggle against apartheid. In the Eastern Cape, the city of Port Elizabeth became one of South Africa's "magnetic jazz poles" and maintained this role up through the 1990s. The harmony of jazz in this region was influenced by Khoisan musical bow songs and the local heritage of this area continued in different manifestations; for example, in *mbaqanga, tula n'divile,* and modern jazz. The fusion of musical influences with the fast pace of town life, and black opposition to the increasingly oppressive government policies of the 1940s, 1950s, and 1960s was expressed in the explosive energy of this urban music. As Lewis Nkosi described it, South African jazz was "carrying the very stench of the brawling bawdy life of the urban African townships. It is a music which has its roots in a life of insecurity in which a single moment of self-realization of love, light, and movement, is extraordinarily more important than a whole of a lifetime."[4] Township jazz in places like New Brighton in Port Elizabeth became an agency for hope and creativity used as a counterpoint to the bleak situation of being a black musician in the era of apartheid. The musical style of township jazz, with all its local South African influences, was a form of resistance; a culturally eclectic cosmopolitan weapon wielded against apartheid's emphasis on "tribal origins" and separation by rigid definitions of race and heritage. As New Brighton jazz musician Lulu Gontsana described it, jazz was studiously absorbed by listening and then merged into a distinct South African style and identity that represented "a thinking environment" that could not be reduced to apartheid's "ethnic cubicles."[5] According to Gontsana, "It was not jazz to play only, it was how to be a human being and to learn to stand on your own."[6]

Marabi was an urban African form of music involving Xhosa instrumentation that helped to combine the styles of "colored" urban performers who had picked up the influence of *vastrap* from white Afrikaner households, black American music, and local African sources that merged in the townships. The peculiarly Xhosa version was known in Johannesburg as *tula n'divile*—Xhosa folk melodies played on the keyboard—and was represented in the Eastern Cape by musicians such as Boet Gashe, who played *itswari* (soirée) music in Queenstown. The emphasis on indigenous influences such as Xhosa lyrics and melodies on South African jazz music produced the style known as *mbaqanga*. *Kwela* represented a cultural response to the rise of industry in South Africa in the 1930s and 1940s; the combination of urbanization and Westernization presented a crisis of identity for the new black working class and the identity that emerged fused African-American music with indigenous elements. Similar to *marabi,* repetition acted as one of the most African characteristics of *kwela* which became popular among the black working class. The black population as a whole responded to the music as recognition that an answer to oppression by race needed these types of creative expression. The formation of the ANC Youth League in the 1940s by Nelson Mandela,

Anton Lembede, Oliver Tambo, Walter Sisulu, and Ashby Mda, among others, represented a push for an alliance between the black elite and working class, and the sharing of "Africanness" as expressed in musical styles such as *mbaqanga* and *kwela* became the basis of a new ideology.

The positive value of identifying as African went hand-in-hand with a demand for political change. The continuing rise of African nationalism—coinciding with independence movements throughout Africa in the 1950s and 1960s—challenged the apartheid government's defining and restricting African identity to that of "tribal" and "rural" by creating this cross-cultural urban identity. The irony of this cross-pollination as a means to stay united and hold on to a shared identity, was that the music that became popular in the cities and townships held strong elements of colonizing influences. The tendency towards multi-part vocal and instrumental participation in the jazz styles of Port Elizabeth in the Eastern Cape, for example, superficially seemed modeled on American big band jazz. This was partially true, but fundamentally this music was also based on over 100 years of choir-singing in the South African Christian and workers' communities. Just as African nationalists were employing the language of democracy they had been taught in mission schools and combining it with their own aspirations to challenge white rule, African musicians were using the language of Western music also taught in the mission schools and combining it with indigenous memory to reinvent a unified cultural identity. Jazz musicians from the Eastern Cape such as Dudley Tito, Patrick Pasha, "The Soul Jazzmen," and Chris McGregor incorporated all the elements that created a unique form of South African urban music, while two significant playwrights from this region Athol Fugard and Gibson Kente further enriched the performance culture of South Africa through subtle and direct expressions of the hardships imposed by apartheid.

Assessing the rise of township music as a danger to the ideology and efficiency of the system of separate development, apartheid authorities devised increasingly rigid policies that targeted the cross-pollination, mixed performances, and united messages of songs and performances of South African cities. The Group Areas Act, Separate Amenities Act, Bantu Education Act, manipulation of culture through "homelands" policies and establishment of a Bantu radio station, together with regulation purposely designed to disrupt black city life such as laws forbidding Africans to perform at places where liquor was served—all created a stranglehold on the development of township life, including performance and music. As one Xhosa woman stated, however, "[the present] is built in the womb of the old,"[7] and a new generation of music that falls under the large heading of "freedom songs" arose in South Africa in the 1950s, and 1960s, whether resurrected from earlier times or written in direct response to the tightening of oppression through apartheid laws and legislation. Xhosa activists and Xhosa poets and musicians (often one and the same) contributed to this dynamic form of cultural resistance and many songs from this period act as historical hallmarks of protest in South Africa. Sung with raised fists at meetings, demonstrations, strikes, boycotts and funerals, *"Nkosi Sikelel' iAfrika,"* for example, was written by Xhosa teacher Enoch Mankayi Sontonga in 1897 (with additional verses later composed by Xhosa poet Samuel Mqhayi), and became the defining anthem of all gatherings in opposition to oppression. Songs that directly challenged the policies of apartheid such as *"Naants' Indod 'Emnyama Verwoerd"* ("Watch Out, Verwoerd") and *"Izakunyatheli Afrika"* ("Africa Is Going to Trample on You") written by Eastern Cape activist Vuyisile Mini in the 1950s and 1960s also became popular, with lyrics that spelled out the frustrations and increasingly militant response of those joining the African National Congress and Pan African Congress in growing numbers before these organizations were banned in 1960.

As a result of the Sharpeville Massacre of 1960, the subsequent fierce crackdown on anti-apartheid activity, and the arrest and imprisonment of Mandela, and other prominent anti-apartheid leaders, many musicians, *iimbongi*, and performers went into exile, and resistance as a whole went underground. Protest music and spoken word during this time was muted but not silenced, with artists raising consciousness overseas and freedom songs and poems maintaining their messages at home in secret meeting places. Songs of lament often marked this period, such as *"Bahleli Bonke"* sung by Miriam Makeba, which asked the question, "Where are the leaders?" naming Mandela, Sisulu and other prominent comrades, before answering, "They are all sitting in jail." *"Thina Sizwe"* expressed the mourning of "We, the black nation" for the land "stolen from us by the white man"; while *"Senzeni Na?"* asked the simple question, "What have we done?" Underground activity carried on through the military wing of the ANC Mkhonto We Sizwe (MK) and through Poqo, the armed wing of the PAC. Poqo was the first black political organization in South Africa that openly accepted the taking of human life as part of its strategy and purposely established the PAC as manifestly more militant than the ANC. In the early 1960s Poqo concentrated much of its efforts in the Eastern Cape, targeting and killing suspected police informants including a number of Transkeian authorities who were viewed as government stooges, and Poqo members sang Azanian Liberation Songs as part of their movement, such as *Izwe Lethu* (This Land Is Ours).

The late 1960s and 1970s witnessed the rise of the Black Consciousness movement led by Eastern Cape activist Stephen Biko and newly politicized youth found expression of their ideology of black celebration in music and performance. The Malombo Jazz Makers went on a domestic tour with Biko as part of the "Into the Heart of Negritude" theater production, an articulation of African National culturalism and the aims of Black Consciousness.

The increase in student and worker activism that reached a climax with the 1976 Soweto Uprising, and the achievement of independence in border states such as Mozambique, Angola, and Zimbabwe, helped to reignite and fuel the struggle. Young people were leaving South Africa to join the guerilla armies of MK in neighboring countries and raising the level of disruption and sabotage within South Africa. There was a new fearlessness—almost recklessness—among the young people of South Africa in the anti-apartheid struggle and this was reflected in and propelled by music and spoken word. The cultural roots of black South Africa were revived during this time as young radicals of the 1970s in regions that included the Eastern Cape took a second look at the authentic lore of their histories that had been formerly scorned by urban sophisticates or tamed and incorporated into the system by apartheid authorities. Tradition was revisited as a source not of unchanging and passive separation, but of creativity and unity. The government response of further repression intensified artistic rebellion even as it provoked more political resistance increasingly buoyed by global attention and influences. There arose an impatience in the younger generation of activists that challenged what it perceived as passivity in the resistance of the 1960s, including the songs. Laments such as "*Senzenina*" fully implicated the Afrikaners in oppression as the agents and architects of apartheid; but the song had, to the newly politicized youth, an uneasy mixture of pain and protest. As one activist expressed it, "There is no more time for wimpish lament, self-pity, begging or praying."[8]

Jazz musicians played songs that challenged apartheid during the 1970s in unlicensed music clubs, primarily in Johannesburg, but also in cities in the Eastern Cape, and African fusion music became popular, combining elements of jazz, blues, and funk, often adding "Afrobeat," the contemporary African style of music created by Nigerian musician Fela Kuti. The existence of many clubs, however, was often short-lived because they could not stand up to the constant raids and restrictions or could not afford to pay off the township police, as well as hold together audiences that were continually intimidated by the authorities. One of the most significant of the ANC's projects formed in exile during this time was the Mayibuye Cultural Ensemble which was based in London. Established in 1975, this ensemble performed throughout Europe with considerable success, incorporating narrative, poetry, and song to communicate a message against the apartheid regime and raise international awareness about the situation in South Africa. The ensemble was also a starting point for developing practical ways to incorporate cultural activity in the struggle for national liberation, particularly the mobilization of music. Its role as a project in exile was eventually taken over in the 1980s by the Amandla Cultural Ensemble, later viewed by the ANC as one of its most significant achievements in the area of cultural opposition. Much of Amandla's repertoire drew from the culture of exile and MK camps, including many freedom songs originating among the amaXhosa that had been created or revived with more militant lyrics added.

In the midst of these developments in South Africa, the homelands of Transkei and Ciskei in the Eastern Cape held a strange and contradictory position with regard to political and cultural resistance. The landscape of geographic segregation had already been established in 1913 with the Natives Land Act, and after the official launching of the system of apartheid in 1948, these regions became "Bantustans," where people deemed indigenous to these areas (the amaXhosa and isiXhosa speakers) were required to reside by law. Transkei, for example, was to become "black" with no more white residents. Greater responsibility was given to the Transkeians as the South African government in Pretoria began to attempt the systematic dispossession of whites in this and other homelands. In 1963 "self-government" was granted to Transkei and the façade of government set up under Kaiser (K.D.) Mathanzima. By the mid-1970s only the larger towns of Mthatha and Butterworth in Transkei remained what were called "white spots" where whites were legally allowed to live. With the granting of so-called "independence" to Transkei in 1976, the institutions of racial segregation, job reservation, pass laws, the Immorality Act and an all-white municipal government in Mthatha were dismantled. Africans began taking over white jobs, more Africans began moving to Mthatha, public facilities began desegregating, new laws prohibiting discrimination were introduced and Africans were allowed to own property in previously white neighborhoods. Transkei also adopted "*Nkosi Sikilel' iAfrika*" as its national anthem. The mass support for this form of separate development quickly faded, however, when the reality of the true nature of independence sunk in, not least in the loss of jobs for Transkeians in the Republic (since they were now foreigners), the continued and increasing inequality of distribution of resources between the homelands and the Republic, and the high rate of poverty and poor health care in the Transkei for which the South African government was no longer officially responsible.

As revolt and resistance against apartheid expanded in the 1970s and 1980s, Transkei managed to contribute in significant ways to opposition, ironically possessing more freedom to criticize through her independent status. Although Mathanzima operated as a puppet of the South African regime and maintained a ban on all anti-apartheid organizations, Transkei became an underground stronghold of the ANC and the majority of the Transkei population—especially the professionals—were known to be "card-carrying" members of the ANC and PAC. The establishment of African responsibility and authority in Transkei had given rise to an articulate middle-class African elite which could express dissent—social, political, and cultural—and provide means for resistance in the Republic. This resistance was displayed in labor unions and student activism in schools and training colleges, and at the University of Transkei (UNITRA—now Walter Sisulu University). It also contained a powerful and sustaining element of cultural protest expressed in freedom songs sung at demonstrations, music and performances at gatherings and events, and praise-singing that challenged the authority of those viewed as government patsies such as Mathanzima.

Meanwhile, the 1980s in South Africa as a whole marked a time of greater internal disruption and greater international pressure on the apartheid government. Prime Minister P. W. Botha combined a superficial easing of apartheid restrictions with tightening security and a raised level of violence against the resistance movement. Protesters took to the streets in increasing numbers and greater confidence despite the repressive tactics employed against them. Songs and spoken word during this time were more intentionally political but their messages were often still disguised in metaphor and hidden messages. Eastern Cape poet Alfred Temba Qabula, for example, adapted traditional praise songs to spoken word performances about issues of union organization and cultural resistance, using images such as that of a train to express moving forward in unity.[9] *Iimbongi* Melikhaya Mbutuma, David Yali-Manisi, and Bongani Sitole at different times challenged the status quo in Transkei in the 1970s and 1980s, condemning Mathanzima for his cooperation with the South African government through praise poems at rallies and demonstrations that applied ancient imagery to contemporary circumstances.

A prominent feature of protest song at rallies, funerals, and demonstrations in South Africa during the 1980s was the *toyi-toyi*, a jogging dance that accompanied freedom songs and chants and is said to have originated on the guerilla training grounds in Zimbabwe to keep up the endurance and spirits of freedom fighters. The 1980s in South Africa are often referred to as the time of "The People's War," when songs were designed to articulate a new urgency and a new direction, and the *toyi-toyi* reflected this. As activists described it, to participate in this combination of dance and song was to experience a moment of empowerment and a brief understanding of what it truly means to be free. The *toyi-toyi* became part of all boycotts and demonstrations in the Eastern Cape, particularly among students and workers in Mthatha as activists became increasingly confident in their challenge to apartheid. The *toyi-toyi*'s expression of militant resistance grew even more prominent in Transkei after the military coup in 1987 that brought General Bantu Holomisa to power, a benign dictator with strong ties to the ANC who was more sympathetic to dissension than the Mathanzima family and less willing to bow to the dictates of the South African government.

The 1980s further marked a period of increased international attention to and involvement in the politics of South Africa, and music and performance played a large role in this development. The cultural boycott of South Africa by the United Nations gained momentum and was more effectively enforced during this time. In 1981, the Associated Actors and Artists of America voted unanimously that none of its members should perform in South Africa, and the purpose of the boycott broadened from simply not performing for segregated audiences to ending apartheid altogether. The ban also encompassed groups from South Africa performing in other countries, which brought mixed reactions from black South African musicians. One positive result, however, was a greater concentration on South African music at home, including in the Eastern Cape, such as the Amampondo Drummers whose name comes from the Pondoland kingdom of the Eastern Cape. The band used marimbas to make music reflecting their roots and became widely popular in the 1980s, producing an album with Archbishop Desmond Tutu and playing at Mandela's 70th birthday concert at Wembley Stadium in England.

The strain of "The People's War" and the economic consequences of disinvestment and sanctions combined with a suffering domestic economy led the South African government to face the fact in the late 1980s that the system of apartheid was becoming increasingly impractical—even as white authorities still struggled to completely acknowledge its injustice. F. W. de Klerk took over the leadership of the National Party and government, and the first major decision of his office was to announce the unbanning of the ANC and other opposition parties and the release of Nelson Mandela along with fellow activists. Once Mandela gained his freedom, one of the first places he visited was Transkei, the place of his birth and childhood. At each place that he gave an address—on arrival at Mthatha Airport, at rallies at UNITRA and at a soccer field on the outskirts of Mthatha—he was met by song, *toyi-toyiing*, and praise-singing. *Iimbongi* such as Sitole celebrated through oral poetry the return of what were considered the real and legitimate leaders to positions of authority and the new experience of real freedom of speech. At each event where he spoke, Mandela demonstrated the fundamental feature of song and spoken word in Xhosa (and most African) culture, call and response, by raising his fist and proclaiming "*Amandla!*" ("Power!"), to which the crowd would reply, "*Ngawethu!*" ("It is ours!"). Music and spoken word continued to play a role in politics in South Africa during this time, but it was a role that reflected the trepidation mingled with hope that accompanied the painful transition toward democracy, and the challenges facing a movement that until this time had always occupied a place of opposition. Fierce political rivalry arose between the ANC centered in the Eastern Cape and the Natal-based Inkatha Freedom Party—a rivalry secretly fueled by the South African Defense Force—and many feared that the country was teetering on the brink of civil war. Negotiations addressing a new form of government moved through maddening phases of short progression followed by stalling due to outbreaks of violence or assassinations such as that of Chris Hani, the ANC leader tragically killed by right-wing extremists. Music and oral poetry continued to help fuel the unraveling of apartheid and movement towards a new dispensation, not least at demonstrations and funerals that represented the continuing conflict, and songs and poetry often expressed frustration with the process of transition and the continued violence. Xhosa singer and composer Sophie Mgcina argued, "Music is storytelling. It should conscientize and talk about [the things] that are happening in this country. . . . We're not free yet; we've just been liberated."[10]

With the formation of a new Democratic South Africa in the 1994 elections, there came a re-defining of the regions within that country that established the former homelands of Transkei and Ciskei as part of the Eastern Cape region. This region had voted overwhelmingly for the ANC with Mandela as president, but, in the twenty-three years since that election, economic difficulties in areas such as the former Transkei have kept alive the spirit of protest against oppression and its expression in music and spoken word of the problems of a country still dealing with the legacies of apartheid such as inequality of healthcare, housing, jobs, and education. Contemporary artists work to revive the important role of the Eastern Cape in the South African jazz scene and Eastern Cape oral poetry and rap music has continued the tradition of criticizing and challenging authority. Organizations such as the Fingo Revolution Movement (FRM), for example, have acted as a voice of resistance against what is perceived as a failing state. The movement involves a number of rappers and hip hop artists putting attention on the disconnect of the Eastern Cape from developments in mainstream South Africa. Both *iimbongi* and rappers of the Eastern Cape address the problems of poor governance and poverty in their region, and the message of these performers is not only one of criticism of authority but also echoes the message of Steve Biko and the BC movement: that of loving oneself as a black person. According to Eastern Cape musician Zalabe Sebenzile, "We're black and we're conscious of it and despite the politics, sometimes the oppression is within ourselves."[11] This aspect of resistance is expressed in tracks such as "Mind in Chains" by Yahkeem, a hip hop artist and activist born and raised in Port Elizabeth. Similar to discussions about rap and hip hop music in the United States, there is also an emphasis in Eastern Cape hip hop and rap music on authenticity and how that is maintained. One of the founders of hip hop in Grahamstown, Xolile Madinda (sometimes known as "X-Nasty" or "X"), states, "I've got no problem with commercializing rap or even the culture if they're selling truth, but it's got to be authentic."[12]

The core of identity for the amaXhosa and people of the Eastern Cape as a whole, therefore, continues to depend on their exchange with those who hold political, creative, and cultural power. Expression of resistance to oppression through music and spoken word, whether through story-telling, coded messages, or calls to unite, is underlined throughout by the question of identity within the framework of a people's canon of creative work and culture. This ongoing challenge is both beautifully and poignantly evident in the history of music and spoken word of the people of the Eastern Cape.

NOTES

1. Miriam Makeba in conversation with Nomsa Mwamuka, *Makeba: The Miriam Makeba Story* (Pretoria: STE Publishers, 2004), 66.
2. Interview with Dumisa Mpupha, February 12, 2016.
3. David Coplan, *In Township Tonight! South Africa's Black City Music and Theatre* (Chicago: 2008, University of Chicago Press), 5.
4. Lewis Nkosi, "Jazz in Exile," *Transition,* 5(24), 1966, 34.
5. Brett Pyper, "A photo essay for Lulu Gontsana (1960–2005): South Africa's house drummer." *Generations of Jazz—At the Red Location Museum,* Exhibition Catalogue, International Library of African Music, 2013, 43.
6. Pyper, "A photo essay for Lulu Gontsana," 45.
7. Tayo Jolaosho, "Anti-apartheid Freedom Songs: Then and Now," *Smithsonian Folkways Magazine* (Spring 2014). http://www.folkways.si.edu/magazine-spring-2014-anti-apartheid-freedom-songs-then-and-now/south-africa/music/article/smithsonian
8. Alton B. Pollard, III, "Rhythms of Resistance: The Role of Freedom Songs in South Africa," in *"This Is How We Flow": Rhythm in Black Cultures,* Angela M. S. Nelson, Ed. (Columbia: University of South Carolina Press, 1999), 114.
9. Alfred Temba Qabula, "In the Tracks of Our Train," in *The World of South African Music: A Reader*, Christine Lucia, ed. (Cambridge Scholars Press: 2005), 170–71.
10. Gwen Ansell, *Soweto Blues: Jazz, Popular Music, and Politics in South Africa* (New York: Continuum International Publishing Group, 2005), 263.
11. Lee William Watkins, "Keeping It Real: AmaXhosa Limbongi Making Mimesis Do Its Thing in the Hip Hop and Rap Music of the Eastern Cape," *Journal of the International Library of African Music* (Volume 8, Number 4, 2010), 31–32.
12. Watkins, " Keeping It Real," 28.

Chapter 2

"Unite Like a Ball of Scrapings"
Early History to the 1850s

While the recording and writing of history in the Western tradition is a largely linear process based on the unfolding of events and key players, among Africans it is more often an exercise in visiting and re-visiting events in such a way that involves mythology, spirituality, entertainment, and reaffirmation of identity; drawing broad connections and parallels, and sometimes changing standard chronology in order to come closer to the truth. Among the Africans of the Eastern Cape, the storytelling process is marked by constant reshaping, interpretation of human relationships, and creating symbols and meaning out of the universe. The rhythms of existence, ties to ancestors, nature, and the land, and tales of humanity in the early history of these people form the backbone of the musical literature that dominates the story of the region. While the fluid and permeable relationships among the Khoikhoi, the San, and the amaXhosa were steadily encroached upon by colonial powers, the Africans were not passive in their response; rather, their many forms of resistance, which included music and praise-singing, played a primary role in the formation of the colonial system. Over many years the Africans of this region had created a shared understanding of nature, community, and spirituality that Europeans found hard to penetrate, and, in the early phase of Western infringement on their lives, the creative expression of these aspects of the people of the Eastern Cape began to formulate the essence of their struggle and lay the foundations of a modern form of African nationalism.

The earliest people of this region were the San people—hunter-gatherers whose lives formed a close connection to the land and whose music reflected that connection. Because all labor and its produce were shared as a matter of practicality, San culture was marked by equality and strong solidarity. The more complicated aspects of kinship, identity, authority, and ownership came later with the arrival of pastoralists (Khoi) and the Bantu (amaXhosa). Among the San or "People of the Eland," there existed no central leader with special rights to produce or knowledge. The resources from the land provided great symbolic meaning and were distributed equally. A specific wind was associated with each male and when that wind blew, it was believed to eradicate the footprints of where a man had walked "as if identity ultimately resided in the shifting land around him."[1]

The music of the San was directly tied to magic and spirituality and believed to have come from divine forces and supernatural energy found in the universe. Music expressed the energy of the spirits of the dead and mythological creatures and the San believed that this energy could both help and hurt living human beings. Singing and dancing activated this energy and "heated" it to the point that dancers could enter a trance and communicate with the spirits. It is the consistent belief of the San throughout their history that music and dance have a spiritual basis and are tools shared with the earliest human beings to create a form of communication with the supernatural and to create both physical and spiritual healing. These songs and dances are said to have appeared in dreams or visions and acted as a mitigating response to crisis or conflict for individuals or within the community. The role of music among the San people was, therefore, primarily that of ritual healing.[2] The response to conflict signifies early evidence of the important role of music in resisting adversity.

The San people are believed to have first come into contact with pastoralists in the early centuries C.E. and later on during the fifteenth century with the Bantu. The pastoralists were called KhoiKhoi ("men of men") and those in the Cape were descended from hunter-gatherers. They settled in the Cape near sources of water and created clan-based herding communities which began to mingle with and often absorb the San communities. Similar to the San, the distribution of resources was fairly egalitarian but there were also hierarchies based on gender, age, and wealth of the individual settlements. Over time authority became more centralized and based on size of the livestock holdings and the proclaimed descent from a "great family." The Khoi were the first Africans to come into contact with Dutch settlers in the Cape region in the seventeenth century. The settlers expropriated Khoi land and reduced their numbers through harsh forms of enslavement and extermination, pushing them eastward.

It was through observing the Khoi dancing to the new moon that the word "Hottentot" came to be applied to them by Europeans—a word that later became derogatory. Johann Jakob Merklein wrote of the Khoi in 1653, "When they are merry they leap up and down and continually sing the word Hottentot and nothing else and keep this up for long." Ambassador Limon de la Loubère observed, "They stamp now with one foot, now with the other, as if treading grapes, and say continually and energetically 'hotantot, hotantot,' but in a quite low voice, as if they were out of breath or feared to waken someone. This silent song has no diversity of pitch but only of beat."[3] In 1986, twenty-seven drawings were discovered in the National Library of South Africa that serve as the earliest European representations of the Khoi. These drawings illustrate Khoi activities that include drumming and dancing, which supports the significance of music in Khoi culture similar to the San.[4] The two groups eventually came into conflict based on their differing means of subsistence. The Khoi's pastoral way of life meant that their domesticated animals encroached on the land where the San hunted, laying bare the pastures where wild game had lived. The San retaliated through cattle raids which led to counter-raids on the part of the Khoi and sometimes war between the two groups. While some of the San retreated into the mountains others gradually joined the Khoi as servants, herders, or fighters which led to the overall mingling of populations, accounting for the term Khoisan and the fusion of language between the two.

The Xhosa people, known as the amaXhosa, developed from the clans of the Cape Nguni. Some were original Cape Nguni, but not all were Xhosa people. The royal families in the area included Mpondo, Bomvana, Xesibe, Thembu and Xhosa, and others, known as intrusive chiefdom clusters, moved to the area in the last 200 years: such as the Mfengu and Bhaca. Lineages also included the Zizi, Bhele, Hlubi, and Ntlangwini. All groups are part of the Bantu family and they refer to people as *abantu*. The early history of the southern Nguni still has many gaps and knowledge of the early amaXhosa is limited. One speculation is that they came down from the East Coast of Africa and their earliest known name was Abe-Nguni, later becoming known as Ama-Xhosa, deriving this name from the early chief Xhosa. This was around the sixteenth century during their entry into the Natal region.[5] A number of clans subsequently joined with the Xhosa as southern Africa during this time was marked by constant migration and others, mostly the Khoisan, became involuntary members through invasion. According to Xhosa oral history, the Xhosa royal families descended from the patriarch Tshawe, and only those of the Tshawe family could be chiefs. Other groups that subsequently joined or were conquered by the Xhosa were known as "commoners," including the Khoi and San, and while they may have come into this new society on the basis of economic inferiority, they were given full rights as any other Xhosa, whose rule was not centered on hereditary service or the color of skin. These circumstances, as Eastern Cape historian J. B. Peires points out, refute the claims made by white colonists that the amaXhosa were invaders no different than European settlers.[6]

There is a record of the earliest contact with Europeans in 1593 and that record indicates that the amaXhosa were already in the Cape by the middle of the sixteenth century and may have been there for several hundred years. It is also known that by 1736 the chief Phalo was ruling the Xhosa. Around

1720, the two sons of Phalo split the Xhosa nation into AmaGcaleka and AmaRharabe (the latter were later known as AmaNgqika after Rharabe's grandson). Other Bantu clans who had lost independent status elsewhere, including Khoi clans, joined with the Xhosa and became commoners—although there was a fair amount of miscegenation among these groups. The Xhosa Paramount Togu, who governed from 1590 to 1620, for example, married the daughter of an important Khoi family and their son Ntinde started the Ntinde clan among the Xhosa. Conflict and connections leading to gradual absorption of the Khoi and San people account for the "clicking" consonants of the language of the Xhosa (isiXhosa)—used to great effect in the spoken word and music of the amaXhosa, such as in the traditional song "*Quongqothwane*" ("The Click Song") made famous by Miriam Makeba.

Ownership of the history of the San, KhoiKhoi, and amaXhosa was lost in many ways and for many years as part of the European colonizing process, and only recently has attention to Xhosa oral historians and *iimbongi* helped to begin to restore a more African perspective. Samuel Edward Krune Mqhayi was one of the most respected historians, *iimbongi*, writers, and oral poets among Xhosa-speaking peoples in the early twentieth century and has been revived in this role most recently by Jeff Opland who states, "Mqhayi exploited books as sources, but he prefers the rhythms and flows of oral tradition, even with its occasional slight vagueness about precise dating."[7] Mqhayi argued, "A person who knows nothing of the historical events of his people lives his life with blunt teeth, he can't really get his teeth into anything he does."[8] Mqhayi's family were originally Thembu but were absorbed into the Rharhabe through the great king Ngquika, and at least two members of his family had reputations as powerful musicians and warriors. Ngqika was a self-proclaimed dancer who traveled with a group of performers that he personally selected. At one festival among the Dange, S. E. Mqhayi's ancestor (Mqhayi) stood out and so Ngqika made him part of his council and he became a close adviser to the king. Mqhayi (the ancestor) died in battle during Hintsa's War of 1834. Mqhayi's grandson Ziwani, who was S. E. Mqhayi's father, had a reputation as a strong singer and fought in Mlanjeni's War of 1850–53.[9]

While Mqhayi's life represents a later period of history marking the relationship between white and African in the Eastern Cape, his *ukubongo* (performance of oral poetry and history) provides a clear window into the history of music/spoken word and resistance in that region. For generations, Xhosa children had been raised listening to the oral performances of their clans, as well as learning to recite them and create their own. Poems would be created while herding livestock, for example, and each person would be given their own personal poem. Tone would give specific meaning to a word with rhythm as the binding force and the *imbongi* would be awake and responsive to the atmosphere at any performance or reciting. At clan gatherings, elders would recite poems about the clan history or specific ancestors, sometimes to invoke those ancestors or gain their attention. An *izibongo* would be used to praise or encourage people, to inspire them or move them to action, or to identify them as exceptional. The naming of chiefs and ancestors was of special significance and the appointed *imbongi* wore a distinctive outfit that included an animal skin hat and two spears. Opland describes it as the "most esteemed form of Xhosa literary art," and Mqhayi is still considered to be the finest practitioner of this art.[10] Nelson Mandela was one of many witnesses to Mqhayi's performances and describes the *imbongi*'s words and his own reaction in his autobiography *Long Walk to Freedom*:

> "What I am talking to you about is the brutal clash between what is indigenous and good, and what is foreign and bad. We cannot allow these foreigners who do not care for our culture to take over our nation. I predict that one day, the forces of African society will achieve a momentous victory over the interloper. . . ." Mqhayi then began to recite his well-known poem in which he apportions the stars in the heavens to the various nations of the world . . . and now suddenly he became still, and lowered his voice.
>
> "Now, come you, O House of Xhosa," he said, and slowly began to lower himself so that he was on one knee. "I give unto you the most important and transcendent star, the Morning Star, for you are a proud and powerful people. It is the star for counting the years—the years of manhood." When he spoke this last word, he dropped his head to his chest. We rose to our feet, clapping and cheering. I did not want ever to stop applauding. I felt such intense pride at that point, not as an African, but as a Xhosa; I felt like one of the chosen people.[11]

What Mqhayi and other Xhosa poets from the early twentieth century represent is a form of resistance to nineteenth-century colonialism through reclamation of their history as well as restoring their own method of telling that history. This reclaiming of history through *izibongo* was continued later on by other poets and *iimbongi*, such as David Phakamile Yali-Manisi, who produced powerful messages of resistance—both past and present—through their art, and who carried on the work of Mqhayi by retelling African and specifically Xhosa history in conjunction with current events.

The *izibongo* would be (and still is) full of alliteration and metaphors, although always containing the same configuration. The listener, however, is responsible for the narrative structure which the *imbongi* does not directly provide, and this calls for a previous knowledge of historical context. The purpose in both praise-singing and poetry is always truth, much more so than the uplifting of a particular chief. As Mqhayi describes it, "The *imbongi* traffics in praise and blame as twin aspects of his truth-telling, because ultimately he is not the chief's poet so much as the chiefdom's."[12] The words were ultimately inspired by messages from the ancestors but also contained democratic elements. According to Luvuyo Dontsa, the *imbongi* "served as the true voice of public opinion, being free not only to praise what he saw as laudable, but also to decry what was worthy of condemnation."[13]

One category of this oral tradition is *ibali,* which is historical narrative. Because Mqhayi was strongly committed to restoring rights and equality to his people, he used his talent in this area and his knowledge of history to undo the damage caused by the colonial historical perspective. Drawing on the strengths of *ukubongo*, for example, he replaced the European black and white themes of strength and weakness during European conquest and colonization with more accurate depictions of dominance and exile. According to Mqhayi:

> For any orator or speaker, any national hero, to be well grounded on any topic, he or she must be well grounded in knowledge, talking from fact. How can anyone be well grounded knowing nothing of his own people? Whatever his efforts in support of a national issue . . . he can expect to be struck down senseless by one puny little word so that he fall flat on his face, because he was hopping on one leg all along. . . . The person has been taught that his chiefs are sly and he believes it; he has been taught that the great men of his national steal, that they are thieves, cowards, liars; and he believes it. He does not realize that in doing so they are misleading him into abandoning his fathers and chiefs.[14]

While the historian John Henderson Soga does not possess the magnificent reputation of S. E. Mqhayi (partly because of his absorption of many of the European Christian mission interpretations of his people's history), his recording of Xhosa history in the early part of the twentieth century is useful in emphasizing the significance of oral tradition and he also attempted to restore a more positive image of the Africans of the Eastern Cape than had been promoted by British accounts. He described the amaXhosa as naturally imaginative and creative as well as having well-developed memories because of their method of retaining history. He noted that recorders of Xhosa communities and clans, in tracing the genealogy of chiefs from each generation, could recite back thirty generations, including direct and indirect branches as well as historical incidents associated with the actions or names of certain chiefs.[15] He also emphasized the courage and independence of his people, even after they had been subjugated to white rule: "There is nothing in them of subservience or sycophancy. While neither men nor women surrender anything of their manhood or womanhood, yet they are neither sullen nor vindictive."[16] This statement might seem like a vast generalization, given the history of subjugation of the amaXhosa by white occupiers; however, there is a strong argument for the independence of their identity being maintained through cultural expression, especially in spoken word and music.

During her research on music among the Xhosa of the Transkei region in the 1980s, Deirdre Hansen asked them about the origin of their music and they replied that the beginning of all music could only be attributed to human beings: "To them, music is a purely human phenomenon, something which people have done ever since they were created."[17] Historically, the songs of the amaXhosa represented living compositions that were the product of living languages and illustrate the basis of these creations: the fundamental relationship between melody and speech. Tone is a key element of isXhosa and the meaning of a word is very much based on tone. There is no exact Xhosa word for music or any word that directly translates "to sing." Since historically the amaXhosa have always maintained a deep sense of community, with the idea of a common humanity being incorporated into all meanings of words, each word associated with music has a community element to it: singing with clapping, singing and clapping for others to dance, leading a song, and following a song. The music itself and any instruments used also becomes humanized. To understand these concepts is to also understand, as David Dargie points out, how damaging Western attempts to define and develop Xhosa music have often been; a reflection of the damage that the imposition of Western concepts and beliefs as a whole has done to African culture and the resistance in subtle and direct ways that this imposition has evoked.[18]

Because of the strong elements of community and humanity in Xhosa culture and similar to the music of the San and Khoi, the music of the amaXhosa was produced collectively and maintained a strong spiritual element. As one Xhosa woman describes it, "Speak to me about music and you bring joyous excitement to the Xhosa. People cannot help but get this feeling (*ihlombe*) when they sing; even those who listen to them shudder (*hlasimla*) when they hear music."[19] *Ihlombe* is the expression of the other-worldly emotion evoked by music—moving those listening to a state of ecstasy that makes them join in and producing a rise in volume and pitch based on this strong collective approach. The music forms that have been passed down from early history are marked by unusual singing techniques such as throat-singing, and multiple rhythms that overlay and intersect each other—all contributing to an expression of collective consciousness—although, in certain circumstances, allowing for some individual musical expression; for example, "personal songs." The amaXhosa of the past were known for pushing their performances to the limit and were admired in their culture if they lost their voices in the process. Improvisation was and still is a huge element in Xhosa music, causing multiple versions of the same song to be performed, but there is also a strong standard structure to the performance and coordination of the singing and dancing as it unfolds. The framework of Xhosa music was said to reflect the role of the individual within the community—the solid connection that bound them together. Each person had to sing and dance well as a component of the whole performance, illustrating the importance of successful contributions to the good of the community. There would be multiple forms of participation, with no one "artist" and no real barriers between the "performer" and the "audience." Communal music, *umdudo* and *umgidi*, would be performed at important events, often with divisions based on age or social groups. This communal aspect of music translated into a strong component of resistance, as did the element of improvisation—adapting to changing circumstances while holding on to a united sense of identity.

Many of the traditional songs of the amaXhosa are known as "beer songs"; based on the belief that when people drink beer their ancestors join them. Beer carries a special symbolic importance of social unity in Xhosa culture, with ancestors operating as part of the extended family. Beer songs make references to ancestors or events that involve ancestors. In more recent history these songs have often been the source of political or protest music. *Umhala wasetywaleni* ("Umhala the Beer Song") is a song for ancestor rituals and includes this stanza:

> So it is said in this home
> I do not feel happy about this nation
> The world is not right
> I am dissatisfied with this place
> So say father and mother
> Oh! (My) father's homestead is destroyed
> And I am unhappy . . .[20]

Songs of the amaXhosa were usually linked to action—both in message and in movement. Early European accounts describe song accompanied by dance, often beginning at sunset when the night was clear and the moon was shining. There would be no musical accompaniment and rhythm would be found through clapping, stamping, whistling, humming and the striking of sticks. Exaggerated breathing would also provide rhythm and vocal accompaniment, as in the *mbayizelo* dance songs *No talili* and *Molweni nonke* performed by a group of Ngqika people and recorded by Hugh Tracey in 1957.[21] European observers had a hard time appreciating these performances. H. Lichenstein wrote in the early 1800s that the Xhosa melodies were "insufferable to a musical ear and their song little better than a deadened howl."[22]

Historically, songs and spoken word in service of resistance often found their most direct expression among the amaXhosa in war. War was carried out in a standard pattern of both ceremony and strategy among the Xhosa and involved singing and dancing, as well as war cries. On the appointed day of battle, warriors would gather at the Great Place—a meeting place of elders and leaders—and begin singing war songs which would focus on one theme but vary in execution. The first group to turn up would start the song and as subsequent groups arrived they would join in. When all the various groups had assembled, the entire army would stand to sing *um-hobe*—the main war song.[23] The point was not so much to celebrate the bravery of the soldiers, but to create a strong community of warriors. The songs that were sung often involved inserting certain names to fit the occasion; for example, the *igwatyu* (national song) was described by Reverend J. Solilo as "a song to strengthen cowards. When it is heard, it mentions cowards by name, so that tomorrow he will be too embarrassed to run away."[24] During battle there was no universal war cry; some were standard but changed to suit the circumstances of each battle. Each cry was in metaphoric language and usually took the form of predicting subsequent events or a reading of what was happening at that moment; for example, a call for more distant soldiers to focus on an area: "*yeyele ngomkono e-Xesi*" ("It has got bogged by the foreleg at e-Xesi"). This cry meant that the enemy had been slowed up in one area—the foreleg being only one part of the body of soldiers. Calling out during the course of battle was standard practice among the Xhosa, acting as communication to both fellow warriors and to the enemy. According to Peires,

> Even in the bitter fighting of the later frontier wars, the Xhosa attempted to express themselves in war, to personalize it, to communicate with the enemy through it. Secure on mountainous heights or behind rocks and bushes, they shouted at the white men, reproaching ("he called out to us . . . and asked why we were burning his house?") or taunting . . . the Xhosa were hoping to draw the Europeans into the bush. But there was more to the challenges than this. In some way, it seems, it was important to the Xhosa to show that they were truly men.[25]

The wife of the South African author William Charles Scully transcribed a description of the music of the Bhaca people (those on the northern frontier of the Eastern Cape) that includes musical notation of a war song as well as other songs associated with the Bhaca. According to the description, the war song was "of great antiquity" although the words had apparently lost their meaning. As part of the culture of clans and groups, each chief would adopt a song composed in his honor, and several of those of the great chief Madikane (who was killed by the Thembu and Gcalekas in 1824) were noted in this account, including one that noted "an assegai thrown among the Zulu, plays. You are a young animal to the Zulu." The author noted, "In Madikane's song there is an undertone of sadness, as well as a finish."[26] Many years later, in the 1960s, the musician Johnny Clegg witnessed a performance by Bhaca workers at a hostel in Johannesburg that echoed that ancient ritual:

As I walked up, I could feel in the concrete the stamping of the feet, and as I got closer the humming was so powerful. . . . There was a fierce, terrible commitment . . . a magnificent, horrible, terrible commitment which was being divulged. . . . And it was such a foreign movement, it was such a foreign thing . . . and I felt like I was being inducted into some kind of cult. . . . Nobody, nobody knew that in the middle of Hillbrow in a courtyard, a traditional Bhaca war dance was being stamped out every Tuesday and Thursday night.²⁷

Regarding the War of the Axe of 1846–1847, R. T. Kawa in *Ibali laMamfengu* wrote, "Sometimes this war is referred to as the War of the Gwatyu, because it was then that the armies of the amaTshiwo [amaXhosa] were heard singing that war-song (*ingoma*) which was so very notable that it is called the *Ingoma yeGwatyu*." A similar song, *Idabi laseCacadu* ("The Battle of Cacadu"), celebrates the success of chief Stokwe Ndlela of the amaQuathi during the Thembu rebellion of 1881. Ndlela, attempting to capture the town of Lady Frere, apparently died in a cave. The song celebrates him in the form of a chant:

> *Hoo-yina! Hoo-yina!*
> *Niphina ngedabi laseCacadu*
> *Mhla iindonga zeCacadu zakhakamnqa*
> *Kuba amanzi ajika aligazi*
> *Zinqoza iinkanunu ezidalingede*
> *Wayelapho uStokwe ka Ndlela*
> *Unoqengqelekile utyeshomibi kanye!!!*
> *Ukhala Mqadi Wafa yintuka!!*
> *Inkomo kaSothuku Nogangatha!!*
> *Iqhayi elibaleka nomtya walo!!*
>
> Where were you at the battle of Cacadu?
> The day the riverbanks of Cacadu were astonished
> Because the water had turned to blood.
> The cannons were clearly to be heard
> And there appeared Stokwe the son of Ndlela
> He who rolls, avoiding dangerous patches!!!
> The chief rafter who respects the main pillar!!
> The beast of Sokuthu and Gangatha!!
> The proud man who escapes with the rope which was meant to bind him fast!!²⁸

It is important to note that songs passed down from the early history of Xhosa battles will not be as they were, as they have been continually changed or revised to suit the occasion of the performance. As David Dargie explains, "This constant variation means that it is not possible to write out a song in the manner of a Western composition. Even if a total performance is transcribed, it is almost certain that every other performance of the same song will be different."[29] What remains from each performance is the history behind it, including stories of resistance, and in the last three hundred years, this usually means resistance to European encroachment.

While songs within the Xhosa tradition are often linked to war, particularly in response to colonial invasion, there is a deep-rooted tonal connection to two indigenous instruments: the *uhadi* bow and the *umrhube* which gives Xhosa music a unique character. While the Bhaca battle cries can be geographically and culturally linked to the tradition of battle songs among the AmaZulu, the *uhadi* sound tends to be gentle, soft, and introspective. Initially, it was the Xhosa cattle herders who typically played the *uhadi*, but increasingly it became the instrument of Xhosa women, as did the practice of throat-singing. While Xhosa music tends to be largely choral in nature, it is based on the six-note scale of Xhosas bow instruments, and that small change of a six-note to seven-note scale can make a clear difference in sound between African and Western. Xhosa music, like much of African music as a whole, is also cyclical in style, but each cycle involves a slight change recognized by the singers and the audience.[30] These aspects of Xhosa music display a subtlety of expression not initially appreciated by Western observers, and represents one instance of resistance through preservation of identity.

Contemporary European sources reveal a pattern of failure in British colonial strategies in the Eastern Cape until the mid-1800s. The abolition of slavery in the Cape Colony created instability and contributed to the retreat of the Dutch-speaking settlers in the event known as The Great Trek. This period was also marked by a series of major wars between the British colonists and the amaXhosa. It is no coincidence that connected to these developments was the increased depiction of Africans by Europeans as "the other"—a development repeated all over the African continent with the rise of exploration based increasingly on acquisition, and colonization. European infringement on the Eastern Cape in the nineteenth century was sparked by the escalating violence of the Frontier Wars—a physical expression and tool of imperialism and capitalism infused with and influenced by the Social Darwinist version of racism. The fierceness of resistance on the part of Africans was complicated by British manipulation of divisions within Xhosa-speaking communities, but the majority of chiefs and their subjects often shared the accurate perception of a previous form of slavery being replaced by a newer more regulated and institutionalized version.

Chapter 2

NTSIKANA

Much like interpretations of the Bible and the writings of Karl Marx, the motivations and music of Ntsikana kaGaba have been described in numerous ways through the influences of the environment and time of explanation. Ntsikana and Makhanda Nxele are Xhosa prophets that seemingly marked a division in historical outlook that came about during the Fourth and Fifth Frontier Wars in the nineteenth century (1811–1819). While Nxele has come to represent a militant approach to colonial aggression, Ntsikana has often been associated with a more pacifist approach connected directly to Christian culture. Both, however, have come to be identified with African (and Xhosa) nationalism. The Fourth and Fifth Frontier Wars forced a reckoning among the Xhosa-speaking people in understanding the nature of the Europeans, especially the European strategies of dominance and war: they were more directly exposed to the experience of total war and were also fast forming the conclusion that Europeans were fundamentally not like Africans. The answers that both Nxele and Ntsikana provided were to questions regarding the intrinsic nature and motivations of Europeans, and solutions to white encroachment on their communities.

The characteristics of the experience of war with the white man represented a new phenomenon to the Xhosa leaders, as did the colonial economy and forms of political control. Chieftainship among the amaXhosa was the primary and most respected form of authority, but the goal was not dictatorship. No decision could be made without a discussion with councilors, and this included those of the king. The disruption, increased distance between clans, and migration patterns exacerbated by the arrival of the Europeans led to a crisis of governance among Xhosa leaders because there was no standard method of dealing with this new development. In pre-colonial Xhosa society, rule was largely based on the principle of whoever controlled the cattle, controlled the community. This principle marked the unity of politics and economics among the amaXhosa, and the complex systems of commerce and capitalism brought by Europeans disrupted that basic organization of society as much as war and conquest did. The method and aims of war also represented a major clash of cultures during the nineteenth century. In pre-colonial society, the amaXhosa did not engage in war as a fight to the death; but rather as a limited conflict that would lead to a transactional agreement. War aims between the two cultures were very different and again illustrated the distinction between an emphasis on property versus emphasis on resources. The Europeans, feeling vulnerable as settlers, wanted clear demarcated boundaries, whereas the Xhosa wanted to continue with open frontiers. This difference led to cattle raids by the Xhosa which led to retaliation on the part of the colonists, and ultimately war. As contemporary *imbongi* Dumisa Mpupha describes this difference: *"Ilizwe lethu lomakele"* (Our land has been ruined). He goes on to explain, "It has walls. We need to destroy these walls to make our land right again."[31] Mpupha also notes the difficulty *iimbongi* find historically in praise-singing to white people dating back to their first encounters. Apparently, even before British colonial conquest of the Eastern Cape, whenever Xhosa men dreamed of white men the latter took the shape of a bad omen, the *impundulu*, which was a supernatural bird used by witches to send to members of a family. Later on, in the townships and rural areas, Xhosa people would feel a particular deep and spiritual unease when a white person sat next to them in the dark, especially at night when there was no electricity. Even when white researchers came to request performance of a praise song from the *iimbongi*, that unease could remain; in the words of Mpupha: "The Devil is beside you wherever you go and now you want me to do praise singing."[32]

Disparities between the British and amaXhosa in battle, conquest and occupation found expression in the words, proclamations, and songs associated with the prophets Nxele and Ntsikana in response to the early Frontier Wars. The Fourth Frontier War was short and intense, with forces under Lt.-Col. Graham following the orders of Sir John Cradock to drive out the Xhosa occupying the area west of the Fish River, including destruction of kraals and gardens. Destroying resources as opposed to absorbing them in battle made no sense to the Africans of the Eastern Cape. The scorched-earth tactics of the British were new to the amaXhosa as were the technical advantages of this new population. The Xhosa people called the white people *abantu abasemanzi*—The People from the Water—connecting them to the mysteries of the ocean, but while they increasingly viewed them as vastly different beings, the amaXhosa did not automatically view white people as somehow superior. The Scottish missionary John Campbell, for example, described those Xhosa who were exposed to Europeans in Cape Town: "[They] expressed surprise at many things which they saw, but never think the white men are more wise or skillful, for they suppose they could do all the white men do if they chose."[33] European war tactics, nonetheless, had created a crisis of leadership among the Xhosa and brought prophets such as Nxele and Ntsikana to great prominence, as they seemed better equipped to explain the phenomenon of white invaders. "There they come!" warned Nxele, who, in his prophecies had promised to turn bullets into water. "They have crossed the Qagqiwa and they have crossed the Nqweba; only one river more, the Nxuba and then they will be in our land. What will become of you then?"[34]

The tension between the two interpretations to resistance attached to Nxele and Ntsikana is similar to the tension faced by the ANC more than one hundred years later between those arguing for armed resistance to apartheid and those holding out for peaceful action and negotiation. The dichotomy of strategy connected to the two figures of Nxele and Ntsikana is also similar to that attached to Martin Luther King, Jr. and Malcolm X regarding nonviolent versus violent strategies of the U. S. Civil Rights Movement in the 1960s. In each case the issue often boiled down to these two questions: 1) Should we use the principles of Christianity introduced by our oppressors to maintain the high moral ground and pressure them to change through pacifism and negotiation? Or, 2) Should we not defend ourselves through armed resistance against the direct and indirect violence that is being perpetuated against us? These questions informed the constant interpretation and re-interpretation of Ntsikana, Nxele, and also the nineteenth-century prophet Mlanjeni's proclamations, songs, and predictions to suit the times. Connected to these questions are more complex aspects of the significance of both prophets. Ntsikana in many ways represents the process among Africans of absorbing an outside influence and making it their own; then turning it as a weapon—a form of black nationalism—against the oppressors who first introduced it. Nxele has tended to represent the more direct and robust rejection of white people along with the damaging effects of European culture, viewed as a form of pollution from which the amaXhosa must cleanse themselves. These interpretations, however, do not preclude active resistance by those who converted to Christianity. During the war of Mlanjene, for example, Xhosa warriors were exposed to Khoi rebels who fought alongside them reading their Bibles on a regular basis and singing hymns in preparation for battle.[35]

Nxele and Ntsikana began as diviners but both were exposed to and absorbed the Christian beliefs of Europeans and could, therefore, form a bridge between the familiar beliefs of the natural order of the Xhosa world. Ntsikana ka Gaba was born around 1780 and is considered to be the first Xhosa Christian. In 1799, when he was still a young cattle-herder, he heard the preaching of the missionary Dr. J. van der Kemp and fifteen years later those words took root in a vision of light Ntsikana had that caused him to get up and dance, reportedly causing a great wind to blow that stopped the dance. The story passed down recounts that this happened three times and Ntsikana announced that something was telling him to pray; he then stayed up all night singing the "*Elele homna*" chorus. According to John Knox Bokwe who later transcribed Ntsikana's hymns, the prophet pronounced that a spirit that was Christianity entered his body and he washed off his clay (symbolic of his previous beliefs) and chanted words that roughly translated to "Hallelujah, Amen!" It was a conversion that occurred with no European missionary present. Ntsikana then began to proselytize to his people and to the chiefs Ngqika and Ndlambe, conducting regular religious services for them. The original hymn was passed down orally and first published by Lovedale

Press in 1876.[36] Now known as *"Ntsimbi ka Ntsikana,"* it survived not only as a Christian hymn but as a Xhosa song, sometimes sung as an expression of resistance, thus illustrating how Xhosa songs have been continually re-adapted to fit different circumstances.

Central to the interpretation of Ntsikana's hymn as a strong influence on African nationalism is the belief that Ntsikana came to Christianity on his own and independently as opposed to having been brainwashed by European missionaries promoting the subjugation of black people through their religion. While he preached salvation through pacifism and obedience to the will of God, his hymns and messages were expressed in the imagery, language, and musical traditions of his people to the extent that they could maintain pride in their heritage as opposed to rejecting it in the presence of something new. This interpretation lays stress on the African trait of absorbing a belief but not losing oneself in the process. According to Janet Hodgson, Ntsikana introduced the Christian God to his people within a traditional Xhosa framework: "By allowing transformation to take place from the roots, instead of being grafted on, he drew on what to his people was already really real so as to get a deep-seated response."[37] Ntsikana is therefore important because he illustrates the beginning of indigenous theology in Southern Africa.

In both singing and speaking, Ntsikana is described as having "a deep, but clear, and sweet, bass voice; when he sang his great hymn you could not keep the tears from flowing out of your eyes."[38] The British explorer A. Steedman described Ntsikana's hymn as a "wild and plaintive melody having a pathos and deep-toned express which was exceedingly affecting."[39] As a call to worship, Ntsikana would sing the hymn that came to be known as "Ntsikana's Bells" at dawn and his followers would gradually gather and participate in the singing in a pattern of call and response. Ntsikana was expressing this new message of faith in a form familiar to the amaXhosa—the *izibongo*—and, therefore, acted as a transitional figure between the culture of pre-colonial history and the new religious influences. Despite the pacifist message of Ntsikana's music and preaching, many of the metaphors in his hymn spoke the language of battle, such as the *kaka* (shield), *nqaba* (stronghold or fort), and *hlati* (forest as a place of refuge from the enemy). He also used the name "conqueror" for "Christ" and it is suggested by Hodgson that this figure presented to his followers was a version of the character "Broad Breast" from the Xhosa oral tale "The Story of *Mbulukuzi*" passed down from previous generations. Ntsikana's message, however, was one derived from the concepts of unity and pacifism; that the "end" would be "the beginning of peace for which there has been no preconcerted council, or arrangement of man. The reign of Broadbreast will commence and continue in the lasting peace of the Son of Man."[40] Unity—*yamanyama* (the scrapings of animal skin rolled into a dense ball)—was the persistent message of Ntsikana's songs and words and the amaXhosa used these words later as inspiration; for example, in the founding of *Manyano lo Buzalwana Bholanga lwama Xhosa* ("Union of the Brotherhood of the amaXhosa Nation") in 1909.

The message of peace and submission to God put forth by Ntsikana contrasts with that of the prophet Nxele who presumably acquired knowledge of Christianity and European culture by working for an Afrikaans farmer in the Cape Colony. The expulsion of the Xhosa across the Fish River in 1812 seemed to fuel Nxele's desire to understand the Europeans and their particular power, and he made careful observation of them in Grahamstown. Preaching a Xhosa version of Christianity, he seemed at first to not make much impact on his compatriots; but as his messages moved away from European religion and took on the growing conflict between Xhosa and the colonial government, he began to influence the war strategies of the Xhosa, and personally led them into battle in Grahamstown in 1819. Incorporating religious elements he had absorbed from the colonists, he produced a new interpretation of events in terms of a conflict between *Thixo* (God of the white people) and *Mdalidiphu* (God of the black people) in which the latter would prevail. The knowledge Nxele gained of European culture, religion, and war is maintained by Peires to be the probable reason he predicted Xhosa immunity from the colonists' bullets.[41] Nxele made the strategic mistake, however, of leading the attack in daylight and, after an initial advantage gained by breaking into small groups, the Xhosa warriors eventually succumbed to the steady fire of the British forces. Nxele surrendered himself as a sacrifice for his people and this led to British cessation of the war. Ntsikana, on the other hand, had counseled against going to war and called on his people to turn from their assegais to a form of spiritual ownership expressed by singing *Inqukuva* (The Round Song, the title of which translates to "ox without horns") and submitting to whatever happens no matter the consequences—a version of placing oneself in the hands of God. While Nxele told of a higher protection that would turn European bullets to water, Ntsikana also declaimed a spiritual protection based on an all-powerful God that was stronger than the oxhide shields the Xhosa used to guard against and frighten their enemies. What Nxele was calling for was a form of salvation in the here and now. Ntsikana's form of salvation related to a more distant future.

The breach between Ntsikana and Nxele is connected to the two Xhosa leaders King Ngqika and Prince Ndlambe, and the differences of interpretation of the influence and intentions of both prophets is reflected in the writings and spoken word of later Xhosa historians and *iimbongi*. According to Mqhayi, Ngqika leaned toward the advice of Ntsikana, whereas Ndlambe was influenced by Nxele. Ntsikana was a hereditary councilor to Ngqika, while Nxele acted as war doctor to Ndlambe. Mqhayi addressed the criticism attached to Ndlambe in turning away from Ntsikana to maintain his connection to Nxele, and defended Ndlambe by stating that the latter was following the custom of sticking to one topic and not constantly changing. Mqhayi reports that Ndlambe said to Ntsikana, "Each ear will hear different things because I am still listening to Nxele." Mqhayi argued that Ndlambe's words helped future generations to understand which of the two prophets became the nation's adviser: "If Nxele had been blocked by the chief, we would be plucking each other's hair out today, some claiming it was Nxele who was blocked from helping the nation, and others saying no, it was Ntsikana."[42]

In his praise-song "Holy Ntsikana" (on events that occurred c. 1800–21), D. L. P. Yali-Manisi argues a different interpretation of the division between Ntsikana and Nxele. He describes Ntsikana warning the Rharhabe that people were coming "with hair of silk like maize filaments" and that they carried a "book" (Bible) and a "holeless button" (money). According to Yali-Manisi, Ntsikana advised Ngqika and his clan to "accept the book" but "reject the button," the latter being "the mother of death and sin. Yali-Manisi disparages Ngqika's concessions to colonial authorities whom he asked for assistance against his own people who were then evicted from their land. Ngqika's role in the British strategy of divide and conquer, the *imbongi* states, set the stage for future degradation and humiliation of his people:

> *Namhla siziimpula zikaLujaca,*
> *Siphakathi kozipho nenyama . . .*
> *Le Afrika namhl' idandalazile.*
>
> today we're left empty-handed,
> set between a rock and a hard place . . .
> Today, this Africa stands exposed.

But Yali-Manisi goes on to make the cry for resistance and nationalism:

> *Siphuthum' izwi lomfo kaGabha,*
> *Elathi: ze nibe yimbumba yamanyama!*
>
> "Let's reclaim what Gabha's son [Ntsikana] said:
> you must unite like a ball of scrapings!"[43]

In his praise-poem "The Battle of Amalinde 1818," Yali-Manisi connects the cause for this division and defeat more directly to Nxele, referring to *Ukudibanisa ngeentlokwe' abantwana bezikumkani* (A head to head clash of royal sons):

> *Sibonile ke Kamb' into 'yenziwe nguMakana*
> *Ukudibanisa ngeentlokwe' abantwana bezikumkani*
> *Ukudibanis' uNgqika noNdlambe bengenatyheneba*
> *Ukuze balwe kuf' abantu bengagxalelananga nganto*
>
> We've seen what Makanda [Nxele] wrought,
> a head to head clash of royal sons,
> Ngqika and Ndlambe, free of antipathy
> fought, and men died for no reason

In this praise poem Yali-Manisi states clearly that "we do not blame Ntsikana," claiming that, at first, "we lay the blame on Lwaganda [Ngqika]" for calling on the English but then goes on to correct that assertion, claiming the blame "rests squarely" on Nxele who had falsely claimed the white population would be swept into the sea leading to the destruction and defeat of his people:

> *Kanti nay' uLwagand' asimbekanga tyala*
> *Sesimbek' ecaleni*
> *Naal' ityala kule nkwenkwe kaGwala*
> *Kuba yathi uyakutshayelwa wonk' umkhosi womLungu*
> *Uyokulahlwa elwandle*
> *Ngelishwa neshoba*
> *Baf' abantu bakwaPhalo*
> *Bebulalana bengenanqala*
>
> Yet we don't really blame Lwaganda,
> we place him to one side,
> the blame rests squarely on Gwala's boy [Nxele]
> who claimed the white troops would be swept aside
> and cast into the sea.
> Through disaster and deception
> The people of Phalo died,
> Killing each other without animosity.[44]

Ntsikana preached pacifism to his followers, but his son Dukwana died fighting against the British, even after having worked for a Presbyterian mission for fifty years, and different versions of Ntsikana's hymn were used in later years as a call to arms against the colonists in subsequent Frontier Wars. It tended to be the preferred hymn sung among those who began to convert to Christianity—in contrast to the music brought by Europeans, thus acting as a subtle form of resistance. The journalist and composer (and father of John Henderson Soga) Tiyo Soga reported that it "was always a favorite with the Chumie people . . . the effect which it produced in our little assembly was thrilling. It must have awakened memories of the past."[45] An anonymous contributor to the publication the *Kaffir*[46] *Express* wrote of Ntsikana's composition in 1878, "We have heard only one Kaffir hymn, which deeply moved the congregation of worshippers . . . [they] look on it with a kind of national feeling, especially now that they droop their heads from the loss of national freedom, and the dominance of the white man."[47] Because of its indigenous origins, Ntsikana's hymn continued to act as a cohesive force among the amaXhosa, encouraging a form of resistance in the form of maintaining identity which contributed in later years to the rise of Black Nationalism and Black Consciousness. In a collection of songs recorded by children of the township Crossroads in the Cape Flats in the 1970s, the songs were described as coming from their "hearts and souls," and included a song of protest that linked Ntsikana with the prophet Mlanjeni. The song was explained as one that went back "to our roots, and to [Ntsikana's and Mlanjeni's] teaching," calling on "the courageous people of the black nation" to arm themselves, using education and the belief that these prophets would return to help them reclaim "our black Africa." After Ntsikana's death, there was, for a while, a dearth of indigenous-composed Christian music, with later hymns introduced in the European style. According to Hodgson, these later hymns "exemplify how, after Ntsikana's time, the amaXhosa were molded by mission education into a Western framework of Christianity." Hodgson argues that these hymns acted as a straitjacket "which constrained the spontaneous expression of their religious feelings in worship."[48]

The point made by Hodgson of European missionaries attempting to shape the future of the amaXhosa through education and particularly through music is an illustration of the method of control of indigenous populations the colonists employed by creating a "civilized" Christian middle class of Africans. There is an ongoing discussion of the importance of tone in isiXhosa when applied to music and how the missionaries often distorted true meaning by adopting straight translations of Western hymns and imposing Victorian hymnody on Xhosa music. This development later proved to be a double-edged sword for white authorities in South Africa because just as the messages of the Bible and Western democracy were incorporated and turned into criticism against them by Africans, so, too, was the style of music re-incorporated to produce songs of liberation and black nationalism.

While controlling the translations and hymnody of Xhosa songs meant that, to begin with, European missionaries were able to influence the message of the music or even replace it, this was not so much the case with *izibongo*, where white influence was less likely to infringe on the independence of meaning and intention of the praise singer. Music might be co-opted by European missionaries, but praise-poems operated independently of white encroachment—not just in purpose and meaning, but also with regard to subject matter. Until the *izibongo* of Mqhayi, praise poems of the nineteenth century tended not to be focused much on white people or their culture. As described by Jeff Opland in "The Image of the Book in Xhosa Oral Poetry," the topics covered were more likely to be community concerns, and the role of white people was only addressed indirectly as far as they affected local people or local politics. Chiefs would be described in negative or positive ways based on their dealings with the white authorities. If they resisted white encroachment they would be praised, as in the case of Mathanzima, son of Sandile:

> *Ixonti lase Bholo*
> *Intw'ede yaf'ingazang'irafe*
>
> Long-hair from Bholo
> Who never paid tax all his life[49]

Or Sigcau, son of Sarhili:

> *Nguzwi—linzima elibizwa pakati*
> *Uxalis' imantyi ngokupendula*
>
> Called Powerful Voice at home;
> He disturbs the magistrate by answering back[50]

Chiefs might also be criticized for collaborating with the white population:

> *Kulamahlat' inkawu zimangele,*
> *Kuba nizibamba nizis' em-Lungwini,*
> *Zibe zingadlanga nto yamlungu*
>
> In these woods the monkeys complain:
> You seize them and send them to whites,
> Though they ate nothing belonging to whites[51]

Chiefs could further be held accountable for accepting alcohol from Europeans. The actions of Maqoma, the son of Ngqika, are described as "strewn with broken bottles" (*kundlel' ezinamaqekez' ebotile*).[52]

An indirect comparison of the pure intentions of Xhosa spoken word versus the corrupting influence of written words and books of the Europeans also appears in the portrait of a chief Rhambalamatye son of Tokhwe who collaborated with the white authorities:

Ngu-Balakisi, uso-Rafukazwe liyabatalwa,
Uso-Bukwe kancwad' ebal' izi-alam.
Ngu qoqo fusakazi, umnyenyeka,
Umbela kama-Xanti,
Upikis' abantu bemqongqota.
Uruxesh' onenkani wakulo-Nyanti,
Ugomb' ihlwihlwili,
Ugzoboz' izulu ngesibili

Barracks, Storehouse of taxes,
Book of books recording the poor.
He's a dark refuge for absconders,
He tortures with bars,
Denies those who confront him.
He's a stubborn caterpillar of Nyanti's,
who draws clots of blood with his lashes,
even heaven falls to the force of his blows.[53]

THE GREAT CATTLE KILLING

The growing intensity of the Frontier Wars culminated in the tragic development known as the Great Cattle Killing of 1856–57, which decimated large sections of the Xhosa-speaking population and destroyed the last vestiges of organized armed resistance to colonization of the Eastern Cape. The music and oral literature of the amaXhosa reflected this clash, using the tradition of prophecy and poetic history with nuances of magical realism to explain the disruption of Xhosa society and culture. As explained by historian Clifton C. Crais, for example, "the millenarian Cattle-Killing Movement of 1856–7 constituted a mode of controlling the future through a representation of the past in the present."[54]

Sometimes described as "a national suicide" of the Xhosa people, the Cattle Killing continues to play a large role in the culture and history of the amaXhosa, finding its way into songs, stories, and literature such as the profound and acclaimed novel *The Heart of Redness* by Zakes Mda. The event centers around a fifteen-year-old girl named Nongqawuse who reported her experience of having visions and meetings with the "spirits of warriors long dead." According to the account relayed by W. W. Gqoba who was seventeen at the height of the Cattle Killing, Nongqawuse received the message from these spirits: "You are to tell the people that the whole community is about to rise again from the dead. Then go on to say to them all the cattle living now must be slaughtered, for they are reared with defiled hands . . . say to them there must be no ploughing of lands." She was told also that the people should instead dig pits and build new huts. Nongqawuse brought this prophecy to her people and claimed the strangers she spoke to were "new people" and messengers of Sifuba-Sibanzi ("Broad-Breast") and Napakede ("The Eternal One").[55] They promised fresh cattle and food for all that had been destroyed and that a "red army" from the sea would conquer the white people oppressing them. Peires proposed in his book on the Cattle Killing, *The Dead Will Arise*, that these messages and visions were probably Xhosa concepts infused with Christian ones of resurrection that came partly as a last-ditch hope to combat despair in the face of aggressive colonization and devastation to the cattle population through lung sickness.[56] The "red army" was possibly linked to rumors of defeat of the British by the Russians in the Crimean War.

A number of the Xhosa chiefs and leaders came to believe the prophecy and some were even convinced of similar visions when brought to the headwaters of the River Kamanga to view the "spirits." According to Gqoba, "The army in the sea never came out to meet the chiefs" and their message was not heard by them, but Nongqawuse relayed their words, repeating the command to kill their cattle, dig pits, and throw away their corn. She went on to say there was another great chief, mounted on a grey horse: "His name was Grey, otherwise known as Satan." The ones who failed to slaughter their cattle would become subjects of "the chief named Satan" and these people "would not see the glory of our own chief, Napakade, son of Sifubasibanzi."[57] Nongqawuse's story was reaffirmed by the experiences told by another young girl Nonkosi who led people to a pond at the Mpongo River professing visions of people dancing on the water.

The visions split the Xhosa communities already struggling with Governor Grey's colonial policies and their own divisions. Many carried out the instructions conveyed by Nongqawuse while others resisted. A great divide arose between "believers" and "unbelievers"; in Gqoba's version they were known as *amaTamba* ("the Submissive") and *amaGotya* ("the Unyielding"). Despite the participation of a large section of the Eastern Cape population in the cattle killing, the day of salvation according to Nongqawuse's prediction did not bring relief to the Believers: "Nothing happened. The sun did not set, no dead person came back to life, and not one of the things that had been predicted came to pass."[58] The failure of the prediction was initially blamed by the Believers on the Unbelievers for not following through with the spirits' instructions, and the catastrophe itself was attributed over time by the majority of the Xhosa to Governor Grey. Although there is no direct evidence of Grey's involvement in the prophecy, he did take full advantage of the situation. He used the ensuing disaster and starvation to take over Xhosa land and to turn a large majority of amaXhosa into a labor force for the colony. Chiefs involved in the cattle killing had charges brought against them by colonial authorities and they were convicted and sent to prison on Robben Island.

Other chiefs, such as Sarhili, were pushed out of their territory and, although some resistance continued in the Frontier War of 1877, the Cattle Killing broke the back of Xhosa resistance and from that time on the Xhosa found themselves increasingly absorbed into the British colony.

For a people who feel very strongly the connection of their ancestors' actions to their own present-day actions, and who further see themselves in constant dialogue with their ancestors' spirits, the nature of an event such as occurred for the amaXhosa in the mid-nineteenth century has never just been a thing of a distant past. The Great Cattle Killing is an event constantly revisited by Xhosa historians, poets, *iimbongi*, and writers as well as one that continues to exist collectively in the memories of the amaXhosa as they apply its meaning to contemporary circumstances. The song "Nongqawuse," for example, is one that is still performed by contemporary choral groups, providing the words of the prophecy and describing the events that took place. Mqhayi declared: "Because this story is so familiar, everyone rips his own chunk from Nongqawuse, letting his imagination run free on his own scrap, ignoring what is left over. Whoever wants to condemn something or destroy it associates it with the name of Nongqawuse."[59] He went on to ask the question of whether "all black people" should be held accountable as opposed to Nongqawuse. He also believed that her prophecy was, over time, fulfilled.

Regarding the spirits' command that food be thrown away as it would be replenished, Mqhayi argued that, later on in the early twentieth century, even though many people did not farm themselves they still had access to maize grown overseas. With respect to the prediction that new cattle would arise, he pointed out that, in his day, people who did not raise goats or cattle could still eat meat. In addressing the prophecy that the dead would arise, he claimed that, with the arrival of Mfengu, the Xhosa began to produce many more children than they had before: "Those 50,000 who died during the Nongqawuse disaster have been restored many times over by these illegitimate children alone."[60]

Mqhayi's poem about Nongqawuse is a reply to those who claim her prophecies went unfulfilled:

> *Kuba nanamhla lise zweni lakowalo.*
> *Umadibanis' umzi ngebhanti –*
> *Ngebhanti yobunye nokolo . . .*
> *Ukub' olubingelelo besinga lwenzanga*
> *Besingayi kulungelwa nto napambili . . .*

> . . . to this day she's in her own country.
> She binds the nation with a belt—
> A belt of faith and unity . . .

> If we had not made this sacrifice,
> Nothing good would lie in store for us . . .[61]

Mqhayi does not blame either side in the division that occurred over Nongqawuse's actions:

> *Makafe ama Tamba alungisile*
> *Yifani ma Tamba nide natyapa.*
> *Into yesizw' iqiniswa ligazi.*
> *Xa indishoy' andigxeki ma Gogotya,*
> *Nani ma Gogoty' andinideli,*
> *Kuba akubingelelwa ngamhlamb' upela.*
> *Nani ngelenu nizukisile,*
> *Ngamana nakula ngokukula*
>
> Let the Believers die, they've behaved properly
> die, Believers, you've done well.
> A national matter is strengthened by blood.
> This is not to mock the Unbelievers,
> I don't despise you, Unbelievers:
> A whole flock is never sacrificed.
> You too have raised your voices in praise
> May you grow from strength to strength. . . .[62]

Mqhayi claimed, "Today our fathers have certainly risen"; that there was not more hunger, "no more grubbing for roots in famine," and that progress was taking place gradually: "we sleep on one step, awake on one higher." The message of national unity attributed to *iimbongi* such as Mqhayi found expression near the end of this poem when he called on his people to hear Broadbreast's message that "the nation must be reconciled" (*Ut' isizwe make sibuyelane*).[63]

While Mqhayi interpreted the events of the Cattle Killing in a time of lingering optimism regarding the uniting power of African nationalism through education, *imbongi* D. L. P. Yali-Manisi was less optimistic in his interpretation of this event, declaiming in the era of apartheid when the Bantu Education system crushed much of the confidence that had arisen among many mission-educated Africans of previous generations and put roadblocks in the path of Pan-Africanism. Manisi called the Cattle Killing "a problem that crippled the land of Phalo" and saw it as an event where "men abandoned their senses completely." Of Nongqawuse he stated that he admired the "girl I've never met":

> *Kuba ndiyamthand' uSathana*
> *Ngokubuswa ngamagwangqa!*

> I'm a loyal fan of Satan:
> He's got the whites at his beck and call!⁶⁴

Yali-Manisi's tone reflects the bitterness of experience of material and psychological oppression, claiming *Yayilishoba kwaloo nto* ("The whole thing stank from the start"), and left an indelible mark on his people's land and their history:

> *Ukuqalekiswa kwesizwe sikaXhosa . . .*
> *Azi babeye phi n'abantu balo mhlaba?*
> *Zaziye phi n'izigwakumbesha?*

> A blight on this land of Xhosa . . .
> Where were the thinkers in this land?
> Where were the men of distinction?⁶⁵

He also takes a dim view of the outcome of the Cattle Killing:

> *Waxakeka k'umhlaba kaPhalo*
> *Yiyo leyo ke leyo ngxaki yasenzakalisayo!*

> Phalo's land was utterly crushed:
> that is the problem that wrought our destruction!⁶⁶

But the blame, in Yali-Manisi's opinion, rests ultimately on a combination of early missionary teachings dulling the senses of the Xhosa and manipulation on the part of colonial authorities such as Grey. Manisi mocks the prim but duplicitous missionary who wears a clerical collar on his front while at the same time concealing a cannon behind his back that

> *Evela phantsi kwendleb' iphum' esilevini,*
> *Kant' iqhawul' iminqambulo kwabangaphambili*

> Comes down from his ear and out through his mouth
> And smashes to smithereens all those before him.

Manisi goes on to describe the Africans overwhelmed in their confused response as the missionaries, led by Grey, concoct a false message of peace and calm while divvying up the land; and Grey, according to Manisi:

*Ibimele mgama yakh' umkhanyo,
Ijong' isiphumo sokufa kwezidumbu*

He stood to one side, shading his eyes
Counting the corpses in mounting piles.[67]

The Cattle Killing was clearly a watershed event in the history and memory of the amaXhosa, finding expression in songs and poems that maintain its significance. The drama and psychological effects of Nongqawuse's prediction and its aftermath illustrate the ways in which the people of the Eastern Cape continue to wrestle with interpretations of their past as it informs their present. The devastation caused by this event to the amaXhosa and the colonial conquest of the nineteenth century also set the stage for different forms of oppression and resistance in the coming years.

As illustrated in the history of the first encounters of the Africans of the Eastern Cape with Europeans, a fundamental difference between the two cultures lay in telling a history through music and spoken word (*ibali*) that focused on a shared understanding of truth, and the Social Darwinist motivation of colonizers that lay stress on strength versus weakness, victors and vanquished. Already, in the face of physical conquest, the Xhosa people were demonstrating a long view of events that contributed to their skill at adaptation even as they often found themselves divided in their initial response to hardship and dramatic change in circumstances brought on by the Frontier Wars and consequent loss of resources and independence. The communal aspect of music and spoken word, meanwhile, increasingly became an important tool of resistance, as did the structure and coordination inherent in traditional performances and the songs of warriors. The lack of an automatic sense of inferiority illustrated by Xhosa writers and poets of the nineteenth century also runs as a thread through the history of the struggle, while indigenous theology, and differing strategies for resistance demonstrated by Ntsikana and Makhanda Nxele, begin to add layers to the identity of the amaXhosa. The tension between holding on to history and the essence of themselves while absorbing the influences of conquest and colonization in the nineteenth century initiated the basis of protest among the people of the Eastern Cape in the twentieth century, with calls for unity (*yamanyama*) creating an expanded Xhosa identity that brought together the separate clans and found new tension in the degree to which members of these families accepted the political dominance and cultural and educational influences of the West. Recounting the history of the events of the eighteenth and nineteenth centuries through music and spoken word inevitably sowed the seeds of nationalism, as did Africans taking on the language of European politics and beliefs in ways that could be eventually used to confront their oppressors.

NOTES

1. Clifton C. Crais. *White supremacy and black resistance in pre-industrial South Africa: The making of the colonial order in the Eastern Cape, 1770–1865* (Cambridge University Press: 1992), 14.

2. Claudia Cancellotti, "Music, Culture & Identity: Pasts, Presents & Futures of San Musical Tradition," paper presented at 18th Symposium on Ethnomusicology, International Library of African Music, Rhodes University, 2004.

3. Major R. Raven-Hart, *Cape of Good Hope, 1652–1702: The First Fifty Years*, 2 vols. (Cape Town: Balkema, 1970), vol. 2, p. 377; Major R. Raven-Hart, *Before Van Riebeeck* (Cape Town: Struik, 1967), 22; both cited in Noël Mostert, *Frontiers* (New York: Alfred A. Knopf, 1992), 110.

4. "The Khoikhoi at the Cape of Good Hope," National Library of South Africa, Library of Congress, World Digital Library. https://www.wdl.org/en/search/?collection=the-khoikhoi-at-the-cape-of-good-hope

5. John Henderson Soga, *The Ama-Xosa: Life and Customs* (Lovedale Press, 1932), 12–13.

6. J. B. Peires, *The House of Phalo* (Berkeley: University of California Press, 1981), 19.

7. Samuel Edward Krune Mqhayi, *Abantu Besizwe*, edited and translated by Jeff Opland (Johannesburg: Wits University Press, 2009), 22.

8. Mqhayi, *Abantu Besizwe*, 28.

9. Mqhayi, *Abantu Besizwe*, 3–4.

10. Mqhayi, *Abantu Besizwe*, 8.

11. Nelson Mandela, *Long Walk to Freedom* (New York: Little, Brown, 1994), 36.

12. Mqhayi, *Abantu Besizwe*, 11.

13. Luvuyo Dontsa, "Performing arts and politics in South Africa," paper presented at the 6th Symposium on Ethnomusicology (International Library of African Music), 14.

14. Mqhayi, *Abantu Besizwe*, 28.

15. Soga, *The Ama-Xosa: Life and Customs*, 88.

16. Soga, *The Ama-Xosa: Life and Customs*, 86.

17. Deirdre Doris Hansen, "Music of the Xhosa-Speaking People" (Ph.D. Dissertation, University of Witwatersrand, Grahamstown, 1981), 56.

18. David Dargie, "Xhosa Music Terminology: How Traditional Thembu Xhosa Musicians Speak and Think About Their Music" (Fort Hare: University of Fort Hare Music Department, 2005), 2–4.

19. Laurie Levine, *The Drumcafé's Traditional Music of South Africa* (Johannesburg: Jacana Media, 2005), 82.

20. David Dargie, *Xhosa Music: Its techniques and instruments, with a collection of songs* (Claremont, South Africa: David Philip, 1988), 117.

21. Catalog # ILAM TR026, Compiled, recorded and edited by Hugh Tracey (Grahamstown: International Library of African Music, 1957).

22. H. Lichtenstein, *Travels in Southern Africa in the Years 1803, 1804, 1805,* translation by A. Plumptre, 2 volumes (Cape Town: 1928–30), Volume 1, 345. Cited

in Janet Hodgson, *Ntsikana's Great Hymn* (Cape Town: Center for African Studies, UCT, 1980), 68.

23. Soga, *The Ama-Xosa: Life and Customs,* 67.

24. William Govan Bennie, *Imibengo* (Lovedale: The Lovedale Press, 1935), 219. Cited in Peires, *The House of Phalo,* 139.

25. Peires, *The House of Phalo,* 139.

26. W. C. Scully, *By Veldt and Kopje* (London: T. Fisher Unwin, 1907), 297–98.

27. David Coplan, "A Terrible Commitment," in *Perilous States: Conversations on Politics, Culture, and Nations,* ed. George E. Marcus (Chicago: University of Chicago Press, 1994), 313.

28. J. B. Peires, Battle of Cacadu, Email, 2018.

29. Dargie, *Xhosa Music,* 10.

30. Interview with Dr. Boudina McConnachie, Lecturer and African Musical Arts (AMA) Activist at Rhodes University and International Library of African Music, January 31, 2021.

31. Interview with *imbongi* Dumisa Mpupha, International Library of African Music, July 2, 2017.

32. Interview with Dumisa Mpupha.

33. John Campbell, *Travels in South Africa* (Andover: Flagg and Gould, 1816), 97.

34. *The Natives and Their Missionaries* (Lovedale: 1908), 34.

35. J. B. Peires, *The Dead Will Arise* (Johannesburg: Ravan Press, 1989), 135.

36. John Knox Bokwe, "Ntsikana, the Story of an African Hymn," in *The World of South African Music: A Reader,* Christine Lucia, ed. (Newcastle, UK: Cambridge Scholars Press, 2005), 21–25.

37. Hodgson, *Ntsikana's Great Hymn,* 3.

38. J. K. Bokwe, *Ntsikana: The Story of an African Convert* (Lovedale: 1914), 30–31.

39. A. Steedman, *Wanderings and Adventures in the Interior of Southern Africa* (London: 1835), 224. Cited in Hodgson, *Ntsikana's Great Hymn,* 68.

40. Hodgson, *Ntsikana's Great Hymn,* 41, 56.

41. Peires, *The House of Phalo,* 143.

42. Mqhayi, *Abantu Besizwe,* 86.

43. D. L. P. Yali-Manisi, *Iimbali Zamanyange—Historical Poems,* edited and translated by Jeff Opland and Pamela Maseko (Pietermaritzburg: University of KwaZulu-Natal Press, 2015), 35–41.

44. Yali-Manisi, *Iimbali Zamanyange,* 43–51.

45. J. A. Chalmers, *Tiyo Soga: A Page of South African Mission Work* (London: 1877), 16–17. Cited in Hodgson, *Ntsikana's Great Hymn,* 77.

46. Originally derived from the Arabic term meaning "non-believer," the term "Kaffir" (or "Kafir") was used by Europeans during the colonial era in Southern Africa in reference to the languages of the Nguni peoples. The words "Kaffraria" and "British Kaffraria" also defined the part of south-eastern Africa inhabited by the amaXhosa, to whom the later uses of "Kaffir" in relation to the Nguni peoples often referred specifically. Historically, the term has acquired a derogatory connotation

and has been an actionable slur since 1976 under the offense of *crimen injuria*: *"the unlawful, intentional and serious violation of the dignity of another."*

47. "Kaffir Poetry," in *Kaffir Express IV* (*47*, August 1, 1874), cited in Hodgson, *Ntsikana's Great Hymn*, 77.

48. Hodgson, *Ntsikana's Great Hymn*, 80–81.

49. W. B. Rubusana, ed. 1911, *Zemk'inkomo magwalandini* (Frome and London: 1906), 251, cited in Jeff Opland, "The image of the book in Xhosa oral poetry," in *Print, text & book cultures in South Africa* (Johannesburg: Wits University Press, 2012) pp. 286–305.

50. Rubusana, *Zemk'inkomo magwalandini*, 234.

51. Rubusana, *Zemk'inkomo magwalandini*, 273.

52. Rubusana, *Zemk'inkomo magwalandini*, 261.

53. Rubusana, *Zemk'inkomo magwalandini*, 285.

54. Crais, *White supremacy and black resistance in pre-industrial South Africa*, 5.

55. W. W. Gqoba, "The Cause of the Cattle-Killing at the Nongqawuse Period," in A.C. Jordan, *Towards an African Literature: The Emergence of Literary Form in Xhosa* (Berkeley: University of California Press, 1973), 69.

56. J. B. Peires, *The Dead Will Arise*, 310–12.

57. Gqoba, "The Cause of the Cattle-Killing at the Nongqawuse Period," 73.

58. Gqoba, "The Cause of the Cattle-Killing at the Nongqawuse Period," 74–75.

59. Mqhayi, *Abantu Besizwe*, 74. See also Adam Ashforth, "The Xhosa Cattle Killing and the Politics of Memory," *Sociological Forum*, vol. 6, No. 3 (September 1991).

60. Mqhayi, *Abantu Besizwe*, 76.

61. Mqhayi, *Abantu Besizwe*, 78–79.

62. Mqhayi, *Abantu Besizwe*, 80–81.

63. Mqhayi, *Abantu Besizwe*, 84–85.

64. Yali-Manisi, *Iimbali Zamanyange*, 204–5.

65. Yali-Manisi, *Iimbali Zamanyange*, 206–7.

66. Yali-Manisi, *Iimbali Zamanyange*, 210–11.

67. Yali-Manisi, *Iimbali Zamanyange*, 210–13.

Chapter 3

"Turn Phalo's Land on Its Head"

Late Nineteenth and Early Twentieth Centuries

The Cattle Killing movement in many ways broke the back of African political independence, particularly in the Transkei region, along with the bulk of direct resistance to colonial rule and European cultural encroachment, with repercussions throughout the Eastern Cape. Sporadic resistance, however, still carried on through the end of the nineteenth century and the seeds of a re-defined form of nationalism and identity worked within the confines of Western imperialism to create a new version of cultural and later political defiance. This constantly reclaimed sense of history, culture, and identity became an underlying theme of twentieth-century South African history and made complete co-optation and dominance of the majority black population by the white minority an elusive goal. What began for European colonizers as a somewhat ad hoc settler policy in the eighteenth and nineteenth centuries grew, through a general lack of understanding of the Xhosa people, into an increasingly entrenched set of policies of segregation that rested on shaky foundations and contradictory objectives. That this system, based almost entirely on racism and separation (while at the same time relying heavily on African labor), lasted as long as it did arguably had more to do with economic luck than successful long-term policies. Maintaining division among Africans and people of color in general was often the fallback strategy—one that tended to fail when faced with periods of unity among those fighting the system.

The divide among amaXhosa between "believers" and "unbelievers" that developed during the Cattle Killing era and aftermath found continuing expression in the growing classification of *abantu basisikoweni* (school people) and *abantu ababomvu* (red people) during the late nineteenth and early twentieth centuries. With the rise of influence of the mission societies throughout the Eastern Cape, the school people were defined as those who acquired some European education and began to assimilate with the colonizers. The red people were those who held on to Xhosa customs and culture and who often referred to school people using the derogatory term *amagqoboka*—"people having a hole," meaning the converts had created a hole in the nation that allowed the Europeans to enter. The red people were seen to be demonstrating their preference for the pre-colonial and more familiar aspects of Xhosa life, such as coloring their bodies with red ochre and wearing blankets instead of European clothes, whereas the school people often began to attempt a form of equality with the colonists by adopting their beliefs and ways of life. The line between these two groups was not rigid and there were subtle expressions of crossover from both sides; but the overall division initially illustrated a rift between those who admitted defeat in the final stages of colonial conquest of the Eastern Cape and those who still looked for some form of independence. As the lines between these two groups blurred over successive generations, however, ideas of nationhood took root among the Western-educated class of Africans as a new way of defining independence and retaining culture using the language of the Europeans.

The division between school and red was always complex and could play out in such circumstances as the interactions of Eastern Cape Africans with white people at their place of work versus interactions with fellow Africans in a village. This contradiction serves as another illustration of the "double consciousness" among black people defined and described by the African American intellectual and Pan-Africanist W.E.B. Du Bois. This division was also complicated by a so-called ethnic separation between the Mfengu—loosely defined as refugees from the Mfecane or the population disruption caused by a combination of Zulu expansion and colonial pressure on southeast Africa in the 1830s and 1840s—and the amaXhosa of the Eastern Cape. The refugees from this "scattering" that mostly fled to the Transkei were set up as a buffer between the British steadily encroaching on Eastern Cape territories and the Xhosa communities who continued to resist them. They came to be known as Mfengu (or "Fingoes" to the colonists) and tended to be the first wholesale converts to Western religion as the missionaries provided protection and economic security to these mixed groups. The standard narrative (still open to more recent contradictions and reinterpretation) is that the Mfengu leaned more readily towards an alliance with Europeans as they had no homestead or defined nation, and, therefore, were more open towards colonial education. In certain praise poems, references were made to the Mfengu: after having been taken under the wing of Xhosa chiefs, the refugees were described as turning their backs on these chiefs to make friends with "their fathers, the white men."[1] The amaXhosa, to begin with, were more likely to be reds, but over time there grew an increasing number of school Xhosa. The period of 1870–1890 witnessed a rise in school people which contributed to an increase in their confidence and a move towards more independence from mission schools and from mission sponsorship. This period also marked a certain amount of economic independence as many of these mission-educated people were still able to support themselves through farming. The amaXhosa increasingly faced a harsh choice, however: either attempt a precarious hold on a fast-disappearing world of the pre-colonial era or adapt to the strange and discordant world of Western society.

To begin with, the school people tended to be more prosperous than red people as they had access to land and trade—this was before oppressive legislation began to limit their economic freedom. From 1880 to 1910, Africans with a European education also had the ability to influence politics through participation in elections, and with the growth of these Western-schooled Africans in the Eastern Cape came a new type of leadership that used the language of Christianity and democracy to challenge the hypocrisy and oppression of their European conquerors. The mission-educated poet Jonas Ntsiko, for example, declared in 1884, "We'll die surrounded by a smiling Gospel" and explained, "The Gospel preacher yields and talks in riddles/Not pointing out the evil of it all."[2] Ntsiko was not rejecting Christianity, so much as placing a requirement on it to be what it claimed to be and suit actions to words. He and other mission-educated leaders sought justice within the new Western framework. In his work "To Arms!," Ntsiko attacked "the white hyena":

> Its belly hangs heavy and drags on the ground
> All gorged with the bones of warrior kings,
> Its mouth is red with the blood of Sandile
> Wake, Rock-rabbits of Thaba Bosiu[3]
> She[4] darts out her tongue to the very skies,
> That rabbit-snake with female breasts
> Who suckled and fostered the trusting Mfengu
> Thereafter to eat them alive[5]

The poet and composer William W. Gqoba described the colonizers' perspective as one based on power and exploitation: "If [the Africans] cry for Greek and Latin and Hebrew give them a little. But make no mistake about the wages. Keep the wages low. If they are employed in respectable jobs, flatter them by addressing them as 'Mr. So-and-So,' but as ordinary laborers they are to be addressed as plain 'Jack' or just 'Boy'!"[6]

According to A.C. Jordan, who was also educated at a mission station in the Eastern Cape, Africans at this stage of colonization were at a crossroads: to those who received some Western education, the new road seemed more desirable but cloudy. To the developing generation of African intellectuals, the roads were both fairly clear and, while these leaders preferred the new one, they were "keenly aware of the changing attitudes of the conqueror. The fullness of life that was promised [them] is not to be realized in the foreseeable future."[7] Many in this new generation, according to Jordan, began to see the previous generations' culture as backward, acting as a form of restraint on modern aspirations; at the same time, they recognized the contradictory nature of colonial promises and policies. This frustration and double consciousness found expression in poetry and song, as in the verses of Ntsiko.

Pushback against colonial institutions had also come from Reverend Tiyo Soga, the first African ordained in the Presbyterian church in South Africa and, according to Mcebisi Ndletyana, "the first nationalist-intellectual and a progenitor of black consciousness."[8] Mission-educated in Alice during the later period of the Frontier Wars, Soga left his homeland to study in Scotland at Glasgow University, returning to the Eastern Cape in 1857. He became a strong champion of his people, upholding the beauty and importance of their culture and identity, melding his Christian education with his roots to promote fellow Africans. In 1857, in Port Elizabeth, he became the first African priest to preach at a white church and frankly expressed his views as to what his audience anticipated:

> I have no doubt that some came with the object of hearing and then laughing at the ridiculous blunders and nonsense of a Kafir preacher. Such thoughts often passed my mind, and became motives to courage and boldness of speech. There are times when the very means which malice and prejudice make use of to ensnare, annoy, or put down man, become sources of strength.[9]

Soga had a strong passion for African literature and worked to develop it in the final years of his short life in the 1860s, despite resistance from the Mission Society which did its best to keep him focused on conversion of Africans. Soga's hope was that he could "endeavour to lay the foundation for a native literature of which our people are in great need."[10] He also wrote and compiled hymns using Scottish melodies, incorporating fables, myths, legends, praise, songs, and customs to preserve the culture of his people and the messages within their music and literature which were often lost in the language and environment of mission work.

One of the most prominent institutions to participate in the "civilizing mission" of the Cape Colony was Lovedale, founded in the Eastern Cape in 1820 and named for Reverend John Brownlee's Tyhume mission (known as Old Lovedale). First established as a mission station attended by followers of Ntsikana after his death, under the auspices of the Scottish Presbyterians it became an educational missionary school and training college from 1841; one of the most famous on the continent. The goal of Lovedale and other similar institutions was to spread literacy and Christianity among the amaXhosa, and from 1854 the colonial government began subsidizing missionary schools to train Africans for work in industry or as interpreters, teachers (for Africans), and clergy. The vision of Cape Governor George Grey held that teaching Africans British law as well as educating them in the British style would motivate them to improve themselves materially. The idea was to create an African middle class with the same values as the settlers in such a way as to pacify the Xhosa community and preserve colonial society. The emerging African intellectuals were a product of this mission and the new middle class of Africans was originally intended to act as a buffer between the colonists and the local populations. These new intellectuals, however, did not become automatic imitators of their Western sponsors. They, instead, re-defined themselves in an attempt to combine the best aspects of both worlds, and became in many ways the pioneers of the creation of a modern African identity and a new South African nationalism. Among these African missionaries were writers, poets, and composers such as Tiyo Soga, Elijah Makiwane, Walter Rubusana, John Knox Bokwe, Simon Sihlali, John Tengo Jabavu, Pambani Mzimba, and Samuel Mqhhayi (discussed in Chapter 2). Leaders within their communities, these men began to impose their own culture on their conversion to Christianity and subsequently preserve the language and customs of their people through theological, poetic, and musical interpretation of these new beliefs. Observing the denominational divisions among the European missions, they questioned the pronouncement of absolute truths within Christianity and maintained much of what was precious to them from the history of their own belief systems. Tiyo Soga is held to have laid the foundations of black consciousness through pride in African history and identity. Mqhayi is seen as a powerful voice of African literature and preserver of history. Rubusana was influential in politics and establishing the importance of isiXhosa in instruction.

Western education was often used to push back at Western hypocrisy, as illustrated in the writings of these men in African-language publications, in praise-singing, and in the composition of hymns. Soga, the first African ordained in a Presbyterian church in South Africa, contributed regularly to the first real isiXhosa newspaper *Indaba*, a monthly paper published by Lovedale. In the first issue of *Indaba* he wrote, "Let us bring to light our ancestors: Ngconde, Togu, Tshino, Phalo, Rharhabe, Mlawu, Ngqika and Ndlambe. Let us resurrect the ancestral spirits of the Xhosa and Fingo nations to bequeath to us a rich heritage."[11] In his later years, Soga used his education to promote the national pride and consciousness that had been censored by his teachers and attacked colonial promotion of commercial interests, highlighting its false justifications for wars that were primarily about land acquisition; for example, he compared the crimes of cattle-theft among Africans with the "refined thieving of forgery, embezzlement, and voluntary insolvency" among white people.[12] In his work, Soga emphasized the preservation of South African history and spent much of his time interviewing the older Xhosa generation on history, fables, legends, customs, and the genealogy of chiefs, promoting African unity above the divisions of ethnicity.

Gqoba openly studied and expressed in poetic dialogues and articles the converging of African and Christian societies, asking if, in adopting Christianity, Africans had traded their fundamental identity for a confusing mixture of European lies and social positions that were out of reach. Mzimba broke from the Free Church of Scotland to form the African Presbyterian church and became a pioneer in the independent church movement. He claimed not to be angry with white missionaries. "But it is clear to me that even the native in Africa here must stand for himself in the religious matters as in other countries, and must not always be on the back of the white man."[13]

While the *iimbongi* continued to view life through the social institutions of their own communities, the Christian converts began to filter their knowledge of pre-colonial customs through their new-found knowledge of Western institutions. Jordan compared these two viewpoints in the context of colonization's period of treaties, annexations, and displacement: "the encroachment of the white man on the land of the Africans, the breaking of alliances between one tribe and another, boundary disputes, the undermining of the power of the chief by missionary and magistrate."[14] From the mid-nineteenth century on, the subject matter of *izibongo* started to include governors, missionaries, and magistrates, with references to "Smiti" (Sir Harry Smith), "Kondile" (Reverend Henry Calderwood), and "Tshalisi" (Charles Brownlee). Smith had been governor during the arrest of Sandile, and Calderwood and Brownlee were both magistrates of the Ngqika region after its conquest. Tiyo Soga's son J. H. Soga viewed Brownlee as an ally, but the *iimbongi* of Ngqika did not, complaining that "the land has been spoilt by the Calderwoods" and "we trust not Tshalisi who seems to be friends with the Germans."[15] The references were made in terms of how the actions of white people impacted the Xhosa, and chiefs were often praised for resisting white dominance or criticized for either surrendering to them or collaborating with them.

In these *izibongo*, the rifle of the colonizers plays an increasingly important role, often as the destructive force behind the written words in treaties and in the Bible of the missionaries. When the Gcaleka were expelled from their region after a dispute with the Mfengu that the British exploited, their chief Sarhili's frustration was expressed with bitterness:

> *Zindinqenil' izizwe zade zaxelelana*
> *Zindinqenil' izizwe zade zacel' umlungu,*
> *Ukuae ziti-nje zakulil' izinandile,*

> *Abizw' u-Fulele kutwe wayek' ama-Mfengu,*
> *'kub' ohlwaywa ngu yise, owawafak' ekwapeni mhlana afika;*
> *Kukuze lixole ngo-Ncha-Yecibi, isizwe siwel' u-Mbashe.*

> . . . Nations who feared me plotted against me,
> Nations who feared me appealed to the whites.
> So when the guns rumbled
> Frere warned you off the Mfengu,
> Who'd been harmed by your father's welcome:
> After Ngcayechibi's war, the nation crossed the Mbhashe.

In a description of a corrupt chief collaborating with whites through the administration of taxes and favoring his cronies at the expense of the poor, the book is held up as a symbol of the corrupting and oppressive influence of white people:

> *Ngu-Balakisi, uso-Rafukazwe liyabatalwa,*
> *Uso-Bukwe kancwad' ebal' izi-alam.*
> *Ngu qoqo fusakazi, umnyenyeka,*
> *Umbela kkama-Xanti,*
> *Upikis' abantu bemqongqota.*
> *Uruxesh' onenkani wakulo-Nyanti,*
> *Ugomb' ihlwihlwili,*
> *Ugqoboz' izulu ngesibili*

> Barracks, Storehouse of taxes,
> Book of books recording the poor.
> He's a dark refuge for absconders.
> He tortures with bars,
> Denies those who confront him.
> He's a stubborn caterpillar of Nyanti's,
> Who draws clots of blood with his lashes,
> Even heaven falls to the force of his blows.[16]

Izibongo made references to Maqoma, known to be a great warrior and orator. A hero of the Battle of Mthontsi in the War of Mlanjeni 1852, stories were told of Maqoma's dignity after rough treatment by Harry Smith. Maqoma, unfortunately, later succumbed to alcohol so that he is praised but also described as one "whose track are strewn with broken bottles," one of many references by *iimbongi* to the destructive force of liquor brought by the whites.[17]

The rising class of African intellectuals was also expressing its frustration with the colonizers through prose in Xhosa publications such as *Isigidimi SamaXhosa* (*Xhosa Messenger*). The Wars of Dispossession were pointed out as contrasting with Christian ideas of peace and goodwill toward humankind.

Suspicions increased over the actions of colonizers who spoke "with a double tongue." The swift changes were seen as challenging the African's fundamental manhood and the writers and poets were concerned with this phenomenon such that it became the focus of their expression. A Xhosa description of the Europeans, "the people who rescue and kill," refers to the colonizers' perceived tendency to protect on the one hand and destroy on the other. While at first promoting a system that rewarded educated Africans through leadership and participation in politics, African intellectuals increasingly became disillusioned with events at the turn of the century whereby, instead of reaching equal middle-class status in the European world, they began to see themselves as victims of change; losing their precarious hold on a little bit of power, economic stability, and social standing in the face of increasing industrialization, capitalism, and urbanization. Almost on the heels of the final stages of colonization and conquest came the discovery of diamonds and gold in South Africa and the rise of the mining industry with its requirement of large sources of cheap labor. While at first, in the words of A.C. Jordan, the "military conquerors lurked behind the missionaries," the captains of industry now began to dominate the colonized regions to the great detriment of the rising African middle class and the African population as a whole. This form of injustice was particularly bitter to the school people. Having been perceived by their own people as turning their backs on many aspects of their communities, they found that, still, in the words of Tiyo Soga, "the white people laugh at us."[18] What continues to be notable in this period of Eastern Cape history is that, while the Western-educated Africans were able to express some of their responses to colonization and preserve elements of their own culture in publications sponsored by mission-run institutions such as the Lovedale Press, they were also hindered by censorship of these writings in ways that the *iimbongi* were not subjected to. It was clearly easier for white authorities to suppress written words published in English than to control a form of artistic expression that was spontaneous, oral, and expressed in isiXhosa.

William Gqoba provides a detailed illustration of the conflict between those Africans who converted to Christianity and accepted Western education and those who held on to their own customs and beliefs in one of his "Great Discussions" between two characters, *Present-world* (non-Christian) and *World-to-come* (Christian). *Present-world* celebrates nature and life on earth, "so rich that even the Christian looks this way and that, and finally join the ranks of the non-Christians who openly and joyfully welcome everything that life can give." This character points out that the white man, for whom *World-to-come* abandoned his chiefs, "made no difference between the Christians and the non-Christians. He (white man) subjected them all to the same laws." *Present-world* goes on to argue that life for non-Christians is more satisfying because they can look forward to a life of peace with their ancestors in "the land of the shades" whereas Christians have to worry about going to hell:

> You deserted your chiefs and came to the whiteman;
> You destroyed our rule and sided with the enemy;
> But now your faith is lean and shrivell'd
> Even like a chameleon whose mouth is smear'd
> With nicotine on a sultry summer's day.[19]

Present-world makes a very strong case in this work by Gqoba, but, in fact, it is *World-to-come* that wins out in the long debate, perhaps as an expression of Gqoba's own Christianity, but also as an acknowledgment of the overwhelming power of the Christian colonizers.

In his "Great Discussion on Education" Gqoba creates a character called Tactless who expresses disillusionment with the so-called civilizing forces:

> We thought . . . that this way of life was going to be a refuge for those who had been smelt out as sorcerers, for suffering womanhood, for young children who had none to protect them. For these and many other blessings we gave up our independence. But no the main thing is taxes; a tax on firewood, a tax on water, a tax on grass even. . . . In good faith we allowed white traders to come and live among us, sharing our pastures with us. Today the land belongs to them.[20]

Tactless, however, acknowledges the attraction of white material goods as well as the self-destructive aspects of this attraction: "We must get them, no matter how much pain this costs us. If you want honey, you thrust your hand and grab it no matter how vicious the bees; no matter how painful the stings." The Great Discussion ends by telling the African people not to fight back, however, but to "go seek learning" and "love the white people."[21]

Much of the *izibongo* of the colonial period was preserved in Rubusana's work *Zemk' iinkomo Magwalandini*, an edited compilation of prose, praises of chiefs, and missionary and Xhosa history. Grounded in the Eastern Cape and written in isiXhosa, this work can be described as a kind of call to arms in its expression of the language, history, and culture of various Xhosa kingdoms, as well as providing stories of Ngqika and the Wars of Dispossession. Rubusana also wrote *History of South Africa from the Native Standpoint* and translated the Bible into Xhosa. Rubusana and his fellow intellectuals further represented a generation of Africans forming their own organizations such as the Native Vigilance Association in order to more directly represent their own people. In 1897, as a response to growing realizations of the limits of publishing through colonial institutions, he and others set up their own newspaper *Izwi Labantu* (*Voice of the People*) with the goal of providing expression of the political aspirations of Africans in the Eastern Cape in the late nineteenth century. Particular focus was placed on the effect of discriminatory land tenure laws that not only hindered the economic independence of Africans, but also acted as a check on their ability to vote. From 1836 black men living in the Cape Colony had the opportunity to participate in municipal elections after the constitution of 1853 established the principle of no color distinction in the franchise. Every male citizen over 21 that either owned property worth £25 or earned a salary of £50 annually (or a salary of £25 and free board and lodging) was entitled to vote. As the Western-educated class of Africans became more aware of the gap between Christian doctrine/Western political ideals and the actual realities of colonial conquest, they initially and collectively made the decision to accept the new order and try to impose change within it. Participation in elections was one method of achieving a power-sharing role with white people, assimilating European culture in order to be recognized as a new class separate from "traditionalism."[22]

Izwi Labantu was established in many ways as a counter voice to John Tengu Jabavu's paper *Imvo Zabantsundu* (Native Opinion) set up in 1884, which often seemed guided by white English-speaking politicians who increasingly supported laws that restricted the eligibility of African voters. White liberal financing of Jabavu's paper caused him, in Rubusana's opinion, to continue to support policies that betrayed his fellow Africans. Jabavu had gained prominence in the 1880s as a spokesman of African opinion, and in 1887 he led protests against the Parliamentary Voters Registration Act, an act which served to restrict African votes after the incorporation of Transkei territories into the Cape Colony, causing 20,000 residents to be struck from the roll, the majority of them black. The black population still represented 30% of the electorate in 12 of the constituencies, and 20% in 10 constituencies in 1891, leading to more demands in Parliament for new laws that would further restrict the black vote. The resulting Franchise and Ballot Act of 1892 raised property qualifications for voting and introduced a literacy test. Jabavu's protests on this second occasion of Cape restrictions, however, were muted as he had become involved with party politics through his connection with Rose Innes and two other Cape liberals, all of whom were members of Cecil Rhodes's cabinet backed by the conservative Afrikaner Bond. Jabavu increasingly moved away from the growing sections of African opinion represented by the likes of Rubusana. Supported by many in the Mfengu population, he began switching his loyalties to the Bond, swayed by their (false) promises of franchise rights for Africans in return for African support.[23] This division came to a head in the early twentieth century and led to an undermining of the power of the black electorate in the Cape Colony. In 1909 Rubusana became the first African elected to the Cape Provincial Council but Jabavu challenged him for his seat in 1914, which split the African vote and gave the seat to the white candidate.

Even as he had exposure to and was influenced by figures such as Jabavu who increasingly looked to colonial assimilation as the key to retaining power, in terms of preservation of Xhosa history and culture in the face of European encroachment, it was Mqhayi who worked tirelessly to maintain not only the prominent role of the *iimbongi* but also redefine the scope and subject matter of praise poems. As described by Mncedisi Qangule, "[Mqhayi] often wrote of history and abstract ideas such as truth, hope, and love, using the morality of his time as the foundation stone for constructing a revitalized African morality."[24] Moving beyond the local focus of previous *iimbongi*, Mqhayi made white people central subjects of many of his praise poems as opposed to background forces affecting events. He also incorporated the European style in his *izibongo*, wrestling with the Western use of rhyme and rhythm in contrast to the Xhosa style that did not concern itself with these elements.

Similar to his fellow mission-educated peers, Mqhayi's primary concern was of justice as a foundation for society, and he often focused on how law and justice operated in pre-colonial Xhosa communities. Sharply critical of colonial education, Mqhayi credited it with providing some benefits of "civilization" but, like his peers, he highlighted the fact of its use to promote the selfish interests of colonialism and imperialism:

> *Ukuhamba behlolela iinkose zabo ezibahlawulayo umhlaba.*
> *Bahamba nalo ilizwi ukuba lihamba liba yingcambane*
> *yokulawula izikhumbani nesizwe, yathi imfuno yayinto nje*
> *eyenzelwe ukuba kuviwane ngentetho*

> Human movement in search of land grabbing land from chiefs,
> Using the word of God as a tool
> And instrument to rule Kings and nations
> An education so inferior
> Became an institution to prepare slaves for new masters[25]

"Perhaps above all," writes Qangule, "Mqhayi will be remembered as a protest poet who stoked the fires of nationalist resistance."[26]

Just as there was pushback in the late nineteenth century against colonial infringement on Xhosa society through prose and poetry among the Africans, there was also reaction within the sphere of music. John Knox Bokwe, viewed generally as the father of black South African choral composition and known particularly for transcribing and arranging the hymns of Ntsikana, became increasingly discontented with the eradication of meaning in Xhosa music through its subjugation to European hymns. Unhappy with the Western musical destruction of the poetic beauty of Xhosa compositions, he worked on combining historical melodies that were more accurate in tone regarding songs and Xhosa patterns of music. Using his knowledge of both Xhosa and Western music he performed his own compositions while training as a Presbyterian minister in Scotland in order to educate the British on the reality of life for Africans in the Cape Colony. One of these pieces was the political hymn "Plea for Africa" which included verses such as these:

> Give your love to Africa! They are brothers all,
> Who, by sin and slavery, long were held in thrall.
> Let white man love the black; and, when time is past,
> In our Father's home above all shall meet at last.
> Give support to Africa! Has not British gold
> Been the gain of tears and blood, when the slaves were sold?
> Let us send the Gospel back, since for all their need,
> Those whom Jesus Christ makes free, shall be free indeed.[27]

In 1891 at the Lovedale Jubilee, Bokwe expressed approval of what he felt his people had gained through Christianity and colonization, but he also focused on the "evils" that Europeans had brought to his people: "It is a strange and sad fact that the sons of colonists, according to the native mind, swerve from the upright courses of their fathers. They deteriorate. . . . There is the fact; answer it."[28] Bokwe's politics became increasing anti-colonial, and he grew to focus on unity among his people. As articulated in his own words, "Let Us Help Each Other," his music became part of the struggle against white oppression. ANC leader Walter Sisulu later expressed the opinion in 1987 that "Plea for Africa" inspired the anthem *Nkosi Sikilel' iAfrika*.[29]

Converts such as Bokwe were often troubled by the destruction of the poetic beauty and meaning of Xhosa language, particularly by Victorian hymnody; a phenomenon that motivated Bokwe's own compositions, which have been described as "the first good Xhosa verse set to music."[30] The European missionaries who initially came to the region lacked the knowledge and motivation to understand the subtleties and nuances of Xhosa music and performance. Their main concern had been to eradicate "uncivilized" aspects of music and dance and preserve the language of amaXhosa largely in order to sing European hymns. According to one of the more sensitive missionaries, "Much of the early hymn-making for the Christian Church in Africa was an unhappy yoking of unidiomatic vernacular prose, clipped into the right number of syllables to fit a line."[31] By controlling the translations and hymnody of the songs of the amaXhosa, European missionaries were able to influence the message of the music and even replace that message with their own. Tone was especially important, adding to the perceived distortion of meaning in adopting straight translation of Western hymns in isiXhosa. This change in meaning through tone and translation added to the larger picture of resistance through black nationalism and race, as later activists sought to restore the true essence and message of their people's music and performance. It should be noted again that this problem of censorship through translation, similar to the situation of censorship in writing, was largely bypassed in the continuing performances of *iimbongi* because, unlike Victorian hymns being translated into Xhosa, their work was less likely to be translated into English. Even when it was translated, white ears could not always comprehend the coded references and obscure metaphors, which meant that authorities were unable to infringe on the independence of meaning and intention.

Just as in the post-Reconstruction period of U.S. history when Western-educated black leaders became increasingly disillusioned with the promise of equality held out to them at the end of the Civil War, mission-educated Africans in South Africa became more awake to their own lack of opportunities under colonial control, despite their conversion and cooperation. A number of them began to form their own organizations, such as the National Education Association based between King William's Town and Fort Beaufort, and *Imbumba Yama Nyama* (the South African Aborigines' Association), formed in Port Elizabeth. The rise of what was referred to as Ethiopianism or African religious separatism became marked in the early 1890s as part of a reaction of Africans against white-controlled churches—churches that preached progress and cooperation but practiced restriction and exclusion. Africans established their own churches in frustration with white paternalism: turning the language of democracy and liberalism back on their oppressors, the rising population of black nationalists and breakaway church leaders pointed out that Africans had already lived in centralized political states before the arrival of the Europeans and thus had prior claims to independence and nationhood. Inspired by black intellectuals from the United States such as Du Bois, this population adapted modern ideas from their Western education but strongly rejected the hypocrisy that accompanied them. To many black leaders, racism was not a fundamental element of a system they had been forced to adapt to, but a sign of the white population's ignorance of and blindness to the true potential of black people. As one writer to *Imvo Zabatsundu* protested:

> It is all very well for politicians to be complaining about the existence of blacks, for this is what might have been expected in Africa—a black man's country. We should have thought that coming to a black man's country, Europeans would accommodate themselves to their surrounds and try to make worthy neighbors of the Natives instead of fretting and fuming over their large numbers and legislating with a view to rid them off the face of the earth.[32]

At the end of the nineteenth century a transatlantic conversation grew between Africans and African Americans in which the black population in the Eastern Cape were significant participants. One of the earliest groups to initiate that conversation was the Virginia Jubilee Singers, a collection of black performers from the United States that toured South Africa between 1890 and 1898. This group represented in many ways the intersection of music and political debate regarding the future of black people in South Africa and their connection to the African diaspora. The South African tour included performances and interactions in the Eastern Cape, such as Port Elizabeth, Grahamstown, and Lovedale Institute in Alice, and crucial discussions over strategies of uplift underpinned the cultural exchange of musical styles and experiences of racial oppression. The arrival of the Jubilee Singers came at a time of growing disillusionment among black leaders with the promises of Cape Liberalism and also coincided with an increased exodus of many black Christian leaders from the control of white establishment churches to join the Ethiopian movement. The tour of the Virginia Jubilee Singers symbolized in numerous ways the combination of issues that black populations on both sides of the Atlantic were grappling with; for example, preservation of culture versus advancement toward equal status in an unequal society, and advancement through vocation versus advancement through liberal arts learning and confrontation.

The founder of the Virginia Jubilee Singers Orpheus McAdoo was born in 1858 in Greensboro, North Carolina, the oldest child of enslaved parents. Similar to many black leaders in the Eastern Cape of South Africa, McAdoo navigated his advancement through Western education, an early example being the influence of his mother, Bessie Eunice, who was the only enslaved person on the estate who could read. He was a graduate of Hampton Institute in Virginia—a school created as a form of higher education for former slaves—and taught for several years there, as well as touring with the Hampton Male Quartet, one of the most famous quartets of that time. One of Hampton's more well-known graduates, Booker T. Washington, promoted the self-help philosophy for advancement represented by the institute. This philosophy put greater emphasis on vocational training for its black students, as opposed to the liberal arts curriculum of white colleges and of other black centers of higher learning such as Fisk University in Nashville, Tennessee. After performing with Frederick Louden's Fisk Jubilee Singers who had their own successful tours in the U.S. and Europe, McAdoo formed his own company as a means of raising money for Hampton Institute. Although McAdoo was influenced by the strategy for black upliftment represented by Hampton and Washington, it should be noted that Louden was an outspoken activist for the campaign for the Civil Rights Act of 1875, and he and the Fisk Jubilee Singers worked to raise national support for the Civil Rights Campaign (the Supreme Court ruled the Act unconstitutional in 1883). A description from the Hampton Archives of the Fisk Singers observed that it was "the opportunity of these singers to present both the New and the Old world that which certified what had often been doubted—whether the Negro had a soul."[33] McAdoo, thus, was most likely influenced by the promotion of advancement of black people through direct political means as well as through entertainment and the arts.

The Virginia Jubilee Singers were billed in South Africa as a minstrel group, but their performances and repertoire were notably different from the previous shows of South African whites in blackface that had toured the country, such as the Christy Minstrels. These local performances had been given to mostly white audiences, and the performers, influenced by the white minstrel shows that came to Europe from the United States, expressed a so-called sympathy and appreciation for black culture. The shows, however, represented more of a parody of black society, and as Veit Erlman argues, it was a way for the performers to act out white fantasies about black people and deal with their increasing fears of losing established white structures to African resurgence and independence.[34] The typical minstrel show reduced black people to basically two crude caricatures: the ugly and raggedy rural persona associated with slavery and the "uppity" fancy-dressed character in white gloves, shoes, and a white tie associated with urban black people. The Virginia Jubilee Singers introduced a new element in the minstrel shows to black and white audiences, including a greater involvement of African American spirituals. After their first appearance in South Africa, they were described in glowing terms by *The Cape Argus*:

> Singing such as is given by the Virginia Concert Company has never before been heard in this country. Their selection consists of a peculiar kind of part song, the different voices joining in at most unexpected moments in a wild kind of harmony. At one moment once has the full force of all the voices, and the next is straining the ears listening to a melody which seems to be fading away. It would be useless for others to attempt to sing music of this description; it is without doubt one of the attributes of the race to which they belong, and in their most sacred songs they seem at times inspired, as if they were lifting up their voices in praise of God with hopes of liberty.[35]

What was more important in the show to white audiences—the reinforcement of stereotypes—was less significant to black audiences who responded to the music and dance influences. Both responses to these shows represent white versus black approaches to racist oppression: white uneasiness with their role—as Dale Cockrell notes in his article on the Jubilee Singers and minstrel shows in South Africa, "we often ridicule those whose treatment troubles us the most"[36]—versus black expression of the sorrows of oppression, love of and pursuit of freedom, and resistance to despair through self-entertainment represented in the spirituals and dance numbers. McAdoo usually introduced the shows with lectures on black culture in America that seemed to reinforce the Hampton model of self-help—a message that was approved by white U.S. educators in the Virginia Jubilee Singers' international tour as it spread the influence of the segregation model and was, obviously, appreciated by white authorities in South Africa. To black audiences, however, the message of separation and subservience was superseded by the inspiration caused by the performers as black people who had figured out how to achieve some level of progress in an oppressive society. The performances also awoke in the African audiences the desire to study in the United States as a powerful tool for challenging inequality in South Africa. Jabavu wrote in *Imvo Zabantsunda*:

> As Africans we are, of course, proud of the achievements of our race. [The Virginia Jubilee Singers'] visit will do their countrymen here no end of good. Already it has suggested reflection to many who, without such a demonstration, would have remained skeptical as to the possibility, not to say probability, of the Natives of this country being raised to anything above remaining as perpetual hewers of wood and drawers of water. The recognition of the latent abilities of the Natives . . . can not fail to exert an influence for the mutual good of all the inhabitants of this country. The visit of our friends, besides, will lead to the awakening in their countrymen here of an interest in the history of the civilization of the Negro race in America, and a knowledge of their history is sure to result beneficial to our people generally.[37]

Izwi Labantu wrote of ten African students who were accepted at Lincoln University in Pennsylvania and Tuskegee Institute in Alabama: "We hope that more of our young men will emulate this example and proceed to England and the United States for the education denied them in this country."[38] The message of segregation that white authorities on both sides of the Atlantic hoped would be spread by McAdoo's group was contradicted by a conversation among Africans that focused on shared nationhood by black populations in South Africa and the United States. This conversation represented Du Bois's creation of ideas of blackness as opposed to Washington's message which was interpreted in South Africa as promoting black people as subjects but not citizens.

Although he would express pro-colonial opinions, mainly because of his unusual position in South African society (before the South African War, black nationals from the United States were given "honorary white status"), McAdoo was aware of these forces and the role his group played in such conversations, just as he was well-aware and critical of the experience of black people in South Africa. He wrote to the head of Hampton Institute General S. C. Armstrong:

> Everyone seemed captivated with the singing; never heard such singing in all their lives, and they said, "and just think that black people should do it." The latter remark will give you some idea of a feeling of prejudice; well, so it is. There is no country in the world where prejudice is so strong as here in Africa. The native today is treated as badly as ever the slave was treated in Georgia. Here in Africa the native laws are most unjust; such as any Christian people would be ashamed of. Do you credit a law in a civilized community compelling every man of dark skin, even though he is a citizen of another country to be in his house by 9 o'clock at night, or he is arrested. . . . Black people who are seen out after 9'oclock must have passes from their masters. Indeed, it is so strict that natives have to get passes for day travel. . . . These laws exist in the Transvaal and Orange Free States, which are governed by the Dutch, who place every living creature before the native.[39]

When the singers toured the Eastern Cape, they were much appreciated by white audiences and the group was paternalistically described in the *Grahamstown Journal* as "the only true exponent of American Coon Songs in South Africa."[40] The uniqueness of their demeanor and situation did cause some confusion in that region. The *Kaffrarian Watchman and Government Gazette* of King William's Town gave this account of the mixing of cultures:

> While the Jubilee Singers were here the natives could not quite understand what sort of people they were. Some of them hesitated to class them as Kafirs, as they seemed so smart and tidy in appearance, and moved about with all the ease and freedom among the white people that a high state of civilization and education alone can give. Occasionally, however, a Kafir would salute a "Singer" in his own language and when he failed to get a reply he would look puzzled, exclaim *Kwoku*! And walk away wondering how his "brother" did not return the salute.[41]

The black audiences at the Virginia Jubilee Singers' shows in King William's Town were described as "enraptured with the singing. . . . Their admiration of their American cousins must really have been very great, for on the day the troupe left the town one of the classic crowd was heard to say in the deep drawling style—'We shall never again hear such splendid singing until we go to Heaven.'"[42]

After performing in Grahamstown, the group gave up several paid performances in order to make the 60-mile trip on bad roads to Alice and perform for a black audience for two days and three nights at Lovedale—described by McAdoo's brother Eugene as "this African Hampton."[43] Eugene McAdoo went on to describe the trip to Lovedale and the experience there:

The school is about sixty miles from Grahamstown, and there is no railroad. The regular mail coach was too small to carry our large party—so a long, covered "Dutch Wagon" was chartered. This was drawn by eighteen huge oxen. . . . . After two days and three nights our sixty miles were accomplished, and we were in the beautiful little town of Alice, and just across the river . . . enclosed by a splendid cactus hedge, was the school. . . . The many nice buildings, the boys at work on the lawns and in the work-shops, the girls at their different labors, made me imagine that I was at Hampton. . . . We were soon shown into the Assembly Room where we were to sing and the girls and boys came in much in the same way as do the students here [at Hampton]. There were nearly five hundred of them, and their faces were a picture of interest and anticipation. We sang for them for nearly a couple of hours, and then they favored us with some of their songs, which we thoroughly enjoyed, for their voices were indeed good.

Eugene McAdoo went on to describe Lovedale as "a great power for good" and claimed that in Alice the troupe found "a more respectable class of natives than in any other part of the country we visited."[44]

Lovedale was, in fact, very similar to Hampton particularly in its approach to curriculum after the mid-1880s, in that black students were not allowed to study Latin and Greek—a policy that had been introduced by Dr. James Stewart—and they, therefore, could not qualify for Cape University and the British Civil Service Exam. General Armstrong established a curriculum at Hampton that borrowed from British colonial models in Asia and focused on producing teachers, farmers, tradesmen, and domestics, deliberately shunning the liberal arts education of white northern universities and black southern colleges such as Fisk and Atlanta. Although McAdoo and his singers largely represented the "up from slavery" model of advancement, their presence and performances inspired African elites to become leaders that more directly challenged the status quo, including members of the South African Native National Congress (SANNC—later ANC). One of the Virginia Jubilee singers, Will Thompson, stayed in South Africa, joining future ANC leaders Isaiah Bud M'bell, Sol Plaatje, and Henry Ngcayiya to organize a protest movement against segregation in public transportation.[45]

The presence of the singers also opened up a debate concerning the degree to which black American assistance should be relied on to raise up the position of Africans. As a result of his experiences in South Africa, McAdoo told Armstrong that he planned to give a $70 scholarship to "an earnest Christian boy" to study at Hampton, which met with approval at that institution (sadly, the young man Titus Mbongwe was killed in a train accident in England while on his way to Hampton). South African white authorities, however, were not so happy over this project, and McAdoo was asked to explain before a committee of white officials whether he was "singing to educate Negroes" or for his own business. One minister stated, "If it is to educate the Kaffirs and

Zulus, you will never succeed in Africa." McAdoo reported this incident back to Hampton, stating, "There is no sympathy between the whites and blacks. There is as much prejudice here regarding the natives as there is in Georgia. They don't believe in the blacks being educated." He went on to state his response to the committee's question as to the purpose of the scholarship: "I told them it was my own enterprise and when once I got the money, like any else, I could do what I liked with it."[46]

Five young men in King William's Town found out about McAdoo's plan through *Imvo Zabantsundu* and applied to Hampton, two of them writing to Armstrong:

> We have meet Mr. O. M. McAdoo, and we speak to him about the School, and we told him about our trying and efforts to be educated here in Africa . . . we have no fathers to take us to school, and we are very poor, we can do nothing of ourself, it's why we trouble you, dear sir . . . from the year 1889 we was desire to be, are in the college, unfortunately we were on account of being very poorest because our parents they are on a position red blankets. . . . Mr. Orpheus M. McAdoo he gave an interesting account of your educational, and we ask him if we must start away with him, and he said we must send our application.[47]

As well as illustrating the transatlantic connection fostered by McAdoo's group, the application also demonstrates the increasingly blurred line in the Eastern Cape between the definitions of red and school at the turn of the century.

The South African tours of the Jubilee Singers inspired black South Africans in the Eastern Cape to form their own singing groups and the spirituals soon became a standard in the performances of African choirs. The spirituals appealed to Africans because of their expression by fellow black singers from the U.S. of a striving for freedom and a looking back to an ancient time of justice and happiness. It was a music demonstrating a shared language among black people with its emphasis on particular values, problems in maintaining those values, and the strategies used to keep them alive.

Charlotte Manye (later Maxeke) represents the influence of McAdoo's group and the resolve among a number of black South Africans to pursue this strategy of uplift and employ it to fight for freedom. Manye was the daughter of a Tlokwa father and Mfengu mother and grew up in Uitenage and Port Elizabeth. She had already gained a reputation as an outstanding singer in her own right while teaching at Wesleyan School when she was exposed to the Virginia Jubilee Singers and, inspired by their example, became a member of the African Jubilee Singers formed by Albert Walklett and modeled after McAdoo's group. Touring with them in England, Manye moved on to a black minstrel group that landed her in the United States where she attended

Wilberforce University with Du Bois as one of her professors. Echoing the sentiments of Pan-Africanism inspired by her experience in the U.S., she wrote, "I wish there were more of our people here [in the United States] to enjoy the privileges of Wilberforce and then go back to teach our people so that our homes can lose that awful name 'the Dark Continent,' and be properly called the continent of light."[48] When she returned to South Africa, she gave a powerful speech at the SANNC's 1902 Congress, even though women were still not allowed to be members. Her musical talents and educational success kept Manye Maxeke at center stage of black activist politics and she became a prominent member of the women's branch of the ANC, maintaining that position until her death in 1939. Charlotte Manye Maxeke stands out as a lone female voice during the rise of black nationalism and political activism in the Eastern Cape and South Africa as a whole, as she gained prominence at a time when women still played a secondary role in African resistance movements and in the music that accompanied these movements. In many ways she helped open the door to female participation in African activism in the twentieth century. Her husband Marshall Maxeke was one of the students she helped get scholarships for study in the United States (they married soon after) and Marshall Maxeke organized the first AME church hymn book in Xhosa.[49]

The debate over the role of U.S. assistance played out among black leaders in the Eastern Cape in the face of a growing mining and capitalist economy that tightened restrictions on Africans and dampened their hopes for advancement. One example of this debate is found on the pages of *Imvo Zabantsundu* with regard to the influence of the Virginia Jubilee Singers. A contributor writing under the pseudonym "Dorotil' mgwevu-ngezihlathi" ("The Grey-Bearded Doctor") wrote:

> *Kuphela izolo nemihla tina Afrika ungafika siwungula uboya sibusa ekaya ize intaka siyishiye endle isala ityiwa zizizwe. Ezona zinto zigqite nokucula kulamadoda ase Amerika abezifanele namhla ukuba zifundo ezikulu kumakowetu zezi.*

> It was not so long ago that we Africans left our homes for other nations to devour. These things are of great significance and the singing of these men from America should stand as a lesson to us.

"Dorotili" compared institutions of the United States with colonial institutions in regard to advancement of black people, and saw those in his own environment as holding back his people in contrast to those in the United States. Jabavu printed this commentary, but added his own rebuttal: "*Kulingile ukutaba amava namavo kumawetu awaya engazingulele e Merika, Kodwa masiwasebenzise pakati Kwetu ukuze asincede*" ("It is all good to take from what our brethren from America but let us use it to help ourselves where we are").[50]

To "Dorotili" the answer for advancement lay in the transatlantic connection represented by the Virginia Jubilee Singers and McAdoo's offers of scholarships. Jabavu's response was that advancement should be homegrown. These two approaches to African aspirations were echoed and reflected not just in the synthesis of musical influences that groups such as McAdoo's represented, but also in the religious independence movement prominent in the Eastern Cape. In 1884 Nehemiah Tile, a Wesleyan minister from the Thembu region of the Eastern Cape, broke from his church to establish the Tile Thembu Church. Other clergy began breaking off in the 1880s and 1890s also to found independent churches. While in the United States, Charlotte Manye wrote a letter about the American Methodist Episcopal (AME) church as a leading institution for black upliftment and the letter was shown to Xhosa clergyman Mangena Mokone who began a correspondence with AME church leaders, including AME Bishop Henry Turner. When Mokone requested more information on the church, Bishop Turner sent him "a Discipline, a hymnal, and other books."[51] Through this AME influence, Mokone established Tiyopia, the Ethiopian church, based on the prophecy from Psalm 68: "Princes shall come out of Egypt; Ethiopia shall soon stretch out her hand to God." Mokone's fellow clergyman Reverend James Mata Dwane managed to raise the funds to travel to the United States, where he was appointed General Superintendent of the new AME church in South Africa. Dwane was one of the most respected church leaders in the Eastern Cape, converting to Christianity at age 19, studying at Healdtown for the ministry, and becoming ordained in Port Elizabeth. He had early leanings towards African nationalism in a connection to *Imbumba Yama Nyama* and his appointment as superintendent minister of circuit in Cala district in 1885 coincided with Tile's separation from mission religion to create his own Thembu church. Forming an alliance with Mokone, Dwane took over the leadership of the Ethiopian church and became part of both separatist church and political leadership among black South Africans.

Along with Mzimbe, Mokone, and Dwane came another separatist church leader in the Eastern Cape, Edward Tsewu, who trained as a teacher at Lovedale and was ordained as a minister of the Free Church in 1883. After working among African laborers in Johannesburg, he formed his own Independent Presbyterian Church and joined forces with the AME church during the visit to South Africa of Bishop Turner. These independent churches included the influence of AME music, incorporating spirituals into their repertoire, melding this influence with their own African/European lyrics and melodies, reviving dance as a part of religious ceremony, and reaffirming an identity and consciousness based on a shared language of oppression and freedom.

When he separated from the white mission church Tsewu took with him a large Lovedale congregation to form the Presbyterian Church of Africa, a circumstance that caused great disruption in the work of white missionaries and aroused concern among the white population over what they viewed as a movement based on race consciousness.[52] The separatist churches began to be viewed with growing alarm by white authorities, and the original complacence and encouragement of American connections, thought to be beneficial to promoting segregationist ideologies, gave way to increased suspicion and restriction of African American religious and musical influences. Messages of self-reliance that had initially met with approval by educators in places such as Lovedale were now viewed as subversive, and the spirituals sung in the AME and Ethiopian churches were seen as carrying dangerous subtexts related to freedom and Pan-Africanism.

These separatist churches and their leaders remained strong in the memories of the Eastern Cape protest leaders of more recent times who viewed them as early champions of black independence and black nationalism. Twentieth-century *imbongi* David Yali-Manisi composed *izibongo* in praise of Dwane and Mokone during the era of apartheid, linking their work to modern African liberation movements and acknowledging their influence. In his praise poem to Dwane, Manisi referenced Dwane's time overseas:

> *Azol'amaza nomoya,*
> *Yeyela ngophond' eMelika*
> *Yagquba yeza nolutho . . .*
> *Washiy' iWesil' igungqa*
> *Wadal' umzi weTopiya*

> And the waves and winds went silent,
> As he gored America,
> He rummaged and came with something . . .
> You left the Methodist shaking,
> As you gave birth to the House of Ethiopia.[53]

In praise of Mokone, Manisi connected the drama of the struggles from the nineteenth century to those his people were experiencing in the twentieth:

> *Hi mfondini kaMokone!*
> *Thetha nosapho likaNtu,*
> *Luyek' amanyondonyondo,*
> *Le nto asinguwo mdlalo.*
> *Kukho ingqumbo ezayo,*
> *Kukho umsindo ozayo;*
> *Kukude ke ezulwini,*

Kuseduz' esihogweni.
Vuthisan' iBhay' Emi,
Lihambele phambil' izwi
Livulindlel' aAfrika,
Yokuhanjwa yimidaka.

You son of Mokone!
Talk to the black African,
To shed the bad,
For this is no child's play.
Great wrath is coming,
Huge anger is upon us:
Heaven is not so near,
But Hell is next door.
Burn the cloth Emi,
Let the Word move forward
And open Africa's path,
For black Africans to trample.[54]

Eastern Cape music at the turn of the century undoubtedly represented the influences of its own history along with that of African American culture, and there was clear cross-pollination, including complex approaches to white interference in ownership of culture and the music that expressed it. Students at Hampton with memories of slavery had mixed feelings over spirituals and were often reluctant to sing these songs because of the painful recollections they evoked;[55] while Africans in the Eastern Cape struggled to hold on to meaning and identity in the music that had been appropriated and redesigned by missionaries. Western-educated African choirs were trained by the method of tonic solfa notation first introduced to mission choirs in Grahamstown by Christopher Birkett in 1855, and subsequently used throughout the Eastern Cape, eventually spreading to most of sub-Saharan Africa. The technique was used to teach sight singing based on a movable system of naming notes, starting with the tonic, with each note given a name plus notation and a hand symbol based on its relationship to other notes and its rhythm. Xhosa singing, like the language of isiXhosa, relies very much on tone and is based on the early instrument the uhadi bow which employs two notes and harmonics. Xhosa singers tend to be able to harmonize automatically as they hear the two notes and blend a multitude of sounds accordingly, with emphasis on resonance. There is no "key" in this form of singing and the method of tonic solfa was able to adapt to this tradition by creating a standard relationship of notes regardless of key.[56] On the one hand, the introduction of tonic solfa subjected African music to European rules; on the other, it provided a degree of flexibility that helped to preserve African melodies, musical structures, and performances. The use of tonic solfa parallels the spread of Christianity in the Eastern Cape and southern Africa as a whole, as both were used as mediums for harnessing African culture to European management, yet both these influences were eventually used to reinforce African purpose and identity. Tonic solfa developed into a medium for thousands of indigenous compositions for the next 150 years, and at the turn of the century, this phenomenon meshed with the growing influence of African American spirituals, creating a combination of influences that was especially prevalent in the choirs of those churches that broke away from white control.

Nkosi Sikilel' iAfrika is one of the strongest representations of this combination of forces and influences; a song that symbolizes musical resistance in South Africa probably more than any other. The mixture of spirituality and collective resistance in its message has allowed it to survive various iterations and usages, adapting to each circumstance of social and political upheaval and unification in South Africa's modern history. Its composer, Enoch Sontonga, a Thembu of the Mpinga clan, was a poet, choirmaster, lay preacher, and photographer who was born in 1873 near Uitenage and educated at Lovedale. He wrote the first two stanzas in isiXhosa in 1897 and the song was first publicly performed in 1899 at the ordination of Reverend M. Boweni, the first Tsonga to become minister in a Methodist church in Johannesburg. Sontonga died young (age 32) in 1905, but at the time of his death his song had already become a prominent choice of choirs, while also developing into an expression of protest. At the first meeting of the SANNC in 1912, it was sung after a closing prayer by the Ohlange Institute Choir under the direction of Reuben Caluza. One of the founding members of the SANNC, Solomon Plaatje, recorded *Nkosi Sikilel' iAfrika* in 1923 accompanied on the piano by the daughter of John William Colenso, Bishop of Natal, and it became the official song of the SANNC in 1925, after this organization changed its name to the ANC. Mqhayi wrote the additional seven stanzas published in his poetry collection *Imihobe Nemobongo* (Anthems of Praise) in 1927, and the song was also published in 1927 by the Lovedale Press in the form of a pamphlet and in the Presbyterian hymn book (*Incwadi yamaCulo aseRhabe*) in 1929.

The lyrics of *Nkosi Sikilel' iAfrika* fused Protestant influences with the importance of cleansing in African culture, which gave it a double meaning that could be adapted to different circumstances. When first performed, the dual message and the song's melody represented the tension between the teaching and musical practices of white Lovedale authorities and the developing culture of AME churches in South Africa. The appeal in the song is to a higher being, one above the authority of white men and one that provides blessings and justice. According to David Coplan and Bennetta Jules-Rosette, "The 'melancholy' . . . musical yearnings of the song emerges from both Sontonga's likely social discontent and from his efforts to bring together two musical and cultural traditions with an air of solemnity and reverence."[57] Sontonga was probably connected to the AME church movement for justice and social advancement and his song reflects a blending of Christian and African influences known as *isidolophu*, a type of urban syncretism that expressed the social and national consciousness of the black middle class in South Africa's cities. The year of the song's first public performance was the same year as the outbreak of the South African War and also coincided with the conflict between AME missionaries and the United Free Church of Scotland in Lovedale. White clergy and Lovedale authorities viewed the African and African American AME missionaries as "evangelical Pan-Africanists" who stirred up division and conflict within Protestant churches in the area and subverted their tight control over African education. No doubt, *Nkosi Sikilel' iAfrika* symbolized frustration and resistance in an emotional yet poetic manner that appealed to Eastern Cape leaders such as those in the ANC, who wrestled with the hypocrisies of white South Africa appearing to include them in one instance then exclude them in the next. Coplan and Jules-Rosette observe, "The sense of lament emerging in the final line of Mqhayi's verses of *Nkosi* . . . reflects the religious, racial, and political conflicts that had already surfaced when the song was first performed in 1899."[58] The song also expresses the desire for unity that echoes Pan-Africanism and its words exert a call to action. Throughout its history, words such as "save" and "remember" have been substituted for "bless" with the implication that over time Africans were diminished or banished. The timing of its creation also reflects the history of resistance in the Eastern Cape. The song emerged and grew popular just as African leaders in South Africa, more particularly in the Eastern Cape, were feeling the full weight of betrayal by Cape Liberalism in the wake of the South African War, and British politicians seemed more concerned in their victory over the Boers to create a union with the Afrikaner republics and black labor reserves for the rise of industry than hold fast to their promises of greater equality and extension of the franchise to the black population.

One major issue at the turn of the century that sparked organized African resistance in the Eastern Cape and revealed the influence of the rise of black nationalism and religious separatism concerned the Glen Grey Act of 1894. This Act and reaction to it in the Eastern Cape represents in many ways the culmination of elements of resistance dating back to initial European encroachment in that area and the Frontier Wars that centered on issues of land and power. These issues were still central to Africans at the turn of the century, but now opposition to white dominance had added elements of the rise of black nationalism and unity among previously disparate groups whose divisions had been manipulated and exploited by colonial authorities and incorporated into mission education in the nineteenth century.

The Glen Grey Act was promoted by Cecil Rhodes, who was at that time Cape Prime Minister and Minister for Native Affairs and who hoped to extend this legislation into the Transkei region and have it eventually adopted throughout southern Africa. Rhodes extolled the so-called advantages of the Act, claiming it would stabilize pay for teachers, develop districts for magistrates, and create a better road system and currency circulation for those in trade. Justifying the new system on the basis of race and paternalism, the Act would triple the total tax paid in Transkei reducing the expenses of administration in this region; furthermore, the system would create and limit a population of producers and land-holders, while denying land to others who would then be forced into the labor market. An African administration being answerable to a white magistrate would create local participation which would cancel out black access to the Cape franchise. In Rhodes's opinion, this type of local politics would be more suitable for a black population than involvement in national government for "those children just emerged from barbarism." A council system, he argued, would "keep the minds of the natives occupied. . . . Having proposed that they should form councils, so that it should not be a farce, let them tax themselves, and give them funds to spend in the manner of building bridges."[59] The main intent was clearly to increase the labor supply for the mines.

The concerted reaction in the Eastern Cape and Transkei to this Act was so overwhelming that at least two of the stipulations were never completely carried out; the land tenure aspects and labor tax specifically were defeated through boycotts and collective refusal to pay the tax. The creation of local councils was eventually pushed through (creating the groundwork for the Bantu Authorities system of apartheid) but only after a long hard fight against highly organized and uniquely unified resistance. The Cape government had mistakenly assumed it could count on compliance from the Mfengu population based on their history as colonial allies and military collaborators, and had not recognized the growing division between headmen and the people. A magistrate in Butterworth observed, "At the present moment these men are far worse off and not so loyal as they were twenty years ago."[60] With the development of an African press where opposition to Cape policies and general treatment of the black population found increasing voice, the Mfengu population gained exposure to and experience in modern political activism. The 1887 Voters Registration Act was referred to by political leaders in Transkei as *tung' umolomo*—"the shutting of the mouth,"[61] and headmen connected with Cape administration were viewed in that region with increasing suspicion.

Imvo Zabantsunda and *Izwi Labantu* played a significant role in this conflict by creating a language of opposition and explaining the measures and effects of the Glen Grey Act, and this development did not escape the notice of Cape magistrates; an Elliotdale magistrate complained of this influence, stating, "We have to look forward to a Native Bond, which will prove a far greater difficulty than the Africander [sic] Bond, and with growing advancement of the Native Tribes will discover their power."[62] When a delegation of leaders presented to the Cape Parliament the grievances of the Qumba population regarding the Act, they emphasized the fact that a lack of popularly elected representation would divorce them from the Parliamentary system; "they would have not representation in the Government of the country, and no franchise."[63] The collective effect of mass organization against the Act connected different groups throughout the Eastern Cape, including those that had been historically antagonistic towards each other. The Idutywa magistrate observed the "remarkable development" that Gcaleka, Ndlambe, and Mfengu "dropped all race feeling and tribal jealousies and agreed on a united course of action."[64]

Defiance of the Glen Grey Act in the Eastern Cape represented among African populations the evolution of new forms of resistance, the rise of new ideologies, and the falling away of certain ethnic divisions caused or manipulated by colonization. The Act, however, also contributed to a more recently developed class division between headmen and the people they were put in charge of, and a divide between the politically organized and some of the new middle-class Africans who had been influenced by the benefits of the council system and were more focused on personal achievement. The conflict further illustrates the crucial role the Eastern Cape played in the development and nurturing of African nationalism in South Africa. Much of the elite resistance leaders were educated at Lovedale—and later on at the University of Fort Hare—and the Eastern Cape came to be historically viewed as the spiritual heartland symbolic to the struggle and to African nationalists. At the turn of the century the history of the Frontier Wars assumed a significance in African nationalist language that was spoken and sung, representing a fight to preserve not only land, but the amaXhosa as a nation and their culture. This trend found expression in literature, newspapers, songs at demonstrations, and *izibongo*. It also connected with the formation of separatist churches as Africans attempted to reconcile their own heritage and beliefs with Christianity. As Mzimba expressed it, "All would admit that for Africa's redemption, the African must be the chosen instrument."[65] Legislation such as the Glen Grey Act demonstrated how segregationist policies could backfire and create new traditions of unity that would undermine white dominance.

The intersection of music, religious separatism, African transnationalism, and resistance in the Eastern Cape can also be illustrated in two movements occurring in the early 20th century that resonated with disillusioned rural populations and carried echoes of the Great Cattle Killing movement of the 1850s. Focusing on the idea from African Americans of external liberation, a group of millennials known as the Israelites staking a claim to land in Bulhoek outside of Queenstown, and the Wellington movement that took off primarily in Transkei, were influenced by the transatlantic message of Marcus Garvey and his United Negro Improvement Association (UNIA). Outside of the U.S. and the Caribbean, the Garvey movement took root in South Africa more firmly than anywhere else. Its slogan "Africa for the Africans" had already been a feature of the religious separatist movement in South Africa and, to the white population, suggested a more radical and fearful solution on the part of Africans to their position in South Africa: no accommodation with white authorities and a reversal of the Land Act. Garveyite Africans in South Africa did not actively push this agenda, although seven branches were set up by 1926, including one in East London, and the movement failed to develop into a mass organization in South Africa. The ripple effects of Garvey's movement in South Africa, however, were strong, notably in its influence for a while on the ANC (possibly including changing the organization's name from SANNC to one that had a more pan-Africanist sound), and in the formation of the Industrial and Commercial Workers' Union (ICU). The latter concentrated much of its organization in the 1920s on rural areas in South Africa and connected with local African movements that predicted and prepared for a rescue mission from the *Ameliki* (Americans). The religious tone of these movements had a natural accompaniment of music influenced by African American gospel and spiritual songs and carrying messages of freedom.

After the War of the Axe of 1846–47, a group of Moravians were granted land in a place that became known as Shiloh, and over the course of the late nineteenth and early twentieth centuries, Africans in that Eastern Cape region suffered continual loss of territory. These circumstances set the stage for the Israelite movement led by Enoch Mgijima with the land conflict further fueled by the restrictions of mission Christianity. Mgijima had become an evangelist in that area, preaching a millennial message with Garveyite overtones. He started out as a Wesleyan Methodist, but gradually built up a substantial number of personal followers and his services involved communal prayers, rhythmic music, and powerful sermons. In opposition to the local mission council and inspired by the African American Church of God and Saints of Christ (CGSG), Mgijima's followers called themselves Israelites and began to build their own church. Israelite Walter Dinca expressed the root causes of their dissatisfaction with white mission authorities: "Can any sane black man follow this religion which is out to exterminate the Natives of this country?"[66] Mgijima joined the CGSG during the rise of the separatist movement in South Africa, the church having been founded in Kansas in 1896 by William Saunders Crowdy who believed that Africans were descended from the lost tribes of Israel and were, therefore, Jewish. By the time of Crowdy's death there were fifty branches of his church in the United States and twelve in South Africa, with a membership of about 2,000. Denied entrance to South Africa himself, Crowdy sent Albert Christian as a representative of his church. Music played a role in these circumstances as Christian had already visited in 1899 as a member of the Virginia Jubilee Singers. He later worked in Port Elizabeth as a black Baptist minister. Returning in 1903 as a missionary for Crowdy, Christian established churches in New Brighton and Uitenage outside Port Elizabeth and gathered converts from the colored and African population. Mgijima never met with Christian, who left South Africa in 1905, but he came into the CGSC through John Msikinya who had been educated in the United States at Lincoln University, and Mgijima soon gained a prominent position. Because the prophecies of the CGSC were ones of peaceful transition, it eventually broke ties with Mgijima's movement whose followers occupied Shiloh in a village where Mgijima lived known as Bulhoek outside of Queenstown. Building homes and planting farms in contravention of the land ordinances, Mgijima called on his flock to gather at Ntabelanga to wait for the final reckoning. Over 3,000 members heeded the call, partly in despair over a series of natural disasters, the pressures of inflation and taxes during World War I, and the flu epidemic of 1918. As Robert Edgar expresses the situation in "The Prophet Motive," to a large number of this suffering population, "it was increasingly clear that there was something radically wrong with the world, and that they were no longer in control of their lives."[67] The retreat to Ntabelanga was a retreat from this devastating world and a method of starting over as a part of God's plan, since black people (and Jews) were God's people. The white regime, however, took a dim view of this occupation, regarding it as one more dangerous and separatist challenge to its authority, and in 1921 government forces drove the Israelites out of the village, killing 163 Israelites and wounding 92 more. It was the first modern political massacre in South African history.[68]

Music was prominent in these prophetic nationalist movements in the Eastern Cape. The herbalist Nontetha Nkwenkwe, who predicted the arrival of black Americans coming to "cut the throats of the Europeans and converted natives who are under the existing churches," called for black solidarity, ordered children out of the white-controlled schools, and encouraged the singing of passages from Revelations that were interpreted as immediate predictions of judgment on the Europeans. She accumulated a devoted following, many of them women, and when she was arrested and jailed in 1922, her supporters gathered in protest, congregating outside the courthouse in King

William's Town to sing hymns and chant prayers. The government response was to commit her to a psychiatric hospital first in Fort Beaufort and later in Pretoria, where a delegation of her followers walked 600 miles to see her. They were arrested in violation of the pass laws and sent back to the Eastern Cape. In adherence to her proclaimed prophecies, her followers also defied a government order to kill a swarm of locusts that had descended on the region in 1923. An acting magistrate in Middledrift described the followers' method of passive resistance:

> As we approached about 40 of them threw themselves on the ground and commenced praying and singing. At first they declined to take any notice of my requests but after separating the women (who were the most virulent) the Headmen requested the men to proceed to destroy locusts which were in enormous swarms around the kraals. This they all declined to do in a most emphatic manner.[69]

This form of confrontation carried on in the face of several attempts by authorities to enforce the order. Eventually, assisted by the local chief and headman, the movement was raided at their meeting place in Ngcabasa and 135 people were arrested. Resistance once more took the form of singing and praying by Nontetha's adherents as they lay on the ground. While in jail, the believers held services, and continued to pray and sing, many describing dreams of liberation by African Americans. Nontetha eventually died in isolation in 1935, but her prophecies and following represented yet another expression of the desperation of Africans in the midst of increasing corruption, devastation, and disease. One of Nontetha's disciples recalled, "There was always hope throughout that the Americans would free us. As oppressed people, we always had hope that we would be released."[70]

A further Garveyite influence in the Eastern Cape came in the person of Wellington Elias Buthelezi. Buthelezi was a Zulu from Natal who claimed to be an African American doctor from Chicago and minister of the AME who had come over in one of Garvey's ships to continue the work of the UNIA. Wellington's speeches, however, did not only include Garveyite principles of black pride, unity and liberation. Riding in a Dodge sedan with a personal chauffeur, he toured the Transkei in 1926—often greeted by singing from local girls' choirs—and spread the message of miraculous redemption from European oppression through a rescue mission launched by black Americans. Reviving rumors from the Versailles conference that power over South Africa had been transferred to the United States, he claimed that the initial agreement made by Prime Minister Jan Smuts had been overturned by the new Prime Minister James Hertzog and that Hertzog was now preparing for war against a black-dominated U.S. in order to preserve white supremacy.

Wellington would encourage Africans to look into a glass instrument and see U.S. planes arriving to drop fireballs as weapons and pushing white people into the sea. His proclamation was an appropriation of the UNIA's message of African independence and he used it to encourage African demands for land and freedom of movement, pushing back against state, missionary and white social authority. The message carried echoes of the Cattle Killing movement of the 1850s as followers were instructed to paint their houses black, kill their white pigs, and destroy anything they owned that was white or came from pigs. The predicted destruction brought by aircraft fired the imagination of local Africans anticipating fire raining from the sky not just on the white population but on all nonbelievers. As fantastical as the prophecy sounded, it acted as a powerful antidote to the government strategy of division through narrow definitions of African "tribes" in that it propelled many rural Africans to take on a transnational identity that connected them to America, and further portrayed African Americans as liberators. As the historian George Frederickson has pointed out, millennialism often expresses a cry against injustice and a reflection of a general desire for liberation.[71] The prophetic nature of this movement was familiar to a people who already had a history of the importance of dreams and visionary associations calling for liberation as expressed in their own songs and in African American spirituals, and these elements merged with the UNIA platform to take root in African minds. The Garveyite movement had previously sparked numerous rumors in East London that "Americans" would come in ships with weapons to launch violent attacks on the white population, and the movement acted as a way to translate local grievances and beliefs into an international cause. Music formed a backdrop to these developments, with members of the South African branches of the UNIA singing missionary Christian hymns that asserted their commitment to principles of African independence including "From Greenland's Icy Mountains" and "Onward Christian Soldiers."[72] When Wellington's prediction failed in 1927 he claimed this was because not all the pigs had been killed. He was later arrested and banned from Transkei.

While the messages in song and spoken word of different millennial and religious movements expressed one form of resistance to white domination, the assertion of a self-defined African identity in the early twentieth century was another. An outburst of Xhosa literature published in the 1920s provided a powerful voice for African nationalism and the reclamation of identity, and was aided by the establishment of African languages programs in South African universities. As noted above, this period also marked an intense phase of radicalization of black leadership as the disappointment of South African Union legislation, the severe restriction of black access to rural property and urban access through the Natives Land Act (1913) and the Urban Areas Act (1923), and the aftermath of World War I added fuel to resistance fire. After the failure of an ANC delegation to Versailles to even get a hearing in the postwar conferences, one of its leaders, Reverend Z. R. Mahabane, expressed the collective impression of the delegates that Britain "had finally washed her hands of the innocent blood of the Bantu races, divested herself of all responsibility—although like Pilate in sacred history," Britain would never be "absolved from responsibility in the shameful 'selling away' of a whole nation."[73]

As urban popular resistance rose in the Rand, the two rival African papers *Abantu-Batho* and *Umteteli wa Bantu* based in Johannesburg propelled the literary careers of Xhosa poets, most notably Mqhayi and Nontsizi Elizabeth Mgqwetho, a unique woman *imbongi* and poet who was a friend and compatriot of Charlotte Manye Maxeke. At that time, women were not recognized as *iimbongi*, although they had always played an important role in *intsomi* (Xhosa folktales), but Mgqwetho established herself as both a prominent poet and *imbongikazi* (female *imbongi*), publishing over 100 poems in *Umteteli*, and giving performances on the Rand, often at concerts organized by Charlotte Maxeke and the Women's League of Congress. The first poem of hers published in *Umteteli* was written in the style of an *imbongi*, calling up those who had died in battle and quoting from the *izibongo* of Sandile.[74]

In April 1920, Mgqwetho sang praises at City Deep Hall to commemorate the valor of those who had battled the police in demonstrations. In June 1922 she gave a poetic presentation in a farewell ceremony for Reverend B. S. Mazwi—a performance that was met with great acclaim and an enthusiastic response from the audience, and she was prominent again that month in the program for the Ntsikana celebration in Johannesburg. According to the report, after a "long and absorbing" speech by Manye Maxeke,

> Kute gqi u *Miss Nontsizi Mgqweto, Imbongikazi watiwa* introduce *ngenteto emfutshane ngu Mr. Govo, u Miss Mgqweto* umemelele *ebonga lomhla ka Ntsikana ongcwele. Ute umbhali wala macapaza eba uzama ukubhala ngesandla esikaulezayo, kwabonakala ukuba zonke ezonto ziyampazamisa ekulapuleni i* tengu-macetyana, *akabanga* saloba *wapulapula njengabanye, elubeke pantsi usiba. Yamemelelake lontombazana ama Xoza abonakala ebambelele ezidleleni entywizisa. Emra kwemizuzu engamashumi amabini ugqibile u Miss Mgqweto waya kuhlala.*

Suddenly, up stepped Miss Nontsizi Mgqwetho, the Woman Poet who was introduced in a short speech by Mr. Govo. Miss Mgqwetho exultantly praised this day of Saint Ntsikana. The writer of these notes tried to scribble in a hasty hand, but it was obvious that all those things were distracting him from hearing the fork-tailed drongo, so he ceased the attempt and listened like the others, with an idle pen. This young lady sang out triumphantly, and the Xhosa were seen with their hands to their cheeks, crying out loud.[75]

Establishing herself as an *imbongikazi*, Mgqwetho announced in December 1924: *"Ndine minyaka emitandatu, namhlange, ene nyanga ezimbini ndibonga, ndenze iisitonga sisinye; ndibangela le Afrika"*—"It's now six years and two months since I exploded on the scene as a poet singing praises to Africa," which indicates the possibility that she had been performing as an *imbongikazi* since 1918.[76] She praised herself in the manner of *iimbongi*, using metaphor and imagery from nature and indicating change in African culture brought about by urbanization that also awoke reaction:

> *Taru! Nontsizi dumezweni ngentsholo*
> *Nto ezibongo ziyintlaninge yezwe*
> *Indlova ke ayisindwa ngumboko wayo*
> *Awu! Taru! Sikukukazi piko e Afrika*
> *Esikusela amatole aze angemki*
> *Emke nezinye intaka eziwadlayo*
> *Uyaziwa lilizwe nambakazi yezulu*
> *Enqene nazi Mbongi zada zaxelelana.*
> *Wugqwetele Mgqwetto lo mhlaba ka Palo*
> *Beta izizwe ngesitunzi zi dangale*
> *Uliramncawa akuvelwa ngasemva*
> *Nabakwaziyo babeta besotuka.*

> Mercy, Nontsizi, renowned for your chanting
> Your poems are the nation's bounty.
> No elephant finds its own trunk clumsy.
> Awu! Mercy, old hen's wing in Africa!
> Hen screening her chicks
> From birds of prey,
> The nation knows you, sky-python,
> Poets sneer but discuss you.
> Turn Phalo's land on its head, Mgqwetho,[77]
> Whack nations and sap their standing.
> Wild beast too fierce to take from behind,
> Those who know tremble in tackling you.[78]

The thrust of much of Mgqwetho's work was directed towards calling Africans to action against oppression and to create unity amongst themselves, which meant that it often combined criticism of white oppression with criticism of black inaction and division. Her work also evoked the internalized division between red and school—Christian and indigenous belief—in *"Ingxoxo yomGinwa kumaGqobhoka!"* ("A Red Debates with Christians"), a poem that echoes Gqoba's debate between "Present-World" and "World-to-Come." In the voice of a red, Ngqwetho denounced the hypocrisy of Christian converts, yet admitted a small degree of truth in Christianity in the final line, expressing the increasingly blurred line between what is rejected from European culture and what is absorbed:

> . . . Niko ngaku Tixo nasebuqabeni
> > Nigqobok' emini kuhlwe nizincuka . . .
> Sotinina tina xa bese njenjalo
> > Sibambe lipina kulo mpambampamba
> Neratshi likuni nina magqoboka
> > Nambatis' u Tixo ngengubo yengwenya.
> Nina magqoboka ningodludla nazo
> > Nayek' izik'ak'a nanxib' ezomlungu
> Nite nzwi nendlebe butywala bomlungu
> > Kodwa yen' umlungu akabudl' obenu . . .
> Nakufika kuti tina bomaqaba
> > Tina sakunoja siti niyinyama.
> Anditsho ukuti Izwi lika Tixo
> Ukuteta kwalo akunanyaniso.
> Camagu!

> . . . You wear red blankets in God's very house,
> > You're Christians by day, hyenas by night . . .
> What do we make of this curious conduct?
> > Which voice do we choose from among this babble?
> Pride is one of your Christian companions,
> > God wears a cloak of crocodile hide.
> You Christians are suckers for every fad,
> > You cast off skin garments and dressed up like whites,
> Your ears are tinkling for white man's booze,
> > But whites won't touch a drop of yours . . .
> If you ever try to come near us again,
> > We Reds will roast you like meat.
> But I'm not saying the word of God
> > is entirely barren of truth.
> Mercy![79]

As part of a tribute to resisters who had battled with the police in Johannesburg entitled *Yeha! Watshonona! Afrika! ELundini* ("Alas! Africa, you fade into the horizon!"), Mgqwetho both praised and admonished the Christian God:

> *Ngxatsho ke Yehova*
> *Tixo woyihlo betu*
> *Yinina ukuba ugqubutele*
> *Ubuso Bako kuyo I Afrika. Taru!*
> *Nabo bebanjwe bonke*
> *Nabantwana bayo*

Kumbula Omawenze kona
Ngalo izwe letu. Camagu!
Sinyateliswa ngamahashi
Sipahlwe nazingozi
Awu! Nkosi Tixo pantsi
Ezantsi e Afrika. Awu! Camagu!

Well done, Jehovah,
God of our fathers,
Why screen your face
From Africa? Mercy!
There they all are in prison,
Even her children.
Remember what you must do
About our country. Peace!
They spur their horses to trample us,
We're ringed by dangers.
Oh! Lord God below,
Down in Africa. Oh! Peace.[80]

Mgqwetho also highlighted the plight of African women in her poems, extolling Charlotte Maxeke for her activism as "the Mother of African Freedom" and supporting the growing trend of boycotts among rural women. Describing the toll taken on women as a result of oppression and urbanization, she asks:

Wazinyatelana Intombi zezwe lako
Zangamak' obokana Ezweni lako
Baza amehlo kade ndandidibona
Kulapo namhla wotshabalala kona . . .
Intombi zezwe lako sisivato sako
Ogudazilingeke Ezweni lako.
Zitsho kamnandi ekumbini lentaba
Ndingazicinga kuti gongqe nenkaba.

Are you trampling your nation's girls,
to enslave them in your land?
Open your eyes, I've long seen it coming:
Here, today, we're facing ruin . . .
Your nation's girls are treasures,
Their beauty a source of pride,
Their sweet voices ring from the mountaintops.
The thought leaves me short of breath.[81]

As Opland points out, however, Mgqwetho, while performing and writing in praise and support of women, would assume the persona of the male *imbongi* and the attitudes that accompanied it in specific praise poems, for example,

> *Tarhu, mHleli ngesithuba sezimbongi!*
> *Ndisahleli ndingumfana andimbongi*
> *Ndingumphathi-thunga lezinxiba-mxhaka*
> *Into elwa ngezulu iinduku zihleli.*

> Thanks, Editor, for the poets' column.
> I'm still here, a young man and no poet;
> I bear the milk-pail to distinguished veterans,
> I fight armed with thunder alone.[82]

During the 1920s Mgqwetho switched loyalties from the ANC to Charlotte Manye Maxeke and her husband Marshall Maxeke's more moderate breakaway movement, but her work continued to highlight the loss of African independence, the exploitation of black labor, the decadence of city life, and the patriarchal society she lived in. Mqhayi, meanwhile, maintained his support for the ANC, consistent with his earlier participation in SANC-sponsored Vigilance Associations of the Eastern Cape, and his work in the 1920s focused on increasing attendance at political meetings and raising funds for specific purposes such as the visit of the ANC delegation to Britain. He often used battle metaphors to rouse his fellow Africans to action: "*Kuni manene nama nenekazi ase Johannesburg ndihlaba umkosi*" ("To you, ladies and gentlemen of Johannesburg I am sounding the war cry"), and he urged opposition in powerful language:

> *Yizani nixobe tu! Ningabi sezela ukuza kuva ukuba nditinina. Ubuciko abseko kumzuzu sixwitana notshaba ezinkundleni! Yitini ukuza ezintla nganisweni zam nize senizimisela ukubinza—indlue iyatsha ngasemva aliseko ituba lokubasisa, kufuneka imali Pesheya.*

> Come armed to the teeth! Don't come to hear what I'm going to say. Eloquence has no place: for quite a while we've been plucking feathers from each other and our opponents in the courts! When you come to my meetings, come prepared to stab—the house is on fire at our backs, there's no time to spin stories, money is needed overseas.[83]

While Mqhayi was hailed at this time as *Imbongi Yesizwe Jikelele* (The Poet of the Whole Nation), and Mgqwetho was called *Imbongikazi Yesizwe* (The Woman Poet of the Nation), a third Xhosa poet, John Solilo, also had significant recognition in the 1920s. Unlike Mqhayi and Mgqwetho, Solilo did not perform as an *imbongi*. A solid convert to Christianity, he gained prominence as a clergyman, but his poetry adopted the style and tone of *iimbongi*. Similar to Mgqwetho, he used Gcoba's "Great Discussion" between a Christian and non-Christian as inspiration for his own poem "*Ingxoxo (Inyembezi ezingena msuli)*"—"A debate (Tears with none to dab them)" to illustrate the vast and depressing difference between black and white perspectives:

> *Ingxoxo pakati ko-Mlungu noMxosa.*
> *Itatwa njengoku ngati bayota*
> *Bobabini zikweni linye, bade basuke beme beteta*
> *Umxosa—*
> *"Nyawuka mlungu, undisitile.*
> *Ilita ndiyalifuna, kwane bandezi*
> *Uva wedw' intsito, noku hamba kwe gazi.*
> *Nam ndingumtu, mandipil' elizweni.*
> *Undicinezele, ndihleli kakubi.*
> *Ndiya kuqabelisa*[84] *kuwe, unyaw' olumdaka."*
> *Umlungu*
> *"Pang' eqingeni, sidenge*[85] *soMxosa*
> *Ulifa lam, ndikunikwe Pezulu . . .*
> *Ungeka gqoboki ukolis' uMdali*[86]
> *Pika ubene, andiku-nyauka.*
> *Sel' amanzi' uncame kafile."*
> *Umxosa*
> *". . .*
> *Yon' iBayibile, wayi libala.*
> *Ungabi*[87] *sayi pata, uyazi hlazisa.*
> *Wanikw' umsebenzi, ufundis' abantu*
> *Wen' uyarweba, ngeraf' ezininzi*
> *Ziyatshab' izizwe, ngoku fun' uSindiso.*
> *Ulahl'iBayibile, weza neBotile.*
> *Int' ozenzayo, zingama sikizi*
> *Ivangeli yako, kukutiy' ukafile."*
> *Umlungu*
> *"U-dom kafile, ungavumi kufunda.*
> *Zifunda ngamava zonke intlanga,*
> *Pambi kwako ndidlal' imidlalo.*
> *Pambi kwako ndilim' amasimi.*
> *Ndiya kuqesha wen' usebenze.*
> *Nditeta noMdali*[88] *we' ubukele . . ."*
> *Umxosa*
> *". . .*
> *Amalumko, ako, ayacengceleza,*
> *Ngezono zetu, noku deleka kwetu."*
> *Umlungu*
> *"Peza mxosa, akukwaz' ukuteta.*

Uyagaba-dela, ubinz' esiqwini . . .
Asiso sono, ukubet' imbongolo,
Uyiqub' ihambe, ikusebenzele.
Intlung' ozivayo, ziku fanele,
Xa uzunz[89] *imbongolo, nok' unengqondo . . .*
Umxosa
" . . .
Bendiba Yingozi, Ukupata kakubi
Ndib' akuqondi, intlung' endiyivayo.
Kant' undenz' imbongolo, mtana wezulu.
Akusa fundisi, inceba ipelile.
Uvis' ubuhlungu, utshutshis' abanye.
Uziketela okuna utanda lentona?"
Umlungu
"Ndiyapeza Mxosa, ukuteta ndikukatule . . .
Ndibafundis' abantu intlalo engcwele.
Bota ke Ntsundlu."

A discussion between a white man and Xhosa.
We imagine them warming themselves at a fire,
Both in the same place, then they stand and talk.
The Xhosa
"Move back, white man, you're blocking my heat.
I want light, but you're in the way.
Only you feel the warmth, the coursing of blood.
I too am human: let me live in the land.
You've held me back, I don't rest easy.
My grubby foot will dispatch you."
The white
"Do what you will, you brainless Xhosa,
You were granted to me from Above . . .
Until you convert and please the Creator,
Protest till you bust, I won't give way.
Take it or leave it, Kafir."
The Xhosa
" . . .
That Bible has slipped from your mind.
Don't touch it again, you'll bring shame on yourself.
"You were given the task of teaching others,
But you've turned into merchants raking in taxes,
Lacking salvation, nations perish.
You spurn the bible and bring the bottle,
Your conduct is disgusting.
Your gospel is Hate The Kafir."
The white

"You dumb Kafir, refusing to learn.
Every nation learns from experience.
Far more than you I take my ease.
Far more than you I cultivate fields.
I employ you and you do the work.
I address the Creator, you just gawk."
The Xhosa
". . .
All your wisdoms explore in fine detail
Our sins and contempt for us."
The white
"Steady now, Xhosa, you're not a good speaker,
you're out of your depth and growing aggressive . . .
"It's no crime to thrash a donkey,
and drive it to work for you.
You deserve the pains you experience
if, having brains, you act like a donkey . . ."
The Xhosa
". . .
I believed brutality perilous,
it held you indifferent to my pain.
Yet, child of heaven, you think I'm a donkey.
Bereft of compassion, you're no longer a teacher,
You wreak suffering, persecute others
Is this your choice, is this your desire?"
The white
"Xhosa, I've had enough talking, I'm done . . .
I like to be known for fair treatment of others
instructing them in a holy life.
Greetings, then, Darky."[90]

The message within Solilo's work, despite his depictions of the great divide between African and European society and aspirations, was one of reconciliation on the part of the black population. He did not, however, promote assimilation, instead placing stress on education as a tool for advancement and social transformation. Solilo consistently exhorted preservation of African identity and called on the white population to come to terms with what in modern terms would be called black pride. He made these sentiments clear in "*Ingoma yaba-ntwana base Africa*" ("Song of the children of Africa"):

> *Makatet' otand' ukuteta,*
> *A-ndiva ntwimbi ndifung' imidaka*
> *a-Ndiyi ndawo, ndofel' e-Afrika.*
> *Maka-ncame notiy' ukafile.*

Ndiyayitanda ngenen' iAfrica.
Kodwa Yngxak' ukuhlala nomlungu.
A-kavumi sivane ngentlalo,
Sihlale sokelan' umlilo . . .
Masivane mlungu ngeAfrica,
Swendele ungena kunyotulwa.
Ndoda ndife ndiyibang' i-Africa
Izwe lam lokuzalwa ngubawo.

Let them say what they like,
Unaffected I swear by black people,
I'm not going to leave, I'll die in Africa.
Let the Kafir hater know that.
I'm a loyal lover of Africa,
But living with whites creates problems.
They refuse to live in harmony,
To share their fire with us . . .
White man, let's come to accord on Africa.
You're rooted and can't be dislodged.
Until I die I'll lay claim to Africa,
The land of my birth, of my father.[91]

By the early nineteenth century, the colonial system had evolved in such a way as to keep the black population increasingly separate from the white society while defining the existence of black people largely in terms of working to benefit and produce profit for the white population. African populations such as those of the Eastern Cape fought consistently against this, using music and spoken word—not only resisting concrete exploitation of their land, work, and means of survival, but also resisting the metaphysical exploitation and erasure of their history and culture. The imposition of European language was countered by isiXhosa maintained in *izibongo* and religious and liberation songs. The imposition of the European version of events was answered by the determined maintenance of collective memory through creative expression. The rise of African nationalism encompassed these forms of resistance while forging connections with black religious and political movements overseas such as those in the United States, and underpinned the communal sense of self that continued to be manifested in artistic form in the first half of the twentieth century.

Three strands of musical and poetic resistance had, meanwhile, evolved within the Eastern Cape communities in response to tightening regulations and restrictions on land, movement, and political and economic survival. Prominent sections of the black middle class maintained a strategy of using music and spoken word to prove the worthiness of black people within a society where white people held all the power. A new generation of educated Africans and those from the breakaway religious movements in town and country employed songs and *izibongo* in the service of direct protest and to reclaim African nationalism and identity. At same time, in the burgeoning urban culture of places like Port Elizabeth and Queenstown, music and performance were being reinvented as part of a new fast-paced life that used entertainment as a means to survive and outsmart the torture and indignities of oppression.

NOTES

1. A.C. Jordan, *Towards an African Literature: The Emergence of Literary Form in Xhosa* (Berkeley: University of California Press, 1973), 61.

2. Harold Scheub, review of *Towards an African Literature: The Emergence of Literary Form in Xhosa* by A.C. Jordan, *The Journal of American Foklore,* Vol. 90, No. 357 (July–September 1977), 347.

3. Mountain in Lesotho

4. Queen Victoria

5. A.C. Jordan, *Towards an African Literature*, 94.

6. A.C. Jordan, *Towards an African Literature*, 66.

7. A.C. Jordan, *Towards an African Literature*, 63.

8. Mcebisi Ndletyana, *African Intellectuals in 19th and early 20th century South Africa* (Cape Town: HSRC Press, 2008), 57.

9. Ndletyana, *African Intellectuals in 19th and early 20th century South Africa*, 25.

10. Ndletyana, *African Intellectuals in 19th and early 20th century South Africa*, 27.

11. *Indaba*, August 1862, 9–11. Cited in André Odendaal, *Black Protest Politics in South Africa to 1912* (Totawa, NJ: Barnes and Noble Books, 1984), 29.

12. Ndletyana, *African Intellectuals in 19th and early 20th century South Africa*, 26.

13. Donovan Williams, "African Nationalism in South Africa: Origins and Problems," *Journal of African History*, XI, 3 (1970), 381.

14. A.C. Jordan, *Towards an African Literature*, 60.

15. A.C. Jordan, *Towards an African Literature*, 61.

16. W. B. Rubusana, ed. 1911, *Zemk'inkomo magwalandini*, (Frome and London: 1906), 285, cited in Jeff Opland, "The image of the book in Xhosa oral poetry," in *Print, text & book cultures in South Africa* (Johannesburg: Wits University Press, 2012), pp. 286–305.

17. A.C. Jordan, *Towards an African Literature*, 63.

18. Scheub, review of *Towards an African Literature*, 349.

19. A.C. Jordan, *Towards an African Literature*, 65.

20. A.C. Jordon, *Towards an African Literature*, 66.

21. A.C. Jordan, *Towards an African Literature*, 67.

22. Odendaal, *Black Protest Politics in South Africa to 1912*, 4.

23. Odendaal, *Black Protest Politics in South Africa to 1912*, 13–14.

24. Mncedisi Qangule, "Samuel Edward Krune Mqhayi," in Ndletyana, *African Intellectuals in 19th and early 20th century South Africa,* 57.
25. Qangule, "Samuel Edward Krune Mqhayi," 63. Translation by M. P. Qanqubi.
26. Qangule, "Samuel Edward Krune Mqhayi," 64.
27. David B. Coplan, *In Township Tonight! South African's Black City Music and Theatre* (Chicago: Jacana Media, 2008), 43–44.
28. *Christian Express* (Lovedale, September 1891), 150.
29. Grant Olwage, "John Knox Bokwe, Colonial Composer: Tales about Race and Music," *Journal of the Royal Musical Association,* volume 131, No. 1 (2006), 26.
30. Coplan, *In Township Tonight!,* 32.
31. Alexander Sandilands, *120 Negro Spirituals* (Lesotho: 1951), 3.
32. *Imvo Zabantsundu,* December 15, 1892, cited in Veit Erlmann, *Music, Modernity, and the Global Imagination* (New York: Oxford University Press, 1999), 176.
33. "Foreword"—fragment of biography of Fisk Jubilee Singers, author unknown, n.d., Hampton University Archives.
34. Veit Erlmann, "'A Feeling of Prejudice.' Orpheus M. McAdoo and the Virginia Jubilee Singers in South Africa 1890–1898," *Journal of South African Studies,* Volume 14, no. 3 (April 1988), 335.
35. "Jubilee Singers at the Vaudeville," *The Cape Argus,* Cape Town, July 1, 1890.
36. Dale Cockrell, "Of Gospel Hymns, Minstrel Shows, and Jubilee Singers: Toward Some Black South African Musics," *American Music,* Volume 5, No. 4 (Winter 1987), 428.
37. *Imvu Zabantsundu,* (October 16, 1890), cited in Erlmann, "A Feeling of Prejudice," 344.
38. *Izwi Labantu,* August 27, 1901, cited in Erlmann, *Music, Modernity, and the Modern Imagination,* 174.
39. "A Letter from South Africa: Black Laws in the Orange Free State of Africa," *Southern Workman,* Volume 19, No. 11 (November 1890), Hampton University Archives.
40. *Grahamstown Journal* (April 10, 1897), cited in Veit Erlmann, "A Feeling of Prejudice," 338.
41. *Southern Workman,* Volume 20, No. 1 (January 1891), Hampton University Archives.
42. *Southern Workman,* Volume 20, No. 1 (January 1891), Hampton University Archives.
43. Cockrell, "Of Gospel Hymns, Minstrel Shows, and Jubilee Singers," 426.
44. Editorial by Eugene McAdoo, *Southern Workman* (January 1894), Hampton University Archives.
45. Robert Trent Vinson, *The Americans Are Coming! Dreams of African American Liberation in Segregationist South Africa* (Athens, OH: Ohio University Press, 2012), 19.
46. *Southern Workman,* Volume 20, No. 2 (February 1891), 146. Hampton University Archives.

47. Jeremiah Mendze, John D. Zamzam, K. Charles Kumkani, and Samuel Cakata to Armstrong, October 28 and 31, 1890, quoted in *Southern Workman,* Volume 20, No. 2 (February 1891), 146. Hampton University Archives.

48. André Odendaal, *The Founders: The Origins of the ANC and the Struggle for Democracy in South Africa* (Lexington, KY: University Press of Kentucky, 2013), 213.

49. Tsitsi Ella Jaji, *Africa in Stereo: Modernism, Music and Pan-African Solidarity* (New York: Oxford University Press, 2014), 49.

50. *Imvo Zabantsundu* (September 18, 1890), 2–3, cited in Kwezi Mkhize, "Empire Unbound: Imperial Liberalism, Race and Diaspora in the Making of South Africa," Ph.D. dissertation, University of Pennsylvania, 2015, 64, 67. Translation by Mkhize.

51. Charles Spencer Smith, *A History of the African Methodist Episcopal Church: Being a Volume Supplemental to A History of the African Methodist Episcopal Church* (Philadelphia: A.M.E. Book Concern, 1922), 182.

52. Odendaal, *The Founders,* 199.

53. Vuyisile Msila, *A Place to Live: Red Location and its history from 1903 to 2013* (Stellenbosch: Sun Press, 2014), 116. Translation by Msila.

54. Msila, *A Place to Live,* 117. Translation by Msila.

55. Sallie Davis Thoroughgood, an original member of the Hampton Singers, expressed the eventual reconciliation of painful memories with the potential power of slave songs: "We learned to value the old songs of our race when we saw the power they had over people of the highest intelligence, and as we remembered how our parents and grandparents had sung them in fear and suffering and hope and faith, right out of their hearts. Dr. Edward Everette Hale [author and Unitarian minister] says that these songs are the only real American music." *Southern Workman* (March 1882), 682. Hampton University Archives.

56. Interview with Dr. Boudina McConnachie, Lecturer and African Musical Arts (AMA) activist at Rhodes University and International Library of African Music, January 31, 2021.

57. David B. Coplan and Bennetta Jules-Rosette, "Nkosi Sikele' iAfrika and the Liberation of the Spirit of South Africa," *African Studies,* 64 (December 2, 2005), 291.

58. Coplan and Jules-Rosette, "Nkosi Sikele' iAfrika and the Liberation of the Spirit of South Africa," 293.

59. Cape House of Assembly Debates, 26.7 1894, 366–67, cited in William Beinart and Colin Bundy, *Hidden Struggles in Rural South Africa: Politics and Popular Movements in the Transkei and Eastern Cape 1890–1930* (Berkeley: University of California Press, 1987), 140.

60. Cape of Good Hope Parliamentary Papers, G.3–1894, *Report of Commission on Labor Supply,* 3 volumes, Volume II, pp. 110, 76, cited in Beinart and Bundy, *Hidden Struggles in Rural South Africa,* 142.

61. André Odendaal, "African Political Mobilization in the Eastern Cape 1890–1910," Ph.D. Dissertation, University of Cambridge (1983), 153.

62. Archives of the Chief Magistrate of the Transkeian Territories 3/82 Confidential report by J. M. Morris, RM Elliotdale to CMT, 18.2 1895, cited in Beinart and Bundy, *Hidden Struggles in Rural South Africa,* 157.

63. Cape of Good Hope Parliamentary Papers, A.1–1903, *Report of the Select Committee of the Glen Grey Act*, 77, cited in Beinart and Bundy, *Hidden Struggles in Rural South Africa*, 158.

64. Cape of Good Hope Parliamentary Papers, A.16–1895, *Copies of all Petitions*, etc., p. 25, CRM Idutywa to CMT, 7.2–1895, cited in Beinart and Bundy, *Hidden Struggles in Rural South Africa*, 158.

65. Mzimba in Dexter Taylor, ed., *Christianity and the Natives of South Africa: A Year Book of South African Missions* (Lovedale, n.d.), 89, cited in Williams, "African Nationalism in South Africa: Origins and Problems."

66. *Queenstown Daily Representative*, October 13, 1920; cited in Robert Edgar, "The Prophet Motive: Enoch Mgijima, the Israelites, and the Background to the Bulhoek Massacre," *The International Journal of African Historical Studies*, Volume 15, No. 3 (1982), 412.

67. Edgar, "The Prophet Motive," 420.

68. Edgar, "The Prophet Motive," 422.

69. J. W. Ord, Acting Magistrate, Middledrift, to Magistrate, King William's Town, 23 October 1923. Justice Department 268 2/950/19 (State Archives Depot, Pretoria).

70. I am indebted for most of this information on Mkwenkwe to the research done by Robert Edgar and Hilary Sapire, and their book *African Apocalypse: The Story of Nontetha Nkwenkwe, a Twentieth-Century South African Prophet* (Athens: Ohio University Press, 2000), 8–31.

71. George M. Frederickson, *Black Liberation* (Oxford: O.U.P., 1995), 168.

72. Robert A. Hill, ed., *The Marcus Garvey and Universal Negro Improvement Association Papers*, Volume XI (Durham: Duke University Press, 2011), 9:337.

73. *Three Presidential Addresses*, (Lovedale Press, n.d.), cited in Mary Benson, *South Africa: The Struggle for a Birthright* (International Defence and Aid Fund, 1985), 42.

74. Jeff Opland, *Xhosa Poets and Poetry*, 2nd ed. (Pietermaritzburg: University of KwaZulu-Natal Press, 2017), 248–49.

75. X. Y. Z. "Isikumbuzo sika Ntsikana E Johannesburg: Isiqendu III" *Umteleli*, June 17, 1922: 6, cited in Jeff Opland, "Abantu-Batho and the Xhosa Poets," in *The People's Paper: A Centenary History and Anthology of Abantu-Batho*, ed. Peter Limb (Johannesburg: Wits University Press, 2012), 205–6. Translation by Pamela Maseko.

76. Jeff Opland, ed. *The Nation's Bounty: The Xhosa Poetry of Nontsizi Mgqwetho* (Johannesburg: Wits University Press, 2007), 252–53.

77. Opland explains Mgqwetho's use of paronomasia, a characteristic of *izibongo*, in this passage: "Here and elsewhere, Mgqwetho evidences verbal dexterity as she juxtaposes her name and the verb *ukugqwetha*, [to] hold or turn a thing (book) upside down; fig, to alter, change; to pervert, making black white, and vice versa," A. Kropf, *A Kafir-English Dictionary*, 2nd edition, edited by R. Godfrey (Lovedale: Lovedale Mission Press, 1915), 133; Opland, *Xhosa Poets and Poetry*, 251.

78. Opland, *Xhosa Poets and Poetry*, 249–51.

79. Opland, *Xhosa Poets and Poetry*, 262–64.

80. "Imbongikazi Nontsizi Mgqwetto, 'Yeha! Watshonona! Afrika! ELundini!'" *Abantu-Batho*, 24 April 1919, in Limb, 416. Translated by Jeff Opland and Pamela Maseko.
81. *Umteteli* (31 January 1925: 8); Opland, *The Nation's Bounty*, 158–59.
82. *Umteteli* (28 June 1924: 6), Opland, *Xhosa Poets and Poetry*, 267.
83. Opland, "*Abantu-Batho* and the Xhosa Poets," in Limb, 221–22.
84. *kunqabelisa*
85. *sindenge*
86. *uMda*; "TS has *noMdali*." Note by Jeff Opland and Peter T. Mtuze, eds., *John Solilo: Umoya wembongi, Collected poems (1922–1935)* (Pietermaritzburg: University of KwaZulu-Natal, 2016), 180.
87. *Ungebi;* "TS has *Ungabi.*" Note by Opland and Mtuze, *John Solilo*, 180.
88. *noMbali*; "TS has *noMdali*." Note by Opland and Mtuze, *John Solilo*, 180.
89. *nzenz'*
90. Opland and Mtuze, *John Solilo*, 178–85.
91. Opland and Mtuze, *John Solilo*, 142.

Chapter 4

"You Sent Us the Light, We Sit in the Dark"

1920s–1940s

The migration to cities of much of the African population through the rise of capitalism, mining, and the effects of World War I led to the development of a town culture that further complicated the evolution of resistance among the black population in the Eastern Cape. Conversations about opposition to oppression included what to absorb from Western culture, what to hold on to in terms of African identity, and how to create a redefined identity based on African nationalism. Much of this debate took place and often began in the university known as Fort Hare (its original name when founded in 1916 was the South African Native College), situated two miles from Lovedale near Alice. Fort Hare was the center of black higher education in the Eastern Cape and produced many black intellectuals and activists, including Nelson Mandela, Oliver Tambo, and Govan Mbeki, as well as fostering African nationalism in the mid-1930s to late 1950s. Reflecting the growing sense of African identity in the post–World War I era, students began to take up politics and social issues as part of their experience of Fort Hare in the 1930s. Among the student body came the awareness that liberation could not depend solely on education and that the missionaries were not necessarily on their side. Mbeki recalled, "Fort Hare was producing Black Englishmen . . . they had no contact with the people. . . . We said in the language of the student in those days 'bugger it,' we must not be Black English people. So we changed courses . . . I majored in political science and psychology. . . . A move away from the old tradition."[1] The 1930s to 1940s also saw a rise in focus by Fort Hare students on direct action in response to suppression and racist legislation and incorporation of Marxism, socialism, and nationalism in debates and discussions.

The challenging discussions in Fort Hare and throughout the Eastern Cape on nationalism, identity, and oppression spilled over into the language of music and spoken word as the influence of jazz from the United States made itself felt in the townships. This language merged with the amalgamation of musical expression from different cultures that came together in the mines and informal gatherings of a growing black urban population. Music and *izibongo* continued to tell the story of oppression while also sharing coded messages—at a time of continued harassment and restriction—that united mass movements, and worked to preserve plus reinvent identity as a response to white definitions of "native" and "black." These creative and political developments challenged the legislation and government policies developing in the first half of the twentieth century that were steadily working towards greater racial separation, the curtailment of the rights of black people, and control of most aspects of black society.

The motivations behind the Natives Land Act of 1913 and the Natives Urban Areas Act of 1923, apart from setting up urban labor centers, included creating a system of mutually exclusive cultures upheld in white segregationist language that stressed and even celebrated "native" culture and "indigenous" music. Urban culture emanating from Johannesburg and influencing Eastern Cape cities such as Port Elizabeth and Queenstown undermined that narrative by blending African and European influences and expressing a language of resistance that was often more social than political. Mission-educated black leaders many times found themselves caught between defending the morality of "tradition"—complicated by the injection of Christian influence—and responding to the radicalism growing in the streets of the townships that was fueled by new forms of music and spoken word. To the new black middle class, educated in mission schools and initially still fighting for footing in the political arena, there remained the hope that the black population could lift white people out of their ignorance on the issue of race, and one of the ways of doing this would be through music and performance. The approach of the *iimbongi* was different, as noted before, because of the nature of their work which continued to focus on raising consciousness among Africans and preserving historical identity. Meanwhile, as disillusionment set in as a response to the increased restrictions through government legislation placed on African movement and political participation, urban culture tended to develop its own economic strategy for dealing with these challenges. As Christopher Ballantine expresses it in his extensive research and writing on music and urban culture in South Africa, the plan among many just trying to survive in the city became less about convincing white authorities to change the system, and more about figuring out ways black people could play the system.[2]

The Urban Areas Act of 1923 expressed a sentiment known as the Stallard Doctrine (Charles Stallard was a member of the Transvaal Provincial

Council) that effectively confined Africans to the margins of society: "The Native should be allowed to enter the urban areas when he is willing to minister to the needs of the white man, and should depart therefrom when he ceases so to minister."[3] The Act did not, however, engineer the retreat of black populations from the cities, despite the rise of slumyards and the level of poverty and deprivation in those areas. It merely added restrictions and hardship to those populations through government crackdowns, economic uncertainty, and acts of injustice. Black urban dwellers coped with these challenges by creating informal cooperatives that combined a culture of communal life with industrial conditions. Mbeki recalled his first visit to Johannesburg from the Eastern Cape and his exposure to police raids on the slumyards: "[It] aroused my anger as nothing else did and determined me to join the struggle to end such a system."[4]

Music and performance became one of the few areas of survival through free expression after increased government banning of other means of subsistence for black people in the cities that included small businesses and independent professions. Even places of public performance such as theaters were unavailable, so that the shebeens became a mainstay for music and dance, where beer and liquor were produced and sold under the government radar and where women as proprietors of these establishments found a niche in the informal economy. Jazz bands also found venues at political meetings such as those of the Industrial and Commercial Workers' Union (ICU) and the ANC. The music played at social occasions was seen as uniquely urban, usually involving a keyboard and banjo or guitar and a style based on repetitive harmonic patterns that echoed the blues from across the Atlantic. The cyclical style was more African, however, and reflected what was known as "root progressions." The songs would combine Sotho, Xhosa, and Zulu music, often taking ceremonial songs and mixing them up with contemporary influences while throwing in African and Christian hymns. The lack of social and political freedom for black people in South Africa was countered by a musical freedom expressed in jazz. According to pianist Edward Sililo, "We'd just take a separate portion of the [hymn tune] and then jazz it up—dance that music!"[5]

The mixture of styles in the music that emerged in the townships reflected the mixtures among the people who inhabited these urban spaces, immortalized as *abaquafi* in the Zulu songs of Reuben Caluza; a word that translates as "cultural driftwood" and originates from the Xhosa term *abaphakathi*, which meant those who were not clearly school or red. The dominant musical style arising in these areas during the 1920s that most clearly illustrates this mixture is *marabi*—a blend of local and international elements that underpinned the development of township jazz. The similarity of African and African American experiences as expressed in music came together in *marabi* with African roots and repetition of chord patterns; but South African jazz was not formulated out of blues, having its own unique style, and the melodies of *marabi*, as pointed out by Solilo, came from everywhere. The earliest forms of this music stemmed from Cape colored musicians' *vastrap* rhythm and a guitar style known as *tickey draai*. Xhosa musicians took these elements and added their own both in music and in movement and swagger. The Xhosa version was known as *tula ndivile*, from the words of a song first popularized by migrant workers in Durban during the late 1920s. *Tula ndivile* roughly translated meant "You keep quiet, you haven't heard what I've heard, I'll tell you!" and established the instrumental panache of Xhosa musicians that pulled together the disparate influences of Afrikaner, Colored, black American, and southern African music. The musician Wilson "King Force" Silgee declared, "*Tickey draai*, plus *tula n'divile* equals *marabi*."[6] Dan Twala, in an interview with David Coplan, describes the influence of the amaXhosa on township music: "When they came to the mines, they came with this coon thing[7]...you see they had their own way of coming together in a crowd . . . marching up and down. They were the most popular people, really; their costumes were a bit brighter and they had a sense of showbiz, being performers and all that."[8] One of the most famous of these innovative musicians in Johannesburg was Tebetjana (Sotho for Little Xhosa) who started out playing guitar and kazoo with colored musicians in Vrededorp and later became a full-time musician in the 1920s. The name of one of his most famous songs *Utebetjana ufana Ne'mfene* ("Tebetjana resembles a Baboon") became directly connected to the *marabi* style.[9]

As American jazz rose in influence in South Africa in the 1920s and 1930s, Queenstown in the Eastern Cape became known as "Little Jazz Town" with its proliferation of ragtime song and dance groups, such as the Darktown Negroes and "Fingers" Matshikaza's Big Four, performing for white audiences and middle-class Africans at evening parties. "Fingers" believed the unique music that came out of Queenstown had its roots in the Xhosa choral tradition:

> We had more singers. And it seems as if we excelled because when that art is common, everybody wants to sing and they don't want to give another person a chance from another town. And they are highly competitive to improve....
> Almost every house had a piano. And somebody in a choir, almost every family.[10]

Boet Gashe became one of the most well-known jazz organists in Queenstown, with the city operating as a stopping point for workers travelling to the mines in Johannesburg. As Coplan describes them, the "booze houses" where Gashe performed were "full of jazz and women," and his music was known as *itswari* (soirée) consisting of three chords played in repetitive sequence. Todd

Matshikiza, also from Queenstown and the son of "Fingers," later painted a vivid picture of Gashe's performances in the South African magazine *Drum*:

> Gashe ... was bent over his organ in one corner, thumping the rhythm from the pedals with his feet, which were also feeding the organ with air; choking the organ with persistent chords in the left hand, and improvising for an effective melody with his right hand. He would call in the aid of a matchstick to hold down a harmonic note ... and you get a delirious effect of perpetual motion ... perpetual motion in a musty hole where a man makes friends without restraint.[11]

Gashe later moved to Johannesburg where he became renowned, like many other Xhosa piano players, for his impressive versatility.

Marabi and jazz music in general was not overtly political and carried no direct messages of resistance, but *marabi* culture was viewed as a threat to the formal order of South African society by white authorities, and initially as a disruptive and decadent influence on black society by middle-class Africans. The urban identity expressed by *marabi* musicians and those who drank and danced in the shebeens and unregulated spaces where their songs were heard was connected to the flouting of authority and to communism in the minds of white officials, and to immorality in the minds of the black bourgeoisie. A former *marabi* pianist and jazz trumpeter recalled, "The police used to come there just to stop the noise. They just come and rush ... whip you out of the room. Then we run away ... jump through the window. Everybody—plus the owner of the house!"[12] A further threat, in the minds of the white population, was competition, as the black bands were immensely popular with white and black audiences and often outshone the white bands. As a means of controlling this situation, local authorities and white club owners would cancel contracts with bands such as the Jazz Maniacs and Merry Blackbirds, or prevent them from being booked. These restrictions formed part of a general pattern of enforcing regulations that increasingly limited the spaces where black people could operate freely and get around segregation, particularly nightclubs. The government used laws to further restrict jazz music such as the Liquor Amendment Act of 1934 that banned black musicians from playing where alcohol was served.

As many of the mission-educated black men and women had accepted the narrative that adopting European culture while maintaining African identity was the key to civilization and progress, *marabi* and jazz represented something mixed up, wild, and uncontrollable to them that would hinder that progress and turn white politicians against them. An effort to use music as a means to change white minds regarding the potential and value of black society, they felt, was part of the path to equality and recognition, and the unruly music of urban culture seemed to undermine that strategy. What was needed instead, many leaders argued, was an African music based on folklore and tradition that uplifted their people and provided them with a respectful place in South African society. The argument carried undertones of emphasis on an evolving identity that was more national than local as expressed by Frieda Bokwe Matthews, the daughter of John Knox Bokwe and the wife of activist Z. K. Matthews. Frieda Matthews was one of the first women to graduate from Fort Hare (her husband was one of the first Africans to earn a B.A. there) and she went on to Trinity College of Music in London. Despite her Western-style formal music training, she gave an impassioned plea for more education in the field of African music, arguing that European influence had caused problems in finding indigenous music in Africa that did not have that influence, but that many African features still held their own within this new combination: "I believe that the way in which a people sing has much to do with the nature of their music."[13] Matthews described one of the most crucial aspects of African life as the gathering of all generations to sing and dance and she criticized mission attempts to eradicate that feature of their lives. To Matthews, it seemed that previous generations of Africans had been taught by colonizers "how to work and stop playing. . . . And as African song was almost inextricably interwoven with play, dancing, story-telling, witchcraft, hunting, fighting, wherever these forms of activity disappeared, music followed the same course. Most of the songs that have disappeared are those that dealt with the most colorful aspects of African life."[14] Matthews also linked music to the survival of her people, and predicted that music would continue to maintain their existence in the face of "civilized labor policies and all that goes to making [their] lot a most undesirable one in South Africa." It was an argument that, while focused on the indigenous elements of African music, also carried with it the role music often ended up playing in the oppressive and uncertain lives of township people: "In music the African finds not only enjoyment but also consolation in troubles both out of his own internal life and out of juxtaposition with white people. . . . You can never utterly destroy the hopes of a people who can sing."[15]

The rising black middle class that worked to preserve what were often viewed as rural values saw the black urban culture and the music that accompanied it as contaminating and destructive. Many of them had connections with the American Board of Missions which would single out post Africans and offer them opportunities connected to Western culture that were presented as a path to political progress; these included achievements in music, literature and art, and carried with them specific criticism of *marabi* culture. While other modern forms of music might be accepted, *marabi* music was viewed as particularly detrimental to newly arrived migrants to the townships, as in the song "*Iqilika,*" a Xhosa word for a strong home-brewed alcohol prominent in *marabi* culture. The song, first recorded by Griffiths

Motsieloa, and arranged by the Rhythm Kings jazz band, provides an inventory of damage done to naïve newcomers to urban life who got a taste of *Iqilika*. It asks where the sons, daughters, mothers, fathers, and "the grey old men" of Africa are, answering that they came and died in Johannesburg under the influence of alcohol:

> There's the *iqilika*
> There it is, there it is.[16]

As the black middle class attempted to tread a thin line between upholding their identity through culturally acceptable music that often meant alliances with white society, and shunning the urban mixture of music in a way that might seem as though they were shunning their own people, many became involved in a "Bantu National Music" project that tried to remain true to their roots and avoid European influences and European interpretations. In the 1920s African teachers created adult choirs in most towns and by 1931 Mark Radebe and Hamilton Masiza had formed the South African Bantu Board of Music (SABBM). The board organized the first series of Eisteddfods (music festivals from the Welsh tradition), that included concerts in Port Elizabeth. The point of this activity was "to preserve and develop the individuality of Native music, and, concurrently, to encourage the finer refinements of European music."[17] Two other objectives included creating a compilation of African indigenous music and sustaining African composers. The festivals were intended to be alcohol-free and involved poetry, stories, essays, song lyrics as part of a competition, and deliberately excluded *marabi* and other forms of similar music. These musical situations within the black communities, thus, created a dichotomy of loyalty and contradictory cultural views, as the preservation of cultural identity bumped up against Western-leaning prejudices, such as those criticizing African polyphony and miners' unique dances. Since the urban environments tended to mix up all these different views and loyalties as well as throwing together black working and middle classes plus recent rural immigrants, there was no clear-cut divide between those who stuck to the "Bantu"/Western culture of music and those who sang and danced to jazz and *marabi*. By the 1930s, when increased repressive legislation had cleared many of the inner-city locations and destroyed a good deal of *marabi* culture, jazz continued in popularity, carrying with it the dance culture. Z. K. Matthews noted that enthusiasm for choral singing in places like Lovedale and Fort Hare was on the wane during that time because students and teachers were "too busy dancing."[18] There was the further challenge of creating African unity in the face of mounting oppression, which took on a new urgency in the late 1920s and 1930s. Middle-class black leaders tried to uphold the culture known as "New African" but often seemed hindered in their encouragement of "traditional" music in the service of unity by internalized feelings of inferiority fostered by their European education and their disdain for the fast pace of urban slumyard life.

Much of the focus of the middle-class criticism of township culture was on a perceived decline in the morals of women, who were held to be the backbone of African society. Due to the rise of the informal sector of living, making money, and playing, black women began expanding their role in society beyond what they had been in pre-colonial and colonial times. It was still a precarious existence for them, with prostitution being one of the more desperate means of existing in townships. Holding prominent positions in the areas of music, housing, and beer brewing, however, increased their power, challenging the stereotype of subjugated women and providing them with a potentially progressive role. Beer formed the center of *marabi* economics and women were part of that central position because their role in the rural communities had always been the brewers of beer. They brought their brewing skills to cities in the Eastern Cape and turned social tradition into an enterprise, adopting the part of shebeen queens. Music acted as a draw to their establishments with *tula n'divile* songs adding to the excitement and relaxation that these spaces provided; it also provided a reason to charge admission. Operating as proprietors of the shebeens gave women a more solid and permanent identity in urban life and music was directly connected to that identity, modernizing and re-shaping it.

The shebeens had an overlapping relationship with another system of survival developing in the townships that originally came from rural areas: the stokvels. Deriving its name from the "stock fairs" or cattle auctions of British settlers in the Eastern Cape, where African farmers and rural workers demonstrated their trading and commercial skills, stokvels developed during the rise of the mining industry to accommodate the problems of overcrowding and disease—particularly the death tolls and costs of burial. Stokvels acted as cooperatives formed to help meet the funeral expenses of family members and these evolved into meeting places to discuss local and regional issues. Over time, women became the mainstay of these associations, similar to their proprietary role in the shebeens. The associations were marked by parties on Sunday afternoons, where "sisterhoods" would march in formation accompanied by a brass band often playing *marabi* music. Shebeens tended to mirror the stokvels, except that liquor was served in the former. As the 1930s saxophone player "King Force" Silgee described it,

> Marabi; that was the environment . . . you get there, you pay your ten cents, you get your share of whatever concoction there is—and you dance. It used to start on Friday night right through to Sunday evening. You get tired, you go and

sleep, and come back again, bob a time you get in. Piano with the audience making a lot of noise—trying to make some theme out of what is playing.[19]

It was this change in the standard role of women brought by the rise of township life that many black middle-class men (and women) were initially censorious of, and they bemoaned the deterioration of morals among women who came to the cities and the knock-on effect they saw that it had on families and African society as a whole. But the increased power of women in Eastern Cape towns such as Port Elizabeth, East London, and Queenstown often helped them maintain family order within urban society. As women struggled against white authorities and black patriarchy to gain a foothold in this fast-paced environment, they expressed more publicly calls for recognition of their significance in the fight for freedom and nationalism. Dr. Alfred Xuma, who would later become president of the ANC (see below), lamented the effect of laws and regulations on these women merely trying to survive: "When I see hundreds of Black women going to jail every Monday, I do not think of them as criminals. I blame the system under which they live. It must be changed . . . these laws for 'natives only' are unexcelled anywhere in the world in their manufacture of criminals."[20] The musician Welcome Duru recalled witnessing the police raids on his mother's home as she brewed beer in Korsten Location and New Brighton in Port Elizabeth. According to Duru, the police "came with a military zeal to destroy the brew that many of my mother's customers relished. I can still remember how some of her customers reveled as they wiped their wet moustaches after satiating their desiccated throats." The experience of police invading his home and destroying his mother's beer barrel aroused in Duru an antagonism towards them, similar to Mbeki's reaction to his first experiences in Johannesburg: "How I hated the motorcycles that police used, they conjured the destroyers of my mother's livelihood. . . . I always recall the distraught expression on Nolhalha's [Duru's mother's] face after every destructive police visit."[21]

When African families such as Duru's were driven out of Korsten and moved to New Brighton in the 1930s, beer drinking, brewing, and entertainment became more regulated, only allowed in "wet areas" in Red Location. Authorities cracked down on but never completely eliminated *marabi* culture which, along with jazz, had been a staple feature of the Korsten community. House parties known as *iDoyili* were central to social life in Korsten where the *hotap* (autoharp) was played, an instrument created out of a paraffin can with its top taken off and strings stretched across. The subject matter of the songs usually focused on their experiences in the location, such as rent increases and other hardships. Later on, the piano and organ became more prevalent, with the keyboard style of Boet Gashe taking over with a mix of Xhosa melodies and American ragtime.[22]

In dealing with the challenge of beer brewing in the locations and municipal areas, most towns followed the Durban model of control by creating a monopoly on the practice to pay for urban development and administration. Port Elizabeth, however, proved to be an exception with several complications. Originating in the early nineteenth century from the establishment of Fort Frederick which was set up to defend the coast from invaders and white farmers from the African population, the city had grown into an active port and trade center, with segregation as an early feature. From 1847, established townships were created for Africans, including "Fingoe Location" in 1855. After the Cattle Killing of 1857, Port Elizabeth experience a large influx of AmaXhosa and, as the town grew, white authorities increased their efforts to re-settle Africans to more distant areas, especially since a growing population of white inhabitants wanted the land. The African population established a pattern of strong resistance to these policies early on and consistently challenged government attempts at segregation. Many of the old locations were subsequently destroyed by authorities in the early twentieth century, with a large section of the population relocated eight miles out of town to New Brighton. The 1902 Native Reserve Location Act, meanwhile, required all designated (non-exempt) Africans to live in determined locations.

The pattern of resistance continued, nonetheless, in the establishment of Korsten Village on the edge of the city limits where Africans were still able to own land and build houses—one reason for the roots of liberation attitudes in this region as Africans, for a while, enjoyed the opportunity for freehold land and governing themselves in Korsten. City officials countered this development by extending Port Elizabeth's boundaries and creating more townships. The township of New Brighton experienced overcrowding and housing shortages, and a lack of rigid enforcement of residence laws and policies led to the rise of a sizeable black population within the city. While Korsten represented one form of defiance in its freehold existence, New Brighton represented another through inhabitants that police found difficult to control. When authorities attempted to crack down on New Brighton residents, many of them merely retreated to Korsten. City officials' efforts to enforce restrictions on black locations in Port Elizabeth were also hampered by a lack of investment in the resources required to carry out township policies. A pattern emerged in the early twentieth century of New Brighton residents either migrating to the outskirts of town to escape the oppression represented by superintendents—especially crackdowns on the brewing of beer—or resisting and protesting against white authorities in public gatherings.[23]

Since New Brighton township had been founded through the Native Reserve Location Act it ran along the lines of rural regions, which allowed the private brewing of beer with some regulations. At the same time, there were numerous strongly religious residents who objected to this practice and the culture it created in New Brighton. City authorities devised a rotation system where one half of the location was not allowed to make beer and the other half was divided into three sections that alternated beer brewing for six-day periods. This arrangement was not based in law and was enforced by local police through impromptu house searches and fines. Women in the township actively protested this method of enforcement and formed their own networks that operated under the radar of the authorities. Such was the determined resistance of these women that the superintendent overseeing New Brighton in the 1920s and 1930s often recommended not changing the system for fear of the strong backlash from the female population. City authorities also attempted to place other restrictions on New Brighton residents, including their social lives, supposedly for their "benefit." No communal gatherings, with the exception of within public halls, schools, or churches, were allowed without permission after 10:00 p.m. Mondays through Fridays, and after 11:00 p.m. on Saturdays.[24] Municipal councils, however, were slack in responding to African needs in city locations such as New Brighton. While philanthropic societies and the Port Elizabeth Joint Council placed an emphasis on the uplift of Africans, the black participation in these organizations came mainly from mission-educated middle-class residents joining with white liberals and there was no real support from the majority of local Africans. "What is the good of it all, we suffer," a disgruntled resident reportedly stated at one of the meetings.[25] The growth of industry in Port Elizabeth, such as the development of the General Motors factory, accompanied by increased restrictions on black labor and living conditions, contributed to the increasingly determined development of African organized opposition to local and national oppression.

Meanwhile, in the 1920s, *iimbongi* such as Mqhayi maintained a presence in the rise of African nationalism performing in public places and publishing their *izibongo*. Mqhayi had taken a teaching position at Lovedale in 1922, but resigned in 1925 over conflict between the meaning behind his classes and the philosophy of the school. He also became the chairman of the Ciskei Native convention while acting as councilor to the Ndlambe chief Silimela Makinana, son of chief Makinana who was prominent in the last Frontier War of 1877. Mqhayi continued to translate while writing and performing praise and historical poems that focused on past events of conflict and war, and on prominent figures in the religious and political arenas of black society, often using his platform to insert criticism of the rising oppression inflicted on his people and relating it to the past. In 1925, for example, when the Prince of Wales came to visit South Africa, Mqhayi performed an *izibongo* that combined praise with irony and expressed the poet's disillusionment with Britain:

> You sent us the truth, denied us the truth:
> You sent us the life, deprived us of life;
> You sent us the light, we sit in the dark,
> Shivering benighted in the bright noonday sun[26]

In 1928, he wrote *Idabi lama Linde* (The Battle of Amalinde), which reiterated his contention that this battle should not be mistakenly be referred to as Thutula's War—a name based on a supposed internal affair between Xhosa rulers—because the war was, in fact, due to "*Ukutelekiswa ngu Mlungu*" (white provocation). In the last line Mqhayi claimed that the king Ngqika abused his power: "*ngeloxesha u Ngqika wayengento ku Ndlambe; amandla ake u Ngqika wawabulala ezizweni ngokusuke asinikele kumntu omhlope. . . . Sibe njalo ke idabi lama Linde Kwanezipum zalo!*" (Ngqika's power destroyed other nations because he had handed himself over to the whites. . . . And that's the story of the Battle of Amalinde and its consequences!).[27]

In 1929, Mqhayi described the ANC in such a way that he both praised and criticized the efforts of the organization. The ANC was struggling in direction and support at that particular time and Mqhayi pointed out the debilitating issues he perceived in the organization of rivalry and disagreement between leaders. He also attempted to correct the record on the perception of the ANC's efforts from the time of its earliest inception in 1887 as the South African Native Congress to the present. One particular point he emphasized was the push he became part of to oppose the Union of South Africa in 1909, believing Africans would be squeezed out of representation and participation in South African society by the Afrikaners: "*asipulapulwanga isicelo setu, sati kanti nati sasinyanisile—uyabona ke u Manyano lusenzakalisile!*" (our petition was not heard, yet we were right—you can see the Union has worked to our disadvantage!).[28] In 1930, Mqhayi praised Charlotte Maxeke as a woman who excelled in conflict resolution: "*Nanamhlanje akuko ndoda ingahlula lomfazi ngokulwa ukuvisa umntu omhlope into etetwa ngumntu ontsundu. Lentokazi yafunda imfundo enzulu kwi Koleji zase Melika* (To this day no man can get the better of this woman in a fight, and in explaining to a white person what a black person is saying).[29]

In 1929, in what became known as the "Black Peril" election, Prime Minister J. B. M. Hertzog portrayed Jan Smuts, leader of the South African Party, as an "apostle of a black Kaffir state" that would lead to extinction of the white population. Smuts, however, while on a tour in Britain, placed emphasis on separate development that would supposedly benefit the black and white populations. He blamed missionary schools for spoiling and "detribalizing" Africans in such a way that they now demanded citizenship, and he portrayed segregation as the means for Africans to preserve their heritage. These political platforms encouraged Garveyites and African nationalists in South Africa to pursue resistance based on leadership from the UNIA, but Mqhayi was not a fan. To Mqhayi, African Americans should serve as role models but not be looked upon as liberators. He reminded Africans of the failure of the Wellington movement and referred to Garvey (calling him "this ugly Gavi") as a jailbird, stating that Africans should not "rely on gentlemen overseas" to free them: "Our nation is alive, and on top of that, perfectly healthy; we must work amongst our own people in our own nation. That's where our salvation and that of our nation lies."[30]

All of these forces: elements of jazz and *marabi* culture, black national identity and middle-class aspirations, the rising importance of women, along with the rise of mass action, political opposition to government legislation, the persistent messages of *izibonga*, and the continuing influence of Garveyism and religious separatism, came together in the late 1920s and early 1930s particularly through the impact of the ICU and the break-off organization Independent ICU (IICU) headquartered in the Eastern Cape city of East London. In 1926 Hertzog had introduced the "Color Bar" bill or Mines and Works Amendment Act which made certain higher-level jobs unavailable to Africans regardless of their skills or qualifications. He also tightened restrictions that increased segregation and racial discrimination. The Native Administration Act of 1927 made the Governor-General the Supreme Chief, so now the government had total power over the appointment and firing of African chiefs. This legislation had the effect of pressuring chiefs not to support the ANC, which had already begun to suffer a loss in power and support. When a ban was issued on holding meetings in "tribal" areas without the Native Commissioner's permission, political activity moved more directly to the cities. A further "hostility clause" mandated the imprisonment of up to one year or fine of £100 (or both) of any person deemed to be encouraging hostility between the black and white populations. The leader of the ICU Clements Kadalie called for a day of prayer in answer to Hertzog's "Color Bar" bill and Thomas Mbeki, a former communist member of the ICU and a principal lieutenant of Kadalie's, challenged this call: "The failure of the A.N.C. was due to too much prayer and no direct action. For God's sake, don't turn chameleon. Are you going back to the masses to ask them to pray, or will you tell them to depend on their numerical powers?"[31] At this point, Kadalie had not properly read the mood of his people and instead went to Europe to talk to the European trade unions.

The Eastern Cape was no stranger to labor unrest. The earliest recorded worker resistance in South Africa occurred in Port Elizabeth in November 1845 when Mfengu beach laborers called for higher wages. In 1901, during the outbreak of the bubonic plague, black female domestic workers protested inoculations through the first General Workers Strike, and in 1920 African and colored dockworkers rejected an offer of a pay rise and participated in a strike led by Samuel Makana Masabalala whom the police arrested without charge and with no bail. When workers stood outside the police station to demand Masabalala's release, twenty-three of them were killed by Port Elizabeth police and a white mob.[32] Masabalala was acquitted and joined the ICU. He eventually became a member of the ANC's national executive committee.

By the end of the 1920s, Kadalie had a greater appreciation for the strength of forces within black urban and rural societies and he adopted a different outlook in reaction to increased repressive legislation on the part of the South African government. His new strategy of resistance involved the rise of African nationalism with its religious separatist elements, the particular complaints of urban dwellers—including women—and alliances with resistance movements in the countryside, particularly in Transkei and Ciskei. The East London branch of the ICU had been fairly active in 1928, with Mac Jabavu, son of J. T. Jabavu, as one of the regular speakers at the Sunday meetings. It was when the ICU began to struggle due to a leadership divide in the middle of 1928 that Kadalie established the IICU (with Masabalala as a fellow activist) in East London which, with its emphasis on unity, loyalty, and paid subscriptions, quickly gained prominence in the Eastern Cape. Relying on police records of political activities in the East London town clerk's file, William Beinart and Colin Bundy provide a vivid account of the IICU in East London and the mass action of the late 1920s and early 1930s—a movement of strikes, rallies and demonstrations that included music and the culture of spoken word: "In them one can hear speeches—tedious and gripping, halting and eloquent, shot through with sardonic humor, pent-up anger, and startling metaphorical flights—accompanied by prayers, hymns and nationalist songs."[33] Kadalie had a new combative language to inspire the rural and urban workers, stating in reaction to the recent oppressive government legislation, "Hertzog hates me and I hate him like hell, the bugger. I am a bad native and I will remain a bad native . . . they call me an agitator and I will remain an agitator."[34] Fellow activist Joel Magade reinforced Eastern Cape support for Kadalie: "The white people do not like Kadalie because he is making the AmaXhosa understand that they have been exploited for years and years and oppressed by the whites."[35]

Kadalie's movement had been injected with the continued influence of Garvey's UNIA and strong feelings over the very real grievances of higher taxes, increased restrictions, and the Color Bar Act, which, among other things, excluded Africans from jobs on the railroads. Wellington Buthelezi had by this time been ejected from the Transkei and in 1927 Marcus Garvey warned that Wellington was not a representative of the UNIA and therefore could not collect money or set up UNIA chapters.[36] Although he ended the facade of his UNIA connection, Wellington continued to preach against white oppression, building black opposition and Pan-African Christianity that focused on freedom. The difference between Wellington's approach in the late 1920s and the majority of Kadalie's movement was that Wellington now leaned on the Booker T. Washington philosophy of entrepreneurship and interpreted African culture and self-help as the new strategy for nationhood. In the Northern Transkei region of Mount Fletcher, however, while Kadalie was rejuvenating the IICU in 1928, the headman Edward Zibi, who had been Vice President of Wellington's Basutoland and the Eastern Cape UNIA division, planned an armed rebellion based on the expectation of the arrival of allies from the United States. Zibi made his kraal a gathering place of UNIA musical events and church programs and he and his followers called themselves "Americans." These supporters, whose numbers included a large contingent of women, cut telephone lines, held up traffic, and attacked white people in Tsolo and Africans on "death lists." They also held monthly concerts. Eventually, a mobile squadron was sent from Mthatha to restore control and the magistrate evicted Zibi from the district. UNIA activity, however, carried on in that region.[37]

The energy of the UNIA and religious separatism made itself felt in the mass action and language of Kadalie's movement. Activist Alfred Mnika admonished supporters: "Don't behave any longer as if you are constructed machines, but wake up and realize that you are human beings and that you have feelings to other human beings . . . this black nation of ours has to be recognized as a nation." In another speech he called on his people to "be like Garvey," who, in spite of his imprisonment, "still worked hard to better the conditions of his fellow black men."[38] Hymns at IICU meetings were given new more political lyrics, and speeches and rallying cries of leaders in the IICU often used the poetic language of *iimbongi* and recalled the history of violence imposed on the amaXhosa to fire up their audiences. One speaker in East London stated, "When the white man came to this country we gave them everything, whereas we should rather have killed them or died in endeavoring to do so . . . we have learned enough now, it is time we were left to govern ourselves."[39] Particularly in the rural areas, *izibongo* language peppered the rallies of the IICU; at one point Mnika declared, "I am Mnika, *Mwari isibongi*. I belong to Hintsa's family." Speeches in the countryside also included millennial references and echoes of the supernatural. According to Joel Magade of the local ICU Branch committee that joined the IICU, there was in the Kentani district, "a crow which can speak and it tells the AmaXhosa to join the organization, and it says there is a great war coming." Speakers invoked the spirit of Nongqawuse (see Chapter 2), using the reference to inspire unity: "I tell you that if you don't follow the prophecies of your ancestors . . . then bad luck will fall on you." Political messages mixed with millennial prophecies were disseminated at prayer meetings where women were predominant and messages took on a theatrical tone. At one meeting a woman named Selina Bungane claimed to be a prophetess: "She again has received a message from the Almighty God that Kadalie should go to Gcalekaland in the Transkei and organize the AmaXhosas at the Great Place of the Paramount chief Nqangomhlaba. . . . I want to tell you this: there are some dangerous locusts riding on the ass and they will bite all those people who refuse to accept Kadalie's teaching."[40]

The involvement of the rural population of the Eastern Cape meant that some sort of strategy had to be created by the IICU with regard to the headmen and chiefs. Urban organizers tended to view the chiefs as backward and collaborative with the white administration, but these organizers needed alliances with them in order to swell support in the countryside. A number of Transkeian chiefs were open to the ideology and policies of the IICU and Kadalie's movement made the most of these connections. In 1928 Mqhayi created a praise poem that touched on the Transkei paramount chief Ngangomhlaba's visit to East London:

> *Yema magqangq' i Mansipaliti*
> *Aroz' amajon' o Mkosi,*
> *Yahlahlamb' i Ntambula ka I.C.U.*
> *Yati: Ngambu-ngambu-ngambu!*

> The whole municipality stood to attention,
> The army soldiers stood in rank,
> The I.C.U. tambourines thudded excitedly:
> Ngambu! Ngambu! Ngambu![41]

Opposition movements in the Eastern Cape were often dominated by women, especially with the increased migration of male workers to the mining areas, leaving women to support households in areas where trade and production went largely unregulated. Women's unions of the churches (*manyano*), formed at the turn of the century, established through organized worship a form of economic as well as religious independence. A system of mutual aid developed through these women and was especially useful during times of oppression and hardship. D. D. T. Jabavu expressed admiration in particular for the women of the Herschel district in the northern section of the Eastern Cape:

> The people with insight here are the women. They are the ones that wear the trousers because the men fear the whites who have become rich from them. The women have their unions (*banomanyano*) where they discuss their affairs; they keep these to themselves and do not reveal the finances to men.[42]

In 1922, before the formation of the IICU, women such as Annie Siyiyo in the Herschel district led a total boycott of local stores where traders had been charging high prices for necessities and paying the women low prices for the goods they produced. The traders had police arrest and charge women who used force to interrupt purchase of goods at their stores, but these arrests and appearances in court only served to strengthen and unify the movement and it spread to the Qumbu district. The women called themselves "strikers," echoing the language of mass movements among workers in the urban regions and there was evidence of African nationalism and Garvey's message in the meetings and attitudes of the women leading the action. The strike was also firmly rooted in local concerns and activity, however, and, at first, the women were willing to accept local progressives as mediators in the conflict.[43] The traders eventually agreed to regulation, but over the next few years the sentiment of the Herschel movement began to turn against the progressives and the mission churches, with protest increasingly directed against taxes used for education and highly effective boycotts of schools. In 1926, police were called in to deal with a group of protesters who had taken over a school, and twenty-seven women were arrested. When a verdict of guilty and a penalty of £5 or two months' sentence was announced in an overcrowded courtroom, chaos ensued: "From 200 to 300 native women present rose as one, brandishing sticks and shouting at the top of their voices, their evident intention being to rush the police and effect a rescue of their friends." The police regained control, but more women came together in the evening: "The mob camped out on the bare patch at the back of the gaol, singing, dancing and shouting."[44] The movement backed off from violence after that incident but continued to press to curtail state intervention, joining forces with elements in the ANC, African nationalists, and religious separatists.

Although recognition of the strength and importance of women in mass action came slowly at first to the IICU in East London, leaders such as Kadalie soon saw their potential, especially as harassment of shebeen owners formed a major part of a growing number of local grievances the IICU encompassed in their platform. For those who came to the towns and cities from the countryside, drinking beer and enjoying the social activities of their culture—including singing and dancing—were often crucial to their survival. Location dwellers were increasingly resentful of municipal restrictions on alcohol and were particularly possessive of the right not to have their homes and social events invaded by the police; a situation where women were especially vulnerable. Women were also prominent in rural activism, and in many regions of the Eastern Cape where IICU action was strong due to their previous boycott experiences, it was the women who kept the population fed during strikes and boycotts—and often the ones who kept them singing. In the strike of 1930, mass meetings were held to fire up the masses, using mixed messages that combined nationalism with religious separatism and maintained the elements of poetry and song. "If you are prepared to die," proclaimed one speaker, "sing 'Onward Christian Soldiers.'"[45]

Kadalie and his strike committee were arrested eleven days after the action of 1930 began. Even though Kadalie had been pressured to deliver a message to end the strike, mass action continued for the next six months. Activism spread throughout the Eastern Cape and as areas such as the Transkei saw an increase in support for the IICU, and boycotting and strikes continued for the next two years. It was only in 1933 that the IICU faded as a result of internal divisions, fragmentation in the townships, and the pressures of combining urban and rural grievances while still maintaining support. The effects of this mass action remained in the Eastern Cape, however, and showed up in future revived efforts that used music and spoken word to fuel resistance. According to Soloman Crutze, "The groups had a certain Africanism in their set-up . . . because the suffering of the African was common, and the ICU had as its goal to alleviate the suffering of the African, therefore the African music and the ICU went together."[46]

Throughout the 1920s and early 1930s, Hertzog had been steadily promising his constituents segregation, and in 1935 he formed a coalition government with Smuts to gain the majority in Parliament, with the main opposition coming from the National Party led by D. F. Malan. It was an advantageous time for Hertzog and the segregationists, as black opposition in the form of the ANC, the communists, and the ICU had weakened considerably and the ANC paper *Abantu-Batho* had been forced to close down. Voices of opposition continued in various forms, but were often singular and scattered. The popular composer Benjamin Tyamzashe ("B ka T") who grew up in the Eastern Cape and attended Lovedale, for example, wrote two musical pieces that reflected the controversy caused by increasing government restrictions on black representation: *Ivoti* ("The Vote") and *Hay Abant' Abamnyama* (Lo! The black people). The pieces focused on the government's intention to remove the Cape franchise and expressed the increasing frustration felt by those black leaders who had hoped to negotiate and work on increasingly equal terms with government officials.[47]

One of Hertzog's bills did effectively aim to end the registration of black voters in the Cape, while fading out those already registered. Black representation was to be relegated to the purely advisory Natives' Representative Council. A deputation of black representatives made up mostly of moderates and clergymen met with the Prime Minister to try to dissuade him from policies that increased and entrenched segregation, but were instead forced to accept a compromise that curtailed black voting rights even more than had been proposed. Hertzog's argument was chilling: "It is not that we hate you, but if we give you the right to vote, within a very short space of time the whole Parliament will be controlled by Natives. I must tell you point-blank I am not prepared for this."[48] Meanwhile, the All Africa Convention (AAC) met in Bloemfontein to push for greater unity among Africans, Indians, and Colored populations in fighting against racist policies. Charlotte Maxeke announced, "Non-Europeans . . . while thanking Europeans for their support, must go ahead themselves."[49] It seemed though that several of the leaders who met with the Prime Minister were unwilling to challenge the South African government directly. Dr. Xuma and James Moroka, on the other hand, had joined the deputation to try and stop the agreement and led the group in rejecting a compromise that would have made the proposal look like it came from the black population. Said Moroka, "We must have *nothing* to do with it. If they are going to take our rights away let them do the dirty job themselves!" ANC leader Reverend Zaccheus Mahabane, who had done his theological training near Queenstown and first worked in the ministry outside of Herschel, also fought against the compromise. In a meeting of concerned Africans about Hertzog's legislation he declared that white men were creating the specter of a "black menace" and that the introduction of these new laws were perpetuated by fear; the white population was scared that eventually the black man in rising numbers would attack them. A voice at the back of the meeting called out, "He will one of these days."[50]

The political repercussions of Hertzog's actions were felt among the students at Fort Hare, along with disillusionment with their white professors and administrators. "Those were serious days," observed Mbeki. "The students were alive. They were debating these issues [Hertzog Bills]. . . . We turned around to our missionaries to find an answer. . . . They were afraid to come out openly against Hertzog."[51] National and international struggles were connected to local and campus controversies; for example, A. C. Jordan, a student at the time, wrote a poem in Xhosa criticizing the Italian invasion of Ethiopia.[52] In 1935 members of one of the university houses organized a mixed dance in contravention of the policies of the administration. Students recalled later, "We wanted to invite the women who were working as domestics in the institution to come in and that infuriated the authorities." Apparently, there was a standoff between university officials and the house committee because "they played the piano and played some drums, and in one of those items the gentlemen took ladies and had a mixed dance and that was such a big broil." When the warden tried to stop the festivities, he was told to go to bed.[53] Increasingly, students at Fort Hare were connecting their situation with the broader issues in South Africa and feeling the need to take action. Cutting their teeth on local activism within the institution, students protested campus issues that resulted in meetings to discuss strategy. Former student Devi Bughwan noted, "It would always lead to a total free-for-all about the state of the country, the oppression, the apartheid. That is how in my recollection the mass meetings became platforms for fiery tirades against the government at the time."[54] African nationalism played a significant role in the increased politicization of Fort Hare students, often as one side of a debate with those leaning more towards the approach of Marxism. Cultural reclamation became a major aspect of student awareness as shown in Phyllis Ntantala's description of her fellow students' excitement over Xhosa epic poetry: "[They] were beginning to question some of the myths on which they had been fed, and beginning to see the old people in the villages to find out what happened this year and that." Mbeki made a special trip to hear Mqhayi recite *izibongo* at Ntab'ozuko near King William's Town—one example of a younger generation of educated Africans wrestling with the dichotomy of hopes for a better future and reclaiming identity combined with disillusionment with the present state of affairs.[55] Later on, Mbeki took over the editorship of *The Territorial Magazine*, launched in the 1930s and renamed *Inkundla ya Bantu* (Bantu Forum) in 1940. The former Fort Hare student, influenced by the historical approach of figures such as Mqhayi, started a project through *Inkundla* that created a "Gallery of African Heroes"—short biographies of prominent people in African history—and invited readers to contribute. The first hero featured was the great Xhosa King Hintsa, kidnapped by British forces in 1835 and shot while trying to escape. Mbeki wrote this biography for the project, using Mqhayi's historical poetry as a source, and told the tale within the contemporary context of African nationalism. According to Mbeki, "Hintsa died free that his people might have freedom and have it more abundantly."[56]

Playing on time-honored and effective prejudices among white people over miscegenation, Hertzog got his bill passed in 1936 and this law, among others, aroused growing unrest among ordinary black people while exposing the dangers of moderation among ANC leaders. Pixley Seme, now leader of the ANC, struggled to maintain unity within the organization and to re-organize its structure, but the leadership as a whole seemed removed from the problems facing urban and rural black working-class populations. Reverend James A. Calata, Secretary General of the ANC, worked to keep contact with the people alive. A Xhosa who lived in Cradock in the Eastern Cape (and grandfather of Fort Calata, the activist murdered by the apartheid government's secret police in 1985), Reverend Calata was part of the surge of activism among black people spurred by the elimination of representation on the common voters' roll. Working at the St. James Mission Church in Cradock, the Reverend had a reputation for enthusiasm for choral music, along with youth work and education, and was determined to revive the flagging ANC leadership. Calata convinced Mahabane to come back as president, and tried to unite the branches of leadership, including those of chiefs in the rural areas: "I am afraid we are still very far from salvation as long as we have men who look more after their own interests than that of the nation."[57]

The Great Depression of the 1930s created a large number of poor white people (*bywoners*) in South Africa who had been driven from their land to the towns where they were unable to find work. The government responded by creating relief schemes and job creation programs similar to those in other countries except that these schemes excluded the black population. The railroad company, for example, fired its black workers and replaced them with white workers. There was basically no government support for the black population and poverty rose in many of the reserves including Ciskei and Transkei, causing increased migration to towns and populating slumyards that were already overcrowded. The situation in Transkei became dire, and the Native Affairs Department tried to resolve some of the consequences of overstocking and land erosion through ill-conceived policies of culling and improvement schemes. As these policies failed to appreciate the level of human poverty created by the reserve system they were largely unsuccessful and met with fierce local opposition. Overall job opportunities diminished for black people and pass controls inhibited urbanization.

As the political and economic environment became ever more challenging to black people in the 1930s, the social divide between middle-class indigenous/religious music and urban jazz/*marabi* grew blurred as politics permeated all walks of life, including entertainment and urban community gatherings. As Christopher Ballantine observes of that time, "Politics . . . now invades music, and music in turn now welcomes politics explicitly into its own constitution."[58] As police raids on *marabi* culture through crackdowns on activities like brewing liquor increased in the 1930s, what became known as "This War" was expressed in the songs of township musicians. John Mavimbela sang in Xhosa about arriving in Johannesburg looking for work and immediately being arrested for having liquor:

> it is painful
> to sleep in jail[59]

The adoption of all forms of African music gradually became a feature of political activity in the 1930s, helping to sow the seeds of militant protest that erupted in the 1940s. Jazz bands had already begun to play at political gatherings of the ANC and ICU and the adoption of a unique combination of African elements in musical expression echoed the rise of New Africanism. In 1935, *Bantu World* reprinted an article by African American singer Paul Robeson from the *Daily Herald* that declared, "I am going back to my people in the sense that for the rest of my life I am going to think and feel as an African—not as a white man. . . . It is not as imitation Europeans, but as Africans that we have value. . ."[60] Journalist Walter Nhlapo echoed these sentiments: "We will rather sing the English National Anthem well and blunder with ours. What is wrong with us?"[61] To reinforce this emphasis on identity, jazz bands began to play numbers composed by Africans and incorporated the *tsaba-tsaba* dance style into their music, a style that combined *marabi* and American swing. Dancing to this music involved a "rubber legged" step combined with a pelvic motion with a man and a woman moving towards each other. Just before they touched, someone would call out "*Tsaba!*"—a signal for the couple to back off. The evolution of style in township music in the 1930s included more African types of melody that resulted in the unique form of African jazz or *mbaqanga*, and different aspects of African culture began to appear as subjects for songs and performance in popular groups such as the Lucky Stars and De Pitch Black Follies. The Lucky Stars performed the Xhosa male initiation ceremony *abakwetha* as part of their act, and the repertoire of De Pitch Black Follies included "*I Qaga*" (a Xhosa song about a beetle), "Xhosa Poet," "Ntsikana's Vision" and hymns by John Bokwe and Tiyo Soga.[62] By the 1940s, township music involved African tunes and rhythms, Latin American rumba and conga, and the combination of these elements in *tsaba tsaba*. Ace Buya's Modernaires started out translating songs from the United States into isiXhosa, and gradually began using *tsaba tsaba* to create their own music. Buya and Victor Ndlazilwana's Woody Woodpeckers recorded songs of Xhosa migrant workers and adapted these cultural songs to close-harmony jazz.[63] This evolution of homegrown African music marks a dramatic change, as it absorbed the social and political philosophy of New Africanism and helped pave the way for the rise of more direct activism such as the formation of the ANC Youth League in the 1940s.

Concentrating on themes he developed in his *izibongo* and writings of the 1920s, Mqhayi contributed to the development of New Africanism in the 1930s through biographies and praise poems that continued to celebrate and commemorate African history and culture, particularly that of Xhosa-speaking people of the Eastern Cape. These compositions reflected the form of opposition to oppression that asserts and proudly upholds identity in the face of erasure, negation, and co-optation. The stories he proclaimed and wrote included instances of white duplicity in nineteenth-century dealings with Xhosa leaders and the courage of those leaders and the amaXhosa in fighting back against colonization—stories that were certain to draw parallels with more recent government oppression of his people and likely to fuel already existing indignation and resolution. In his account of the battle of the Waterkloof of 1852, for example, Mqhayi told the story of Sir Harry Smith who had become governor of the Cape in 1847 and, when traveling through Port Elizabeth, reportedly "wanted to place his foot on Maqoma's neck" (*wafuna ukubeka unyao lwake entanyeni ka Maqoma*). The powerful chief and warrior's response was, "*Ufuna ukwenza umsebenzi wobunja wena kuba uyinja; akakutumanga lonto us Vitoliya*" ("You insist on behaving like a dog because you are a dog; Queen Victoria did not send you to do this"), after which, Smith left. In the same account, Mqhayi described how Colonel John Jarvis Bisset laid a trap for Sandile, inviting the Ngqika chief to meet and negotiate peace terms and then capturing him and holding him prisoner: "*Ayizange ipele lonto ku Sandile, ukuti kanti inkosi le ikwa yinto exokayo elixa ibifanele ukuteta ngokungoyiki*" ("Sandile never forgot that, that this chief could lie, under guise of secret discussion").[64] This account, no doubt, served as a reminder of the perfidy of white power and its history in light of legislation imposed on black people in the early twentieth century.

Mqhayi then described how Sandile refused to consent to Smith's assertion that he be deposed as part of the peace terms of the War of the Axe (1846–1847): "*Asinto wake wayivuma nage mpumlo leyo u Mgolombane*" (Not even by the flaring of a nostril did Mgolombane [Sandile] consent to that). Mqhayi went on to praise Sandile in poetry that echoed the continuing challenges of black leaders in South Africa,

> *U Ndand' ako vece*
> *U Xesi magqahala*
> *U Nchunch' ayiseli kwabalekayo*
> *Isel' ezadungeni*
> *Ngokoyik' umlom' ukugoba*
> *Ubantu bantlaninge*
> *Bazalis' umhlaba*
> *Kazi woz' atinina min' abahlanganisayo*

> Who flutters over Vece,
> The rocky Keiskamma,
> A free-handed host who drinks no running water,
> Who drinks from a pool,
> Scared to stoop his mouth.
> His people form multitudes,
> Filling the earth:
> But how will he ever assemble them?

Then, as Mqhayi tells the history, Sandile's army went after Brownlee's two sons—one was shot and died in hospital; the other killed in an ambush and decapitated.[65]

In 1930 Mqhayi described and praised Tyala Nteyi, a nineteenth-century Gcaleka hero who was admired and respected by both his own people and white authorities due to his efforts for peace and his bravery in war, highlighting this unique concurrence on character in a divided country.[66] To emphasize this point in light of present circumstances, Mqhayi added:

Asizange ke sifumane sinqinelane ngolohlobo nomlungu. Usakuti umfo anga-lunga kuti, ati kanti ke kubo selenezote; aze ati umfo elungile nje kubo, kanti selelityanti kuti—injualo ke intlalo yetu nomlungu . . .

We are not often in agreement on the evidence like this with the whites. Usually when a person is acceptable to us, he is an abomination to them; and when a person is acceptable to them, he is not loved by us. This is how things are with us and the whites . . . [67]

Mqhayi resurrected stories of Xhosa war victories, referring again to Lieutenant-Colonel John Fordyce's decisive defeat by a Xhosa force at the Battle of the Waterkloof, while also giving his own opinion on the cause of the Great Cattle Killing:

Mandishiye lento ka Nongqause kweliti—umzi omhlope uti lento yayilicebo lika Sarili lokuba umzi wama Xosa ulahle inkomo nokutya uze uti xa uzazijora yind-lala, awufunze kubelungu, uye kungena ungasenanto uyijongileyo ngasemva. Tina siti elilicebo labelungu, lokwapula umqolo wama Xosa kuba wawungavumi ukwapuka zizo zonke imfazwe namanye amayelenqe. Kodwa ke ngenye imini soze sihlale pantsi sitete, ivele inyaniso.

Let me stop talking about Nongqawuse—the whites say this was [Gcaleka chief] Sarhili's plan to get the Xhosa to abandon their cattle and their food and, when they were raving from starvation, he would drive them to the whites, so they would be assimilated and not look back. But we say this was a white scheme to break the back of the Xhosa because of their resistance in all the wars and various plots. But one day we will sit down to talk, and the truth will emerge.[68]

Mqhayi's passage voices the divide between black and white populations, not only in their battles with each other, but in their interpretation of the truth. At the same time, it expresses the hope still alive among many black leaders in South Africa in the 1920s and 1930s that some form of reconciliation and dialogue was possible.

In recognition of the importance of women in the history of the amaX-hosa, Mqhayi wrote a tribute to Thembu Queen Suthu in 1932, citing her contribution to the history of the Rharhabe as well as her assistance to white people during the War of the Axe and Mlanjeni's War. He also wrote of Aggie Lekalakala, who broke through the barriers to education for women to become a prominent teacher in Queenstown. Throughout the 1930s, Mqhayi continued to extol the virtues of significant black intellectuals and leaders such as P. J. Mzimba, Elijah Makiwane, John Knox Bokwe, William Wauchope, Walter Rubusana, John Tengo Jabavu, and Charlotte Maxeke. Wauchope had died in the sinking of the the *S.S. Mendi* in the English Channel in 1917 during World War I—a tragedy that took the lives of over 600 black volunteer soldiers on their way to join the war effort—and Mqhayi included in a tribute to Wauchope this passage: "*Khumbula mlesi ukuba abafana bakowenu benze izimanga kuyo kanye loongozi, izimanga zokusindisa iqela lama doda amhlope awaye zindosana phezu kwawo, afa wona azsinda zona!*" (Never forget, reader, that the young men of your country worked wonders in that crisis, wonders in rescuing large numbers of white men who were their superiors, and lost their own lives in saving others!)[69]

In praise of John Henderson Soga in 1936, Mqhayi made this assertion:

> *Nbubanin' ofunzelene nathi maXhosa*
> *Eyakuxakwa sidang' entungo?*
> *Ngubanin' onomona sithi,*
> *Akayi kuba nasigaqa-na?*
> *Zizwe walumkelen' ama Xhosa!*

> Whoever challenges us Xhosa,
> Won't the roof pendants frustrate him?
> Whoever's jealous of us,
> Won't he turn into a lump of clay?
> Nations, beware the Xhosa![70]

As described in Chapter 2, it was Mqhayi's message of the power of the Xhosa nation that served as one of Nelson Mandela's first exposures to African nationalism, evoking pride in his Xhosa identity when Mandela was a student at Healdtown in 1939. In 1940 Mqhayi once again gave a moving tribute to Charlotte Maxeke after her death in October 1939. In a biblical reference to Deborah's song of triumph against the Canaanites in the book of Judges that recalled Maxeke's great musical talent combined with her political activism, Mqhayi named her "*I Tye lesiseko se Tiyopiya!*" (Foundation stone of Ethiopia!) and urged his people to erect a monument to her memory:

> *Az' angaz' alityalwe kowabo;*
> *Az' angaz' alityalw' emhlabeni;*
> *Az' angaz' alityalw'e Afrika!*

> May she never be forgotten by her people;
> May she never be forgotten on earth;
> May she never be forgotten in Africa.[71]

The 1940s and the advent of World War II brought a new generation of black leaders in South Africa that observed the increasing divide between African realities and African expectations. In the wake of its racial policies and restrictive legislation the South African government not surprisingly found itself struggling to recruit Africans to the Allied cause. Calata observed, "If the Government of South Africa does not get Africans to volunteer for service they must examine the situation from within. I am afraid they are themselves to blame for the present attitude of mind of the Africans."[72] In 1940, meanwhile, the ANC elected Dr. Xuma as its new president. Born in Manzana in the Ngcobo district of the Eastern Cape, Alfred Bathini Xuma had been educated at Clarkebury, a Wesleyan missionary school in Transkei, and led a student strike in 1911 to protest discrimination in the administering of teaching certificates to white versus black educators. He studied in the United States at Tuskegee, the University of Minnesota, and Northwestern University where he earned his medical degree, and went on to pursue medicine in Europe and Scotland. Returning to South Africa to practice as a doctor, Xuma was drawn into politics through his concern for the miners he treated who suffered from respiratory diseases as a result of their working conditions and the lack of proper compensation for them on the part of mine owners. In 1930 he made a name for himself as a prominent African leader in a speech he gave at Fort Hare, calling for an end to segregation, citizenship for all South Africans, and a multiracial dialogue with educated Africans taking the lead:

> What we need most is a revolution of the people's thoughts, their ideas, their ideals, and their spirit to recognize the African as a human being with human desires and aspirations which must be satisfied; to concede to the African "his reasonable demand to be considered a human being with full scope for human growth and human happiness."[73]

A member of the All Africa Convention and a prominent voice in refuting Hertzog's bill to remove Africans from the Cape electoral roll, Xuma was drawn to the international Pan-African movement while studying for a degree in public health in London in the late 1930s. After his election as president of the ANC, Xuma worked hard to re-organize the organization—drafting a new constitution assisted by the activist lawyer of Afrikaner descent Bram Fischer plus Calata and Z. K. Matthews, and initially exciting enthusiasm among the younger generation. The reorganization of the ANC had been inspired by the Atlantic Charter of 1941 which upheld the principle of self-determination for all nationalities and was interpreted by African nationalists as support for their liberation (although British Prime Minister Winston Churchill showed himself less enthusiastic about this interpretation than his co-signer President Franklin Roosevelt). International events such as the Italian invasion of Ethiopia in 1935 also fueled African nationalist feelings in South Africa that contributed to Dr. Xuma's efforts.

In 1944, Mqhayi praised the efforts of Xuma while calling on his people to stay focused:

Ngozintsinga ngathi ziintsimbhi
Uyalithwal' ikhulu lamadoda;
Awaxhom'onk' awoManyano.
Ngomithambho ngathi ziingcingo;
Zokuxhom' umXhosa nomZulu—
Kujing' umSuthu nomTshwana.
Emadodenii kwedini kaXuma!
Kad' izizwe zixhuma ziphethuka!
Xa kulapho sifun' ukunamanama . . .
Vul' amehl' ungab' ulahleke!

The one with guts like iron
Can carry a hundred men;
Lifting all the Manyano members.
The one with veins like wire;
To lift a Xhosa and Zulu—
A Sotho and Tswana will swing.
Join the men, Xuma's kid!
The nations have long been jumping and swerving!
And so we need to focus on something . . .
Open your eyes, and don't lose your way!"[74]

Dr. Xuma's wife, Madie Hall Xuma, meanwhile, was busy reinvigorating the Women's League of South Africa and working alongside her husband to keep political and social activism alive. An African American from Winston-Salem, North Carolina whom Alfred Xuma had married in 1940, Madie was a staunch supporter of women's rights, a member of the AME church, and an initiator of YWCA groups in North Carolina and South Africa. In a speech she gave at the Wilberforce Library Society in Transvaal, Madie argued that one of the most devastating consequences of slavery was the brainwashing of black people to accept their inferiority and second-class status. In 1943 she wrote, directed and produced a play to benefit the ANC titled *American Negro Review: The Progress of a Race* which was based on an original performance from Winston-Salem with a cast that had included renowned African American contralto Marian Anderson. In this play, music and dance were used to express the evolution of the story of black people from slavery to freedom and their eventual achievements in the areas of science, politics, sports and the arts. A narrative of black advancement, the performance raised over £200 for the ANC. Madie Xuma also produced *The Green Pastures*, a popular musical on black American life and the empowerment of black people that consisted of biblical characters, including Noah, Moses, Adam and Eve, Cain, Joshua, and God—all depicted as black. Popular spirituals punctuated the dialogue and lines were spoken with a rural southern dialect.

The play was intended to appeal to the hopes of black South Africans, but South African authorities were not happy with the implications and messages of the performance. In December 1943, Madie Xuma was informed by the Secretary of the Interior that her work was not suitable for public audiences "as the play is calculated to give offense to the religious convictions or feelings of a section of the public."[75]

While Madie Xuma worked at using musical performance to spread the message of empowerment to black populations all over South Africa, music continued to be a strong social force in the Eastern Cape townships, despite government crackdowns and restrictions. T.C. White Hall, a prominent place of meeting in New Brighton, served as the heart of cultural activity for black people in Port Elizabeth. Jazz and dance bands played to full crowds while church choirs and choral groups also performed. A number of male vocal groups became popular in New Brighton in the 1940s, including the Abancedisi Choristers and the Broadway Brothers, who made appearances at T.C. White Hall. They also performed in Korsten, South End and Uitenhage, with shows usually on Saturdays that included long hours of nonstop music from swing to *marabi*. Jimmy Matyu recalled the excitement of these shows in Port Elizabeth in the 1940s and 1950s, along with the battle to enjoy them in the face of mounting restrictions:

> I still remember the fashionably dressed dancing women who worked as "sleep-in" domestics in the former exclusively white suburbs anxiously checking their watches so they did not miss the last bus at 9 p.m. to their servant quarters in the backyard. . . . Yes, in those days it was easy for a law-abiding black to have a criminal record for failing to produce his *dompass* or night pass when demanded rudely by an overzealous policeman.[76]

Other choirs that formed in New Brighton in the 1940s included the Mexican Vocal Company, founded by James Ntshinga (a headman in the Native Administration), the Port Elizabeth Male Voice Choir led by Gilpin William Tshangana, and the United Artists Choir. These singing groups were usually backed up by a piano and occasionally a rhythm section. Performances also showcased the actor/comedian/singer Andrew Smith Tsewu as well as a young group of singers known as the Tiny Tots which had been formed by Mrs. Nyaluza, a schoolteacher at Methodist Primary School. Welcome Duru and his brother Kenneth got their start in musical performance with the Tiny Tots, as did other future jazz musicians including Robert Maduba, Bulelo ("Bully") Makwezela, Dilesa Vikiva, and Nomaniso Dlula. The lyrics of the Tiny Tots songs often played around with isiXhosa double meanings, while gramophone records and the cinema exposed the singers to American performers such as the Andrews Sisters, the Mills Brothers, and the Inkspots, all of whom became strong influences on the group. Performances of the Tiny Tots included gumboots and tap dancing. Unable to afford tap shoes, the youths would use bottle lids held between their toes.[77]

With several members graduating from the Tiny Tots, Duru's group the Basin Blues started performing in the 1940s in Port Elizabeth. Duru had grown up first in Korsten and then New Brighton when his family was relocated in the 1930s and he claimed that the Basin Blues started in the initiates' school he was part of: "There we did nothing the entire day. We would sit down as *bakhwethas* [initiates] and sing tunes. It was not long before I noticed a sense of harmony. I knew then that when we came out I would form the vocal troupe—that was how the Basin Blues were formed."[78]

As a youth Duru lived in the section of New Brighton known as McNamee Village (named for township Superintendent J. P. McNamee) on Mendi Road—an address that later became famous as a stopping point for black musicians travelling to Johannesburg. McNamee Village had a competitive relationship with the other two sections of New Brighton: Newtown, later called White Location (*eLalini Mholophe*), and Red Location (*eLalini Ebomvu*). While playing at T.C. White Hall in Red Location, bands would often be bullied by the local youths who would throw plants that caused strong smells to waft through the hall and cause mass sneezing and general mayhem among the audience and musicians. According to Duru, the McNamee youths held their own against the gangs of the Red and White locations: "That is the reason why the McNamee men tended to be bound together by music as well as belonging to certain cultural groups."[79]

In 1943, the same year that Madie Xuma's play was shut down by South African authorities, the ANC, influenced by the Atlantic Charter, adopted the statement "Africans' Claims in South Africa" which set out a bill of rights calling for abolition of all discriminatory legislation, the redistribution of land, African participation in collective bargaining and universal adult suffrage. In 1944 Anton Lembede founded the ANC Youth League, together with former Fort Hare students Nelson Mandela, Albert Sisulu, and Oliver Tambo. They were joined by other ANC young professionals, including Jordan Ngubane who voiced the frustration over their present circumstances:

> The progressive decline of living conditions for the African has given rise to feelings of great suspicions of the Whiteman's motives. Poor health services, low wages, shortage of land for Africans, the color bar, inferior education and the consistent assertion of White superiority over the African in every aspect of life are all regarded as one huge plan to undermine the African's resistance to disease, weaken his will to be free and are, therefore, an indirect attempt to exterminate the African people with a view to making South Africa a hundred percent Whiteman's country."[80]

The ANC Youth League based its ideas on African nationalism and the belief that Africans could only be freed by their own efforts, as opposed to making continued and seemingly fruitless appeals to white governments. It was greatly influenced by several external developments: the fact that a world war had been fought against racism and for democracy, the movement for India's independence from British colonial rule, and the rise of nationalism throughout the African continent. The new militancy of the African trade unions in the 1940s and the activities of the South African Communist Party (SACP) also helped to inspire the rise of the ANC Youth League. Workers began to play a more important role in the ANC—particularly in the League.

As an anti-pass campaign gained traction through the energy of both the ANC and South African Communist Party, the years 1942–1944 marked a time of sixty illegal African strikes, including a series of bus boycotts. In 1946 mine workers led a general strike that involved close to 70,000 workers in the mining regions, and the Transkei Voters Association and the Transkeian Organized Bodies joined the anti-pass campaign, opening their meetings with the newly written Anti-Pass Hymn.[81] The South African government under Jan Smuts brutally suppressed the strike, but the movement in combination with the initial success of the anti-pass campaign increased fear and paranoia in the white population and these events became a major factor in the outcome of the 1948 elections. The ANC, meanwhile, stumbled in maintaining momentum, particularly in the anti-pass campaign, and support for the organization tapered off such that by 1948 it had fewer than 6,000 members—holding on to many followers, in the Eastern Cape region—and no fully developed plan of action. This would change after the 1948 election, when the shock of the newly energized National Party coming to power and launching a series of laws and policies that marked the beginning of the period of apartheid, re-energized the ANC and black opposition as a whole. The spirit and scope of African nationalism was continuing to redefine and underpin resistance in the Eastern Cape, and music and spoken word kept pace with these developments. The freedom of African jazz clapped back at increased government restrictions; the revisiting of indigenous culture and reviving Xhosa version of history in music and spoken word marked a defiance in the face of cultural colonization; and performance connected with protest amid a growing realization among black leaders that attempting to negotiate with an authority that exercised so much power did little to advance the cause of their people. The new assertiveness that those such as Dr. Xuma had brought to African protest politics in the 1940s and that was built upon by the ANC Youth League laid the foundation for more militant action and greater challenges to white liberal perspectives—an assertiveness seen by much of the black population as desperately needed in the wake of the apartheid election of 1948.

Meanwhile, in 1945, the great poet, writer, historian, and *imbongi* Mqhayi died unexpectedly. Walter Nhalpo expressed the reaction of much of the black population to this news:

Bantudom has lost one of her most beloved creative minds...

His literary works are to the Xhosa what the Strauss Waltzes were to Vienna, and what Napoleonic victories were to the French. A memorial should be erected to him so that the father can point Mqhayi to his son, the mother to her daughter, the host to his guest and say with pride: "herein lies the immortal Mqhayi."[82]

In 2013, the author and academic Xolela Mangcu went in search of Mqhayi's grave in King William's Town, only to discover it sadly neglected near a rubbish dump.[83]

NOTES

1. Daniel Massey, *Under Protest: The Rise of Student Resistance at Fort Hare* (Pretoria: UNISA Press, 2010), 32.

2. Christopher Ballantine, "Music and Emancipation: The Social Role of Black Jazz and Vaudeville in South Africa between the 1920s and the early 1940s," *Journal of South African Studies,* volume 17, no. 1 (March 1991), 135.

3. Transvaal Local Government (Stallard) Commission, 1922. TAB 1217, National Archives of South Africa.

4. Colin Bundy, *Govan Mbeki* (Athens, OH: Ohio University Press, 2012), 31.

5. Christopher Ballantine, "Fact, Ideology and Paradox: African Elements in Early Black South African Jazz and Vaudeville," *African Music,* Volume 7, No. 3, (1996), 49.

6. David Coplan, *In Township Tonight!* (Chicago: University of Chicago Press, 1985, 2007), 117–18.

7. The word "coon" is a reference to the term originally used in South Africa to describe music and parades that developed among Africans and the colored population, mainly those tracing their roots to slavery in the Cape, with performances influenced by American minstrelsy.

8. Coplan, *In Township Tonight!* 116.

9. Coplan, *In Township Tonight!* 118.

10. Gwen Ansell, *Soweto Blues* (London: Contiuum International Publishing Group, 2004), 11.

11. Todd Matshikiza, *Drum* (June 1957).

12. Christopher Ballantine, "The Identities of Race, Class and Gender in the Repression of Early Black South African Jazz and Vaudeville (circa 1920–1944)," paper presented at the 11th Symposium on Ethnomusicology, University of Natal, 1993, International Library of African Music Archives.

13. Frieda Bokwe Matthews, "African Music in South Africa," in *The World of South African Music: A Reader*, ed. Christine Lucia (Newcastle: Cambridge Scholars Press, 2005), 39.

14. Matthews, "African Music in South Africa," 39–40.

15. Matthews, "African Music in South Africa," 40.

16. Ballantine, "The Identities of Race, Class and Gender," 9.

17. *Mteteli wa Bantu*, June 6, 1931, cited in Coplan, *In Township Tonight!* 139.

18. Coplan, *In Township Tonight!* 154.

19. Paul la Housse, *Brewers, Beerhalls, and Boycotts* (Johannesburg: Ravan Press, 1988), 43.

20. Xuma, Evidence to the Native Economic Commission, 1931, *Izwi Lase Township*, January 1984, No. 7, p. 8. University of Witwatersrand Historical Papers.

21. Vuyisile Msila, *The Black Train Rising: The Life and Times of Welcome Duru* (Lynwood Ridge, South Africa: Siyomba Projects, 2010), 3.

22. Gary F. Baines, *A History of New Brighton 1903–1953: The Detroit of the Union* (Lewiston, NY: Edwin Mellen Press, 2002), 228; Lestie Hughes, "The Social and Cultural Significance of Dudley Tito's Music: A Postmodern Investigation," M.A. Thesis (University of Port Elizabeth, 1999), 27.

23. Baines, *A History of New Brighton 1903–1953*, 227–29; Jennifer Robinson, *The Power of Apartheid: State, Power and Space in South African Cities* (Oxford: Butterworth-Heinemann, 1996), 89–105.

24. Robinson, *The Power of Apartheid*, 92.

25. Record of Evidence to the Natives Economic Commission, Tshangana, March 18–April 10, 1931, p. 5992, TA K26, Volume 7, Central Government Archives, Pretoria.

26. Anthony Sampson, *Nelson Mandela: The Authorized Biography* (New York: Knopf, 1999), 23.

27. S.E.K. Mqhayi, *Abantu besizwe: Historical and biographic writings, 1902–1944*, edited and translated by Jeff Opland (Johannesburg: Wits University Press, 2009), 310–23.

28. Mqhayi, *Abantu besizwe*, 330.

29. Mqhayi, *Abantu besizwe*, 342.

30. *Imvo Zabantsundu*, February 25, 1929. Library of Congress.

31. Mary Benson, *The Struggle for a Birthright* (London: International Defense Aid Fund, 1966), 49.

32. Red Location Museum Exhibit, 2013.

33. William Beinart and Colin Bundy, *Hidden Struggles in Rural South Africa: Politics and Popular Movements in the Transkei and Eastern Cape 1890–1930* (Johannesburg: Ravan Press, 1987), 270.

34. Police Report collected in CA 1/ELN volumes 86 file C3(1) and 87 file C3 (2), September 20, 1929, cited in Beinart and Bundy, *Hidden Struggles in Rural South Africa*, 290.

35. Police Report, February 5, 1928, cited in Beinart and Bundy, *Hidden Struggles in Rural South Africa*, 284.

36. *Negro World*, July 30, 1927. Library of Congress.

37. Affidavit of Richard Nortje, May 13, 1929; affidavit of Richard Welsh, May 13, 1929; Welsh, May 15, 1929; NTS 1681, file 2/276 Part 1, NASA, CT.

38. Police Report, February 19, 1928 and May 13, 1928; cited in Beinart and Bundy, *Hidden Struggles in Rural South Africa*, 283.

39. Police Report, January 6, 1930; cited in Beinart and Bundy, *Hidden Struggles in Rural South Africa*, 293.

40. Police Report, September 3, 1930; November 12, 1930; December 28, 1930; October 5, 1930; cited in Beinart and Bundy, *Hidden Struggles in Rural South Africa*, 312–14.

41. Mqhayi, *Abantu besizwe*, 294–95.

42. William Beinart, "*Amafelandawonye* (The Diehards): Rural Popular Protest and Women's Movements in Herschel District, South Africa, in the 1920s," paper presented at the University of the Witwatersrand History Workshop (January 31–February 4, 1984), 19.

43. Beinart, "*Amafelandawonye*," 20.

44. Beinart, "*Amafelandawonye*," 31.

45. Police Report, January 12, 1930; cited in Beinart and Bundy, *Hidden Struggles in Rural South Africa*, 296.

46. Interview of Solomon Crutse by David Coplan, July 26, 1978, in Coplan, *In Township Tonight!* 161.

47. Mavis Noluthando Mpola, "An Analysis of Oral Literary Music Texts in IsiXhosa," Ph.D. Thesis (Rhodes University, 2007), 65.

48. Benson, *The Struggle for a Birthright*, 68.

49. Benson, *The Struggle for a Birthright*, 66.

50. Benson, *The Struggle for a Birthright*, 69.

51. Massey, *Under Protest*, 34.

52. Bundy, *Govan Mbeki*, 40.

53. Massey, *Under Protest*, 35.

54. Massey, *Under Protest*, 39.

55. Bundy, *Govan Mbeki*, 41.

56. Bundy, *Govan Mbeki*, 52–54.

57. Benson, *The Struggle for a Birthright*, 73.

58. Christopher Ballantine, "Music and Emancipation," 145.

59. Christopher Ballantine, "The Identities of Race, Class, and Gender," 7.

60. *Bantu World*, July 13, 1935.

61. *Bantu World*, July 13, 1935.

62. *Bantu World*, February 12, 1938.

63. Coplan, *In Township Tonight!* 186.

64. Mqhayi, *Abantu besizwe*, 362.

65. Mqhayi, *Abantu besizwe*, 362–64.

66. See "Death of Tyala," in Charles Brownlee, *Kaffir Life and History* (Lovedale Mission Press, 1896), 362–65.

67. Mqhayi, *Abantu besizwe*, 370–71.

68. Mqhayi, *Abantu besizwe*, 384–85.

69. Mqhayi, *Abantu besizwe*, 476.

70. Mqhayi, *Abantu besizwe*, 504–5.
71. Mqhayi, *Abantu besizwe*, 524–26.
72. Benson, *The Struggle for a Birthright*, 75.
73. Dr. A. B. Xuma, "Bridging the Gap Between White and Black in South Africa." Address to the Conference of European and Bantu Christian Student Associations at Fort Hare, June 27–July 3, 1930, in *From Protest to Challenge: A Documentary History of African Politics in South Africa 1882–1964, Volume 1: Protest and Hope 1882–1934*, ed. Thomas Karis, Gwendolyn Carter, and Sheridan Johns III (Stanford, CA: Hoover Institution Press, 1972), 227.
74. Mqhayi, *Abantu besizwe*, 528.
75. Iris Berger, "An African American 'Mother of the Nation': Madie Hall Xuma in South Africa 1940–1963," *Journal of Southern African Studies*, volume 27, No. 3 (September 2001), 557.
76. Vuyisile Msila, *A Place to Live: Red Location and Its History from 1903 to 2013*, (Stellenbosch: SUN MEDIA METRO, 2014), 131–32.
77. Baines, *A History of New Brighton 1903–1953*, 230; Hughes, "The Social and Cultural Significance of Dudley Tito's Music," 29. Hughes identifies the woman who started the Tiny Tots as Mrs. Gulwa.
78. Msila, *The Black Train Rising*, 54.
79. Msila, *The Black Train Rising*, 22.
80. Jordan Ngubane, *Inkundla ya Bantu*, July 17, 1944.
81. Bundy, *Govan Mbeki*, 65.
82. Mqhayi, *Abantu besizwe*, 16.
83. Xolela Mangcu, "Retracing Nelson Mandela through the Lineage of Black Political Thought," *Transition*, No. 112, Django Unpacked (2013), 107–8.

Chapter 5

"A Spirit That Could Not Be Broken"

1950s–1960s

While the establishment of the apartheid regime in 1948 marked a new period of oppression, the 1950s ushered in an era of increased popular protest and resistance in the Eastern Cape. The harshness of the apartheid laws in many ways fueled not only the determination of pushback but the intensity of musical and poetic expression. Port Elizabeth, for example, became a flash point for both organized resistance and jazz music. Vuyisile Msila writes that life in Port Elizabeth during that time had many moments of inspiration: "While people lived in poverty and squalor, cultural activities continued to enrich their lives. They continued to experience their lives as cultural beings. This was a spirit that could not be broken."[1] In New Brighton township activists formed street committees and collected donations to pay whenever possible those involved in protest administration and leadership. Robert Mkxotho Matji, for example, through donations, was able to quit his job as a factory worker and become a full-time secretary for the ANC and a key activist in the Defiance Campaign. Govan Mbeki, expelled from Durban in 1955, was invited to work as a local editor and office manager for the communist publication *New Age* in Port Elizabeth, where he continued to foment activism and organize ANC cells in response to increased apartheid restrictions and crackdowns. Dr. James Lowell Zwelinzima Njongwe, a Fort Hare graduate from Qumbu in Transkei, became a prominent organizer for resistance in the Eastern Cape as part of the ANC National Executive Committee. *Iimbongi* also continued to provide commentary on the changing situation, particularly regarding the evolution of chiefdoms and local African authorities within the structure of apartheid. The emergence of those such as Melikhaya Mbutuma and D. L. P. Manisi as voices of opposition among *iimbongi* in the 1950s and 1960s illustrated the stark choice given to traditional praise-singers of whether to swallow their criticism of state-installed and compliant traditional leaders or continue to speak truth to power and face the possibility of censorship, banning, and imprisonment.

At Fort Hare, student activism was influenced by the revival of the ANC in response to the Nationalist Party elections of 1948, the aftermath of World War II, and the subtler effects of the guidance and lectures of one of their professors, Z. K. Matthews. Matthews' son Joe, who described daily life in the presence of his father as one of "a lot of argument and discussion," became chairman of the Fort Hare branch of the ANC Youth League, helping to organize protest activity such as the boycott of Governor-General G. Brand van Zyl's visit to the campus. According to Frieda Matthews, the students' position on the visit was, "How can we welcome the head of state of which we are not citizens?"[2] Students at Fort Hare increasingly made a direct comparison between their lack of power within the college and that of people of color in South Africa as a whole. They also took note of the shrinking access to real education that apartheid brought, and the control that white authorities maintained over the historical narrative. One student, Andrew Masondo, complained of the perspective he was supposed to accept through mission school education: "I thought the history we were taught was biased. You know I couldn't understand how people who came here and didn't have cattle suddenly talked about other people stealing their cattle."[3] According to former students, protest at Fort Hare was often directed at the poor quality of food at the university. V. R. Govender believed these particular demonstrations helped form the musical element of resistance: "We took pots and pans, boom, boom, boom, and that's how the songs came about."[4]

In the post–World War II era, nationalism came to the forefront of the African political response to apartheid, with calls for more confrontational protests from leaders such as Mandela, Anton Lembede, Walter Sisulu, and Oliver Tambo—strong voices in the ANC Youth League. In describing their policy and program of action in 1948, these leaders made clear the elements of African identity in their description of white oppression and its historical basis:

> More than 150 years ago, our fore-fathers were called upon to defend their fatherland against the foreign attacks of European Settlers. In spite of bravery and unparalleled heroism, they were forced to surrender to white domination. Two main factors contributed to their defeat. Firstly, the superior weapons of the white man, and secondly the fact that the Africans fought as isolated tribes, instead of pooling their resources and attacking as a united force.[5]

The Youth League called for the end of European domination of Africa, an equal re-division of land, and the establishment of democracy for all in

South Africa, as well as in Africa as a whole. Acknowledging that no group in power was likely to forfeit that power voluntarily, the ANC Youth League promoted African nationalism as "the militant outlook of an oppressed people seeking a solid basis for waging a long, bitter, and unrelenting struggle for its national freedom."[6] Confrontation was increasingly replacing negotiation as a strategy for resistance and national identity acted as an impetus for defiant protest.

Port Elizabeth had already established itself at the center of organized African politics in South Africa, with more combative and labor-oriented activism in the 1940s overtaking the previous black elite–centered strategies of negotiation that had marked the early decades of the twentieth century. While ANC leaders in other cities tended to be middle-class professionals, leadership in Port Elizabeth had a more working-class character with labor and union movements heavily involved. Nationwide resistance movements such as the anti-pass campaign of 1944, the rent boycotts of 1945 and 1951, the dock workers strike of 1945–46, and the bus boycott of 1949 were all marked by strong support from Port Elizabeth activists. Resistance was also on the rise in rural areas of the Eastern Cape, such as the Transkei. Faced with the daunting effects of the Bantu Authorities Act and apartheid restrictions causing increased hardship over land, cattle, and general subsistence, populations in the countryside fought back with legal challenges to evictions, as well as more confrontational tactics.

As township life in the Eastern Cape became more of a struggle as a result of apartheid, music and performance became part of the fast-paced life adopted by Africans treading the thin line between legal and illegal activity in the 1950s. Creative expression provided an outlet for the stress of navigating laws and state-sponsored violence based on the color of one's skin, as did organized resistance; and the two responses often blended together at rallies, performances, and jam sessions that punctuated urban life for black people in the 1950s. Church choirs and choral groups in New Brighton grew in prominence, and places such as T.C. White Hall continued to sponsor musical acts in Red Location while jazz and dance bands played to full crowds. The violence imposed on township dwellers through the apartheid system found an echo in the disruption and violence played out in the music halls and streets by *tsotsis*—youths branded as criminal elements—who added to the dangers of urban life. Msila recalled an incident in Walmer Township in Port Elizabeth while playing with the Basin Blues when *tsotsis* brought axes into Victory Hall and stood with them in front of the stage to intimidate the band into playing nonstop through the night.[7]

Post-war jazz music and performance took off in the Eastern Cape in places such as Port Elizabeth and Queenstown where missionary schools often provided the formal music education that gave black students access to different instruments. Musicians also experienced increased exposure to films and songs from the United States through records, gramophones and movie theaters. Local South African jazz started to take on its own character in these places and a critical mass of talent grew during the 1950s and 1960s. Local jazz musician Patrick Pasha described New Brighton in the 1950s as "a beehive of jazz activity," with bands such as the King Cole Basses making their mark, and the African Rhythm Crotchets, a group of middle-class teachers who performed music to accompany Western dances such as the quickstep, foxtrot, and tango. Both of these bands developed a style based on American swing and added original *mbaqanga* pieces with a more energetic rhythm while combining aural technique with tonic solfa.[8] It was during the 1950s that Welcome Duru, leader of the New Brighton Basin Blues, wrote "*Wenyuk' umbombela*" ("The Train Song"), a classic protest song played throughout the townships and later recorded by Harry Belafonte and Miriam Makeba.[9] Absorbing the influences of singers such as the Inkspots from the United States, the Port Elizabeth Male Voice Choir, Abancedisi Choristers, and the Broadway Brothers all performed at T.C. White Hall, as well as in Korsten, South End, and Uitenhage, playing long hours on Saturday nights with every style of music from swing to *marabi*. The Basin Blues was one of the three leading vocal groups in New Brighton that performed on a regular basis in T.C. White Hall; the other two were the Keynotes led by Norman Ntshinga and the Swing Slickers led by Gogi "Kutman" Kwatsha. Reflecting the raucous life that accompanied these musicians, Kwatsha developed a notoriety for his use of a knife in fights.[10] Other bands included the Junior Jazzman, and the Jazz Maniacs. Not strictly professional, these musicians were nonetheless highly accomplished in multiple ways; Mike Ngxokolo, a schoolteacher and trombonist who played with the Soul Jazzmen, taught himself staff notation and shared his knowledge with fellow musicians. Writing songs for South African Eisteddfods, Ngxokolo went on to become a member of Athol Fugard's Serpent Players. His greatest compositions included *Ah' Zanzolo: Bunjalo Ubomi*—a tribute to the famed Xhosa king Hintsa. New Brighton was also the home of Enoch Fikile Gwashu who wrote novels in Xhosa and composed choral songs, such as *Ndeva Ilizwe*—a song about hearing a voice from the mountains telling of a journey ahead.[11]

In the 1950s, New Brighton bands were strongly influenced by American jazz, including the style of dress—black suits—and a particular form of urban elitism. Lumkile Jacobs, for example, had hoped to join the King Cole Basses, but was rejected based on his rural background. Jacobs instead became a member of the Junior Jazzmen along with Ngxokolo and the trumpet player Sergeant Mjo. Other jazz bands demonstrating the New Brighton sound were Swannie's Swing Aces and the Rhythm Downbeats. Relocations by government authorities influenced the formation of bands such as

Kwazakhele's Lake Town Swingsters and Symphony Band with members who had had to move from Korsten. They played regular performances at ANC meetings in T.C. White Hall and the War Memorial Hall as part of opposition to forced segregation. Queenstown also continued to build a reputation for jazz, infused with influences from the United States and other parts of South Africa. Combining European hymnody and Western classical music with overseas sounds, local South African jazz in this city began to take on its own character.

The 1940s had introduced a new generation of leaders in cities such as Port Elizabeth and East London who possessed a political consciousness influenced by personal and communal experiences and by a collective memory kept alive by music and the spoken word of the *iimbongi*. Action was continually taking place through boycotts and strikes, but a tradition of resistance in the Eastern Cape had been maintained since the Frontier Wars of the nineteenth century. Deborah Posel contends that state attempts to use Africans to help regulate the segregationist system through advisory boards "underlined the breadth and intensity of African dissent. The very bodies created by the state for the purposes of co-opting support from moderate Africans were joining the throngs of the disaffected."[12] The ANC was also now taking greater stock of the importance of the working class in resistance strategies and it was in the 1950s that the South African Congress of Trade Unions (SACTU) was established, connecting economic struggles with political ones and upholding the principles of liberation and freedom. Prominent leaders of SACTU included Vuyisile Mini, an Eastern Cape activist born in Port Elizabeth and known for combining his musical skills with his organizing strengths. Mini joined the struggle against apartheid at age seventeen and later became Secretary of the Dock Workers' Union and Sheet Metal Workers Union—both affiliated with SACTU—and his deep bass and protest songs became standard features of anti-apartheid demonstrations in the 1950s and 1960s. His most well-known song was *Pasopa nansi 'ndondemnyama we Verwoerd* ("Look out, Verwoerd, here are the black people), referring to Hendrik Verwoerd, Minister for Native Affairs and later Prime Minister of South Africa. The song was made popular in a recording by Miriam Makeba, and could be heard sung at numerous anti-apartheid rallies and demonstrations. In the documentary *Amandla!*, singer Dolly Rathebe remembers the power of Mini's song: "When you really wanted to make the whites mad, you sang *nansi 'ndondemnyama we Verwoerd*."[13]

In 1952 Albert Luthuli took over as president of the ANC and began leading campaigns against Pass Laws, the Group Areas Act, the Separate Voters' Representation Act, the Suppression of Communism Act, and the Bantu Authorities Act. His new leadership role coincided with the organization of the Defiance Campaign, a resistance strategy formulated by leaders of the ANC, South African Communist Party, and the South African Indian Congress (SAIC), that called on large numbers of volunteers throughout the country to defy discriminatory laws and invite arrest. On April 6, 1952, a gathering in Port Elizabeth approved the strategy and on April 13, after a public meeting chaired by Raymond Mhlaba of the local ANC, those attending gave unanimous consent to the conference decisions and a significant number of volunteers signed on for the campaign. On May 31st the national executives of the ANC and SAIC met in Port Elizabeth to confirm June 26th as the starting date of the Defiance Campaign. With the support of many churches, ANC President-General Dr. J. S. Moroka held a mass meeting on June 1st of 3,000 Africans and led the pledge to fight for freedom in the face of suffering and death. The majority of the volunteers were respected members of the community who had been trained in nonviolent behavior, and women made up 42% of participation in the campaign, acting as a staple feature of support and preparation for each planned demonstration and series of arrests.[14] Vuyisile Mini also joined the campaign, continuing to contribute to the resistance movement with his music and political leadership, and was imprisoned for entering railway property reserved for whites only. After his release, Mini rapidly progressed up the ladder of ANC leadership and became ANC Secretary of the Cape region.

The press announced the beginning of the Defiance Campaign after the May 31st meeting, and reports included a gathering in preparation for the campaign in New Brighton. Mary Benson vividly describes this meeting:

> There were no bands, no uniforms, no marching to whip up the masses. The black, green and gold Congress flag blew in a strong cold wind. Women led the singing until the leaders arrived and they all solemnly sang *Nkosi Sikelel' iAfrika*. Old bearded men were there, small children in rags watched, and a praise singer, dressed in skins with a cow tail whip and a small assegai, chanted traditional praises to the leaders. From cars the police watched. Professor Matthews told the crowd: "Fighting for freedom is not a picnic . . . it is a very painful process and in that fight there is going to be suffering and even death."[15]

On June 26th, Mhlaba led thirty volunteers through the "Europeans Only" entrance of New Brighton Railroad Station. A crowd followed the volunteers singing *"Senzeni Na?"* (What have we done, we African people?) and many wore ANC armbands and shouted "Mayibuye iAfrica!" ("Come Back, Africa!").[16] Those who marched through the entrance were arrested, refused bail, and stayed in custody. The first week in July, 85 resisters in Port Elizabeth defied apartheid laws and were put in North End Jail which by that time was reported as nearly full, and the number of arrested defiers in the city climbed steadily as the campaign took off. In the first month 389 were arrested, 666 in the second month, and 738 by the end of September.[17] Those arrested who were under the age of 21 were sentenced to corporal punishment and given a warning by the local magistrate that future resisters would get harsher sentences; but the number of volunteers did not decline. On July 5, nineteen volunteers were arrested in the white section of the North End Post Office and the jail became packed to capacity.[18] The first all-female group of volunteers in Port Elizabeth were led by "Nompie" Njongwe (Dr. Njongwe's wife) through the "Europeans Only" entrance at the railroad station and they were the first to receive harsher sentences: forty days in jail with the option of an £8 fine (suspended for six months).[19]

Students from Fort Hare played a major albeit indirect role in the Defiance Campaign. Denied direct participation by Njongwe, who felt that it was important for these future leaders to continue their studies and pass their exams, the students organized the Defiance Movement in Alice and surrounding areas with notable success in the level of participation from the region (70%), setting up defiance of curfew regulations and the black occupation of benches designated for whites only at the Alice train station. Music continued to play a major role in these demonstrations. When, in August 1952, a large number of volunteers were arrested in Alice, Fort Hare students held a rally in front of the courthouse the following day in support of those arrested. Former student Frank Mdlalose recalled, "We'd organize the whole of Fort Hare to come and sing around the courthouse to disrupt things." As police were brought in from King William's Town and Fort Beaufort, "we, as the students, we just sang." The police ended up charging on the student rally, scattering the crowd and attacking them.[20]

During the Defiance Campaign, ANC membership in New Brighton increased from 2,700 to 13,000 within a month, and Korsten and Dassieskraal townships also saw significant increases. Strike action in conjunction with the Defiance Campaign in Port Elizabeth correspondingly marked the growth of union membership and by mid-October the city had clearly become a significant force in the nationwide campaign.[21] The New Brighton Riots of October 1952 disrupted the momentum of the campaign in Port Elizabeth, however, and led to a serious crackdown. Referred to by local residents as the "Paint Riot" because it began when police accused two men at the New Brighton station of stealing a can of paint, the incident escalated as crowds from Red Location attacked the police and railway station. The unrest carried on into the night resulting in the deaths of three whites killed by angry township residents and seven Africans shot by the police. Race relations worsened in response to the riots, and the City Council, which had formerly taken a fairly liberal attitude to township population restrictions, immediately adopted a hard-line approach to influx control, curfews, and political activism, essentially placing the New Brighton area under siege. The government blamed Defiance Campaign leaders and refused to appoint a Commission of Inquiry, instead fueling white fears and prejudices through press reports. Hendrik Verwoerd, who was then Minister of Native Affairs, made no bones about connecting the riots to the Defiance Campaign and went so far as to blame Port Elizabeth authorities for being too liberal in their policies toward the black population. The riots, claimed Verwoerd, held a "double lesson" for Port Elizabeth officials because the Defiance Campaign had been launched from the city and the first outbreak of violence had occurred in that city's "model village"—clearly indicating that Port Elizabeth had been too slow in applying apartheid rules to the townships.[22]

The high level of political activity and resistance in Port Elizabeth was generated by increased resentment over forced removals from Korsten, Fairview, and South End. Apartheid had marginalized these populations and they were not likely to forget. Boycotts in Port Elizabeth that had already begun against government institutions grew more widespread in the 1950s, targeting local stores that were known for mistreatment of Africans or for refusing to employ them. New legislation introduced by apartheid hit these populations particularly hard and complaints had already been growing over the harsh treatment of New Brighton residents by railroad officials even before the New Brighton riots. While Pretoria claimed the uprising at the station had been planned by outside agitators, in a private memo the police in Port Elizabeth admitted there was no evidence of this. The ANC blamed the police: "It was the policy of using the police to terrorize Non-Europeans that had brought about an explosive and dangerous situation."[23]

In 1953 the ANC was banned from holding meetings in New Brighton and activism became riskier. Resistance hit a setback with most senior members of the ANC in Port Elizabeth under banning orders and thirteen of them charged with violating the Suppression of Communism Act, but political activism in the Eastern Cape refused to die and only became more creative. Underground cells were formed through the "M-plan"—a structure largely designed by Mandela as a channel of communication between leaders and their followers. Former activists from the Defiance Campaign known as *amaVolontiya* were assigned street committees to communicate with and organize. Govan Mbeki started a program of political education in Port Elizabeth "without equal in any South African city in the 1950s," according to Colin Bundy. He wrote a widely distributed booklet titled *Isikhokelo ngesimo onkqubo ye ANC* ("Guide to the Nature and 'way of doing things' within the ANC") which summarized the history, objectives, and strategies of that organization, and study groups of ten read excerpts from the booklet each week.[24]

Of the 8,557 Defiance Campaign participants, 5,719 were from the Eastern Cape, and 1,067 of those were women, demonstrating Eastern Cape women's role in resistance politics and coming on the heels of their strong involvement in anti-pass demonstrations; for example, in East London in April 1950.[25] With apartheid authorities cracking down on population influx in the townships in the 1950s, African women's place in the cities became increasingly insecure as the government moved gradually towards a policy of more restrictive measures for black women, including passes. In the wake of the Defiance Campaign, a meeting was held for women in Port Elizabeth led by local ANC and union leader Florence Matomela, one of the first women arrested in New Brighton during the Defiance Campaign, Tswana activist Frances Baard, and the prominent national union leader Ray Alexander who was visiting from Cape Town. The meeting and local developments in Port Elizabeth became a catalyst for the formation of a national women's organization—the Federation of South African Women (FSAW)—and Port Elizabeth remained a strong center for the Federation and the ANC Women's League.[26] The first conference leading to the creation of the FSAW in 1954 was marked by singing and dancing which became a constant feature at FSAW meetings: "The township women brought an energy and exuberance to their meetings that lifted them out of the realm of mere business and turned them into vibrant social gatherings as well. . . . Gone are the days when the place of women was in the kitchen and looking after the children. Today they are marching side by side with men in the road to freedom."[27] The movement focused primarily on politically conscious women who faced the hardship of township life, usually married with children, trying to hold their fragile households together. A quote from one of the FSAW meetings reported: "As wives and mothers it falls upon us to make small wages stretch a long way. It is we who feel the cries of our children when they are hungry and sick. It is our lot to keep and care for homes that are too small, broken and dirty."[28]

Freedom songs dominated the Defiance Campaign, including "Mandela Mandela," that carried the lines:

> Mandela says fight for freedom
> Mandela says freedom now
> All we say is away with slavery
> In our land of Africa[29]

Also heard at rallies during the campaign was Mini's song "*Somlandela*" (We Shall Follow Him). Both songs demonstrated the growing prominence of Mandela as a leader in the struggle against apartheid, while another song by Mini that was popular among Defiance Campaign protesters, *Izakunyathel' iAfrika*, warned apartheid leaders "Africa will trample you underfoot."[30] Reviving the language of war from their ancestors, resistance leaders and their musical accompaniment recognized the power of cultural identity in the message of defiance, and the uniting effect it had on those who increasingly found a collective response related to being "African" or "black."

At the same time that political activism intensified in Port Elizabeth, the *kwela* craze hit New Brighton and spread to townships throughout the Eastern Cape, launching the careers of numerous musicians and acting as a vanguard for a new generation of jazz performers. The 1950s also saw a rise of mass consumerism in the music industry among the black population. Commercial media was increasingly accessible as were portable record players and transistor radios.[31] With its lively combination of pennywhistle and guitar, *kwela* had primarily been an element of street culture until it attracted the attention of record companies. This new form of music expressed the experience of township populations, the word "*kwela*" meaning "get up," usually as a warning to township residents of approaching police. It also reflected the deep roots of those communities with rural traditions mingling with urban influences and expressing a culture denied by apartheid authorities.

To apartheid ministers such as Hendrik Verwoerd, the only reason black people were allowed to live in cities was so they could work for white people, and his legislative efforts reflected that attitude, attempting to divide and destroy urban black communities. *Kwela* acted as a musical means for township dwellers to thumb their noses at efforts to divide them and demean their culture, combining an eclectic mixture of American-based swing, *marabi*, and the rural flute music of young African boys herding cattle and sheep. Because the pennywhistle was a cheap instrument and played by young boys on street corners, *kwela* was initially disparaged by middle-class black people, even as it grew to be a standard feature of music in stokvels and shebeens, expanding on *marabi* and *tsaba-tsaba*. The new form of music also inspired a new type of dance—*pata pata* (touch touch)—later popularized by Miriam Makeba's song by the same name. *Kwela* further reflected the precarious life of black people in townships such as New Brighton, with residents keeping a constant eye out for police and government authorities. In 1956, the song "Tom Hark" was released with an introduction telling the story of a police van drawing near to a group of gamblers on a street corner who quickly pack up their dice and pull out pennywhistles while one shouts in Afrikaans, "*Daar kom die kwela-kwela*" (Here comes the police van), illustrating the double meaning of *kwela* as "Get up, Africa!"[32] *Kwela* also challenged apartheid by crossing the color bar and attracting white listeners, and pennywhistle bands represented a wave of African performers that gained popularity among white populations. These bands further expressed an urban identity that created common cause between the black middle class and the poor and working class. *Kwela* music has been described by Lara Allen as an "African answer to the blues" and its connection to activism described by David Coplan as "musical politics in its most profound counter-hegemonic sense [where] . . . musical assertions of creative humanity were used to advance political consciousness."[33]

While acting as a general conduit for cultural and urban freedom, *kwela* performers also supported the Defiance Campaign and other resistance movements in the 1950s, playing at fundraisers for activists and eventually making African jazz music as a whole another target for government authorities. The National Party platform included cracking down on street performers and using pass laws, liquor regulations, and separate amenities regulations to severely restrict the influence, freedom, and creativity of *kwela* music, and by the 1960s black bands were no longer allowed to hold public performances for black audiences. In the same way that forced removals of the 1920s and 1930s had crushed *marabi* music, increased restrictive legislation and limited audiences hit *kwela*, especially as regards its interracial appeal. The apartheid government's refusal to recognize musical performance as proper employment imposed additional burdens on musical expression and passes were not issued to musicians as self-employed people. Arrests for invalid passes could result in 14-day imprisonment with those arrested waiting for trial, and conviction could mean three to six months in jail. Pass offenders were also often sold as cheap farm labor. Night passes—crucial to most performances—were particularly difficult to obtain and travelling bands were subject to constant harassment by police. If record companies had agreed to register musicians as employees, musicians would not have had to suffer these hardships, but companies refused because a "Bantu Levy" of about £2 per month had to be paid for each employee.[34]

The Separate Amenities Act of 1953 created an even heavier obstacle to black musicians trying to earn a living. Different "races" could not be onstage at the same time and the most desirable performance spots were off-limits to non-white entertainers. Black musicians were also banned from venues that served alcohol. The limited choice now given to *kwela* performers was either survive a wandering existence on the streets or be sucked into the narrow confines of the recording studios. It was yet another strategy of apartheid for shutting down black expression. These circumstances tended to take away any leverage black musicians might have with recording companies who could exploit them at will without fear of legal challenges. If members of a band were savvy enough to challenge a contract they were branded as troublemakers and replaced by one of the many other pennywhistle groups trying to make it. Low levels of education and difficulties many musicians had with English also made exploitation easier for the companies and the inequalities of recording sessions affected the quality of the final product. White musicians could pay for each session and use several takes to perfect their sound. Black musicians had to pay a flat fee and were forced to record as many songs as quickly as possible.[35]

Despite these obstacles, *kwela* and African jazz music was kept alive in the Eastern Cape in cities such as Queenstown and Port Elizabeth, especially during the Defiance Campaign and before the crackdown by white authorities on the lives and movement of black populations in urban areas. The *kwela* craze launched the careers of numerous performers and introduced to Port Elizabeth a new generation of jazz musicians. *Kwela* and jive represented not just a musical expression of identity, but a youthful rebellion against the older generation, especially the middle-class values seen as instilled by white oppression. The popularity of these new styles of music among black people also contributed to the rise in mass consumerism in the music industry and the extension of black urban culture through commercial media. With greater access to music through record players and radios, the preferences in township residents leaned toward homespun *kwela* and jive.[36]

As the apartheid system laid an increasingly heavy hand on the culture and history of Africans, *iimbongi* continued to add their voices to the new wave of resistance in the Eastern Cape. Rising in significance as a successor to Mqhayi in the arena of spoken word and coinciding with the establishment of apartheid, David Yali-Manisi made clear his nationalist sentiments and growing support of the ANC. He and *imbongi* Melikhaya Mbutuma also acted as channels of expression of the standoff between two Transkei chiefs: Kaiser Mathanzima, who cooperated with the apartheid state in the creation of the Bantu Authorities System, and Sabatha Dalindyebo, king of the Thembu who opposed the system and was eventually exiled for his opposition. The Bantu Authorities Act of 1951 marked the establishment of "tribal" homelands, and Mathanzima was appointed "permanent Regional Chief of the Emigrant Thembu districts of St. Mark's and Xalanga" in the Transkei. In 1955, Nelson Mandela (Mathanzima's uncle, although younger) debated with Mathanzima on the legitimacy of the Bantu Authorities System which, according to Mandela, did not act in the interest of the African people who wanted a democratic system, not one based on royalty and manipulated by the government. Mathanzima upheld the policy of separate development, arguing that it was a more peaceful means of liberating his people and that the ANC's way was one that would lead to violence.[37]

Dalindyebo attended Lovedale Institute (and later Healdtown), where he met Yali-Manisi and the two formed a strong and lasting association. While at Lovedale, Mathanzima as a fellow classmate had advised Dalindyebo to continue with his schooling, but Dalindyebo became increasingly politicized—he was expelled from Healdtown for cutting telephone wires and leading a strike—and he came to reject the white version of education. Dalindyebo was initiated in 1948 with the name Jonguhlahoga ("Watch the Country"), and in 1954 he was installed as Paramount Chief of the Thembu, with Yali-Manisi performing along with Mbutuma at the ceremony. From early on, Dalindyebo made clear his resistance to the Bantu Authorities Act, as well as his opposition to Mathanzima's position and alliance with the apartheid government, and he was consequently harassed on a regular basis by government authorities.[38]

Strongly influenced by the poetry and performances of Mqhayi, Yali-Manisi from his childhood to adulthood also paid close attention to the oral history of his region. As he described it to Jeff Opland, he learned his people's story: "its paths and its pains, its way of life when it comes into contact with whites, its way of life before that contact. . . . And in that way I know the history of my nation."[39] Like Dalindyebo, he was expelled from school (Lovedale) apparently for spontaneously extolling the virtues of his people through praise poetry. As Yali-Manisi told Opland, he could not refrain from jumping up and singing eulogies for important African visitors—poems that often held a connection to nature and were performed in a traditional fashion: "This Dr. Shepherd construed as unchristian and unbecoming." Yali-Manisi was once summoned to the Master's office to explain why, when it was his turn to lead prayers, his fellow students did not close their eyes and instead of saying "Amen" would exclaim "Hurray!" The future *imbongi* responded that he did not know why as he would pray like the others, "but there was one thing I could not leave out, and that was to pray for the liberation and salvation of my people."[40]

It became increasingly clear to Manisi, as it had to Dalindyebo, that the education he was receiving was not beneficial to the liberation of Africans:

> As a youth I had the feeling that we as a people had lost all of our rights. So, as I was at school at Lovedale, I learnt that though we were at a missionary institution we were not treated well as human beings. From there I learnt from historical books, and I got the knowledge that all we had was grabbed by the white man. So that remained in my mind till I grew up to be a young man who could make his own decisions.[41]

Manisi had been asked by Mathanzima to work as his *imbongi* in 1949, but the poet eventually broke from the Transkeian chief in 1955, having grown increasingly supportive of the ANC. In 1953, when Manisi performed as an *imbongi* at Qamata, Mathanzima, also present, read a piece in the *Daily Dispatch* about the power granted to the chiefs, showing his approval and asking for responses. According to Manisi, "I questioned him: if at all we are freed by the Nationalist government, why do they choose to give freedom to the chiefs instead of to the people who are fighting for their freedom—the ANC and other organizations? Even in the past, it was not the chiefs who fought for this country: it was the people who are the warriors." Apparently, Mathanzima was not pleased with this question.[42]

When Dalindyebo travelled around the Thembu region in the Eastern Cape, Manisi wrote a poem about the visit which was printed in *Umthunywa* in 1952, just after the government began planting spokes in the wheel of Dalindyebo's succession:

> ... Watch the Nation's son,
> Tough tree of Nomathokuzi's home,
> Other nations could never twist it,
> Even the whites would fear him,
> nations feared him till they appealed to the whites,
> that's why they reported him to Umtata magistrates ...
> A letter came from the whites at twilight
> Denying the prince his rights ...[43]

In 1952 and 1954, Manisi published two volumes of *izibongo* that praised the Xhosa chiefs and narrated stories of the frontier wars. In the preface to the second volume, Dorrington Nobaza (Manisi's great-uncle) wrote, "In this booklet the son of Yali-Manisi urges us to be sensitive to our past, to return to our language and learn to build ourselves up through our traditions and customs."[44]

Just before publication of the second volume, Manisi went to Johannesburg to attend an ANC meeting as a representative of Queenstown. Mandela was also there, even though he was under banning orders, and Manisi was so struck by the ANC Youth leader that he wrote a praise poem to Mandela immediately after:

> You've bridged nations great and small,
> Forging African unity:
> All its nations are gripped in one birth pang ...
> You set Africa blazing;
> The rising sun scorched arrant rogues
> Flushed the thugs with roasted pates ...
> Speak, Mandela's son! Speak, my chief!
> Speak out fearlessly: there're remnants in Africa!
> Hold no fear of sunburnt bellies,
> Shoulder-shruggers and white flag wavers ...
> Speak out fearlessly, Thembu, there are still men!
> Speak out fearlessly, they're still men in Africa!
> Those bones can stir,
> Link up with each other ...
> May the Lord bless you,
> Grant you success

> In confronting the lackeys of evil.
> Let it be so, my chief.[45]

In the poem, Manisi called Mandela *Zweliyashukuma* ("the country's quaking"), putting his description in the context of disruption on the part of small nations fighting for independence from larger nations. Mandela was referred to by Manisi as a liberator in the form of an *ichanti*—according to Opland, a "mythical, secretive, colorful, hypnotic, shape-changing river-snake"—and with striking foresight he depicted the leader as one working not just for his people but for all of Africa, leaving behind his life in Transkei to challenge white "tramps." Manisi ended by encouraging Mandela, with the support of his ancestors, to continue to fight the white regime and awaken the apathy of black people.[46] Manisi, now an active member of the ANC, was well aware that the inclusion of the Mandela praise poem in the second volume of his work would doom its publication and its distribution in the schools, and so he paid for its printing himself. Even so, the Queenstown printer did not distribute the collection, regarding Manisi's reputation for outspokenness as now too extensive to take the risk.[47]

In 1955, the year that Yali-Manisi broke completely from Mathanzima, delegates of the Congress Alliance of organizations opposed to apartheid met in Kliptown outside of Johannesburg to adopt the Freedom Charter, calling for a democratic South Africa with equality for all. *Umteteli wa Bantu* published a poem by Manisi expressing his evolved loyalties and directed at Mathanzima which made Manisi's disapproval clear: "I'm not praising you, son of Mhlobo, I'm inciting you." There was, as stated, no praise of Mathanzima in the verses; only direct criticism:

> great one who struts preening on his own
> overseer whose stench repelled nations . . .
> Discussion is foreign to Mhlobo's son,
> presuming to judge nobles he subverts justice.
> Oh dear; this chief of the Hala!
> Herdsman of stricken Cattle.[48]

The poem affirmed Manisi's support of Sabatha Dalindyebo and of the ANC, and his disapproval of Mathanzima merely increased over time. Manisi was making the point that Mathanzima should redirect his energies towards justice for his people. Mathanzima, however, became increasingly firmly entrenched in the Bantustan system created as part of apartheid's program of separate development. When Manisi stepped down as *imbongi* for Mathanzima, Nelson Mabunu replaced him. Mabunu was a sergeant in the Security Police and also became Mathanzima's bodyguard. According to

Opland, he adopted more the role of entertainer than praise singer, producing *izibongo* that increasingly parroted Mathanzima's speeches.⁴⁹

Mbutuma also made clear his allegiance to Dalindyebo in opposition to Mathanzima from the 1950s through the 1970s, as well as his resistance to the Bantustan system as whole. When the Minister of Bantu Administration Michel Daniel de Wet Nel visited Transkei in 1959, Mbutuma recited a poem that pulled no punches, accusing the Minister of carrying the curse of drought to a rain-soaked region:

> *Ndive ngelizwi ndathi ixelegu alifunwa.*
> *Aa! Zanelanga!*
>
> I heard a protesting voice, and I concluded a despot is not wanted amongst the people.
> Hail! Bringer of barrenness!⁵⁰

The late 1950s and early 1960s represented a culmination of the more radical direction of opposition to apartheid prompted by the ANC Youth League and the Pan Africanist Congress. This development led, in turn, to government crackdowns on opposition and fierce reprisals against those targeted as leaders in the resistance movements. The arrest of 156 Congress leaders in 1956 on suspicion of communist activity and the subsequent Treason Trial led to an eventual acquittal in 1961 of most of the accused and admission by the court that neither the ANC nor the Freedom Charter could be proved to be communist. Vuyisile Mini was among those arrested, and he used his strong voice and protest compositions to sing and raise the spirits of those imprisoned alongside him. Fellow activist and poet Jeremy Cronin observed of Mini, "Probably because of his bass voice, he was one of the best organizers in the liberation movement."⁵¹

Despite the eventual exoneration of the majority of those accused, the Treason Trial used up much of the resources of the ANC and led to the adoption of new tactics and opposition movements. Robert Sobukwe formed the Pan Africanist Party as an expression of township frustration with influx control and a general sense that an alliance with white opposition was not useful to their cause since white people benefitted from the apartheid system. Protest was also organized by the FSAW in response to new legislation requiring the carrying of passes by women, and when the government held firm, requiring that women be subject to the same pass legislation as men in 1961, opposition began to focus on police raids against shebeens which threatened the independence of township women involved in brewing beer. Resistance to apartheid reached a climax with the Sharpeville Massacre of March 1960, when a peaceful march organized by the PAC to protest the carrying of passes caused police to panic and fire into the crowd, resulting in the deaths of 69 people, many of whom were shot in the back. The event and its aftermath, including international condemnation, fueled more government suppression, including banning the ANC and PAC and launching an intense suppression on all forms of opposition. Recognizing the limits of protest strategies so far, Mandela went underground, and he and other ANC leaders formed Mkhonto We Sizwe (MK—Spear of the Nation), the military wing of the ANC, arguing that the violence of the apartheid government was now too severe to be met with only nonviolent resistance.[52] MK adopted the techniques of sabotage and sporadic acts of violence, while Mandela traveled around South Africa to continue the resistance movement, and overseas to gain support from sympathetic countries.

The PAC also launched an underground military campaign. Sobukwe and fellow PAC leader Potlako Leballo were imprisoned, and the armed wing adopted the name Poqo (isiXhosa for "standing alone" or "pure") which later became the Azanian People's Liberation Army (APLA). The songs of Poqo reflected its new program of strategic violence:

> *We bulala*
> *Bulal' icolonialism*
> *Bulal' a mabhulu kwenzenjani*
> *Yiyole*
> *Yiyole, Yiyole le APLA*
> *Yiyole le AOLA kwenzenjani*
>
> We're out to kill colonialism
> We're out to kill the Boers
> APLA is here
> To help us achieve our goals[53]

As the ANC songs hailed Mandela as their leader, calling on him as they called on their ancestors to lead them to freedom, so too did the PAC songs call on Sobukwe:

> *Sizohamba No Sobukwe*
> *Hamba no Sobukwe*
> *We Sobukwe sikhokhele*
> *Sizongen' eAzania*
> *Sizongen' eAzania*
> *Sizongena neBasooka*
>
> We'll follow Sobukwe
> We'll follow Sobukwe

> Sobukwe lead us
> We are entering Azania
> We are entering Azania
> We are entering with bazookas into Azania[54]

Azania was the name given to what would be the reclaimed land for Africans, and the songs of Poqo/APLA often echoed the liberation language of previous Eastern Cape millennial movements, with homage paid to those killed in the armed struggle:

> *Sibane sethu maqhawe AseAzania*
> *Ukufa kwenu akusoze kulityalwe*
> *Ukufa kwenu kuya kukhanyi s'indlela yabo*
> *Bonke abaphantsi kwengcinezelo*
>
> Your light you braves of Azania
> Your deaths will never be forgotten
> Your death will be a guiding light for the course
> Of all those under oppression[55]

As part of the rise in government pressure on resistance of the early 1960s, apartheid authorities increasingly targeted Mandela and his ANC cohorts, which eventually led to their capture and arrest and the Rivonia Trial in 1964 that resulted in life sentences for Mandela and Sisulu, among others. A major clampdown on resistance followed, with many leaders ending up either in prison or in exile in the early 1960s. The Eastern Cape, with its strong reputation for resistance against white oppression, particularly experienced the effects of government crackdowns. In 1963, the state launched a major attack on mass movements in that region, arresting over 1,000 people in the Port Elizabeth area and forcing many of them to serve long sentences on charges of continuing the work of the ANC after it had been banned. Government authorities also began imposing restrictions on Fort Hare University as part of a comprehensive design to silence resistance in the higher education system, and student protest floundered for a while at the university.

Mini was one of those arrested in the government crackdown, along with two other SACTU activists, Wilson Khayinga and Zinakile Mkaba. They were charged with seventeen counts of sabotage and other political crimes, including involvement in the murder of alleged police informer Sipho Mange, and all three were sentenced to death by hanging. In letters smuggled out of the prison, Mini wrote of his final days before execution: "Captain Geldenhuys and two other policemen came to see me. . . . They said there is still a chance for me to be saved. . . . I must just tell them where the detonators and revolvers were, and they would help me. I refused." The police also asked Mini to give evidence against another activist, Wilton Mkwayi, and Mini again refused. Finally, they asked Mini if we would give the *Amandla* salute when he walked to the gallows, and Mini replied that he would. Mkaba and Khayinga also refused to give information to the authorities.[56]

While in prison in Pretoria awaiting his execution, Mini and his condemned comrades sang numerous songs, including *Thath' umthwalo bhuti sigoduke balindile oomama noobab' ekhaya* ("Take up your things, brother, and let's go, they are waiting, our mother and fathers, at home"). Ben Turok, who at the time was Secretary of the South African Congress of Democrats and also imprisoned in Pretoria, first became aware of Mini's presence there when he recognized Mini's laugh: "I marveled at his daring. No one laughed out loud in central prison. It was absolutely forbidden . . . and his comrades joined him. . . . And as the three of them settled into their new surroundings, there issued out of the window of the 'last week cell' beautiful melodies of traditional African music rendered in the most perfect unison of long practiced harmony." Turok observed that they enjoyed singing most in the early evenings, when prison staff was at a minimum and the prisoners were resting: "Mini and his comrades sensed the appreciation of their audience and gave forth in the subtlest cadences, telling in song the heroic stories of Xhosa history."[57]

Turok goes on to describe the evening before the three comrades' execution as "devastatingly sad":

The heroic occupants of the death cells communicated to the prison in gentle melancholy song that their end was near. . . . It was late at night when the singing ceased, and the prison fell into uneasy silence. I was already awake when the singing began again in the early morning. Once again the excruciatingly beautiful music floated through the barred window, echoing around the brick exercise yard, losing itself in the vast prison yards.

And then, unexpectedly, the voice of Vuyisile Mini came roaring down the hushed passages. Evidently standing on a stool, with his face reaching up to a barred vent in his cell, his unmistakable bass voice was enunciating his final message in Xhosa to the world he was leaving. In a voice charged with emotion but stubbornly defiant he spoke of the struggle waged by the African National Congress and of his absolute conviction of the victory to come. And then it was Khayinga's turn, followed by Mkaba, as they too defied all prison rules to shout out their valedictions. Soon after, I heard the door of their cells being opened. Murmuring voices reached my straining ears, and then the three martyrs broke into a final poignant melody which seemed to fill the whole prison with sound and then gradually faded away into the distant depths of the condemned section.[58]

According to Turok, as they were led to the gallows, Mini, Mkaba, and Khayinga sang *nansi 'ndondemnyama we Verwoerd.*[59] After their execution, the three activists were buried in a pauper's grave in Pretoria. In 1998 their remains were exhumed and a hero's funeral was held for Mini in Emlotheni in New Brighton with a special dedication and memorial. A statue of Mini was also erected in Port Elizabeth and the city's Market Square was officially renamed Vuyisile Mini Square in 2010.

As opposition and unrest gained momentum in the Eastern Cape townships in the late 1950s, resistance also was on the rise in rural areas; for example, in Transkei. These developments highlighted the increasingly precarious environment that *iimbongi* such as Yali-Manisi operated in as they tried to maintain their role of political and social critics while feeling the effects of government restriction and manipulation of rural tradition to suit the apartheid agenda. Playing on white fears associated with the rise of the Cold War, the South African government employed the strategy of labelling all opposition as communist-related and all leaders of resistance as communists. In September 1957 Mbeki wrote a story for *New Age* titled "There Is Unrest in the Transkei, but It Is Not Caused by Moscow-Trained Saboteurs." The article addressed the rumors spreading throughout the white population in the Transkei that there were unidentified submarines off the Pondoland coast with strange lights at night. Mbeki acknowledged that there was discontent in the homeland, "but it is born of the intolerable economic conditions which are turning the whole area into one vast refugee paupers' camp." The article went on to relate the severe struggles Africans dealt with over land, cattle, fences, and increased restrictions on their way of life. Farmworkers hired lawyers when they had the means to fight against evictions, but also, in frustration, they tore down fences and attacked unpopular headmen. "If the peasants' peaceful innocence in Verwoerd's longest make-believe colony is disturbed, it is the Nats [National Party] and their apartheid laws who are the saboteurs."[60] Another story on Transkei by Mbeki published in 1959, "The People Are Dying—Land, Stock Taken from Transkei Peasants" echoed Yali-Manisi's disillusionment with traditional leaders such as Mathanzima. Mbeki described the extensive powers awarded by the Bantu Authorities Act on "a ruling aristocracy of corrupt chiefs," and sympathized with a rural population resentful of the new taxes, such as the ten-shilling General Levy, which they called *Impundulu*—a legendary Xhosa bloodsucking bird. Mbeki reported that public meetings in this region had been banned unless led by one of a "large army of Bantu Authorities officials" with praises sung by a "soulless stooge" at the end of these gatherings.[61] In Mbeki's opinion, the situation in Transkei as a result of the Bantu Authorities Act was merely the latest in a long line of schemes "to solve the desperate needs of a land-hungry people without giving them land." Mbeki warned that the last word lay with his people, "and they have not spoken yet,"[62] and he organized cells that would link urban and rural resistance. According to one of his workers, Andrew Masondo, "We, the Eastern Cape, developed a very good way of organizing the rural areas," moving back and forth between the townships and farms to connect participants in the opposition movement.[63]

One of the cells organized by Mbeki operated out of Fort Hare University, and it did not take long for the government to target Fort Hare for its role in the resistance to Bantustan policy. In 1959, apartheid began inserting itself into South Africa's university system with the Extension of University Education Act and the Fort Hare Transfer Act. The legislation limited the admission of black students to specified universities and the government took control of Fort Hare, ending the admission of non-Xhosa students to the institution. Apartheid authorities viewed Fort Hare students as a particular threat to their separate development plans; the Minister for Bantu Education Daniel de Wet Nel regarded the students as indoctrinated and "being turned into agitators."[64] According to de Wet Nel, the government needed to keep Fort Hare under control because the university refused to adopt apartheid and directly opposed it, eradicating explicitly the methods the South African government had formed to apply its policies.[65] In the minds of apartheid officials, the role of non-white universities should be to foster the growth of Bantustans, and to act as agents in furthering the plan of separate development. The threat of this new legislation united students and staff at Fort Hare in protest, a development which the government responded to by inserting undercover police at the university who offered up to £10 to any students that agreed to provide information on staff or student leaders involved in resistance to the Separate Education Bill.[66] In 1958, student activist Ambrose Makiwane led a protest march into Lovedale in response to the proposed education bills, the Bantustan system, and the Treason Trial taking place at that time.[67] According to Makiwane, the education legislation was unacceptable, "because it makes for better and more rapid development towards the degradation, mental regimentation, and slavery, and aims at making the student mind mere pulp that can be manipulated to suit the whims and fancies of a fatal ideology."[68] By 1959, however, it was clear that these protests would not stop the new legislation as the government took control of Fort Hare in following year. Students responded by forming an underground resistance. When the new government-appointed rector Johannes Jurgens Ross took over along with the new registrar, they were met with banners that read, "We don't want fascists here," "Leave Fort Hare alone—away with indoctrination," and graffiti demanding, "Ross, Get Out!"[69] The car of the head of the University of South Africa (UNISA) was vandalized, students threw eggs and tomatoes at the registrar, and the South African flag at Fort Hare was secretly replaced with the flag of a skull and crossbones (the flagpole was also oiled to prevent anyone climbing up).[70] But as students kept up resistance, the government steadily replaced pre-legislation faculty with Afrikaner professors. Black faculty representation fell from 35% to 19% and police presence and government security grew on campus.[71] As government control increased, more students found themselves expelled or refused admission, even as they continued to organize and protest. Nontombi Dwane, a student at Fort Hare at this time, described the turmoil: "You got to Fort Hare . . . and you find a boiling pot, and then you are thrown in the middle of it."[72]

Most organized resistance at Fort Hare went underground in 1960 when the apartheid government banned the ANC and PAC following Sharpeville. Students maintained contact with national resistance movements and many were highly active in the M-Plan. After the arrest of Mandela, Sisulu and others and the Rivonia trial in 1963–64, however, activism at Fort Hare began to decline as many of the national resistance leaders were either imprisoned or went into exile. Under instructions from the ANC, students started leaving Fort Hare in 1963, and political activity at the university stalled from 1963 to 1968. Makiwane left Fort Hare in 1960 during the state of emergency following the Sharpeville Massacre, but found himself first expelled by the government from Port Elizabeth and then from East London. Bantustan authorities were also now working more closely with the apartheid government, as Makiwane discovered: "In the meantime Mathanzima was attempting to get the government to keep me in my father's farm . . . he tried to use Chief Sabata [Dalindyebo] who was then the Paramount Chief of Thembuland. And Chief Sabata refused."[73]

On the eve of the opening of the Transkeian Territorial Authority in 1962, the Security Branch launched a raid in Mthatha based on the suspicion of ANC and PAC activity. Resistance in the Eastern Cape to the Bantustan system was particularly strong in Pondoland and among the Thembu, and the so-called "independence" promised to Transkeians was met with a great deal of distrust. Critics pointed out that chieftainship had been increasingly connected to unpopular measures, with the Transkei as a prime example. An article in the anti-apartheid publication *Fighting Talk* argued: "Self-rule for the Transkei means rule by the chiefs. It is important to say this because self-government should mean democratic government by the mass of the people."[74] Dalindyebo argued that his Thembu people would not approve the new constitution because they had not been present when it was drafted. Many in the Transkei reportedly feared a loss of personal freedom justified by a so-called battle against communism. In April 1962, Johannes Gumbi, a reporter for *Bantu World,* reported on the effects of a state of emergency in Pondoland and a partial one throughout Transkei: "Many ordinary people of the Transkei reject the self-government that is being offered to them. I heard this over and over again while I was in Umtata." Mathanzima, as head of the Territorial Authorities and future Prime Minister of a self-governing Transkei, encouraged chiefs to fight against the "evil communist element" in Pondoland in his closing address to the Territorial Authorities. He added that "unlawful meetings" were happening in "obscure places under cover of darkness" with the aim of breaking the law and to destroy African nationalism. Mathanzima was ironically using the language of African nationalists that had served leaders in opposition to white rule of the past to promote the apartheid system of separate development. Many, however, were not fooled, and Gumbi noted that greater support for Dalindyebo than for Mathanzima and the other chiefs was demonstrated at this meeting.[75]

The pressures and influences of apartheid legislation, anti-apartheid resistance, and resulting turmoil and crackdowns undoubtedly made themselves felt in the music and performance world of the Eastern Cape. Music continued to be a prominent feature in rallies and marches protesting the raft of policies and acts that served to entrench the apartheid system and strangle opposition, and the South African government was fairly awake to the subversive and uniting potential of black songs and performances. The 1950s had also marked the formation of the Union of Southern African Artists and the increased popularity of black variety performances with white audiences. The original motive for the formation of the Union of Southern African Artists was protection of black performers from exploitation, with activities including lectures, members' events, and free legal advice. The Union also began to organize township jazz concerts that travelled around the country giving performances at weddings and dances, often combining different groups for larger performances. A certain amount of employment was therefore provided for artists, although the focus tended to be on the white market. There was still, during this time, however, a musical culture among the black population that was independent and closely connected socially and politically to local communities. According to cultural activist Robert Mshengu Kavanagh, "music *functioned* in the life of the community and made reference to and judgments about situations such as bus boycotts, riots, rail disasters and political trials, and such music was played at celebrations, political rallies and funerals." Singing groups, Kavanagh argues, were always spontaneously forming.[76] The problem with the promotion of township jazz and large-scale musicals more prominent in large cities such as Johannesburg and Cape Town was that they tended to cater to white audiences and drained black urban areas of talent and creativity based on community. Musicals and performances directed and produced by white liberals often underestimated their black cast's capabilities, playing down, for example, the violent and repressive role of local police in the townships, and upholding the view of Africans as backward before their exposure to white culture. This was not so much the case in Eastern Cape towns such as Port Elizabeth where popular music continued to thrive and musicians more often remained part of the local community. Black performers and artists, thus, faced the challenge of being caught between belonging to an independent creative culture that expressed the social and political conditions shaping their daily lives and being enticed by white-controlled show business that portrayed them as "undeveloped" and "less civilized," simplified their struggles, and often placed the burden of responsibility for their suffering on their own people rather than addressing the system that made it so. While Eastern Cape performers and artists were often more able to maintain independent expression than those artists lured to the big cities such as Johannesburg by the white-controlled entertainment businesses, the price of this artistic independence for performers remaining in places such as Port Elizabeth and Queenstown meant less financial success and less recognition. It was a tough decision for those black musicians and actors aiming for national and international attention.

With increased enthusiasm for black urban theater, therefore, came the challenge of authentic depiction of black culture within an art form that was still largely controlled by white producers and directors and performed for white audiences. One example is the successful musical *King Kong* first performed in 1959, which told the story of the rise and fall of the boxer Ezekiel Dhlamini within the context of Sophiatown—a black township on the outskirts of Johannesburg, often described as the Harlem of South Africa. The white director of *King Kong* saw Western theater as "a civilizing force" on the African and the story told in the musical tended to romanticize the police as protectors of black communities, while demonizing the gangster culture.[77] White audiences could congratulate themselves on attending a multicultural production calling for harmony without facing the wider implications of situations such as the destruction of Sophiatown by apartheid authorities and the relocation of the township population to pave the way for a white suburb.

The one exception within the play to this tendency to cater to white sensibilities, and one that represented a connection to the Eastern Cape, was the involvement of the musician and journalist Todd Matshikiza who wrote two sets of lyrics for *King Kong*: *Ityala lala Madoda* and *Hambani Madoda*. Anthony Sampson, the editor of *Drum* magazine, observed that Matshikiza "felt and showed no strain between his Xhosa tribal background and his European way of life."[78] Matshikiza wrote music as well as lyrics for *King Kong* which combined urban and international influences with Xhosa rhythms and melodies. His lyrics connected local responsibility for black hardship with the greater hardships imposed by an oppressive system. While Western interpretation of circumstance tended to focus on the individual, the African point of view as articulated by Matshikiza was communal and invoked traditional and rural roots of black life, as well as the urban challenges his people faced. *Ityala lala Madoda* references three standard characters in Xhosa folk literature: *UAndazi* ("Mr. I-don't-know"), *uAsindim* ("Mr. It's-not-me"), and *Ualaziwe-mntu* ("Mr. Nobody-knows"). While Matshikiza searched in his musical creation for a broader explanation for the struggles of people in the townships, he also implied that people in Sophiatown suffer because they do not take action.

Hambani Madoda is a song of people standing in a bus queue in the early morning after King Kong was defeated the previous night, and the song expresses the collective experience of the black urban community. As Kavanagh observes, "Here the romanticism and commercialism of the 'musical' and its 'theatrical' plot are swept away by the work of one man in the creative team of *King Kong* who fully understood because he had experienced and above all accepted the culture of the people of Sophiatown and was equipped to express it."[79] The song expresses both the suffering and the determination to fight for freedom within the collective psyche of black people in South Africa, and like *Ityala lala Madoda*, it was sung in a combination of isiXhosa and Zulu, directly addressing black members of the audience, and bypassing the white listeners. In the song women and men are ordered to "keep moving" as they stand in the cold and the rain, packed on the buses, poor and hungry, fearful of being attacked by ruffians and gang members:

> *Hambani madoda*
> *Isikhathi asikho*
>
> keep moving, men
> it's getting late.[80]

According to Sampson, Matshikiza's writing contained a constant musical quality infused with jazz: "Our readers loved 'Matshikese,' as we called it, which was the way they talked and thought, beating in time with the jazz within them." When playing after hours in shebeens where he "thumped jazz from the piano," Matshikiza referred to his music as "drowning the sorrows of nine million black voices."[81]

By 1958, the Union monopolized the market in promotion of entertainment, organizing township jazz concerts in white areas. Increased government restrictions in 1960–61, however, caused the Union to lose its influence as audiences became more segregated. In the 1960s, black and white populations could not mix outside of working hours, black people could not attend public performances in white areas, and black artists could not perform in white areas. In 1963 the Publications and Entertainment Act created a new Publications Control Board that operated with wide-ranging powers to restrict public entertainment. Along with the restrictions placed on black musicians involving limited spaces for performances, regulations and curfews, another form of censorship came through the government-owned and -operated South African Broadcasting Company (SABC) which limited official accessibility to music to thirteen ethnic styles as represented in the stations they were attached to. One of the results of these narrowly defined styles was the reinforcement of a crude rural stereotype of Africans which underlined the perception of their only being a part of city life for reasons of employment. Record companies in turn would rarely agree to record this limited style of music. Black jazz musicians were essentially banned from standard performances, while their music was banned from the airwaves.[82] These circumstances did not prevent Eastern Cape musicians from performing locally but they did limit the scope of this region's music and artists' ability to make a living from it. Curfews and crackdowns also made their lives precarious as they tread a thin line between maintaining their and their fans' enthusiasm and coming up against the authorities who felt threatened by it. Eastern Cape musicians persisted, however, often balancing their performances with day-jobs to make a viable living.

As black opposition became suppressed during the early 1960s, the continuing struggle against apartheid fell back on white liberals and those able to survive the system—a situation increasingly recognized by the younger black generation as inadequate and one which eventually resulted in the rise of the Black Consciousness movement in the late 1960s. In that muted phase of anti-apartheid resistance of the first half of the 1960s, jazz music and the fast-paced precarious life connected to it was often all that black urban communities were able to turn to for solace beyond the burden of simple survival. It was during this time that Port Elizabeth gained a reputation as one of South Africa's "magnetic jazz poles" (Johannesburg and Cape Town being the other two) and maintained this status through the 1990s. The harmony of Eastern Cape jazz had its roots, as noted in earlier chapters, in its musical history and was preserved in different forms such as *mbanqanga* and modern South African jazz. The historical harmonic cycle of early Eastern Cape music could also be distinguished in styles such as *marabi*, *kwela*, and *smanje-manje*, but the music was modern in its representation of the fast pace of life in the townships. Writer Lewis Nkosi described the scene: "From a situation in which violence is endemic . . . has come an ebullient sound more intuitive than any outside of the United States of what jazz is supposed to celebrate—the moment of love, lust, bravery, increased fruition, and all those vivid dancing good times of the body when the now may be all there is."[83] The mixed message of joy and suffering in township life was expressed in unique songs such as *Intlupheko* ("Distress" or "Suffering") by the Soul Jazzmen, and Matshikiza's *Makhaliphile* ("The Brave"), which was dedicated to anti-apartheid activist Trevor Huddleston.

Influenced by Eastern Cape bands that included the King Cole Basses, the Broadway Brothers, and the Barnacle Bills, Count Attwell from Korsten location in Port Elizabeth formed the African Rhythm Crotchets consisting of seven former students from Lovedale, Healdtown, and Tiger Kloof college. Each member had to acquire their own instrument and the band performed in Cape Town, East London, and at all of Fort Hare's graduation balls.[84] "Big T" Ntsele from New Brighton started out playing the bass with the King Cole Basses, Dalton's Keynote Combo, and the African Rhythm Crotchets. He later joined the Question Marks, before forming the Soul Jazzmen with Whitey Kulman. In 1964, Lami Zokufa, originally from Cape Town, initiated "How to read music" workshops in Port Elizabeth and scheduled regular Sunday jam sessions.[85]

Two musicians whose names became synonymous with jazz in the Eastern Cape from the 1960s to the present were Dudley Tito and Patrick Pasha. Profoundly influenced by the Junior Jazzmen, the South African film *The Magic Garden*, and imported bebop records, Tito honed his skills through nightly jamming sessions and busking with Whitey Kulman, eventually representing the Eastern Cape as a member of the Jazz Giants at the Cold Castle National Jazz Festival in Johannesburg in 1962. During the 1960s, he played saxophone with the "G Note Combo," the "Playmates," and the "Port Elizabeth Jazz Pioneers," performing music that represented a mixture of swing, *mbaqanga*, and ballroom in standard performances, while leaning heavily on bebop in after-hours jamming sessions. Tito described himself as "born into" *mbaqanga*, and could transform an American jazz song into *mbaqanga* in the middle of the performance in response to the mood of his audience. Tito eventually became a member of the Jazz Soul Men, hoping to achieve a full-time career in music, but apartheid restrictions held him back. South African pass laws limited touring possibilities, although Eastern Cape police could be unpredictable in their enforcement. Tito recalled one night when his group was stopped by police while returning from a performance in Cradock. The band was ordered out of their vehicle and then mockingly ordered to play; the artists gave a private show to the officers and were subsequently allowed to move on.[86]

Pasha was born in Uitenhage and grew up with a strong sense of community which influenced his approach to the development of township jazz in the Eastern Cape. He played trombone with the Rhythm Aces and took on the tenor and alto saxophone, playing with groups such as the Broadway Yanks in Walmer Location. Like Tito, Pasha was inspired by bebop, and also, like Tito, he represented Port Elizabeth at the 1962 Cold Castle Festival, playing with the Friendly City 6. He stayed in Johannesburg for a while and became part of the show *Back in Your Own Backyard* as it went on a national tour, but Pasha grew disillusioned with the pace of life in Johannesburg, and when *Back in*

Your Own Backyard came to Port Elizabeth, he decided to stay, reuniting with his wife Beauty. His experiences as a musician operating within the confines of apartheid in the 1960s led to his involvement in activism in the 1970s and 1980s.[87]

As apartheid authorities tightened their grip on the lives of the black population in South Africa in the 1960s and increased oppressive legislation threatened what small bit of liberty was left for black people, many musicians and artists faced the stark choice of staying in their country with family and friends, ducking and dodging the worst aspects of apartheid and eking out a low-level economic existence, or grabbing the opportunity to pursue greater artistic and political freedom abroad while suffering the mental anguish of a life in exile. A number of jazz musicians from the Eastern Cape that became household names in South Africa as well as internationally made that choice. Performers such as Johnny Mbizo Dyani, Dudu Pukwana, and Chris McGregor left South Africa in the 1960s to pursue careers overseas, whereas others including Pat Matshikiza stayed in South Africa. McGregor had grown up in Transkei, the son of Scottish missionaries, and was drawn to the music of the region, initially forming a vocal group with friends from Mthatha High School, while also influenced by the styles of *kwela* and *mbanqanga*. After winning a scholarship to the University of Cape Town's College of Music, he absorbed the jazz styles coming over from the United States such as that of Duke Ellington and Thelonious Monk, played at various venues and festivals, including a private function to raise funds for Mandela's Treason Trial, and eventually formed the Blue Notes, the famous jazz band that included Pukwana and Dyani. Pukwana was a pianist and alto sax player from Walmer township in Port Elizabeth who had been playing in bands in that city from a young age, including the Four Yanks and his own band the Jazz Giants with Nick Moyake and Tete Mbambisa. Pukwana and the Jazz Giants dazzled audiences at the 1962 Castle Lager Jazz Festival at Moroka-Jabavu Stadium just outside of Johannesburg, and soon after McGregor invited Pukwana to join the Blue Notes.

Dyani is a particularly poignant example of the harsh choice made by musicians in South Africa between remaining or leaving, especially in terms of working to end apartheid (see Chapter 6). He was born in Zeleni location near King William's Town and grew up in Duncan Village outside of East London, raised by his aunt and her husband. The family was musical and a piano was kept in the house which all the children played. Duncan Village was the second-largest township in South Africa after Soweto but families of three famous musicians lived close by each other: Dyani, Tete Mbambisa, and female vocalist Pinise Saul. Johnny often delivered milk to the Mbambisa and Saul families and hung around to pick up on the music and play with the instruments. Mrs. Ida Mbambisa had a butcher shop with a shebeen in the back, and entertainment would be provided for visitors with music performed by Fats and Tete Mbambisa. Fellow sax player Nick Moyake often came from Port Elizabeth to stay at the Mbambisas, and Dyani and Pukwana would sometimes play together as a duo. The trumpet player Mongezi Feza would also come from Queenstown, sometimes staying in Dyani's house. In 1962, when Tete's vocal group the Four Yanks were scheduled to play in Cape Town, one of the singers fell sick and Tete invited Dyani to come take his place. Dyani was much younger than the other band members but he quickly became popular, picking up influences from famous jazz musicians that were on the scene. After he returned to the Eastern Cape, he made the decision to become a bass player, and joined Eric Nomvete's East London band the African Revellers Review which combined dance music and *mbanqanga*. In 1963, Nomvete invited Dyani to play several parts in a local variety show, *Xapa Goes to Town*, about a country boy from Transkei who travels to Johannesburg to learn modern manners in order to impress his female teacher. Just before the play's opening in King William's Town, *Back in Your Own Backyard* came to East London from Johannesburg with a backing band that included some of Dyani's musical heroes, such as Pat Matshikiza and Dyani's friends from the Eastern Cape Pukwana and Nick Moyake. Dyani ended up joining this production along with Pinise Saul, when two performers dropped out, and he traveled with the play to Cape Town. It was about this time that McGregor was putting together the Blue Notes and looking for a bass player, and fellow band members Pukwana and Moyake recommended Dyani. The two had first heard Dyani back in Duncan Village when the young bass player had asked to sit in on an afternoon session. They lent him a bass, and after the first song, as former ANC activist Pallo Jordan writes, "the others on the bandstand realized that they were not dealing with some brash upstart . . . but rather with a bold but gifted bassist." The Blue Notes took on Dyani and the band recorded 15 tracks for SABC and began a nationwide tour in 1964. It was in the same year that the members made the decision to leave South Africa.[88]

Pat Matshikiza began playing piano at age seven, coming from a musical family in Queenstown that included his father Meekly "Fingertips" Matshikiza and his famous uncle Todd. He attended St. Matthew's College in Keiskammahoek in the Eastern Cape where he became a resident organist. He then moved to Johannesburg where he was guided through the musical world by Gideon "Mgibe" Nxumalo, and became a pianist for Union Artists productions at Dorkay House, including *Back in Your Own Backyard*. In 1964 he joined the Early Mabuza Quartet who won first prize along with the Malombo Jazzmen at the 1964 Castle Lager Jazz Festival. The quartet recorded five tracks, including two compositions by Pat: *Maxhegwana* (Little Old Man) and *Inyameko* (Perseverance).[89]

While holding on to their own local influences, Eastern Cape jazz musicians formed a strong musical connection to jazz performers and composers in the United States, such as Charlie Parker, Dizzy Gillespie and Thelonious Monk. They blended these influences with their own style to create a unique sound as part of a modern jazz movement that spread through the major cities of South Africa. Pallo Jordan observed, "From the beginning modern jazz was a minority taste, patronized by black workers and intellectuals in the urban areas, a growing number of 'off-beat' white students and artists, and the occasional music business impresario." It was tough to be a modern jazz musician in South Africa, given all the oppressive circumstances, but pioneers from the Eastern Cape such as Dyani were still ready to try. "Perhaps it was their youth," notes Jordan. "That most did not have the additional responsibility of raising a family enabled them to steer the perilous course between the shoals of racist laws and discriminatory practice."[90]

Restrictions on black performers in South Africa sparked European and U.S. boycotts, with the overall result that black artists were limited to performing for black audiences just at the time that urban black culture was on the rise. This development included the rise of a middle-class black population that executed a certain amount of spending power. Ironically, because the apartheid government had cut ties between black and white populations in urban areas, and because the Union of Southern African Artists had over the years provided skills and experience for black artists, there arose at this time a popular trend of black theater. White producers that had previously marketed black productions to white audiences now had to please black audiences, which resulted in arguably more authentic scripts and performances that resonated more clearly with urban black culture. It was in the 1960s that Welcome Duru and several performers and musicians including Ngxokolo, Fats Bookholane, Mabel Magada, and Norman Tshinga approached the playwright Athol Fugard about starting a theater group in New Brighton. Fugard's roots were in Port Elizabeth; he had attended Port Elizabeth Technical College, later attending the University of Cape Town where he studied philosophy and social anthropology, and he was influenced in his criticism of apartheid early on by his experience working as a clerk in the Native Commissioner's Court: "I knew that the system was evil, but until then I had no idea of just how systematically evil it was."[91]

Duru and his fellow performers were inspired by Fugard's plays, particularly *Blood Knot* and his direction of Samuel Beckett's *Waiting for Godot*, which was why they approached the playwright. Fugard was initially unwilling to take them on, aware of the challenges of a white man working with Africans in a township in the face of apartheid laws, but he eventually agreed, and adapted Niccolo Machiavelli's play *La Mandragola* to a township setting, renaming it *The Cure*. The script, according to Duru, was examined by the South African police force's Special Branch, an action that early on set up a pattern of scrutiny of the players by government authorities and dogged the players' future projects. They called themselves the Serpent Players, named for an old snake pit in the Port Elizabeth museum that was owned by Rhodes University and used as a stage for rehearsals. Subjected to constant surveillance by the police, the actors often rehearsed in secret at Fugard's house in Schoenmakerskop, and Duru observed that the police "seemed to have realized that Athol and his actors were finding ways of telling what was happening in South Africa. They were somehow telling the story of Apartheid on stage and Athol tried to choose scripts that would interest us and exposed the Black African's living conditions."[92] While performing as Azdak in Fugard's adaptation of Brecht's *The Caucasion Chalk Circle*, Duru was accused of being a member of the ANC and imprisoned for 90 days (Fugard had to take over his part). Other Serpent members were also arrested, including Ntshinga, who was sentenced to ten years' hard labor on Robben Island.[93] The government had already cracked down on multi-racial collaboration in the arts, so Fugard's involvement with non-professional actors in Port Elizabeth represented a way around these restrictions, though one that subjected his players to constant harassment and potential arrest.

Another struggle for Fugard and his Serpent Players was similar to that illustrated by the authorship and production of *King Kong*: dealing with the potential distortion of black township life as portrayed through the lens of a white Western-educated author. In his play *No-Good Friday*, which Fugard collaborated on with Lewis Nkosi in Johannesburg, the emphasis on survival of township culture often placed responsibility for dehumanization on the population dealing with that survival rather than the system that caused the moral dilemmas these populations had to face. Black politicians were linked with gangsters and *tsotsis* and connected to black nationalism, and the collective aspects of black communities were frequently subordinate to the individualism of Western perspectives. When Fugard began working with the Serpent Players, he embraced the township view of his performers with their Eastern Cape take on the subject matter at hand, but the group's work was still heavily influenced by the style of European playwrights such as Brecht, both in the plots used and theatrical direction.

When Duru returned to Port Elizabeth after his first stint in prison, he began working with the Xhosa musician and playwright Gibson Kente. Kente's early experience of music included singing during his attendance at the Seventh-Day Adventist institution Bethel College in Transkei. "Every Sunday was like the typical revival meet in the States," recalled Kente in an interview. "We yelled till we had to speak in whispers the following day. Man, we yelled."[94] Kente confronted the dilemma of white authors writing for black audiences by writing his own scripts about township life, achieving a certain amount of economic independence for himself in the 1960s in order to do so. While Fugard's specialty was drama, Kente's was musical theater, and Duru strongly believed in the importance of both men's influences on theater and performance: "Their plays . . . changed the way township people saw theater. Gibson's plays were for many years musicals that thrilled people in various township halls. The people liked their messages because they appealed to their lives."[95] According to Duru, Kente would train his singers to show intensity of feeling in songs by making them stretch open their mouths while they sang: "He always said that when they sang they should be able to put four fingers in their mouths. He showed them the importance of showing the feeling of the song on their faces as they sang with their mouths wide open."[96]

In 1965, Kente wrote the musical *Sikalo* about a man who tries to escape the confines of life in the township, but ultimately winds up in jail. The play was first performed without assistance from Union Artists; then the Union announced that it would present the play in 1966. Under these circumstances, Kente found himself forced to accept a UA company manager and co-director. When actors complained in September of that year about the management calling in the police and when Kente was told he could no longer direct, he threatened to withdraw the rights to the play in retaliation and the whole cast staged a walkout in response to terms offered as part of the national tour. By the end of the year Kente had announced his separation from UA. Kente's troubles with *Sikalo* continued into 1967. In a February article titled "Why No Sikalo?" *The World* reported that the cast failed to turn up at Kwa-Thema Community Center for opening night and that the play was having problems with "a change of management" after the decision to break with UA.[97]

Kente's efforts at economic and artistic independence and his emphasis on the African perspective of township life represented a changing perspective to resistance as expressed in the rise of the Black Consciousness movement. This movement, sparked by the writings and philosophy of Eastern Cape activist Steve Biko at the end of the 1960s, influenced a trend towards rejecting Eurocentric values and led to greater encouragement of "home-grown" and African-American music and performances that encouraged, for example in jazz, a combination of original *mbaqanga* songs and bebop influences from the U.S. The music was interpreted as an expression of the struggle against oppression, but was not so much about a return to pre-colonial culture as a celebration of black identity. Tito felt this influence, growing up in Red Location where daily life was accompanied by traditional Xhosa songs and *marabi* music played on tin guitars and pennywhistles.[98] When Tito joined the

Soul Jazz Men, the music they played described as "Soul" referred not to the style of soul, but to songs that "touched one's soul."[99]

One of the main concerns of the ruling apartheid elite was the potential progress of the rapidly urbanizing African population towards full citizenship. Apartheid strategy in the 1960s and 1970s was therefore marked by legislation and policies that created more roadblocks to equality and African participation in government. As discussed earlier in this chapter, part of that strategy was the creation of homelands ("bantustans") to promote superficial ethnic divisions that the apartheid government would be able to manipulate and control. Each of these homelands would develop towards "independence," creating a façade of legitimacy that echoed the liberation movements in other parts of Africa. The challenge apartheid authorities encountered to this plan was the substantial lack of enthusiasm for it on the part of Africans; the government, therefore, decided to basically force it on them. The ensuing conflict, despite the crackdown on resistance and exile and imprisonment of many ANC leaders in the early 1960s, sowed the seeds for the rise of Black Consciousness in the late 1960s. Black Consciousness came to represent, among other things, the effort to recover the definition of African nationalism from apartheid authorities and oppose the "traditional" African leaders who collaborated with those authorities as part of the homelands strategy. The latter attempted to frame the conflict on the basis of class and schooling, and foreign communist influence: "We will have to take a firm stand against the now too familiar belittling of chiefs by educated Africans. They will come under our control and they will not do as they please. We shall stamp out communism," announced Chief Jansen Jongilizwe Ntola of Bizana at a Tribal Assembly Meeting in 1962 that addressed the opposition of the Thembu people led by Chief Dalindyebo to the proposed Transkei Constitution. Chief Mathanzima followed up Ntola's assertion with his own claim mentioned earlier of secret meetings being held for planning the end of African nationalism. Chief Dalindyebo, however, maintained his and his followers' defiance, observing at the opening of the Tribal Assembly's session that he was the only one who was cheered by the crowd: "There were no cheers for Mathanzima."[100] This early defiance and challenge to apartheid's strategy of defining and co-opting African nationalism in order to create geographic segregation through homelands presided over by puppet chiefs helped sow the seeds of Black Consciousness in the Eastern Cape. Black Consciousness leaders such as Steve Biko recognized early on that, in order for their movement to gain traction, the gap between rural and urban, professional and working class had to be bridged.

As Transkei continued to follow the apartheid government's plan towards "independence" *imbongi* Mbutuma spoke out against the process and against

Mathanzima's role in it. South African authorities had made Mathanzima "paramount chief of Emigrant Thembuland" to provide him with a status equal to Dalindyebo's, and Mbutuma made clear his opposition in a praise poem delivered in 1963 in which he condemned Mathanzima for his power-grabbing participation in the process, for undermining the legitimacy of the chiefdom, and for allowing himself to be distracted from his proper duties as chief by white persuasion. He accused Mathanzima of "preening himself" high above his people while below trouble afflicted them. In true *imbongi* tradition of speaking the whole truth, however, Mbutuma was also critical of his own chief Sabatha Dalindyebo for allowing these developments in his homeland and turning too often to alcohol:

> *Ndifike esithi imbodlela liselwa lonxano . . .*
> *Yinto endisuke ndawa umxhelo ndanotyhafo,*
> *Koko okhonjiweyo ngomnwe akaze adake . . .*

> I found him drowning his sorrows in booze . . .
> This broke my heart and laid me low,
> but those in high rank are ever with us.[101]

When Mandela came to understand the futility of passive resistance against state-sponsored violence and persuaded the ANC to adopt a policy of strategic use of arms against apartheid, the point was not personal vengeance against the white population but a means of keeping control over popular anger. This approach was taken up by the youth, so that MK soldiers captured and brought back from the former Rhodesia in 1967, for example, were met by ANC prisoners with a new version of the Calypso song "Banana Boat": "Take-o, take-o/Take the country the Castro way."[102] This theme of defiance that formed the basis of Black Consciousness was highly influenced by African students and intellectuals in the 1960s first probing their self-identity against the backdrop of racial oppression, then analyzing apartheid tactics, resistance strategies, and methods of political inspiration. Socially and culturally, and eventually politically, they deliberately reinvented nationalism on their own terms and not based on social and ethnic divisions imposed by apartheid. During this time, even though black universities were heavily censored in their curriculum, ideas and influences from Europe and the United States found their way onto these campuses and infected them with radicalism. Music in the townships also reflected these developments, and soul music with all its connections to self-confidence expressed in the United States—dashikis, Afros, Motown, Malcolm X and the Black Panthers—contained a message that resonated much more powerfully with South African youth than the "traditionalism" manufactured by white "experts." That message and influence was absorbed by the Black Consciousness generation of musicians and combined with local township rhythms and songs to create a self-defined version of nationalism that shunned neo-traditionalism defined by the authorities in the same way that neocolonialism was rejected by black power movements.

Born and raised in Ginsberg location outside King William's Town, Biko was affected early on by the clash between apartheid and resistance when his older brother Khaya was imprisoned for nine months for his alleged participation in Poqo while at Lovedale. Biko was interrogated as a result of his brother's arrest and expelled from Lovedale, gaining admittance in 1964 to St. Francis College at Mariannhill in Natal. It was as a medical student at the University of Natal and as a member of NUSAS, that Biko began to formulate the view that the black population needed to separate from whites in terms of resistance leadership. Thembeka Nobanda, a fellow medical student at the University of Natal and a friend from Mthatha, remembered Biko as someone "who liked to help the underdog . . . He was just always trying to defend somebody. To put things right for somebody who was being hurt." When Nobanda confided in him her anguish over the detention of her boyfriend, Biko sympathized, remarking that it was something that all black men in South Africa were now facing. Later on, during their studies Nobanda noticed how serious Biko had become in his focus on the plight of black people in his country, "and I knew that Steve was lost forever in politics now he was really trying to get some things done."[103] Biko's disillusionment with the NUSAS white leadership led to his break from this student organization to launch the all-black South African Student Organization (SASO) in 1969. "They had this problem . . . of superiority, and they tended to take us for granted, and they wanted us to accept things that were second class," explained Biko.[104] Assisting him with this break were fellow students, including Barney Pityana from Fort Hare who had been a classmate of Biko's at Lovedale.

Biko's early activism as a medical student at the University of Natal helped to revive student resistance at Fort Hare in the late 1960s. When Professor John Marshall of Johns Hopkins University defended the colonization of Namibia as a guest speaker at Fort Hare, he was met with vocal criticism from the students who subsequently wrote up a petition in opposition to the rector Johannes Marthinus de Wet, who had been appointed by the government and was a member of the conservative Afrikaner organization the Broederbond. The petition was the result of the University Christian Movement's (UCM) mission to Fort Hare led by Biko. The students had hoped to start a branch of UCM at Fort Hare, but De Wet opposed its establishment on the grounds that it was too liberal and would mislead students. As anti–De Wet graffiti appeared on the walls of the campus buildings and students held sit-ins, the Special Branch was called in to target specific students. De Wet, meanwhile, requested a meeting with a student delegation, but the students responded by stating that they were a leaderless group and he should, therefore, meet with the whole student body. The campus was subsequently closed on September 6th, but students refused to leave. Thirty police in riot gear were called in who met the students with dogs and tear gas as the students occupied the front of the administration block singing, "We Shall Overcome" and *Nkosi S'ikele iAfrika*. As the police hauled them out, the students chanted, "Justice will prevail."[105] Three hundred and fifty of the 453 enrolled students were suspended; fifty more left. In a press statement, the students declared, "It was a spontaneous demonstration with no leaders and no links with communism, foreign groups, NUSAS [National Union of South African Students] or any other body. The demonstration was due to oppressive conditions on the campus and the interrogation of 17 students by the Security Branch."[106]

Biko and his compatriots clearly created a highly attractive ideology that energized the young black population and synthesized the strands of resistance represented in the homelands, in the schools and universities, and in music. The deliberate strategy of making it an all-black movement gave it time to build strength as it undermined the potential interference of government security. In the late 1960s and early 1970s, South African Prime Minister B. J. Vorster was concentrating his efforts on breaking up multi-racial organizations, so SASO was able to gain traction while the government struggled to assess the motivation of this organization. Black Consciousness, meanwhile, grew as it harnessed pent-up resentment and anger initiated by the government crackdowns of the early 1960s, especially among black students; and its messages of black pride, uniting through self-assertion, working together towards change, and fighting self-defeatism and generations of insecurity created by the racism of colonization and apartheid resonated in universities and spread to schools in the city and the countryside. The underlying connection to nationalism challenged the false cultural creations initiated by apartheid in Bantustans and in institutions that took control of their music and culture such as Radio Bantu. Black people, according to Biko, should not be viewed as foreigners in their own country, requesting access to the white system, but should create a system based on values that they themselves defined.

Just as colonizers of the nineteenth century had imposed their own definitions of ethnicity, tradition, and "tribe" on Africans, freezing those categories in time, apartheid authorities, through Radio Bantu, created false heritages of African music in the 1960s and exploited performers to represent this "neo-tribal" music. Between 1960 and 1962, SABC got rid of various generic or specific African language programs on the radio and put in place English and Afrikaans stations with white cultural emphases, along with Radio Bantu with its 13 different stations for each defined "tribe." Ethnomusicologist Dr. Yvonne Huskisson controlled these stations as part of a strategy to stifle the influence of jazz, which she denounced as "popular, sex-stimulating music" that was prevalent "among all less developed people, groups or races."[107] The Bantu Education Act had, meanwhile, eradicated jazz and other European and U.S. influences along with nationalist elements from the music curriculum in African schools. As Gwen Ansell observes, many artists as a means of survival played along with this development, supporting the fictional versions of indigenous music, dressing in defined costumes of their culture and romanticizing their culture while praising the puppet leaders of their region.[108] One of the things Black Consciousness challenged was this distortion of African culture through a European lens.

The problem for white authorities was that black music could not be completely separated from black politics. Just like political resistance in South Africa, music was a collective experience that invited participation. Every political discussion was marked by music, and the militant influence of MK, even with imprisonment and exile of leaders, remained. Former MK Commander Ronnie Kasrils observes that in the 1960s there came a change in the format of music heard at social and underground gatherings; the songs became "more rhythmical and repetitive—they were essentially becoming marching songs." Words also began to move away from religious and biblical references to political struggles. Lyrics such as "We will follow Jesus wherever he goes" were changed to "We will follow Luthuli wherever he goes," and were followed up with "The jails are full, they show that we struggle for our freedom."[109]

Jazz also persevered in the face of cultural appropriation and became part of the soundtrack to Black Consciousness. The influence of jazz in the Black Consciousness movement could be traced to the festivals of the early 1960s sponsored by beer companies, where jazz musicians stymied the censorship of apartheid authorities by reaching their audiences through performances that had no words but that still touched the souls of those in the audience and inspired authentic nationalism. Nkiho Xaba described a session at a festival from 1962: "When Eric Nomvete, who was from East London, came on stage with his group, it was such an electrifying moment. When he played *Ndinovalo Ndinomingi* (Pondo Blues), (t)here was a silence when he played those rhythms—and then there was a roar and beer bottles started flying all over the place. Because he invokes a spirit that, look, man this is what we want to do—there's no need for us to be going anywhere else but look into ourselves."[110] The song combines sounds that replicate those of playing a ram's horn, Xhosa jazz chords, and call and response patterns in the trumpet and sax solos. As Ansell describes it, "Nomvete's solo sounds like no other player on the planet." She goes on to explain, "African audiences had no problems with certain ways of drawing on tradition; but those ways would be defined by creators and listeners, not by the white authorities, and would speak to a discourse of genuine independence."[111]

It was not easy for jazz musicians playing within the confines of apartheid, and even though their music was difficult to directly censor, the system was still oppressive in all manner of ways, as expressed by Tony McGregor in his description of the experiences of his brother Chris McGregor: "It just became very difficult to be a jazz musician; I think one of the things about jazz is that people who play jazz are generally within themselves free people, and they play a free kind of music. And it becomes very difficult to be free in a society where there are all these laws and regulations governing people's lives to the extent that apartheid laws did."[112]

Chris McGregor's decision to leave South Africa is connected to the separation between the white and black experience that Steve Biko highlighted in his break from NUSAS and decision to form a black-only movement. Tony McGregor explains it happening while Chris played at a festival in Port Elizabeth when the police began to attack members of the audience: "It became quite a tense scene. And Chris realized that just by being there, just by playing that music, and being a white playing in black areas mostly he was actually endangering people's lives. That he might get away with it because he was white, but other people might in fact lose their lives from just listening to the music. And that incident I think happened in 1963 and he realized then that he couldn't stay in South Africa."[113] The rising awareness by black youth of these differences in experience making resistance a necessarily black-controlled phenomenon, and the increased expectations inspired by the Black Consciousness movement as it began to formulate in the late 1960s, engaged with cultural and musical expressions that set the stage in the Eastern Cape and South Africa as a whole for the drama of the 1970s and heightened conflict of the 1980s.

The roots of the rise of a newly defined sense of identity as a result of the experiences of resistance in the 1950s and 1960s in South Africa, that would be increasingly expressed in Black Consciousness in the 1970s, can be traced back to the early modern African intellectuals of the Eastern Cape in the late nineteenth and early twentieth centuries. Africans such as Walter Rubusana and S. E. K. Mqhayi were instrumental in taking pride of culture and language from their people and preserving it through a narrative form that combined oral tradition and Western influences, and these early twentieth-century voices found an echo in the more recent political and creative voices that served to liberate black people from a false psychological containment caused by years of colonization and apartheid. The restrictions and crackdowns imposed on the black population in the 1950s and 1960s that those in the Eastern Cape felt and responded to only caused a momentary lull in the process of defining black identity and black nationalism, before the revival of an increasingly confident defiance would make itself felt, not least in the form of music and spoken word.

NOTES

1. Vuyisile Msila, *A Place to Live: Red Location and Its History from 1903 to 2013* (Stellenbosch: Sun Press, 2014), 139.
2. Daniel Massey, *Under Protest: The Rise of Student Resistance at Fort Hare* (Pretoria: Unisa Press, 2010), 65.
3. Massey, *Under Protest*, 85.
4. Massey, *Under Protest*, 109.
5. "Basic Policy of Congress Youth League." Manifesto Issued by the National Executive Committee of the ANC Youth League, 1948, in *From Protest to Challenge: A Documentary History of African Politics in South Africa, 1882–1964*, ed. Thomas Karis and Gwendolyn M. Carter, vol. 2, *Hope and Challenge, 1935–1952*, by Thomas Karis (Stanford, CA: Hoover Institution, 1973), 326–29.
6. "Basic Policy of Congress Youth League," 326–29.
7. Vuyisile Msila, *A Place to Live*, 163.
8. Lestie Hughes, "The Social and Cultural Significance of Dudley Tito's Music: A Postmodern Investigation," Master's Thesis (University of Port Elizabeth, 1999), 31.
9. Vuyisile Msila, *The Black Train Rising: The Life and Times of Welcome Duru* (Lynwood Ridge, South Africa: Siyamba Projects, 2010), 117–18.
10. Msila, *A Place to Live*, 132–33.
11. Msila, *A Place to Live*, 138–39.
12. Deborah Posel, *The Making of Apartheid 1948–1961: Conflict and Compromise* (Oxford: Clarendon Press, 1991), 38.
13. *Amandla!* Directed by Lee Hirsch, New York and Johannesburg: ATO Pictures/ Kwela Productions, 2002.
14. Gary F. Baines, *A History of New Brighton, Port Elizabeth, South Africa 1903–1953: The Detroit of the Union* (Lewiston, New York: Edwin Mellon, 2002), 264–65.
15. Mary Benson, *South Africa: The Struggle for a Birthright* (London: International Defence and Aid Fund, 1985), 144.
16. Msila, *A Place to Live*, 169.
17. D. Carter, "The Defiance Campaign—a Comparative Analysis of the Organization, Leadership, and Participation in the Eastern Cape and Transvaal," *University of London, Institute of Commonwealth Studies, Collected Seminar Papers*, 2 (1970), 97, Appendix III.
18. Msila, *A Place to Live*, 170.
19. "Mass Support for Defiance Campaign," *The Clarion*, (July 31, 1952).
20. Massey, *Under Protest*, 75.
21. Baines, *A History of New Brighton*, 266–67.
22. "Verwoerd blames Port Elizabeth for Native Riots," *Eastern Province Herald*, October 21, 1952; "Port Elizabeth Warned by Minister," *The Star*, October 23, 1952.
23. "Port Elizabeth Disturbances," *Natal Witness*, October 21, 1952.

24. Colin Bundy, *Govan Mbeki* (Athens, OH: Ohio University Press, 2012), 82.

25. Carter, "The Defiance Campaign"—a comparative analysis of the organization, leadership and participation in the Eastern Cape and the Transvaal," *University of London Institute of Commonwealth Studies, Collected Seminar Papers on the Societies of Southern Africa in the 19th and 20th Centuries*, volume II (October 1970–June 1971); Benson, *South Africa: The Struggle for a Birthright*, 151.

26. Cherryl Walker, *Women and Resistance in South Africa* (New York: Monthly Review Press, 1982), 138.

27. FSAW "Report of the First National Conference of Women," Historical Papers, University of Witwatersrand, 4.

28. FSAW "Report," 14.

29. *Mayibuye: The Spear of the Nation* (recorded 1978, Netherlands), South African Audio Archive.

30. *Mayibuye: The Spear of the Nation*.

31. Baines, *A History of New Brighton*, 236–37.

32. David B. Coplan, *In Township Tonight! South Africa's Black City Music and Theatre* (Chicago: University of Chicago Press, 2007), 192.

33. Lara Allen, "Pennywhistle Kwela: A Musical, Historical, and Socio-Political Analysis," MA Thesis (University of Natal, Durban, 1993), 239; Coplan, 198.

34. Lara Allen, "The Effect of Repressive State Policies on the Development and Demise of Kwela Music: South Africa: 1955–65," paper presented at 10th Symposium on Ethnomusicology, Rhodes University (Grahamstown: International Library of African Music, 1991), 1.

35. Allen, "The Effect of Repressive State Policies," 1–2.

36. Baines, *A History of New Brighton*, 236–37.

37. Nelson Mandela, *Long Walk to Freedom* (Boston: Little, Brown and Company, 1994), 159–60.

38. Jeff Opland, "The Early Career of D. L. P. Manisi, Thembu Imbongi," *Research in African Literatures,* Vol. 33, No. 1 (Spring 2002), 7–8.

39. Opland, 10.

40. Opland, "The Early Career of D. L. P. Manisi, Thembu Imbongi,"11.

41. Opland, "The Early Career of D. L. P. Manisi, Thembu Imbongi,"12.

42. Opland, "The Early Career of D. L. P. Manisi, Thembu Imbongi,"12–13.

43. Opland, "The Early Career of D. L. P. Manisi, Thembu Imbongi," 17–18.

44. Opland, "The Early Career of D. L. P. Manisi, Thembu Imbongi," 20.

45. Opland, "The Early Career of D. L. P. Manisi, Thembu Imbongi," 21–22.

46. Opland, "The Early Career of D. L. P. Manisi, Thembu Imbongi," 23.

47. Opland, "The Early Career of D. L. P. Manisi, Thembu Imbongi," 23.

48. Opland, "The Early Career of D. L. P. Manisi, Thembu Imbongi," 23.

49. D.L.P. Yali-Manisi, *Iimbali Zamanyange—Historical Poems*, edited and translated by Jeff Opland and Pamela Maseko (Pietermaritzberg: University of KwaZulu-Natal Press, 2015), 12.

50. Archie Mafeje, "The Role of the Bard in a Contemporary African Community," *Journal of African Languages*, VI, 3 (1967), 196–97.

51. *Amandla!*

52. Mandela, *Long Walk to Freedom*, 234–46.

53. Alton B. Pollard III, "Rhythms of Resistance: The Role of Freedom Songs in South Africa," in *This Is How We Flow: Rhythm in Black Cultures,* ed. Angela M. S. Nelson (Columbia, SC: University of South Carolina Press, 1999), 106.

54. Pollard, "Rhythms of Resistance,"107.

55. Pollard, "Rhythms of Resistance," 108.

56. "Let the Living Remember," *Dawn*, Umkhonto We Sizwe, Volume 8, No. 6 (1984), 9–10.

57. "Let the Living Remember," 10–11.

58. "Let the Living Remember," 11.

59. "Let the Living Remember," 11.

60. Bundy, *Govan Mbeki*, 89.

61. Bundy, *Govan Mbeki*, 89–90.

62. Bundy, *Govan Mbeki*, 92.

63. Bundy, *Govan Mbeki*, 100.

64. Council Minutes, 1959, Fort Hare Papers.

65. John Shingler, "Crack heard around the world: Leave Fort Hare alone—away with indoctrination," *Student: The International Student Magazine* (1959), 18, Cory Library, Alexander Kerr Collection. PR 43228.

66. Massey, *Under Protest*, 135.

67. Ambrose Makiwane, Cala, March 4, 1999, Interview by Danny Massey, Digital Innovation South Africa disa.ukzn.ac.za/ora19990304000009000.

68. Ambrose Makiwane, "SRC Statement re: Findings of a Commission of Enquiry," August 21, 1958, SRC and other committees, Fort Hare Papers.

69. Shingler, 18.

70. Massey, *Under Protest*, 162.

71. Massey, *Under Protest*, 172.

72. Massey, *Under Protest*, 184.

73. Makiwane interview.

74. "Verwoerd's Crown Colony: The Transkeian Scheme and the Future of the Chiefs," *Fighting Talk*, Vol. 16, No. 2 (March 1962), 3.

75. Johannes Gumbi, "The Transkei Constitution—Changes Needed," *Bantu World*, May 15, 1962.

76. Robert Mshengu Kavanagh, *Theatre and Cultural Struggle Under Apartheid* (London: Zed Books, 1985), 91.

77. Kavanagh, *Theatre and Cultural Struggle Under Apartheid*, 93.

78. Anthony Sampson, *Drum: A Venture into the New Africa* (London: Collins, 1956), 88.

79. Kavanagh, *Theatre and Cultural Struggle Under Apartheid*, 111.

80. Kavanagh, *Theatre and Cultural Struggle Under Apartheid*, 111. (Translation by Kavanagh.)

81. Anthony Sampson, *Drum*, 28, 35.

82. Gwen Ansell, "Of Roots and Rhythms," in Pallo Jordan and Jurgen Schadeberg, eds., *Jazz, Blues and Swing: Six Decades of Music in South Africa* (Claremont, South Africa: David Philip, 2007), 17.

83. Lewis Nkosi, "Jazz in Exile," *Transition Magazine* (Volume 5, No. 24, 1966), 34.

84. Ansell, *Soweto Blues: Jazz, Popular Music and Politics in South Africa* (London: Continuum, 2004), 148.

85. Ansell, *Soweto Blues*, 149.

86. Hughes, "The Social and Cultural Significance of Dudley Tito's Music," 41.

87. Lestie Hughes, "Patrick Pasha: Community Leader, Musician Minister and Mentor of Many," in Diane Thram, ed., *Generations of Jazz at the Red Location Museum*, Exhibition Catalogue (International Library of African Music, 2013), 32.

88. Lars Rasmussen, "When Man and Bass Became One: Johnny Dyani 1947–1986," in *Mbizo—A Book About Johnny Dyani*, ed. Lars Rasmussen (Copenhagen: The Booktrader, 2003); Pallo Jordan, "Johnny Dyani: A Portrait," *Rixaka: Cultural Journal of the African National Congress*, No. 4 (1988).

89. Sam Mathe, "Pioneer jazzman 'Bra Pat,' the Legend," *Sunday Independent*, (January 4, 2015).

90. Jordan, "Johnny Dyani: A Portrait."

91. Kavanagh, *Theatre and Cultural Struggle Under Apartheid*, 63.

92. Msila, *The Black Train Rising*, 123–24.

93. Msila, *The Black Train Rising*, 124.

94. *The World*, (April 4, 1966).

95. Msila, *The Black Train Rising*, 127.

96. Msila, *The Black Train Rising*, 128.

97. *The World* (February 9, 1967).

98. Hughes, "The Social and Cultural Significance of Dudley Tito's Music," 38.

99. Hughes, "The Social and Cultural Significance of Dudley Tito's Music," 40.

100. *Bantu World*, May 15, 1962.

101. Mafeje, "The Role of the Bard in a Contemporary African Community," 214–15.

102. Indres Naidoo, *Prisoner 885/63, Island in Chains: As told by Indres Naidoo to Albie Sachs* (Hammondsworth, Middlesex: Penguin Books, 1982), 215.

103. Interview with Thembeka Nobanda by the author, Mthatha, June 1989.

104. Millard Arnold, ed., *Steve Biko: Black Consciousness in South Africa* (New York: Random House, 1978), 8.

105. Massey, *Under Protest*, 193.

106. "Expelled students deny leading Fort Hare demonstration," *Rand Daily Mail*, (March 13, 1969).

107. Dr. Y. Huskisson, "A Survey of Music in the Native Schools of the Transvaal," Master's Thesis (University of Witwatersrand: 1955), 238, 110.

108. Gwen Ansell, *Soweto Blues*, 111.

109. *South African Freedom Songs*, CD (University of Western Cape: Mayibuye Center, 2000) Disc 1, Disc 2.

110. Sibongile Khumalo interview for *Ubuyile*, 2000, cited in Ansell, 128.

111. Ansell, *Soweto Blues*, 128–29.

112. Interview for *Ubuyile*, 2000. Cited in Ansell, *Soweto Blues*, 134.

113. Interview for *Ubuyile*.

Chapter 6

"A Land in Calamity's Shadow"
1970s–1980s

By the end of the 1960s, the apartheid regime had enacted enough policies and legislation to make clear its vision for separate development in South Africa. Government crackdowns of the early part of the decade were at the same time accompanied by economic growth that spurred more ambitious plans for segregation. The Bantu Education system was expanded to encompass institutions of higher learning such as Fort Hare, with the idea of producing a generation of young people with limited expectations for their future. This new generation was to transition into the homeland system as obedient workers with separate defined cultures and "nations," while apartheid moved to stifle urban protest through territorial segregation. Restrictions on unions and segregation in the cities further worked to ensure accommodation to the apartheid system. The overall purpose of these government strategies was to divide black populations and weaken resistance. After a brief lull in the late 1960s, however, new forms of black resistance began to respond t these institutions and take the place of white liberal opposition, which was increasingly seen as too gradual and too timid. These methods of resistance worked to undermine the fundamental weaknesses of the apartheid plan. The problem with the government's homeland strategy was that the leaders propped up by the authorities in the Bantustans tended to be opportunistic and corrupt, characteristics that those banished to homelands such as Transkei on the basis of a state-defined identity did not fail to notice and which led to pockets of resistance secretly organizing within these homelands and reaching out to ANC, MK, and PAC leaders in exile in border states. The trouble with the Bantu Education system was that it fueled resentment and rebellion among its student population—for example, at Fort Hare—and led to the rise of Black Consciousness whose focus on a unified celebration of African identity undermined separate "tribal" classifications. The issue with apartheid's labor policies was that the world-wide recession of the 1970s hit industries in South

Africa such that workers gained increasing leverage in opposing their conditions of work, pay, and treatment in places like Port Elizabeth, even within the strict confines of the apartheid labor system. The three populations the government hoped to make most compliant through the institutions they created—students, homeland residents, and workers—became in many ways the vanguard of resistance beginning in the 1970s and leading to total disruption strategies of the 1980s. Music, performance, and spoken word raised these factions of opposition to new levels and made itself felt in the Eastern Cape as well as through Eastern Cape performers scattered throughout the country and abroad.

Black Consciousness was the predominant ideology that inspired the resistance that began at the end of the 1960s, and because direct political defiance had become too risky at this time, the first real focus of this movement was on retrieval of culture and reclamation of identity, two aims that were easy to access through a long history of musical and poetic expression and performance. These objectives were also easy to disseminate as government security forces were primarily concerned with multi-racial gatherings and organizations, whereas Black Consciousness fit initially within the state definition of separate development. The goal of reclamation of identity was why, as Steve Biko argued, a separation of students from white-dominated organizations such as NUSAS was necessary, since the white population had little to no understanding of the black experience or of black culture and history. As he explained in a 1972 interview with Gail Gerhart, "Whites saw it as some measure of bravery and sacrifice on their part to speak on behalf of blacks. And all blacks were doing all this time was just to clap and say 'amen.'"[1]

As a Xhosa from King William's Town, Biko's message and that of Black Consciousness came to resonate with the youth of the Eastern Cape and injected students with a new shot of confidence and confrontation. Fort Hare student activists Jeff and Selby Baqwa had been classmates with Biko at Mariannhill College in Natal and shared the influences from that experience that called for an intellectually sharp antidote to oppression on the part of university and government authority. Biko described the origins of the Black Consciousness movement as starting with the Fort Hare Transfer Act of 1959 that had put the apartheid government in direct control of the university, along with the establishment of "tribal" universities. Faced with a stark choice of surviving between the power of the police and the "leftist noises of the white liberals,"[2] Biko had already engineered a break among black students from the white-led NUSAS to form SASO (see Chapter 5). What followed was the formation of the Black People's Convention (BPC) in 1971, representing a coalition of African organizations committed to the ideology of Black Consciousness; and a further wing called Black Community Programs (BCP) which sought to broaden the reach of the movement beyond students and youth to encompass coordinated local self-help projects, such as medical clinics and home industries. The movement had strong connections to black nationalism in the United States, with an emphasis on psychological rehabilitation as preparation for political resistance. Black people, the movement argued, were oppressed not just by force, but through their own sense of impotence and inferiority. The aim was to "conscientize" black people, using slogans such as "Black is Beautiful," and music, poetry, and performance played a significant role. As argued by author and poet Mbulelelo Vizikhungo Mzamane, "Black Consciousness and the cultural renaissance it fostered illustrate the adage that when people live under conditions of severe repression, with no attention paid by the rulers to their political voice, culture often becomes an important medium for expressing their desire to transcend their oppressive situation."[3]

A revived and modernized form of black culture that incorporated Black Consciousness ideology could continue the struggle for liberation, and this development clearly played out in the Eastern Cape. Young activists established that culture could not only be used to oppress a people, it could also be used to liberate them, and Black Consciousness leaders made systematic and deliberate attempts to encourage a restored consciousness through performance. "Its tool," states Mzamane, "was culture itself," with a recognition "that culture is not a static or even a necessarily coherent phenomenon but is subject to change, fragmentation, and reformulation."[4] Theater, especially, entered a new stage of revival, as it had already existed in one form or another as part of the culture and history of Africans, and it was easy to transport and more difficult for authorities to censor than recordings or film. But performance and culture had to be redefined on black terms. Fort Hare activist and Black Consciousness leader Barney Pityana lamented that "Black men want to prove to white men at all costs, the richness of their thought, the equal value of their intellect. This is true and it is to be regretted. It is a negative way of expressing one's value."[5] Pityana and Biko were strongly influenced by Frantz Fanon who made this argument several times in his writings on the effects of colonialism on black people, and they most likely viewed Black Consciousness culture as entering Fanon's "third stage" of the black intellectual's struggle with his own culture:

> After having tried to lose himself among the people with the people, [he] will rouse the people . . . combat literature, revolutionary literature, national literature emerges. During this phase a great many men and women who previously would never have thought of writing, now that they find themselves in exceptional circumstances, in prison, in the resistance or on the eve of their execution, feel the need to proclaim their nation, to portray their people and become the spokesperson of a new reality in action.[6]

In 1971, Biko argued,

> A culture is essentially the society's composite answer to the varied problems of life. We are experiencing new problems by the day and whatever we do adds to the richness of our cultural heritage as long as it has Man as its center. The adoption of Black Theatre and drama is one such important innovation which we need to encourage and to develop. Our love for music and rhythm must be made to assume some relevance even in this present day.[7]

A rise in the spread of Black Consciousness ideology and literature in the 1970s fueled the rise in black identity awareness and led to an explosion of creativity that reflected this awareness. The independence movements in neighboring African countries invigorated the black population in South Africa as people in the shebeens danced, sang, and toasted the liberation of countries such as Mozambique and Angola. The new ideology as expressed in performance put pressure on those such as Gibson Kente who had, until the 1970s, concentrated on depicting the hardship of township life in his plays, but steered clear from more direct political criticism of white power. Kente, throughout his career, emphasized the importance of education among black people in order to prepare them for a new dispensation, but Black Consciousness ideology was now challenging that approach. Biko defended the suspicion and skepticism of rural black populations such as those in Transkei towards Western-educated Christian black people. Education was now seen by many black artists as destructive to African culture. Just as he questioned white involvement in student movements that challenged apartheid, Biko was straightforward on the subject of white involvement in and control of black performance productions: "How many white people fighting for their version of a change in South Africa are really motivated by genuine concern and not by guilt?"[8]

Athol Fugard admitted on numerous occasions that it was guilt that caused him to work with black players, including the founding of the Serpent Players in Port Elizabeth. His plays and Kente's until the 1970s had fallen into the category of what Xhosa playwright, musician, and scholar Zakes Mda called "protest culture." These were plays that addressed the oppressors, with an attempt to sting their collective conscience or open their eyes to the harsh effects of their laws. As Mda observes, though, it was a useless exercise appealing to the oppressor: "He knew what he was doing. And in any case the oppressor never saw these plays, you know. These plays, like the Fugard ones, were played in the city venues where they were seen by white liberals, who were already converted. So they didn't serve any useful function in that sense, except reinforcing already existing convictions."[9] The plays that burst forth in the 1970s through Black Consciousness represented, in Mda's words, "a theater of resistance." Protest theater expressed disapproval of the system: "It was . . . a theater of complaint, depictions of the inhumanity of the system on passive victims." Theater of resistance "no longer placed the onus on the oppressed to prove their humanity. It no longer attempted to appeal to the conscience of the oppressor. It addressed itself directly to the oppressed, with the view of mobilizing the oppressed to fight against oppression."[10] This was a theater that did not mourn the effects of oppression so much as operate as a call to action. Plays depicted this message in professional venues, and, as Mda states, "it was also the theater of street corners, of funerals, of weddings and of political rallies . . . a theater of an artistry that lived beyond the occasion, but also it was a theater of litanies and slogans."[11] A new distinction arose during this time between "Black Theater" and "theater presented by Blacks." Black Theater placed emphasis on revolution and black liberation. All other plays were just dramas presented by black performers. Until he produced the play *How Long?* Kente was criticized by the movement for his plays falling into the second category, often referred to as "township theater."

"The cultural revolution has started," proclaimed SASO. "It is now, for other theatre groups to examine themselves not as an isolated quantity but as a force that reacts within the community it serves. Theatre, for the time being, at least, must serve a dual purpose—to act as a didactic means and to present entertainment, to the black people of South Africa."[12] Black Consciousness moved playwrights such as Kente and Fugard closer to depicting the harshness of apartheid more directly and the younger generation of activists noticed this, praising the Serpent Players and Kente's group for their performances in the early 1970s. Fugard's play *The Coat* was described in the June 1971 *SASO Newsletter* as "a searching experience into the lives of people who are affected by the brutality of the system in South Africa," and during a SASO conference in Durban in August 1971, the Serpent Players performed in the evening and were applauded, along with other theater groups, for showing "precisely the direction of Black theater." The players' performance of *The Bacchae*, a contemporary interpretation of *Antigone*, was further described as pinpointing "the realities of our situation." These two plays, along with *Friday's Bread on Monday* and *Into the Heart of Negritude*, according to SASO, "set us searching for the black soul. These presentations with the Malombo Jazzmen and the modelling of traditional dress were adequate experimentation of the vehicle drama to arouse consciousness. In this the cultural aspect was satisfied."[13]

The Serpent Players and Kente's theater group continued to demonstrate the influence of black consciousness in the early 1970s. In the play *Sizwe Banzi is Dead*, which Fugard wrote with John Kani and Winston Ntshona in 1972, the main character faces a life of poverty through the classification in his government-issued passbook that denies him the legal right to work in Port Elizabeth and sends him to King William's Town where there are no jobs. Sizwe consequently adopts the identity of a dead man, using his passbook to continue to work. This basically means that he has to "kill" himself in order to survive in his own country and support his family, illustrating the precarious existence of black people under the apartheid system. A photographer, however, takes Sizwe's picture and, in so doing, restores his humanity. The play represents a struggle for real identity that the passbook system, and so many other aspects of South Africa during this time, sought to suppress and thereby eradicate black people's true sense of themselves. The characters eventually realize that the one thing they own that the government cannot fully erase is themselves, and they prove to be better men than the white authorities because they understand the value of human life and identity.[14]

Kani had actually taken his time coming around to trust Fugard enough to collaborate with him on *Sizwe* and on *The Island/Hodoshe* the following year. Growing up in Port Elizabeth as the son of a black policeman, Kani and his family were members of the ANC. His brother was arrested and sent to Robben Island and these experiences instilled in him a profound mistrust of white people: "We attend secret meetings in the evenings where we are taught to hate the enemy . . . kill the enemy. We are singing songs about this being our country. . . . And that was actually what kept me going. It was my hatred and my love for my people, my love for freedom." Kani first came into contact with Fugard when he went to see the players perform *Antigone*, and believed the black actors were being "duped" by Fugard: "This white man is here to suck their brains out! He's one of those that say 'I know black people.' And in the meantime he's writing volumes and becomes an authority on them. I was very, very suspicious." Kani gradually came to respect Fugard's theatrical work enough to stick with him and eventually write plays with him, attracted to Fugard's emphasis on the story in performances, and more critical of what he thought was often sacrificed in protest and Black Theater: "One compromised a lot—standard, quality. If the message was correct, if the message was talking about the people, and was informing, educating, exciting, conscientising, it was ready, it was right. But we in the Serpent Players with Athol, were always bound by the story, by the quality, the standard, and if there are politics, those will take care of themselves."[15]

Kente was cautious in his approach to the rise of Black Consciousness in the 1970s. His standard method of criticizing white oppression was to tell stories of the hardship of township life—a strategy that made it easier for him to keep working under apartheid. Like many musicians and *iimbongi*, his message was coded as opposed to direct. As his plays in the first half of the 1970s became more overtly political, Kente found himself more than ever walking a thin line between the apartheid system and the new mood of black nationalism. The former, as always, scrutinized his plays in search of potential subversive undertones or critical description of authority or apartheid, while the latter tended to be critical of his caution and suspicious of any perceived collaboration with the system. Spurred by the momentum of Black Consciousness, however, Kente produced a trilogy of plays that were more confrontational in relation to the system his people lived under than his previous productions. The play *How Long?* holds a theme of escaping slum conditions through education as it tells the tale of a young boy, Afrika Twala, in Soweto who faces numerous problems while trying to keep up his schooling. The play illustrates the frustrating obstacles and unnecessary suffering caused by segregation and the pass system, as Twala's father is beaten and thrown in jail, and his grandmother is evicted and left to die in the street. There is a message of hope that underlines that of black nationhood when a black policeman sees through the system, takes off his uniform, and calls for unity. With a high standard of singing and acting and a strong rapport between actors and the audiences, the play was powerful and spoke directly to the oppressed. As Kente described it, "The people on their own chose to complete the statement adding 'How Long Must We Suffer This Way?' The liberation movements and the ANC in exile used its music as one of its rallying cries. . . . Radio Freedom in Lusaka pounded its songs to Africa. Using the stage to bombard apartheid added a new dimension to the struggle—one that was later to lead to protest theatre."[16]

The second of these plays, *I Believe*, caused audiences to brand Kente "the prophet" because the message of the play seemed to accurately foreshadow the Soweto Uprising of 1976 and its aftermath. The play focused on the frustration of youth in the townships; in particular, a young rebel named Zwelitsha who battles with a security police chief. Kente, commenting on the play, explained, "I was saying 'I believe that if the government can take note of the attitude of the youth, of the simmering impatience of the youth, the anger of the youth—if they can act now, we might save ourselves a lot of hardships in the future.'"[17] The authorities also noticed the message and influence of *I Believe* and issued the playwright a warning. According to Kente their message was: "Mr. Kente, you are the most dangerous person in this country, because your message, whatever it is—you make it stick. People carry it home, they sing about it because it is in musicals. It's very dangerous."[18]

Too Late, the third of the more political plays, centers on the character Saduva, a recently orphaned young man who comes from the Northern Transvaal to Soweto to live with his aunt. The play again highlights the struggles of township life due to apartheid and pass laws, with Saduva's aunt arrested for running a shebeen and Saduva jailed for not having the right permit to live in Soweto. His disabled cousin is killed by the police while trying to defend Saduva, and Saduva is assaulted while in prison. *Too Late* was viewed by many critics as Kente's most successful play and it demonstrated to Black Consciousness activists that the Eastern Cape playwright was now more directly addressing apartheid with a message of black unity. The political content also meant greater interference and harassment on the part of the authorities. Both *How Long?* and *Too Late* were banned for a short while in Soweto, and Kente was pressured to remove a few lines with swear words and a reference to homosexuality in *Too Late*. Kente eventually had to shut down *Too Late* in 1975.

Fugard's Serpent Players were part of three travelling theater groups in the Eastern Cape, the other two being the Imitha Players under Rob Amato in East London, and the Ikwezi Players under Don Maclennan in Grahamstown. Together with troupes from other parts of South Africa, they created a circuit of performances in which they could share their plays and direct their own theaters. The Imitha Players performed their own version of *Oedipus* with Julius Mtsaka in the lead role. Amato describes one of the performances:

> They finally got to the point where Oedipus . . . comes in with his eyes gouged out . . . and he comes in with tomato sauce all over his eyes. . . . And a big, fat mamma in the front row, says, "Agh, come on Julie, we know you're not blind." The whole place packs up! . . . he went and stood over her, and cried, as if saying "Mama, I am talking about pain, I am talking about man, I am talking about ancient things." And she fell silent, and the people around her fell silent and contrite, and the whole house became contrite and quiet. And he went on to the most wonderful climax to end the play. So it worked, but only by a rescue which was of extraordinary proportions."[19]

Mtsaka appreciated his experience in Imitha Players and work with Amato, but he also later commented on the unequal relationship between black players and white directors even in these Eastern Cape groups: "During the time of the Imitha Players and whatever other groups were operating at the time, it was a matter of a black group transferring their power into the hands of a white person in the name of learning. So, the relations cannot be the same." In reply to the argument that the black players were being taught a certain theatrical tradition, Mtsaka stated that "to a great extent it was. But at the same time I could not find any reason why white directors could not say, 'Look, I've trained you. Here's an opportunity for you to take over and direct.'"[20] Skhala Leslie Xinwa, who was also part of the Imitha Players, linked this sentiment to the rise of Black Consciousness during the 1970s, since proponents of this ideology often questioned the involvement of white people in black productions. But Xinwa made a distinction between different white directors and writers, such as Amato and Rob McLaren (also known as Robert Mshengu Kavanagh—see Chapter 5). Xinwa described McLaren as more "grassroots" than Amato, in that McLaren actually stayed in Soweto and mingled with the people there, "understood their banalities"; whereas, according to Xinwa, "Rob [Amato] was never really exposed to that. He met people like us; he never met the real grassroot people, except through the factory, his family factory that he managed in East London."[21]

Mtsaka did get a chance to direct and also played the lead role in *Sacrifice of Kreli* by Xhosa playwright Fatima Dike. Set in 1885, the play tells the story of the amaGcaleka chief Kreli (paramount chief of the amaXhosa and known to them as Sarhili) and his attempts to raise up his people after defeat by the Cape colonial military forces in 1877–78. Kreli hides with his supporters in a deep ravine away from their former territory. The renowned and trusted diviner Mlanjeni is dispatched to the dwelling place of the Gcaleka ancestors to find out what should be done. Kreli makes use of Mlanjeni's return from the ancestral world to inspire his people to restore their old ways, get their children back from the neighboring land of Bomvana, and revive their struggle against the loss of their nation and against division. Mtsaka played Kreli as weakened by his struggles in battle and exile, but still determined. Addressing his restless warriors, he tells them he is their servant and their child; "their mother [and] their father."[22]

The play also has an *imbongi*, Mpelesi, creating a conflict between the message of the diviner Mlanjeni and that of Mpelesi. Mlanjeni, at one point, appears to be dead, but he has actually left to consult with the ancestors and returns to provide a final message before he dies. The message, as Dike explains it, is from the ancestors telling Kreli's people to return and build their homes, restore their crops, have children and live as there is a future for them. Dike remarked years later after the end of apartheid, "And this is exactly what is happening in this country now: we are given a future. We had many of our leaders in prison for twenty-seven years, and never thought they would come out. Suddenly they came out and we were delivered." This observation connects to her description of her people's approach to time: "There is no hour, there is no day, there is no week, there is no month it's just time. The African concept of time is three-dimensional. . . . There is no future. The future is born out of the past."[23]

Dike's play echoed the historical trend of the *iimbongi* by connecting the past struggles of African leaders to the present struggle of the black population under apartheid. This approach fit in with that of black culture in the new context of liberation: that it should be interpreted by black people on their own terms and in the language and history of their choosing, not through the influence and lens of Western society. When Fatima's play was performed in the Cape and Transkei, the language used was isiXhosa. For all other performances, the players used a combination of isiXhosa and English. David Coplan observes that Dike "was clear about the use of English not as a convenience or compromise but as a creative tool for translating the beauty and rhythm of Xhosa into an international poetic medium."[24]

More attention was also placed in black theater on the effects and consequences of those activists imprisoned, especially those on Robben Island. Having previously produced a version of *Antigone*, the Serpent Players created and performed the play *The Island*, which involved the character of Antigone played out by two prisoners on Robben Island as a means of surviving the cruel and barbaric treatment imposed on them by a particularly vicious guard. The prisoners nickname the guard *Hodoshe* after a stinging green fly ("the fly that brings death"). According to Kani, *The Island* was initially called *The Hodoshe Span*, otherwise the authorities would have guessed it was about Robben Island. While Kani's brother was on Robben Island, this guard apparently did his best to break every prisoner he was in charge of. There were several Serpent Players imprisoned on the island at that time and Kani's brother sent a letter letting him know that one of the players was performing a one-man version of *Antigone* while working at the quarry. Those in the Serpent Players who had been on the island such as Welcome Duru and Norman Ntsinga came back with descriptions of what they had experienced: "the work gangs, the clothing . . . inmates injured by wardens, tending one another's cuts with urine for want of a better antiseptic." Prisoners would narrate movies they had seen to each other; "one man used to hold imaginary telephone conversations into a tin can."[25] This gave Kani and Fugard the idea for making a play within a play about imprisonment on Robben Island.[26]

Another Eastern Cape playwright, Khayalethu Mqhayisa, wrote the play *Confused Mhlaba* which centered on the struggles of Robben Island prisoners returning home. Aged 22 in 1974, Mqhayisa had already written and produced nine plays when he published and began producing *Confused Mhlaba*. In the play, a former prisoner coming back to his township in Port Elizabeth decides to adapt to the system, concentrate on getting a steady job, and turn his back on violent resistance as a strategy for change. The play is full of richness and humor and also acts as a commentary on social and political conditions in South Africa. The content was too much for the government, however, and it was banned under the Publications Act No. 42 of 1974. Performances of the play were also halted, and Mqayisa was served notice of these restrictions by the police, which was unusual. When the matter was brought to the Publications Appeal Board by Ravan Press, who had published the play, the authorities supplied bizarre reasons for its actions, placing importance on the idea that *Mhlaba* could mean "land" or "country" in isiXhosa (it can also mean "world"); thus Mqayisa, from their way of thinking, was implying that South Africa was a "confused country" (a pretty mild description considering the level of injustice and irrationality in the system). The board also contended that the play was "strongly emotionally loaded" and it hurt race relations as well as acting as a threat to public safety, "because the police are presented in a bad light."[27]

The government's action in regard to Mqayisa's play reflected the changing dynamic between authorities and the younger generation pushing the ideology of Black Consciousness. Initially complacent towards a movement that seemed to support apartheid's message of separate development, the government began to view student activism and the confrontational philosophy and culture in support of black pride with increased uneasiness in the early 1970s, and once again it moved towards flexing its oppressive muscles, focusing on students. Black Consciousness ideology had found its way to Fort Hare early on, although its graduates recognized that by 1973, the historic Fort Hare of the 1950s was no longer in existence in terms of operating as a place of progressive learning. The new form of activism among its students connected it more closely to other so-called "bush colleges" that had been formed as part of the segregation of higher learning in South Africa, even as Fort Hare students tried to resist the new government version of their university and maintain some semblance of the old model. According to Barney Pityana, "We were always conscious during our generation of . . . resisting the Fort Hare that was being constructed by Bantu education. We had a vision of being part of the historic Fort Hare." Selby Baqwa agrees: "It was still a bush college but it was better. The Zululands and the Turfloops were a much more transparent creation of the system . . . a sham . . . you still felt, if you've been to the Fort, you've been to the place. Even if the prestige or aura is more historical than real."[28]

Initially, there arose a division at Fort Hare between those students maintaining the liberal tradition of the institution and those embracing the new dynamic of Black Consciousness. Pityana, for example, had been raised in the ANC-dominated region of New Brighton and his loyalties to the ANC were strengthened when he attended Lovedale. In 1968, Biko asked Pityana to come to a gathering of students in Mariannhill, but Pityana refused because he did not like the students' approach to combatting oppression. By the time Pityana was expelled from Fort Hare, however, he had begun to understand the Black Consciousness approach, and was able to reconcile his own beliefs with joining the SASO: "I was the one who articulated the idea that we haven't broken from liberals, but we have actually formed a home for black students."[29] In 1970, Pityana was elected president of the SASO, and the *SASO Newsletter* in September of that year reported overwhelming support for the organization at Fort Hare and the decision of students to affiliate with SASO, but Fort Hare Rector J. M. De Wet made the banning of Pityana a condition for the University allowing SASO to function on campus. Pityana, meanwhile, wrote an essay for the SASO newsletter that underlined the ideology and strategy of Black Consciousness, especially with regard to African culture:

> The black people are rediscovering themselves, their dignity and humanity. . . . A radical re-formulation of history has to be undertaken. There must be a more realistic interpretation of the causes of the Frontier Wars. . . . The Blacks should be known to have loved, lived a happy family life, were religious (but not necessarily Christian); they fought wars bravely, painted, sculpted, sung songs and praises, would have established their humanity and their right to receive fair treatment. It is against this appalling ignorance about himself and his history and particular mode of personality that the black soul is revolting.[30]

Fort Hare student Makhenkesi Stofile had also been raised under the umbrella of the ANC, with ANC activist parents and growing up in Port Elizabeth during the years of the Defiance Campaign with strong memories of the musical aspect of protest. He took part in the campaign against Bantu Education, remarking, "It was nice, the singing, the anti-Bantu Education songs and saying we were not going to school on the first of April, the song went." Stofile arrived at Fort Hare as a strong supporter of the ANC and wedded to its ideology: "Either you are going to fight for it or you just have to remain in that problem. We got to know people who got arrested, people got killed, people got detained for nothing. . . . So that was the experience we grew up in, in song, in life, in death sometimes." The approach of SASO, therefore, represented a challenge to Stofile's political way of thinking: "We thought it was a crazy, narrow, nationalistic approach."[31] Black Consciousness, nevertheless, spread throughout the campus of Fort Hare, and in 1972 SASO launched an intense recruitment campaign, such that by the end of the year sixty percent of students were members.

On April 29, 1972, Onkgopotse Ramothibi Tiro, president of the Student Representative Council at the University of the North, Turfloop, gave a speech at graduation that challenged the system of separated universities, asking, "What is there in European education which is not good for the African? We want a system of education which is common to all South Africans. . . . Our so-called leaders have become the bolts of the same machine which is crushing us as a nation. We [black graduates] have to go back to them and educate them. Times are changing and we should change with them. The magic story of human achievement gives irrefutable proof that as soon as nationalism is awakened among the intelligentsia, it becomes the vanguard in the struggle against alien rule."[32] As a result of this speech, Tiro was expelled from his post-graduate diploma course on May 3rd. As students responded with a boycott and sit-in, police were brought in, the campus was closed, and 1,146 students were expelled. Student protests erupted in sympathy all over

South Africa, and Fort Hare joined in the response. Although not directly responsible for these actions, SASO took up the charge and called an emergency meeting at the Federal Theological Seminary at Alice that was attended by 40 delegates from Fort Hare. The subsequent "Alice Declaration" of May 14 announced the students' decision to go on strike, noting "the oppressive atmosphere in the black institutions of higher learning as demonstrated by the expulsion of the Turfloop student body."[33] The initial division at Fort Hare between the *abaKaringes* (rebels) representing SASO who tended to come from the factories and mines in the north, and its critics the *abaThembus*, representing the Eastern Cape liberal families of teachers, principals and nurses, faded quickly and a newly united and determined population of student activists arose in response to the treatment of their friend and colleague Tiro. Students directly challenged Rector De Wet's repressive policies and his increasing use of the police Special Branch to harass students, and the campus uprising echoed the African nationalist surge in protest throughout the country. In the summer of 1972, Jerry Modisane wrote an article in the SASO newsletter titled "Why I walked off Fort Hare in protest," arguing that there was no real education at a "tribal" university, and observing, "one is not given the know-how, technical or otherwise, which will arm one to succeed in the battle against social, economic, educational and even political oppression. Instead, after spending a period of systematic sale of one's dignity and humanity, a certificate is donated to one." Modisane recommended that black students reject the system: "It is not so much us black people who need these tribal institutions. It is actually the oppressors who need them because they are inter alia their best weapon to keep us oppressed. . . . It is therefore obvious I am not rejecting education. As a matter of fact it is because I yearn for real black education that I reject tribal education."[34]

In July 1973 the Fort Hare Local Committee reported to SASO that it had become the "the sole voice of the students, and the only living body which can boast of representing a cross-section of the student body opinion." It went on to inform SASO that this local branch of SASO had been refused permission at Fort Hare to use halls for staging plays and showing films. At the same time neighboring high schools including Lovedale and Healdtown continued to invite local SASO members to visit and share black publications. Also reported was the presence of Jeff Baqwa as guest speaker on Heroes' Day, "when we held a successful evening of Drama, Poetry and Music befitting the day." The report admitted the difficulties facing Fort Hare students in staying affiliated to SASO under pressure from the administration, but affirmed that their local chapter was having an impact, and that music and performance played an important role in defending cultural and national identity.[35]

In August 1973, students at Fort Hare launched a major stay-away in response to suspensions of students and harsh crackdowns on the part of university authorities and the police. Fort Hare began to allow suspended students back but with restrictive conditions, including not holding meetings and not talking to the press. The students responded in defiance by calling a meeting, and as Selby Baqwa remembers, "Before we knew what was happening, the dogs and policemen were on us. I've got marks where I was bitten by dogs."[36] Claiming violence on the part of students, De Wet worked ever more closely with the police to maintain order at Fort Hare. In August, following incidents where police threw tear gas at students and baton-charged them, around 400 students were expelled for the rest of the year, with 300 more leaving in protest. Ntombi Dwane, a former Fort Hare student and teacher at Lovedale during the upheavals, compared the authorities' response to when she had protested as a student: "They beat up students. It was terrible. . . . Whoa, they were brutal. You see, now in the 70s, you know after SASO and all that . . . it was warfare."[37] Many student leaders made the decision not to return, but instead, spread their story across South Africa and make themselves heard and understood. In the opinion of Thenjiwe Mtintso, who went on from Fort Hare to become a journalist for the East London paper the *Daily Dispatch*, the strategy on the part of De Wet to try to suppress the students backfired, and in her case, it only politicized her more: "When De Wet began to bring in the police, that hardened the attitude of students. That hardened all of us, even the *abaThembus*, because when the police came, they didn't say who was *abaKaringe* and who was *abaThembu*. They were hitting all of us."[38] De Wet and the government also went after the neighboring multi-racial Federal Theological Seminary (Fedsem) in Alice where many Fort Hare students would take refuge when chased by the police. After putting much pressure on Fedsem, Fort Hare eventually took control of the seminary through an order of expropriation and Fedsem was forced to move to Mthatha and then Pietermaritzburg.

With so many students expelled or leaving institutions such as Fort Hare, protest momentum began to build outside of universities and filtered down to the youth in community organizations and at middle and high schools. Young people in places like Port Elizabeth undoubtedly played a critical role in the liberation struggle. Known as "comrades" or "young lions," a number of youth organizations sprung up or rejuvenated themselves and became connected to underground movements, most prominent of which were the ANC, AZAPO (Azanian People's Movement), and PAC. Organizations such as the Port Elizabeth Youth Congress (PEYCO) and the Young Christian Workers (YCW) became the driving force behind youth activism in the Eastern Cape, and Port Elizabeth youth were already mobilized by 1976. According to Vuyisile Msila, these youths "wanted to realize the freedom dream at whatever costs. Many lost the opportunity to progress with their studies because they had to hide from the system."[39] Young people from the townships of

Port Elizabeth led marches, addressed injustice at rallies and showed up at funerals. Msila observes, "They were the youths who sang songs in the face of adversity. . . . They burnt down what belonged to the system yet continued teaching one another about the freedom ideal."[40] The government reprisals against university students and SASO came too late to shut down the movement, as many of those raised in the Bantu system felt increasingly frustrated by their limited education and opportunities. That frustration would build and erupt in the 1976 uprisings of Soweto that spread across South Africa and found determined expression in the Eastern Cape.

In the early 1970s, black workers gained some traction through the growth of manufacturing and the rise in the need for skilled employment. From 1973 to 1975, however, this advancement was brought to a halt by inflation caused by an increase in oil prices plus a drop in the gold price, causing a recession. Black labor unrest intensified in different areas of South Africa, including in East London, with factory strikes launched against specific issues. These labor conflicts combined with rising student activism spurred on by Black Consciousness created a situation resembling a pressure cooker ready to explode. The issue that proved the catalyst to the 1976 uprising was the decision by apartheid authorities to teach half of the curriculum in black schools in Afrikaans. This would further restrict black students' already limited access to international education, with Afrikaans viewed as the language of oppression. On June 16th 15,000 schoolchildren protested in Soweto where they were met by police as they moved towards a large sports stadium. The police fired on the crowd, killing a number of students, including young schoolchildren. The youth erupted in response throughout Soweto, attacking all symbols of white oppression as the police continued their attack; and, in the evening, as black workers returned from their jobs, the police turned on them, instantly creating an alliance of labor and youth in the spontaneous revolts that spread throughout the country. More than anything, the events of June 16th served to radicalize young black people as they saw the power in their actions and mourned the loss of friends in the uprising. Schools were targeted by fire burnings, and, as police launched raids on the schools, students burned textbooks and resurrected freedom songs, such as *"Senzini Na?"* ("What have we done?") and *"Lento Andizondi uVorster,"* the latter stating, "The thing I don't understand Vorster/is fighting with an axe/what cowards!" The song compared bringing an axe to a stick fight to Prime Minister B. J. Vorster ordering the use of guns against unarmed students.[41]

Resistance among the youth in the Eastern Cape had already begun before the June 16th uprising as seen at Fort Hare, and also in black and colored schools. By 1976, young people were mobilized. A little over a month after the uprising, at a boxing tournament at Centenary Great Hall in Port Elizabeth, police found themselves unable to control a crowd trying to get in. As the police began firing on the crowd, township residents responded by burning two police cars, and within two days, ten people in New Brighton had been killed and at least 20 injured by the police. Young people began attacking schools in New Brighton and Zwide townships as police responded with teargas. Pupils at Kwazakhele High School led protests and organizing throughout 1976 in Port Elizabeth, with one of the students, Thozamile Botha, later becoming a leader of the Port Elizabeth Black Civic Organization (PEBCO) and an exiled member of the ANC. The school was targeted by the government's Special Branch, and thirty-one of the students were charged under the Terrorism Act in January 1977 and sent to Robben Island.[42]

Much of the newfound confidence of these young people came from the spread of Black Consciousness ideology and it influenced many in the black population as they began to become more aware of their worth, and openly question the status quo, their employers, police, and the education system. The government had taken note of these developments before the uprising; in 1974 it banned a rally organized by the BPC and over 5,000 people clashed with the police. Police responded by raiding the homes of Black Consciousness leaders, detaining many of them and charging thirteen in 1975 under the Terrorism Act, with nine of them sentenced to five to ten years in prison. Biko was not arrested, but he gave evidence at the trial that became a public statement of Black Consciousness philosophy and provided the movement with greater attention and publicity.

Biko during this time had been operating with a small circle of activists in Ginsberg township outside of King William's Town that formed the center of leadership of Black Consciousness. As the movement evolved from the goals of purely psychological and cultural liberation towards more concrete objectives, Biko and his fellow activists began to reach out to the ANC and PAC underground networks, and the police stepped up harassment and arrest of activists in his circle. In 1976, Malusi Mpumlwana, who had been working with Biko, was detained. Thenjiwe Mtintso, the former Fort Hare student who was now a journalist for the East London *Daily Dispatch*, was also detained, suffered harsh treatment and was eventually banned and confined to Johannesburg. Dr. Mamphela Ramphele, the director of Biko's Zanempilo clinic near King William's Town, was banned and sent to Tzaneen in Northern Transvaal.

On August 17th, 1977, Biko drove to Cape Town in defiance of his bans, accompanied by Peter Jones, an accountant. He was hoping to meet with Neville Alexander in an attempt to mend a rift that had grown among BPC members in Cape Town. Unable to see Alexander, Biko returned to the Eastern Cape and was stopped at a roadblock between Grahamstown and King William's Town. He was arrested and taken to Port Elizabeth police headquarters where both he and Jones were interrogated. Jones was severely beaten, starved, and detained for 533 days. Biko was also beaten, suffering brutal head injuries. He was subsequently transferred to Pretoria, riding naked and shackled in the back of a police Land Rover, and reported by the authorities to have died at Pretoria Central Prison on September 12th.

Biko's death caused a national and international outcry. His funeral was held in King William's Town, which turned into a powerful rally, lasting five hours and drawing a crowd of up to 20,000 black people, hundreds of white attendees, and representatives of thirteen foreign embassies, with numerous speakers attacking the government and holding it responsible for Biko's death. With multiple freedom songs ringing out throughout the gathering, black people in attendance reaffirmed their resolve for equality and freedom, and the event set a pattern for funerals of activists killed in South Africa for the next decade and more. The government was forced to hold an inquest, an unusual occurrence and one that embarrassed apartheid authorities, and in 1979 Biko's widow was offered R65,000 (c. $100,000) in an out-of-court settlement. Still, the government maintained that it was in no way responsible for Biko's death. (More accurate details that implicated apartheid authorities were only revealed after apartheid ended through hearings of the Truth and Reconciliation Commission.) Although the government predictably banned SASO, BPC, and BCP, along with Black Consciousness theater, it failed to grasp the strength of the movement and the extent to which it empowered underground activism against apartheid as a whole. The Soweto Uprising and the death of Biko rejuvenated the ANC's military wing MK as large numbers of mostly young black people left South Africa to join the ranks of those fighting and training in exile. Nelson Mandela observed a younger generation of prisoners coming into Robben Island in the aftermath of Soweto who had gone to training grounds in neighboring countries and returned to South Africa to infiltrate the system: "These young men were a different breed of prisoner than we had ever seen before. They were brave, hostile, and aggressive. They would not take orders, and shouted 'Amandla!' at every opportunity. Their instinct was to confront rather than to cooperate."[43]

Resistance continued in the Eastern Cape. By November 1977, all 39,000 primary and secondary students in Port Elizabeth were on strike. As they attacked teachers' houses, police responded with guns and armored tanks, and the schools in Port Elizabeth, Ciskei and the border corridor regions were subsequently closed. Port Elizabeth was described as a place where the police had lost control, with a special task force of white police brought in during the Christmas holidays to keep order. Msila recalled what it was like in New Brighton township: "At night the location sounded like a war zone. . . . Police came in the wee hours of the morning kicking down doors and showing no mercy to the young people as they ferried them in their vans. There were a number of people who were tortured to death."[44] Like others throughout

South Africa, Eastern Cape youth were stirred into action through the events of the Soweto Uprising and the death of Biko. Inspired by the successful liberation movements throughout Africa and the guerilla wars in Namibia and Zimbabwe, they began to see the uselessness of fighting in townships and, in their mounting anger over police brutality, many took up arms to fight more directly. Black Consciousness ideology, African nationalist movements, and the resurgence of protests and riots in the 1970s had given them a sense of combatting apartheid on a more equal basis.

In the midst of all this upheaval, musicians from the Eastern Cape continued to create, perform, adapt and resist. Caught up in the general government reprisals and suppression of black nationalism, jazz clubs and places of performance were constantly raided and closed, and travelling musicians harassed, with authorities beating down but not defeating the creative spirit of the players. Winston Mankunku Ngozi recalled, "In the '70s, work was scarce. We had to travel to Port Elizabeth . . . we were touring all the time."[45] Venues such as the Golden Fountain and the Alabama Hotel, for example, operated in the "grey area" of Korsten location in Port Elizabeth, which was immune to pass laws and presented a crossover style of music that also crossed the color line. A new generation of musicians playing jazz and other forms of popular music pushed through the barriers of ethnic separation and government restrictions, infused with the messages and cultural support of Black Consciousness. The political content of music played during this time ranged from songs increasingly making use of the *toyi-toyi* jogging dance and chanting exported from the training grounds of MK fighters in exile, to familiar *mbqanga* songs and political protest songs. Jazz continued to be a form of resistance, maintaining an urban cosmopolitan approach that mixed influences and provided a subtle yet powerful antidote to the staleness of officially defined "tribal" music. Port Elizabeth's Soul Jazzmen, for example, won first prize at festivals in the late 1970s, mixing jazz, U.S.-imported soul, and *mbaqanga*, and artists in South Africa declared the "freedom" of jazz music.

This freedom is illustrated in the iconic song *Tshona!* released in 1975, written by Eastern Cape musician Patrick Matshikiza. *Tshona!* was later described as symbolizing "the resilience of a creative spirit and the staying power of township jazz against all odds."[46] It was an instant hit during a time that jazz was increasingly in competition with disco and soul. Sipho Mabuse, who played drums on *Tshona!* described the new energy infecting the music of the 1970s in South Africa, noting that black people were suddenly realizing the need to identify themselves and observing that the revolution in Mozambique changed everything:

> We overhauled ourselves into dashiki-clad musicians who were black power saluting and adhering to all of Steve Biko's influences and so on. Biko was very

important. Because that era—where you played mbaqanga or not—the emphasis . . . was not lost, as long as it was coupled with political objectives of the day. And people became proud of who they were: the type of music that we do must relate to the politics of the day; and the lyrics and . . . the music must derive from our environment.[47]

Pat Matshikiza and fellow band members were later invited by Hugh Masekela to come to the United States and perform, but they came to see remaining in South Africa as a form of cultural resistance and maintaining artistic freedom: "I said I would go if the others would, but Allen Kwela said, 'I ain't going because I want to play jazz, not mbaqanga. I know they're calling us to play mbaqanga. That's America. Jazz has got its own clubs there. I want to go and play modern jazz: I can't be playing those other tunes.' So I went home again to P[ort] E[lizabeth]."[48] Pat Matshikiza made the choice to stay in his homeland, but his career suffered from the oppression of apartheid; in the late 1970s, he left the mainstream, changed his identity, and lived in the colored township of Eldorado Park in Johannesburg under the name Patrick Matthews to avoid deportation to the Eastern Cape—actions similar to those of the character in *Sizwe Banzi is Dead*.[49]

As discussed in Chapter 5, other Eastern Cape musicians had already left the country to pursue artistic freedom abroad. Their sound, however, stayed with them as well as their connection to the struggle against apartheid. Miriam Makeba brought the unique Xhosa style and sound to Europe with performances and recordings of "The Click Song" and "*Patha Patha*." She also brought awareness of life in the townships and the oppression of the system in performances of the song heard throughout the locations in the Eastern Cape, "*Khawuleza*" ("Hurry, Mama"), introducing the song with a description of children shouting on the streets to warn their parents and the community of the presence of the police coming to raid their homes, telling their mothers to "hurry":

> *Fihlan' amagogogo*
> *Nang' amapolisa azonngen' endlwini*
>
> Hide the buckets
> Here are the police; they will get into the house[50]

The East London bassist Johnny Dyani also held on to his culture and maintained a message of resistance to apartheid. He had come into his own by the end of the 1960s, after performing in different parts of the world as part of the Blue Notes and other bands. The Blue Notes began experimenting with free jazz, and in a London session that brought Dyani and Louis

Moholo onstage at Ronnie Scott's "Old Place" in Soho, according to Pallo Jordan, "in sensational second and third sets, the reunited Bluenotes set the club on fire."[51] From 1969 to 1971 Dyani played with American jazz trumpeter Don Cherry and also spent some months as artist-in-residence at Dartmouth College with Cherry and Turkish drummer Okay Temiz. In 1972, Dyani formed a trio with Mongezi Feza and Temiz, Music for Xaba, that played combinations of Dyani's originals and Xhosa songs. Mongezi's wife KiJo Feza occasionally sang with the group and called their music "the South African heartbeat, transposed to jazz."[52] In 1973 Dyani led the group Witch Doctor's Son, a band marked by a strong *mbaqanga* sound. Reflecting on jazz during this time, Dyani made clear his loyalty to his roots: "In Europe they admire the Americans so much but the Americans are copying us [South Africans]. It all comes from Africa but the South African musicians are not strong enough within themselves and don't have enough belief within themselves. They let themselves be used."[53] It was a sentiment that echoed the message of Black Consciousness—that black South Africans had to develop their own confidence, and Dyani became increasingly frustrated with his fellow compatriots for not becoming more self-assured and promoting their own unique form of jazz. Dyani maintained connections with the ANC as he performed overseas, and when the ANC participated in the World Festival of African Arts and Culture (FESTAC) Dyani was invited to form part of the South African delegation. He also became the cultural ambassador for the ANC in Sweden.

Port Elizabeth jazz pianist Dudu Pukwana who had also joined the Blue Notes became part of Chris McGregor's next band the Brotherhood of Breath. The tracks on their two albums represented a break from their South African roots, with more improvised music of free jazz and songs like "MRA" that reflected the fast pace of the big cities they toured overseas. Pukwana, however, came back to his roots in the band he formed with Moholo and Feza called Assagai that took up the Black Consciousness message of pride in their African identity. One of the band's most popular and powerful songs was "*Kinzambi*," a track with African drums, stunning saxophone solos and a prominent electric guitar. The song communicated strength to inspire and cause change. Pukwana went on to create his own record company Jika Records with his next band Zila, which included the powerful female voice of his Eastern Cape friend Pinise Saul. One of the tracks, "*Ziyekeleni*" ("Let Us"), demonstrated a return to the origins of township jazz.[54]

Community consciousness in the Eastern Cape townships that had marked activity in previous decades began joining more directly with political activism in the 1970s and 1980s and made itself felt, as always, musically and culturally. Churches continued to be involved in protest actions using scripture as the language of liberation. Traditionally acting as a strong connecting element in the Eastern Cape, church members became more radical in response to increased oppression, and their activism was expressed in creative choral and church music. Ministers were many times targeted by police because of their involvement in providing relief for families of detainees and because they were often at the forefront of religious gatherings that would turn political. Patrick Pasha navigated his multiple roles in Port Elizabeth as a community builder, minister, and musician, viewing all three as crucial to the liberation struggle. The concerts he played in many times served as a cover for political meetings and the songs sung were often songs of protest. When Pasha helped lead a congregation of 20,000–30,000 people in a memorial service for the activist Molly Blackburn in 1986 he was consequently detained for a day. He also got into trouble with the Security Police after he received a telegram from the exiled ANC activist Thabo Mbeki asking Pasha, as General Secretary of the ministers fraternal association (IDAMASA), to admit his imprisoned father Govan to the organization after his release from Robben Island.[55]

As demonstrated in earlier chapters, Port Elizabeth had a historical tradition of organizing and resistance that infected the music and this made itself felt with the rise of black nationalism. Reed musician Zim Ngqawana recalled:

> In Port Elizabeth you had to deal with politics—so much of that black consciousness thing, Steve Biko. They were loyal to it. . . . It was just coming out of the '76 uprising so my blood was still warm. And there were people who had gone through worse things; all this, they talk about to you, what they had experienced. So it was just there for us to absorb. The music articulated this. You know, if you are playing without consciousness, you can hear it from your sound. One note, and you can say: he has not roots.[56]

The Eastern Cape bandleader Tete Mbambisa created a song called "Unity" on the album *Tete's Big Sound* that reflected the consciousness of his people, calling for them to act together, even though the song itself was instrumental. Another song on the same album, "Black Heroes" was described in the liner notes as "a musician's song of lamentations, delivered by sad artists at the graveside, blowing a hymn. This is Tete's infectious dedication to all our great musicians who have left us. A sad piece, a funereal note with a distant drum chanting and calling on the Black Gods to bless their sons and daughters with soul."[57]

Drummer Lulu Gontsana, who grew up in New Brighton in what he called "a thinking environment" with family friends that included Biko and musician Mackay Davashe, turned away from taking music at "white schools" because he believed a proper music education should be "learning in the culture" within his own community. Starting out running errands for the Soul Jazzmen, he eventually became their percussionist, and in the late 1970s connected with the jazz-rock-fusion band Spirits Rejoice. In the stifling environment of apartheid, Lulu described music as "a traveling space" that helped people rise above the restrictive places designated by unimaginative authorities:

> Where I grew up was a very rich scene. There was a club, Monde's Place. The main cats were Peter Jackson and his brother, Duke Makasi, Bra' Dennis Mpale, Early Mabuz, Chris McGregor—the only mlungu [white person] around and speaking fluent Xhosa. . . . Everybody was at Monde's place; it was like a university . . . we learned not just about music but about people, culture, politics. Those old bandleaders insisted we must listen to everything, practice, and develop hip chops.[58]

As a large section of the male population in the Eastern Cape tended to be absent, working in the mines or abroad in exile, women in that region continued to maintain their reputation of strength and fortitude in the face of poverty and oppression. Historically, women in the Eastern Cape had always participated in dance, music, and songs for religious and cultural festivals, as well as commemorations of births, deaths and marriages—every aspect of everyday life among the amaXhosa—often with the standard accompaniment of ululating described as the cry of the heart of women. During apartheid, a number of women joined the ranks of creative artists expressing their culture in music and performance, despite the economic and social challenges that accompanied this expression. Raised in Ngqoko near Lady Frere in Transkei, Nofinish Dywili concentrated her life on Xhosa—specifically Thembu—music, and became well known for her singing, dancing, bow playing and overtone (throat singing) performances. Women in Transkei were known for the performance of *iintsomi*, dramatic songs performed for families and local communities, and these continued through the 1970s and 1980s as one way of holding on to identity. Similar to *izibongo*, moral and philosophical messages would be revealed through metaphors and stories in the *intsomi* as opposed to stated directly; and, also like the praise poems of *iimbongi*, the audience would respond and become part of the performance.[59]

A number of female vocalists from New Brighton township also made their mark on the music scene, such as Vuyelwa Qwesha Luzipho, who began singing with the Soul Jazzmen in the 1970s. Luzipho especially liked singing Big T Ntsele's protest song "Bastard," and recorded the song "*Unolali*" (You Are Sleeping) with the Soul Jazzmen which was disguised as "*Le Ndoda*" (The Man) for the SABC version. Shirley Lineo Lebakeng became a member of the fusion band Black Slave in 1974, a group that frequently performed at ANC rallies. In 1976 she was detained by police and made to appear in court after one of these events. Later on, she joined the Soul Jazzmen. Margaret

Singana from Queenstown became known as "Lady Africa" throughout Southern Africa, moving to Johannesburg and associating with Dorkay House and the South African Union of Artists. She performed with The Symbols, singing the song "Good Feelings" in 1972, and did a famous version of "I Never Loved a Man the Way I Loved You"—one of the earliest openly romantic songs in black South Africa. Nomzamo Mkuzo became a popular singer in the 1970s and 1980s, recording for SABC as the "J-J Quartet" along with her husband the guitarist Jamani Skweyana. Mkuzo sang numerous jazz compositions in isiXhosa about social issues connected to the New Brighton jazz environment. These female performers, like their male counterparts, had to navigate a difficult path to successful careers, but they came from a close-knit community in the Eastern Cape that practiced a tradition of older respected musicians mentoring younger aspiring artists.[60]

Despite many obstacles, black theater also managed to continue and thrive in the late 1970s, possibly as part of the new surge of defiance that marked resistance in South Africa. John Kani observed, "Repression is like some kind of gangrene within you, inside of you, that eats your soul, that forces you to save your soul. I couldn't really say that a repressive society would result in creative art. But somehow it does help, it is an ingredient; it acts as a catalyst to a man who is committed."[61] In 1977, the ban on multi-racial theater companies was lifted and two plays by Zakes Mda at the end of the decade illustrated the present and future effects of the continuing struggle. *We Shall Sing for the Fatherland* was a satire about the outcome of a "freedom war" for two former resistance fighters, and *Dark Voices Ring* was an expression of the long-lasting and devastating effects of apartheid on individuals, shining a light on the motivations for resistance in apartheid South Africa.

Even though Black Consciousness theater was banned by the government along with other organizations connected to the movement, its influence remained in performance. Apartheid's cultural appropriation had poisoned the well of ethnic identities with its own versions of African history and tradition that divided instead of uniting the population and, in the eyes of the new generation, slowed the progress of African people. Africans fought back by combining their own version of the past with modern forms of theater and performance that served to connect them across regional boundaries. Jazz, as noted before, was in itself a form of resistance, combatting the notion of "tribal origins" by insisting on a cosmopolitan approach to music that was culturally eclectic and urban; blending *mbaqanga*, bebop, and free jazz to create a subtle yet powerful act of musical protest. The political content of music in the 1970s ranged from using the *toyi-toyi* beat to familiar township jazz to overtly political protest songs, such as Big T's "*Unolali*" (Superintendent). As Mzamane observes, "Black consciousness and the cultural renaissance it fostered illustrate the adage that when people live under conditions of severe repression, with no attention paid by the rulers to their political repression . . . [or] their political voice, culture often becomes an important medium for expressing their desire to transcend their oppressive situation."[62]

The radicalization of youth in South Africa, especially after June 16th, and not least in the Eastern Cape, was something that Gibson Kente struggled with because, until his trilogy of *How Long*, *I Believe*, and *Too Late*, he had consciously avoided politics. His plays of the early 1970s challenged the system and directly put the blame for hardship in the townships on apartheid while making heroes out of those dealing with that hardship, but Kente was most concerned with education, and when the events of the Soweto Uprising led to a widening of the education gap, he was troubled. Unafraid of physical violence on a personal level, having trained as a boxer, Kente hated violence on a large scale and asserted his focus on humanity. He never really wanted to be a "protest playwright," and later complained that "we sacrificed the aesthetics of the game. We shouted slogans. Real art was trampled on. Protest theater was there to deliver crude messages, too embarrassing for the disciples of art."[63] Despite his attempts to distance himself from politics, Kente was arrested in November 1976 just before a film version of *How Long?* had been scheduled for a private screening in Port Elizabeth, and in the midst of the August and September raids under the State of Emergency declared in response to the June uprising. Authorities banned the film, with a screenplay written by Kente and many in his theater group, and impounded the film reels. The experience of oppression and imprisonment often radicalizes a person, but this was not the case with Kente, and because of the superficial stories in the plays he subsequently produced, he was criticized for artistic reticence. The actor Dixon Motele observed, "I think he was scared. . . . When they released him we assembled, and then he said, 'Folks, we must now forget about politics, and write about something that'll make us live.' We were not very happy about that!"[64] When interviewed in 1979, Kente asserted that he was an artist, not a politician, although he also admitted that it was difficult in South Africa to separate the two; this was why his plays contained an element of what he called "bread and butter politics." When asked his opinion on the state of his country, he replied, "I see the last kicks of a dying horse. But the whites hold the key to peaceful change. If not, they will be responsible for violent change."[65]

While the effects of Black Consciousness played out initially in the universities, colleges, and schools and among the younger generation, the black labor population and those relegated to "Bantustans" or "Homelands" were also affected by this new surge in identity and nationhood as part of resistance, with a focus on taking back the definition of both of these elements from the apartheid authorities. Writing under the pseudonym "Frank Talk," Biko early on challenged the Bantustan system of geographic separation that separated Africans into "tribes" and continued to crowd them into the poorest areas of the country with the false promise of "independence" in their own "homeland." As Biko saw it, "Slowly the ground is being swept off from under our feet and soon we as blacks will believe completely that our political rights are in fact in our 'own' areas." As Biko correctly forecasted, black people would then have no basis for asserting their rights in the Republic, "which incidentally will comprise more than three quarters of the land of our fore-fathers." Specifically citing the case of Transkei, Biko asked, "After the kind of noises made by . . . [Kaiser] Mathanzima, who can argue that black opinion is being stifled in South Africa?"[66]

In 1972, the Black Consciousness movement went on to firmly reject government plans for separate development based on the homeland system. The origins of the plan dated back to Cecil Rhodes' proposal to create a system that would over time provide the British colony in South Africa with an unlimited supply of workers with no right of participation in government. The scheme was updated by Hendrik Verwoerd using Transkei as the first model of Bantustans, not coincidentally, being the region of the Glen Grey Act of 1894 (see Chapter 3). Chief Kaiser Mathanzima had been a willing collaborator with apartheid authorities from his base in Thembuland, and he formally accepted independence of Transkei in 1976, serving as the homeland's first prime minister and then its second president (Paramount Chief Botha Sigcau was Transkei's first president). Gaining general acceptance throughout Transkei of this new dispensation, however, was an uphill battle, and populations within the region remained divided in their feelings over the so-called independence, due to rural resentment of administrative control of farming practices, among other issues, and a firmly-entrenched and long-standing loyalty felt by many in the region to the ANC, the PAC, and other banned organizations.

In 1976, Nelson Mandela received a visit in Robben Island prison from the Minister of Prisons Jimmy Kruger, who was also a member of Prime Minister Vorster's cabinet. The visit was an attempt to get Mandela to support the government's separate development and homeland policies by promising a significant reduction in his sentence if he would agree to move there after serving his time. Mandela recalls, "I listened respectfully until he had finished. First, I said, I wholly rejected the Bantustan policy, and would do nothing to support it, and second, I was from Johannesburg, and it was to Johannesburg that I would return." Kruger returned a month later with the same offer and Mandela once again rejected it: "It was an offer only a turncoat would accept."[67] Mandela admitted, however, that having asserted to Kruger that Soweto was his home and he would never move back to the Eastern Cape through a government arrangement, he did dream of returning one day "to a free Transkei."[68]

The role played by the Eastern Cape homelands in the apartheid government's separate development scheme tended in many ways to underline and fuel resistance to those officials set up to administer the plan, while reinforcing suspicion of anyone seen as connected to authorities. The authorities, at the same, worked to restrict any parties that might "infect" the population with ideas that would work against maintaining a cooperative labor force. Deirdre Hansen encountered division and the struggles of gaining trust and acceptance in the Transkei and Ciskei regions while doing field work in the 1970s for her dissertation on music of the amaXhosa. Magistrates placed restrictions on her activities that included not being able to stay in homesteads in the administrative areas and limiting her field work to daily trips to these areas. She was not allowed to attend any nightly events and had to report to security police each morning to inform them which area she would be visiting that day. This was particularly frustrating as most musical events happened at night; Hansen would instead have to arrange special performances in the daytime which took the music and its meaning completely out of context. She observed that it was "a phony method of carrying out research and one which could produce only negative results." Her presence as a white person in an area that had seen a lot of unrest and was often in a state of emergency made establishing connections with the local population problematic: "I was well aware of the hostile attitude of many people toward the white bureaucracy in general and the Bantu Authorities system in particular. I had seen obvious signs of this in the scattered heaps of burnt fodder, damaged fences and windmills, the sabotaged tractors, and polluted dams which were regular features of the landscape in certain areas."

Hansen came across people who seemed to support the white administration, but also an equal if not greater number who distrusted all white people. She noted that some people, particularly the non-Christians, were certain that she was a spy for the apartheid government, "sent to investigate any illegal activities that might be going on . . . to estimate to what extent the people were accepting or rejecting the government's rehabilitation/resettlement scheme."[69] The scheme included agricultural restrictions such as the culling of stock and limiting areas for cultivation, neither of which had ever been popular with the local population.

As a consequence, when Hansen visited beer huts, she would be asked to show her permit and then witness a half-hearted performance, usually the same song and usually a "school song"—one that was a product of Western mission influences—as opposed to a "red song" that would be indigenous. Her questions concerning the music and the meaning within the words of songs were met with suspicion, which made their significance difficult to understand: "I did not know then that song texts are often full of innuendos, even blatant insults, usually directed at a particular person or group in authority." Hansen eventually decided to ignore the official requirements of her field work, leaving her permit at her headquarters and not letting security police know of her daily routine. At this point, she was better able to judge the level of support for the Bantustan system, often just by listening to the words of songs. She found that there was trust and confidence in the Chief Minister in Eastern Pondoland; but in Engcobo, Mthatha, Kwa Bhaca, MaXesibeni, and Cacadu, she heard songs that criticized President Sigcau for mimicking the white man and behaving like a dictator. Hansen noted, "I was permitted to record the former, but not the latter."[70]

The establishment of an "independent" Transkei in the 1970s, meanwhile, made the position of the *iimbongi* even more precarious as they maintained the treacherous path between speaking truth to power and avoiding harassment, suppression, and detention. David Yali-Manisi tended to focus on three members of the Thembu royal family as the subjects of his *izibongo*: Mathanzima, Mandela, and Paramount Chief Sabata Dalindyebo who remained a political opponent of Mathanzima until his death in exile in 1986. The *imbongi* Melikhaya Mbutuma stayed fiercely loyal to Dalindyebo, while *imbongi* Nelson Title Mabunu maintained allegiance to Mathanzima. Manisi was also critical of Mathanzima, but initially cautious in his approach to Transkei's change of status and Mathanzima as prime minister. Doing his best to perform on the basis of sorting out fact from fiction for his audiences, making sense of all that was happening to them as was often the role of artists in the era of resistance and Black Consciousness, Manisi continued to reference the state of affairs in the Eastern Cape and relate them to the past, particularly in Transkei. According to Manisi, "you cannot be an *imbongi* if you do not know your nation," and this included extensive and authentic knowledge of a nation's history; otherwise, he asked, "what would be the basis of your *izibongo*?"[71]

In August of 1976, Jeff Opland was present at a meeting near Engcobo where Mathanzima, accompanied by Mabunu, made a presentation to a less than enthusiastic audience. Mabunu did his best to work up some passion among the spectators but Opland noted that it was an uphill battle. This was not surprising as the meeting was in Dalindyebo's territory, and occurred two months after the Soweto Uprising. October 1976 marked the celebration of Transkei's independence in Mthatha. Manisi arrived the day of the presentation of the new President (Sigcau) and Prime Minister (Mathanzima), and, as a highly respected *imbongi*, he was invited to perform a praise song. Manisi's praise of both leaders was tempered with warning for the future and leaned heavily on his first loyalty, which was to his people:

> ... for oh this land over which you'll rule
> is a land in calamity's shadow,

> as it shrugs off one form of oppression
> another grumbles and covets it.
> Once we lived with the English,
> who grabbed and sold us to the Boers;
> today the Boers release our bonds.
> One thing we know: there's a jackal here,
> sitting like a shivering chicken . . .
> May you both march in step with the Transkeian nation
> and may Qamata [God] bless you both.[72]

Manisi had recognized that, whatever the future held for Transkei in the new form of separation from the South African republic, this event was significant for his chief and his people, and he was, for the moment, prepared to wait and see what happened. In his poem to Mathanzima, he described the new prime minister as "a leopard hunter who disturbed a python," and an "otter snatcher with tortoise as bait." Manisi later explained to Opland that he used this imagery to depict Mathanzima as having "struggled for something in difficulty and got into greater difficulty; he caught something, but it was not what he was hunting." In other words, Mathanzima was not fully in control of the new dispensation.[73] What Manisi had hoped in attending the ceremony and proclaiming his interpretation of events through his *izibongo*, was that he could impose a sense of moral responsibility on the new leaders and remind them to uphold the needs and aspirations of their people. A few months later, Manisi wrote about Transkei's independence in a published poem entitled *Inkululeko uZimelegeleqe eTranskayi* (Freedom: Independence in Transkei), which he dedicated to Mathanzima. It had mainly been written out of necessity as Manisi had not been able to publish his poetry until that time and it represented a chance for schoolchildren to read his *izibongo*. Manisi's hopes that the new form of independence for Transkei would elevate its leaders to a greater sense of moral responsibility to his people were clearly ignored, however, and Manisi later regretted the book, requesting that it be buried.[74] His dilemma was just one instance of the compromises artists not in exile often found themselves making in South Africa, and the difficulties in holding on to principles.

In July of 1977, Manisi, Mbutuma and Chief S. M. Burns-Ncamashe who was also an *imbongi* gave a presentation at the lecture hall of the Settlers Monument in Grahamstown. When, in his poem to Mathanzima, Mbutuma stated, "My prince . . . poses a problem to his people," Ncamashe explained that, to Mbutuma, Mathanzima had brought difficulties as opposed to advantages in coming to power, because "he owes his position to whites . . . whereas the natural leader, the most senior man, is the paramount chief Sabatha Dalindyebo." Mbutuma had referred in his poem to two birds "soaring in the skies," with Mathanzima being the one that flew higher; "But Mathanzima must be careful," warned Ncamashe, "he may rise but he still remains junior to Sabatha Dalindyebo." Ncamashe went on to describe how Mbutuma was predicting political changes in the country where the white people would ultimately give way to black rule. Ncamashe and Mbutuma also referred indirectly to the offer made to Mandela by the apartheid government of returning to Transkei in exchange for recognizing its new form of independence. They pointed out the potential rivalry between Mandela and Mathanzima, the latter being tainted by his connection to the apartheid government. "The *imbongi* here thinks he entertains certain fears about men for example Nelson Mandela: should Nelson Mandela leave prison and come back to join his people? He will be a problem to a man like Kaiser who shines at the present time just because brighter stars are in prison." While Mathanzima was often called by his family name Daliwonga by prominent leaders and those who visited him, he was also often called Zanengxaki (Bringer of Problems) by *iimbongi* such as Mbutuma because of his collaboration with homeland policy and because he had objections to the release of Nelson Mandela from prison.[75] While in prison, Mandela had meanwhile made increasingly clear his support for Dalindyebo and his disapproval of Mathanzima. At one point, Mathanzima requested to visit Mandela in prison; but, after consulting with his fellow ANC activist on Robben Island, Mandela refused to meet with his Thembu nephew. This was after Mandela learned "with great dismay" in 1980 that Dalindyebo had been deposed by Mathanzima.[76]

At the Settlers Monument ceremony of 1977, Manisi performed a poem that looked at the broader aspects of South Africa and the relationship between black and white people. "How do we come to be set apart?" he asked. "Can't we share the land with each other?" He noted in his poem that while his oppressed people are distressed, the white population "stride freely about," and black people "travel with pounding hearts." Increasingly, Manisi reaffirmed his disillusionment with Mathanzima and the chief's ineffective and corrupt form of governance, believing that this leader was dividing his people more than uniting them:

> He's "I'm your creature, Greed:
> I wolfed down the morsel with ashes still on it:
> Yet my status precludes me from cooking myself . . ."[77]

Manisi was describing in metaphor how Mathanzima, as a chief, would not do his own cooking, yet he was so greedy, he could not resist snatching food from the fire before it was presented to him.

The ANC in exile was in total opposition to the so-called independence of homelands such as Transkei, making this clear in an editorial of 1979 titled

"Down with Bantustans!" that reinforced the view that Bantustans were a fundamental aspect of apartheid: "a reservoir for cheap African labor and an aspect of the military-industrial complex and the militarization of the social and economic life of the Africans." The ANC leadership correctly pinpointed a prime objective of the creation of the homelands, which was to recruit Africans to fight against ANC guerillas. ANC leaders also had little respect for the puppet chief ministers of these nations: "Does Mathanzima with his arrests, detentions, banning orders, total dependence on South Africa and international imperialism qualify to be an 'anti-apartheid' spokesman or even an upholder of the principle of self-determination and independence? We warn those who are supporting the Bantustans . . . beware of the wrath of the people!"[78]

The homelands were poorly financed, except for their bureaucracy and military, giving the residents little choice for supporting themselves apart from becoming part of the migrant labor forces in the mines, and working in the commercial farms, factories, and industrial estates close to the borders with the republic. One unplanned effect of this arrangement, however, was the communication it provided between rural and urban residents and the bringing of authentic culture into the cities which undermined the superficial "ethnic" culture established by the state. Workers from the homelands, meanwhile, returned from the cities with strategies and news concerning the struggle. Transkei, as a result, became a resistance stronghold in the 1980s, with workers and students at institutions such as the University of Transkei (UNITRA—now Walter Sisulu University) operating as active members of the ANC, PAC, and MK.

Ciskei, the other Eastern Cape homeland, was different in many ways from Transkei in terms of its demographics and forms of resistance. While Transkei's geography was mainly rural with administration and government based on historical chieftainships, Ciskei represented a more urban and industrial region, in close proximity to Queenstown, King William's Town, and East London. With a resistance population largely consisting of city workers, the backbone of protest in Ciskei came from the increased power of trade unions and civic associations. The ANC had more dues-paying members from this region and its borders than any other area of South Africa except for the Transvaal. Leadership in Ciskei in the 1970s and 1980s was marked by the rivalry of two brothers, Lennox and Charles Sebe, with the latter ejected in 1984 (he took up residence in Transkei). Lennox attempted to create a Ciskeian form of nationalism to rival the unity of the ANC and the Xhosa identity of Transkei, but his rule deteriorated into a corrupt dictatorship in partial response to the rise in power of the trade union movement and increased popular resistance in the 1980s that leaked into the homeland.[79]

Izibongo increasingly found its way into the mines and among workers in the cities as part of the culture brought from the Eastern Cape and expressed in the rise of trade union resistance in South Africa. The praise poetry that had historically extolled and described the successes and failures of chiefs began to focus on African *indunas* (compound overseers) and bosses who ran the mines. Here, also, resistance and criticism of Mathanzima would be expressed by *iimbongi* to an audience of workers, with a certain amount of immunity that protected the praise singers in places like Transkei as well as more urban areas. To censor or arrest an *imbongi* would contradict Mathanzima's traditional authority and the position of *iimbongi* that was necessary to add legitimacy to the homeland leader's power. In the mines, the Xhosa praise singers represented the interests of the miners, their moral values, and their grievances to black *indunas*. The *izibongo* expressed would also reflect a kind of social commentary among the miners and maintain a shared black culture in the mines known as *mtheto*. *Iimbongi* in these environments could demonstrate the comparative immunity of their position in their observation of the system they worked in; for example, in the Xhosa "praise" of white officials:

> Alas! I fear Thee. Honorable Father!
> You who smile like a witch when it kills
> Useless hat with a hole in the crown![80]

Iimbongi in the mines also operated as peacemakers, using irony and raucous humor to ease tensions among groups that were thrown together under adverse circumstances and that represented a wide swath of nations.[81]

One prominent oral poet known among workers for his performances during the 1970s and 1980s was Alfred Temba Qabula, who was originally from Flagstaff in Transkei. Orphaned after his father was poisoned and his mother died young, Qabula participated in the Pondoland rebellion at age eighteen and survived by hiding out in the forests with friends, scavenging for food. Although he eventually became a migrant worker, ending up in Durban, his family stayed in the country and he maintained that they and their rural life were his main source of inspiration, even though much of his poetry was about the sufferings of migrant labor. Joining the democratic trade union in South Africa, Qabula created poems for performances at mass meetings, trade unions, and community gatherings, and these would be accompanied by chants, music and ululating. In his "Praise Poem to FOSATU" (Federation of South African Trade Unions) he seemed to hark back to his own personal experience of hiding out during the Pondoland revolt while also recalling the historical significance of the forest (*hlati*) in earlier times as a place of refuge from one's enemy. The poem also calls on trade unions such as FOSATU to answer the need for leadership by those disillusioned by the loss of leaders to death, exile and imprisonment, and the poor leadership that is subject to corruption and betrayal; to not disappoint their followers or sacrifice them to their enemies:

> To date your policy and your songs are commendable,
> We don't know what's to happen tomorrow.[82]

The banning of Black Consciousness organizations and leaders did not shut down resistance in South Africa as authorities had anticipated, hoping for a repeat of the effects of the crackdowns of the 1960s. For one thing, the economy could not now support the level of state-sponsored suppression and violence required to flatten rebellion, and the cost of administrating segregation in so many facets of life was also rising. The ANC noted, however, that the apartheid government, through extensive legislation that continued to be enacted through the end of the 1970s and into the 1980s, closed many avenues of free musical expression. According to the cultural journal of the ANC *Rixaka*, recording companies had in the 1960s and 1970s profited off this state of affairs and contributed to the stifling of political expression:

> Only "happy-happy" music that set the nation dancing itself into oblivious disregard of the meaning of commitment was allowed. Banal songs with meaningless lyrics are the ones that get pressed on wax. Choral music—which is a favorite with a vast majority of our people—has been effectively and insidiously denuded of political content . . . apartheid has reduced a black musician to the status of a beggar whereby the road to a job is strewn with obstacles, such as stiff competition among musicians.[83]

Despite these obstacles, musicians and performing artists continued to maintain a tenuous hold on artistic and political integrity, not least in the townships of the Eastern Cape where tight-knit communities were marked by musical and oral expression. The ANC recognized this and sought to harness this energy to the increased resistance among workers and the rising strength of trade unions in the 1980s:

> There are also hosts of individuals, musicians who are part of the movement that won't ever sell its soul. . . . In nearly every township one can think of there is a cultural group that has connections with a church or a youth club or carries on autonomously. . . . Their music celebrates that thing in them that sees the need to fight for freedom. . . . It is some of these groups that appear at commemoration services, celebrations or political meetings to render a song, a poem, or a short drama. . . . The growing militancy of the workers indicates their growing awareness of their strength as a class. Workers' political awareness is high. The

workers and their unions can be of inestimable help in politicizing and organizing their cultural counterparts by inviting or adopting them into their fold.[84]

The increased power of the labor force in Port Elizabeth was connected to the growing dominance of highly capitalized manufacturing industries in South Africa and their dependence on semi-skilled permanent workers, as opposed to migrant labor. This development in the 1980s meant that late twentieth-century capitalism in South Africa was increasingly at odds with the system of apartheid. Mounting international attention accompanied by economic sanctions also created a challenge for political authorities. International pressure was fueled by resistance groups in exile, including the Mayibuye Cultural Ensemble of the late 1970s and the Amandla Cultural Ensemble of the 1980s, both set up by the ANC. The Mayibuye Cultural Ensemble toured all over Europe with performances providing a message of liberation through poems and standard freedom songs such as *Nants 'indod 'emnyama Vorster, Thina Sizwe, Dubula ngembayibayi* (We will shoot them with cannons), and songs about the Soweto Uprising. Increased responsibilities and lack of funds caused the group to struggle and eventually fall apart. Despite the amateur nature of the Mayibuye Cultural Ensemble, however, the passion of the performances and the urgency of the message resonated with audiences abroad and the ANC recognized this.[85] ANC leadership consequently decided to establish a more professional group that directly connected cultural and military resistance, employing ANC members in southern Africa. The Amandla Cultural Ensemble, therefore, consisted of mostly young trained soldiers with an emphasis on fighting and material based on the experience of exile and Umkhonto We Sizwe. The beat of the music became dynamic with the influence of *toyi-toyi* and songs such as *Sikhoklehe Tambo* (Lead us, Tambo) and *Rolihlahla Mandela*. Backing bands that incorporated jazz and township music also were part of the ensemble, and dances representing different ethnic groups although always with an emphasis on unity. The aim was to represent the dynamic nature of Africans in South Africa to the world; to reveal them to be more than victims by using culture as an act of rebellion. The ensemble successfully raised consciousness overseas while also encouraging resistance among exiles in southern Africa through performances at army camps and within South Africa through the illegal sale of its recordings.[86]

The South African government responded to economic and political pressures in the 1980s with the policy of "total strategy" that sought to combine stronger security measures against rebellion with reforms that would satisfy certain demands without undermining the system. Certain "petty apartheid" restrictions were removed, pass controls were relaxed, and the allowance of multi-racial private schools began in 1981, with the goal of creating greater class differences while seeming to reduce racial ones. In the meantime, the line between the military and police in South Africa became increasingly blurred and the State Security Council (SSC) gained more power in the 1980s under the Minister of Defense General Magnus Malan, including control over security and intelligence. Thus, along with the slight lifting of racial restrictions on the part of the government came raids, arrests, detentions and extra-judicial killings as standard features of the army and police. It was as if the South African government was attempting to ride a horse by both kicking it to go and pulling on its reins to stop, with the inevitable result that it lost control. The 1980s became a decade in South Africa marked by state-sponsored violence which was met by popular violence in the townships, as resistance moved towards a strategy of total disruption and the country tumbled towards the precipice of potential civil war.

The harsh detentions and torture carried out against the youth and Black Consciousness leaders in the wake of the Soweto Uprising could clearly not be mitigated by piecemeal and superficial reforms, and the attitude of this generation hardened in the 1980s in response to anyone seen as collaborating with the system. Reprisals and resistance were often fierce among students and workers. By 1985 major rebellion in the townships had spread throughout the Eastern Cape. The newly formed opposition group of the 1980s the United Democratic Front (UDF), often trailing behind local resistance, gained strength in the already defiant locations in Port Elizabeth, which were witness to some of the most powerful revolts of modern South African history. By 1985, these townships were up in arms; and, while the government blamed the UDF, the majority of the resistance was local. Conflict in Uitenhage was especially intense, as on Sharpeville Day when police opened fire on a funeral procession and killed 20 people. The government declared a State of Emergency in the region in July and emergency regulations stayed in place throughout the country until 1990.

The state of emergency was oppressive to those living in Port Elizabeth townships. Curfews kept residents restricted in the evenings with stiff penalties and dangerous consequences for those who defied them, and police were given greater powers of arrest. For a long time, no schools were operating and few students were able to write exams. Students and workers were at the forefront of resistance in the area and revolts spread around the Eastern Cape, with Port Elizabeth described as a "war zone." Barbed wire separated New Brighton from Kwazakhele, which was further separated by barbed wire from the north side of Red Location. Township dwellers were forced to use one entrance in and out of Kwazakhele, which was a border gate surrounded by tanks and soldiers at Maqanda. Msila recalls being stopped for over two hours at this entrance while soldiers carefully studied a novel by Nigerian author Chinua Achebe that he was carrying in his pocket.[87] A rival resistance group, the Azanian People's Organization (AZAPO), had also formed in the 1980s, and conflict between AZAPO and the UDF heightened tension in the Eastern Cape, with many suspicious that a government "Third Force" was fueling the division. Locals reported witnessing collaborators posing as AZAPO members climbing out of police casspirs (mine-resistant ambush protected tanks) at key areas in the townships.[88] The conflict and military oppression in the townships seemed to only increase resistance, however. Stayaways were a constant feature of the mid-1980s in the Eastern Cape, as well as "black weekends" when black townspeople refused to buy from white-owned businesses and would strike the following Monday. A resident of Red Location in New Brighton remembered that people in his township had become militant and politicized: "They felt oppressed. . . . It was easy to organize them in committees because they were already in blocks . . . to promise them that you would liberate them was a huge priority."[89]

PEBCO in Port Elizabeth represented one of the organizations in the Eastern Cape that united workers, originally in response to rent increases. It soon expanded its aims to promote equal rights, protest discriminatory laws, and included the long-term objective of creating one municipality for all of the city, rejecting the system based on separation by race. Heading up boycotts and stayaways during the States of Emergency of the 1980s, PEBCO's leaders were many times detained by government forces, and the organization's influence became so powerful that the South African government was temporarily forced to remove its police force and the South African Defense Force (SADF) from the townships. Activists Sipho Hashe, Qaqawuli Godolozi and Champion Galela, known as the "PEBCO Three," disappeared from the Port Elizabeth airport and it was later revealed that they had been abducted by a government death squad and burned to death, their ashes scattered in the Fish River.[90] The government launched crackdowns on township leaders at the end of 1986, including those in Red Location, detaining street committee members and imprisoning close to 1,000 residents by January 1987, which left PEBCO momentarily crippled by loss of leadership. The organization also struggled in its dual role of pursuing civic and political aims; attempting to address local grievances while also answering the ANC's call for "a people's war" against apartheid. One activist noted, "You found a lot of sloganeering and freedom singing at rallies which later chased away the very people who should attend PEBCO rallies—the older people who occupy houses, the tenants."[91]

PEBCO's support reflected the collective anger directed against those officials forming Black Local Authorities (BLAs) seen as municipal puppets controlled by the white establishment. Protestors burned the houses of these local councilors and many of them faced intimidation and violence. KwaNobuhle Community Council member Thamsanqa Kinikini along with his son and two nephews were killed and set alight by a crowed of angry protesters while hiding out in the mortuary where they worked. The crowd then turned on two employees of a successful businessman who became the first victims of "necklacing," a form of reprisal that involved placing a burning tire on the neck of the targeted "collaborator."[92] The MK leader Chris Hani explained and, to a certain degree, defended the use of necklacing in the ANC publication Sechaba: "The necklace was a weapon devised by the oppressed themselves to remove this cancer [black agents for the government] from our society, the cancer of collaboration of the puppets. It is not a weapon of the ANC. It is a weapon of the masses themselves to cleanse the townships from the very disruptive and even lethal activities of the puppets and collaborators." Making the country ungovernable using these extreme methods, Hani warned, however, required a certain amount of caution as apartheid authorities could use the same methods through provocateurs against activists: "We have our own revolutionary methods of dealing with collaborators, the methods of the ANC. But I refuse to condemn our people when they mete out their own traditional forms of justice to those who collaborate. . . . Why should they be cool as icebergs, when they are being killed every day?"[93]

Msila describes the level of radicalization among the youth in Port Elizabeth that invoked fear among a number of those in the townships, as some of these newly politicized youths "fell victims to their fury when they chased counterrevolutionaries." According to Msila, those who broke boycotts were often made to eat soap or drink fish oil, and he observes, "The protracted conflict between the system and the youth resulted in violent young people." But, to Msila, like Hani and others, the violence on the part of the youth was perceived as legitimate, based on their treatment by the state: "The young people in Port Elizabeth's township [New Brighton] had an indomitable spirit. Despite the repressive power of the apartheid police, they were determined to continue the struggle . . . young people were intent on taking over power and the streets in the black townships reflected this as tires burnt in every street and freedom songs reverberated in every corner of the location."[94]

Through revival of the importance of authentic culture during the Black Consciousness era and in the creation of the Amandla Cultural Ensemble and the push to unite cultural workers with labor in South Africa, the ANC in exile and operating underground in South Africa, along with the UDF, deliberately harnessed the arts to the movement in the 1980s. This decade represented the coming together of different elements, styles, rhythms, lyrics, music, performance and spoken word into one loud and defiant message of resistance and liberation. The unified sound would act as accompaniment to marches, boycotts, strikes, funerals and eruptions of violence, while increasingly echoing overseas with benefit concerts against apartheid and campaigns in solidarity with the movement. South African authorities recognized the danger of the cultural aspect to resistance and began to specifically target performers and "cultural workers" in censorship, raids, and crackdowns. Funerals became important venues for performance and expression in the Eastern Cape, as well as throughout South Africa, as these were harder for the state to suppress. According to one activist, "The government would say, OK, you can have a funeral—one of the few ways that blacks could come together in public—but you cannot have any inflammatory symbolic communication. So the speech-makers would hire a band and would say their political speeches to music, usually just a riff being played over and over in the background."[95]

Performance continued to be dangerous for artists within South Africa in the 1980s, specifically in the Eastern Cape where conflict was increasingly rife and government security forces exercised censorship and often violent intimidation. To protect himself, as mentioned earlier, Pat Matshikiza changed his name and for twenty years retreated into the safe but tedious work of playing music in hotel lounges. He was sent by a Sun Hotels manager to work in Venda and then to the Eastern Cape hotel Amatolo Sun in Bhisho. It was a tough time for Matshikiza:

> I was very, very depressed and I was rebellious. . . . What I didn't like about the job was I couldn't play anything but cocktail music, no jazz, and the people were a little unfriendly. When they walked in, they always told the waitress: don't put us near the piano; we don't want that noise. And that hurt me a lot. . . . Funny enough, after a couple of weeks, some of those people changed. They'd say, "we've come to listen to you." . . . Twenty years playing in hotels, and all that time I was either a prisoner or a pet.[96]

Cultural resistance and artistic expression, always strong among communities in the Eastern Cape, meanwhile coalesced within this region and spread to other parts of the country and abroad as the cultural boycott caused musicians and performers to concentrate on homegrown creations and local audiences. Music incorporating performers' roots, for example, challenged homeland policies by mixing historical and ethnic influences with cosmopolitan sounds, and musicians fought to hold on to these roots without giving in to the false identities of the Bantustan system or cooperation with the façade of independent nations within South Africa. Johnny Dyani was one of the first to absorb this roots music into the modern sound while in exile, and fellow exiled South African musician Abdullah Ibrahim (formerly Dollar Brand) collaborated with Dyani on this new sound, recognizing its liberating influence and observing that it created new avenues of expression: "With Johnny, I touched the Xhosa tradition, and it's massive what you can do with it! We experienced it and expanded on it and it opened a freedom for us. It allows you space."[97]

In 1983 Dyani revealed his new concept of music called *sk'enke* (*tsotsitaal*—slang for "communal sharing"). He specified that it was not *kwela*, not *mbaqanga*, but a combination of folk, jazz, reggae, and punk "to mix everything," bringing more freedom of performance and greater improvisation."[98] Jazz music was used during this time both inside and outside South Africa as a form of protest, but Dyani refused to call his music jazz, preferring to label it as folk and seeing it as a more authentic form of resistance. Up until his untimely death while performing in 1986, Dyani continued to hold on to the music of his Xhosa background; the sounds and rhythms he had used as a child playing on street corners in East London. He incorporated those sounds in a unique form of music that was part of the cultural liberation movement against apartheid. In a tribute to Dyani, the activist Pallo Jordan described the musician's significance to the struggle: "In his music one can hear the rhythms of protest, so eloquently expressed in the work songs of the widow of the reserves, one could be swept up in the spirit of defiance and revolt conveyed in the surging freedom songs. But above all, his music resounded of our musical traditions."[99] Other musicians also focused on the authentic aspects of their culture as part of the struggle. The marimba band Amampondo, for example, resurrected historical sounds specific to the amaXhosa, mixing Western instrumentation with local elements such as kudu horns and Chopi xylophones. The band's sound represented a combination of pan-African influences and styles specific to the amaXhosa to create music that inspired those involved in resistance. The group performed their first concert in Cape Town in 1980 for striking meat workers.[100]

Similar to the Black Consciousness movement in the 1970s, the ANC, in its deliberate strategy of incorporating cultural workers as part of the movement against apartheid in the 1980s, became increasingly intolerant of theater that appeared to only entertain and evaded the topic of oppression, or that challenged the strategies of resistance. With the rise of state-sponsored and increasingly vicious violence against anyone involved in resistance, and the fierce response and suspicion of suspected collaborators on the part of the youth, the 1980s had become a time of intense scrutiny of loyalties and this situation played out in cultural as well as political and social arenas. To the ANC, performance was just as crucial in terms of the struggle as guerilla warfare and political action, and, because the stakes were high, the emphasis had to be on revolution: "Mass student and labour upsurges go hand in hand [with] the kind of theatre that finds its inspiration in the struggle of the people," including performance at funerals and "in the besieged concentration camps euphemistically called locations." Everything that brought black people together was now a political statement.[101] In 1986, the ANC declared that the cultural work of activists in South Africa had become a necessary component of political consciousness: "The songs, the chants, the slogans; the poems, short stories and novels that our writers pen at tremendous risk to themselves—all these are rocks of the foundation of our freedom."[102]

Kente, meanwhile, with two plays of the late 1970s, *Can You Take It?* and *Laduma* (It Thundered), seemed to retreat in the 1980s into safe apolitical township theater, addressing either personal domestic problems of families or, in the case of *Laduma*, appearing to criticize the excesses of resistance.[103] The ANC, taking note of this retreat, singled out Kente as well as Fugard with often scathing criticism. In denouncing the "Jim Comes to Jo'burg" and "Crime Does Not Pay" type of plays, an editorial on "Popular Theatre and Struggle" in *Rixaka* described stereotypes in these plays that included a church or funeral scene with "a highly spirited and lecherous *umfundisi* (priest), a jail scene depicting a *ja bass* servile African policeman who brutalized the convicts and, for laughs presumably, the inevitable shebeen 'queen' involved in gossip and *tsotsitaal* sequences with her hipster patrons." The piece went on to attack Kente as the "Crown Prince" of this type of theater: "a shrewd businessman-cum-playwright who is able to cash in on this genre, milking unsuspecting patrons to the point of overly identifying with the status quo."[104] Kente's plays were denounced as contrived and "screamingly unfunny," and, while acknowledging that these plays often exposed injustice in South Africa, his critics saw them as offering no direction in terms of fighting back.[105] Similarly, in addressing the work of Athol Fugard, while the ANC recognized the importance of the plays of Fugard's Serpent Players, such as *Sizwe Banzi is Dead* and *The Island*, it still put the playwright's work in the category of theater by white liberals who could not fully understand the experiences of black people, did not get at the root of oppression and destitution, and, like Kente's work, seemed to offer no solutions. Athol's plays were instead seen more as tailored to be a success on Broadway "and catapult its protagonists into the world of stardom."[106]

The cultural workers the ANC championed during these more radical times were those who often played a double role as soldier and performance activist. Eastern Cape activist Nomokhosi Mini, the daughter of Vuyisile Mini, was one such figure. Also known as Mary Thabethe or Rally, Nomokhosi was born in Port Elizabeth in 1958, attending school in New Brighton and getting arrested in 1977 for demonstrating against Bantu education. During her arrest, she and other students were beaten at New Brighton police station with batons and sjamboks (leather whips), an experience that further radicalized her and led her to join the Black Consciousness–inspired group the South African Students Movement (SASM). Mini was then detained under the Suppression of Terrorism Act and imprisoned for fourteen days. After her release she went into exile and joined the ANC, becoming a founding member of the Amandla Cultural Ensemble in 1979. She was also put in charge of the political affairs of the women's section of the ensemble. As a soldier, Mini led in the camps as commander and commissar, with duties that included driving tanks, shooting bazookas, and engineering work. After surviving a SADF attack in March 1985 on Novo Catengue camp in Angola, Mini along with five fellow ANC activists were killed by the SADF in Maseru in Lesotho the following December. Described by fellow comrade and close friend Zou Kota-Fredericks as "disciplined, strong, and dedicated," Mini was also apparently good-humored and high-spirited, planning a housewarming party on the day she died. The ANC compared the circumstances of her life and death to that of her father: withstanding police torture in the same manner as Vuyisile Mini, and "as [Vuyisile] Mini had sung for freedom to the gallows, so had Nomkhosi to her death."[107]

In 1980, when Kaiser Mathanzima still enjoyed considerable power in Transkei but chafed under the criticism from and popularity of Chief Sabatha Dalindyebo, he used his power to have Dalindyebo charged under Transkei's Public Security Act and Constitution Act which outlawed any insults to the dignity and injury to the reputation of the State President. As mentioned earlier, Dalindyebo was forced into exile in Zambia and his advocates among the *iimbongi* consequently faced a dilemma caused by the Public Security Act. They could continue to criticize chiefs and heads of state such as Mathanzima, hoping for leniency in their own homeland, but the fate of Dalindyebo demonstrated their position to be risky. When Dalindyebo went on trial in 1979, the *imbongi* Mncedisi Qangule drew a large crowd of protesters outside the courthouse as he denounced the proceedings. Warned by the Mthatha police to be quiet, Qangule returned the next day, again with a crowd of people, running "a commentary of the circumstances of the King's arrest, saying the incident marked the beginning of the end for peace in Transkei." Qangule continued to be harassed and was again arrested and detained in the middle of a performance at St. John's College in Mthatha. According to Qangule, "At the offices of the security police I was warned not to sing praises any more. When I was locked into my cell at the Wellington Prison, I continued singing praises about my detention. This precious talent is bestowed on me by God. Nobody can arrogate to himself the dubious authority of telling me not to use it."[108]

The position for *iimbongi* was, thus, precarious in the 1980s in the face of violent state suppression, on the one hand, and increased suspicion among those involved in resistance of anything smacking of collaboration. If an *imbongi* merely participated in events and ceremonies involving homeland leaders he might be criticized for providing an air of legitimacy to the proceedings; as illustrated by Sizwe Mayoli's poem *Inkululeko yase Sieskei*, which criticized the celebration of "independence" of the homeland of Ciskei:

> An imbongi
> With his forgotten name praised the head of the state
> For leading people to the unknown.[109]

Because of these circumstances, Dalindyebo's main advocate among *iimbongi* Mbutuma ended up changing loyalties, getting himself elected as a member of parliament in Mathanzima's party. When Opland queried Mbutuma on this change, the *imbongi* defended his actions as the best method of helping people in his district. His true feelings about Mathanzima were unaltered, and so he played a double game, working within the system and suppressing his own criticism of the Transkei president by ceasing to perform *izibongo*. The situation began to change, however, as the actions of Kaiser Mathanzima and his brother George became more erratic and corrupt, and as Kaiser Mathanzima began losing support among the Transkei Defense Force and among the black bourgeoisie.

As cultural activists stepped up the pressure of protest in the 1980s, *iimbongi* such as Yali-Manisi incorporated into their poetry the message espoused by the UDF of all the oppressed coming together in resistance. In 1983, Manisi published the epic poem *Imfazwe ka Mlanjeni* (The War of Mlanjeni) that echoed S. E. K. Mqhayi's *Umhlekazi uHintsa* of 1937, a poem calling for the erection of a memorial to Hintsa, Paramount Chief of Gcaleka, killed by British soldiers in the War of 1834–35. Manisi's poem was 55 pages and written as if performed by an *imbongi*, arousing emotion and making a call to action. Like many *izibongo*, it connected the crimes of the past, particularly of stealing land from chiefs and people of South Africa, to a call for justice in the present, and in the language of the present, the poem placed emphasis on unity:

> *Azi xa kunje nje nje ngoku*
> *Kothi kuphi kube kuyini na?*
> *... Masiwalahl' onke la manyingilili*
> *Siphuthum' ukulunga nokulungisa,*
> *... Nditsho kambe ndingxwelerhekile*
> *Kuba kunje nje nje namhlanje ...*
> *Lasikhonkxa sonke ngekhonkc' elinye,*
> *Akwaba mxhosa, mZulu namSuthu;*
> *Silibele kukwabana nj'iinkomozimkile!*
> *Huntshu-u!*

> Now the state of affairs is unbearable,
> How long shall we suffer like this?
> ... let's scrap all these fads and fashions,
> and retrieve our worth and justice ...

> I say this with aching heart,
> for this is the state of affairs today . . .
> all of us chained by the very same jailer.
> There is no Xhosa, Zulu or Sotho:
> our cattle are plundered while we're busy bickering.
> Onward, onward to victory!

In this epic poem, Manisi also took note of the increased conflict, tension, and violence in his country and warned of a reckoning:

> *Lumka! udlala ngenj' ilele nje,*
> *Yoz' ivuk' ikutye ngeny' imini!*
>
> Watch out, if you keep on teasing a sleeping dog,
> It will one day rise and bite you.[110]

Prominent *iimbongi* such as Manisi had often been confident in speaking their truth through praise poems since this was a necessary part of their profession, but the Black Consciousness movement had provided more impetus to direct confrontation, with black activists holding white people's feet to the fire, and increased international attention in the 1980s gave black performers from South Africa a wider platform to share their message of resistance. When English-speaking faculty at Rhodes University in Grahamstown made a point of opposing government policy, Manisi used his art to remind them that they were equally culpable, inviting them to "cross the river" into townships and meet the black population living in "uncongenial dark houses."[111] At a conference in Berlin in 1985, a European academic questioned Manisi on the real extent of his improvisation and spontaneity since he had been given several days to think about the topic of his *izibongo*. Manisi gave a swift and spontaneous response:

> So then,
> Bull that eats other bulls, mumbling the while,
> You speak of the Xhosa and Zulu languages:
> What the hell do you know of Zulu and Xhosa?
> Where do you come from? Mind your own business:
> Leave the Xhosa and Zulu alone
> To tend their Nguni languages,
> For this country's in a mess . . .
> The English ground us underfoot,
> The Boers blunted our horns,
> The French were frosty,
> And today the Germans gawk at us.

Manisi then returned to his seat amid loud applause.[112]

International sanctions against South Africa and disinvestment in the 1980s included cultural boycotts and began to focus specifically on ending apartheid. In 1981 the Association of Actors and Artists of America, which combined all major performers' unions, voted unanimously to not perform in South Africa. The boycotts caused some controversy, but were largely supported by resistance movements as, despite the damage felt by black workers and performers, they provided definite leverage against industries, corporations, and the government. The argument that black people would suffer the most was most often put forward by white people and South African authorities, and proponents of this argument were firmly challenged on their sincerity by voices in the resistance movement. "Since when," asked the ANC leadership in exile, "have the masters become so magnanimous that they spend sleepless nights agonizing over our welfare?"[113]

Manisi took note of this increased attention abroad and incorporated messages to the international community in his performances at conferences in Europe and the United States:

> . . . be sure to tell Reagan
> we're trusting him
> Though we haven't seen anything yet.[114]

The reference was to U.S. President Ronald Reagan's reluctance to endorse sanctions and disinvestment against South Africa. Performing as a Fulbright Scholar at a conference at Columbia University in 1988, Manisi also made a direct plea to the U.S. academics to promote education for his people:

> Support us men, we're in trouble,
> please lend us support
> to free the black in South Africa, please lend us support
> to inflame the minds
> of South Africa's blacks . . .[115]

Manisi put his message more bluntly when asked by an American student what he thought about the U.S. response to the struggle in South Africa: "Well, so far I would say Americans are not actually acting to support the struggle in South Africa. . . . We don't invite Americans to go and fight against South African authorities, but what we need is their education system to be exposed to our people so that they must have the knowledge the white man is getting in South Africa. So in other words I blame Americans for failing to help the black man in South Africa."[116]

It was during the 1980s that the military wing of the ANC Mkonto we Sizwe (MK) gained a foothold in Transkei through the leadership of Chris Hani. A former student at Lovedale and Fort Hare, Hani had joined the ANC in 1962, his family having been at odds with Mathanzima for quite a long time. Mathanzima tried to revoke Hani's scholarship to Fort Hare in the 1950s, citing Hani's father's opposition to the Bantu Authorities and the early politicization of Hani, warning: "We cannot sharpen that axe that will fall on our necks."[117] With the banning of the ANC in 1964, Hani went into exile and became a guerilla, featuring prominently in the Wankie (Hwange) Campaign in Rhodesia (Zimbabwe) in 1967. After being arrested and tortured in Lesotho by that country's security police, Hani was released through the help of the ANC, and in the 1970s rose to the rank of Army Commissar and became a member of the ANC National Executive Committee. Since Lesotho bordered Transkei, Hani soon became influential in establishing a channel into Transkei and ultimately into South Africa. The underground movement in Transkei incorporated numerous activists including former students from places such as Fort Hare and St. Johns College in Mthatha. ANC cells in Transkei had been run in the 1970s by Tata James "Castro" Kati, a former Robben Island prisoner who was part of the Defiance Campaign in the 1950s and worked with the MK underground in Port Elizabeth with Govan Mbeki. After serving his time, Kati was deported to Transkei where he worked in Mthatha district setting up stores of weapons and places of refuge for activists and guerillas. In 1981, the South African security police disrupted Kati's web of comrades, capturing and torturing Kati and other leaders in East London. Kati's wife died while he was in prison, and the attendance at her funeral of nearly 2,000 people demonstrated the level of support for resistance within Transkei. Dalindyebo helped pay for the funeral with money smuggled in from Zambia.[118]

With Kati imprisoned, the ANC underground was revived by Hani mainly through activists at the newly created University of Transkei (UNITRA). The ANC and MK made contact through student connections with Lesotho, and students increasingly organized on the campus of the university. UNITRA was ostensibly an institution controlled and promoted by Mathanizima, with many in the university administration connected to South Africa's government and corporations, but the students and a good number of the lecturers were part of the resistance movement. By the end of the 1980s, the majority of them were members of the ANC or PAC, even before these organizations were unbanned.[119]

MK infiltration of Transkei increased in the 1980s under Hani's leadership. In June 1985 the Mthatha fuel depot was bombed along with the municipal water pipelines and an electricity station. The depot burned throughout the day causing an intense petrol shortage, and the city went without electricity for several days. Security forces targeted Bathandwa Ndondo, a student activist who had been expelled from UNITRA the previous year and had continued as an activist while working for the Health Care Trust in Cala. The Transkei police along with a South African police unit arrested and shot him outside his home on September 4, claiming later that he had been involved in the fuel depot bombings. It was subsequently determined that the explosions had, in fact, been engineered by MK forces under the leadership of Dumisani Mafu and were not connected to Ndondo.[120] Ndondo, however, had become a prominent figure among students at UNITRA, and remained so even after his expulsion. According to Vangeli Gamede who was in the graduate program reading history at UNITRA in the late 1980s, the students spoke often of Ndondo: "When I arrived . . . the name of Ndondo would leave their mouths and they would quote him [because] he was very active in fighting against the Bantustans." Gamede and his fellow students held the belief that the Mathanzimas were really behind the killing of Ndondo as they felt threatened by his effect on the youth.[121] Ndondo's death only served to increase defiance among students, however, and the ANC and PAC continued to exert strong influence at UNITRA. Although the majority of students and faculty tended to lean towards the ANC, Gamede recalls a predominance of loyalty in the history department for the PAC, which had a reputation for attracting intellectuals at the university: "People I became close to were great thinkers at that time." Strikes and demonstrations marked by freedom songs continually erupted at the university and in Mthatha, spilling out into Butterworth and other nearby towns throughout the 1980s. Says Gamede, "I don't remember a single year when the university didn't close down and we would be chased out of residences."[122]

The tension between those categorized as spies and the revolutionary forces was felt among the students at UNITRA and throughout the Eastern Cape, and the killing of Ndondo illustrates the extent and increasing normality of extra-judicial killing being carried out by South African forces in that region, including in Transkei with the aid of Mathanzima. The violent actions of "third force" undercover government agents assisted by "askaris" (black policemen and informants) were further exposed in the killing of "The Cradock Four"—Matthew Goniwe, Fort Calata, Sparrow Mkhonto and Sicelo Mhlauli—in June 1985. Goniwe and Calata were particularly active in building local resistance. Goniwe had been imprisoned in Transkei for four years under the suppression of communism act and later became a rural organizer for the UDF. Calata's grandfather was Secretary-General of the ANC in the 1930s and 1940s, and one of those accused in the Treason Trial of the 1950s. Fort Calata campaigned on behalf of Goniwe when the latter was under pressure from the government for his community activism and the two became close friends and political comrades. Mkhonto was active in the railway union and the Cradock Residents Association (CRADORA), and Mhlauli had left Ciskei after authorities there kept harassing him, eventually also becoming active in the UDF. Goniwe, Calata, and Mkhonto had been returning to Cradock from a UDF meeting in Port Elizabeth when they were set upon along with Mhlauli. The burned and mutilated bodies of the four men were subsequently found four days later and, although the government initially proclaimed their deaths to be the result of actions by "unknown persons," evidence was eventually uncovered of their murder being carried out by state-sponsored death squads. President P. W. Botha responded to the deaths and the subsequent funeral with a declaration of a state of emergency in the Eastern Cape in 1985, but the increased presence of the "Third Force," as the suspected undercover activities of the government were called, seemed to only fuel MK activity in Transkei and the Eastern Cape, which carried on through the mid-1980s. In 1986, bombings linked to the MK occurred at Cala Post Office and the Wild Coast Casino in Eastern Mpondoland (Fort Hare graduate Pumzile Mayaphi was involved in the latter bombing), and in the same year the MK attacked the Mthatha police station.

The MK was intent in the 1980s on connecting their armed struggle to the ANC in the minds of the populace and its members put greater emphasis on the idea of a "people's army," creating a populist element reflected in the songs they sang. The anthem of the MK, *Hamba Kahle mKhonto,* emphasized the intensity of the conflict and the violence felt to be necessary to put an end to the apartheid system in South Africa, especially in combatting state-sponsored violence and extra-judicial killings:

> *Hamba kahle mkhonto.*
> *Wemkhonto*
> *Mkhonto wesizwe*
> *Thina Bantu bomkhonto siz 'misele*
> *Ukuwabulala*
> *Wona lamabhulu*
>
> Safe journey spear
> Yes spear
> Spear of the nation
> We, the members of Umkhonto are determined
> To kill
> These Boers

Training, keeping up morale, and underground activity were marked by songs which included those about MK's actions, ambition, and unity:

> We are going there, the Umkhonto boys have arrived.
> We are going there. Hayi, Hayi. We are going forward.
> Don't be worried, the boys know their job.
> Let Africa return

Young comrades in the Eastern Cape involved in violent resistance were known as *Amabutho* and these youths sang songs that expressed solidarity with MK: "We won't abandon Umkhonto we Sizwe/These Boer blood-suckers won't get us." *Amabutho* also had specific songs that illustrated their awareness of stepped-up violence on the part of the SADF and that marked their own determination:

> The Boer is oppressing us.
> The SADF
> is shooting us like animals.
> Kill the Boers.[123]

Protesters would also address those fighting in exile in their songs or those who had died in the struggle, beginning a phrase with "Hey, guerilla, *nyamazani*" then following it with names; for example, "Hey, Mandela," or "Hey, Hani." *Nyamazani* means a wild animal in isiXhosa, and in this context it became a metaphor for a soldier hiding, fighting and running for his life to bring down or escape the enemy.[124]

In the late 1980s, as the South African government found itself wrestling with violent conflict, a floundering economy, and international pressure, it also faced the unraveling of its homeland system. The era of the Mathanzimas began to confront an increasingly rocky future, with rising support for the ANC and PAC, ironically, among the newly created black middle class that had enjoyed a certain amount of economic flexibility within the confines of the homeland system. With the impending coup that would bring ANC-sympathizer Major-General Bantu Holomisa to power in Transkei, and with the rapid changes moving towards the demise of the apartheid system that occurred throughout the Eastern Cape and South Africa as a whole at the end of the 1980s and early 1990s, cultural expression took on a new impetus, focusing on a liberated South Africa that increasingly seemed more possible but not achievable without continued intense struggle.

NOTES

1. Steve Biko, Interview by Gail M. Gerhart, October 24, 1972, Steve Biko Centre Archives, King William's Town, South Africa.
2. Donald Woods, *Biko* (New York: Holt, 1991), 97.

3. Mbulelo Vizikhungo Mzamane, "The Impact of Black Consciousness on Culture," in *Bounds of possibility: The Legacy of Steve Biko and Black Consciousness*, N. Barney Pityana, Manphela Ramphele, Malusi Mpumlwana, and Lindy Wilson, eds. (Cape Town: Zed Books, 1992), 185.

4. Mzamane, "The Impact of Black Consciousness on Culture," 193.

5. Barney Pityana, "Power and Change in South Africa," in *Student Perspectives on South Africa*, eds. H. W. van der Merwe and David Walsh (Cape Town: David Philip, 1972), 178.

6. Frantz Fanon, *The Wretched of the Earth* (New York: Grove Press, 1963), 160.

7. Steve Biko, "Black consciousness and the quest for true humanity," address given to a Black Theology seminar, Pietermaritzburg, August 28, 1971, *SASO Newsletter* (September 1971).

8. Steve Biko, *I Write What I Like* (Johannesburg: Picador Africa, 2004; originally published 1978), 70.

9. Rolf Solberg, *Alternative Theater in South Africa: Talks with prime movers since the 1970s* (Pietermaritzburg: Hadeda Books, 1999), 33.

10. Zakes Mda, "Biko's Children," in *The Steve Biko Memorial Lectures 2000–2008* (Johannesburg: The Steve Biko Foundation, 2017), 25.

11. Mda, "Biko's Children," 25.

12. "The Theatre and Black South Africa," *SASO Newsletter*, June 1971 (Natal: SASO Publications), 14.

13. *SASO Newsletter*, June 1971, 4; *SASO Newsletter*, August 1971, 4.

14. Athol Fugard, John Kani, and Winston Ntshona, *Sizwe Banzi is Dead* (New York: Viking, 1976).

15. Solberg, *Alternative Theater in South Africa*, 224–28.

16. Rolf Solberg, *Bra Gib: Father of South Africa's Township Theatre* (Scottsville, South Africa: University of KwaZulu-Natal Press, 2011), 26.

17. Rolf Solberg, *Alternative Theater in South Africa*, 83–84.

18. Solberg, *Alternative Theater in South Africa*, 83–84.

19. Solberg, *Alternative Theater in South Africa*, 53.

20. Solberg, *Alternative Theater in South Africa*, 145–46.

21. Solberg, *Alternative Theater in South Africa*, 80–81.

22. Fatima Dike, *The Sacrifice of Kreli* (Alexandria, VA: Alexander Street Press, 2002), 6.

23. Solberg. *Alternative Theatre in South Africa*, 116–17.

24. David Coplan, *In Township Tonight! South Africa's Black City Music and Theatre, 2nd Edition* (Chicago: University of Chicago Press, 2007), 278.

25. E. A. Mackay, "Antigone and Orestes in the Works of Athol Fugard," *Theoria: A Journal of Studies in the Arts, Humanities and Social Sciences*, vol. LXXIV (October 1989), 34.

26. Solberg, *Alternative Theatre in South Africa*, 222–24.

27. Peter Randall, "The banning of 'Confused Mhlaba,'" *Index on Censorship*, 5:4 (1976) DOI: 10.1080/03064227608532569, 3.

28. Daniel Massey, *Under Protest: The Rise of Student Resistance at Fort Hare* (Pretoria: Unisa Press, 2010), 204–5.

29. Massey, *Under Protest*, 207.
30. *SASO Newsletter* (Natal: SASO, September 1970), 10.
31. Massey, *Under Protest*, 208.
32. Thomas G. Karis and Gail M. Gerhart, *From Protest to Challenge: A Documentary History of African Politics in South Africa, 1882–1990, Volume 5, Nadir and Resurgence, 1964–1979* (Bloomington IN: Indiana University Press, 1997), 497–99.
33. Karis and Gerhart, *From Protest to Challenge*, 499.
34. Jerry Modisane, "Why I walked off Fort Hare in protest," *SASO Newsletter* (May 1972), 17.
35. Karis and Gerhart, *From Protest to Challenge*, 531–33.
36. Massey, *Under Protest*, 221.
37. Massey, *Under Protest*, 224.
38. Massey, *Under Protest*, 226.
39. Vuyisile Msila, *A Place to Live: Red Location and Its History from 1903 to 2013* (Stellenbosch: Sun Press, 2014), 206.
40. Msila, *A Place to Live*, 206.
41. Gwen Ansell, *Soweto Blues: Jazz, Popular Music and Politics in South Africa*, (New York: Continuum, 2004), 163.
42. Msila, *A Place to Live*, 208.
43. Nelson Mandela, *Long Walk to Freedom* (New York: Little, Brown and Company, 1994), 421.
44. Msila, *A Place to Live*, 209.
45. Gwen Ansell, *Soweto Blues*, 149.
46. Sam Mathe, "Pioneer jazzman 'Bra Pat,' the legend," *Sunday Independent*, January 4, 2015.
47. Ansell, *Soweto Blues*, 156.
48. Ansell, *Soweto Blues*, 172.
49. Mathe, "Pioneer jazzman 'Bra Pat,' the legend."
50. Msila, *A Place to Live*, 225; Miriam Makeba—"*Khawuleza*," https://www.youtube.com/watch?v=Fqdcz0eYLSQ. Translation by Msila.
51. Pallo Jordan, "Johnny Dyani: A Portrait," *Rixaka: Cultural Journal of the African National Congress*, No. 4 (1988).
52. Lars Rasmussen, "When Man and Bass Became One: Johnny Dyani 1947–1986," in *Mbizo—A Book About Johnny Dyani*, ed. Lars Rasmussen (Copenhagen: The Booktrader, 2003), 10.
53. Lars Rasmussen, *Mbizo—A Book About Johnny Dyani*, 85.
54. Nick Mencia, "Biography of Mtutuzeli Dudu Pukwana," *South African History Online*. https://www.sahistory.org.za/article/biography-mtutuzeli-dudu-pukwana-nick-mencia.
55. Lestie Hughes, "Patrick Pasha," in *Generations of Jazz—At the Red Location Museum*, ed. Diane Thram (Exhibition Catalogue, Grahamstown: International Library of African Music, 2013), 34.
56. Ansell, *Soweto Blues*, 176.
57. Ansell, *Soweto Blues*, 165.

58. Brett Pyper, "A photo essay for Lulu Gontsana (1960–2005): South Africa's house drummer," *Generations of Jazz*, 45–48; Ansell, *Soweto Blues,* 177.

59. *Women Marching into the 21st Century: Wathint' Abafazi, Wathint' Imbokodo* (Cape Town: Human Sciences Research Council Press, 2000), 144; Harold Scheub, *The Xhosa Ntsomi* (Oxford: Clarendon, 1975), 16.

60. *Women Marching into the 21st Century*, 169; Diane Thram, "New Brighton's Vibrant Female Vocalists," in *Generations of Jazz*, 36–39.

61. *S'Ketch*, Winter 1975, cited in Coplan, *In Township Tonight!* 26.

62. Mzamane, "The Impact of Black Consciousness on Culture," 185.

63. Tshokolo wa Molakong, "The curtain rises again for Gibson Kente," *True Love and Family* (August 1993), cited in Solberg, *Bra Gib*, 34.

64. Kenneth Chikanga, "Theatrical tour de force," *Citizen*, (February 17, 2001).

65. Solberg, *Bra Gib*, 40.

66. *SASO Newsletter* (June 1971), 11.

67. Mandela, *Long Walk to Freedom,* 419–20.

68. Mandela, *Long Walk to Freedom,* 441.

69. Deirdre Doris Hansen, "The Music of the Xhosa-Speaking People," Doctoral Dissertation (University of Witwatersrand, 1981), xx–xxii.

70. Hansen, "The Music of the Xhosa-Speaking People," xxxii–xxxiii. In his work on *iintsomi* performances in Transkei and the KwaZulu-Natal region, Harold Scheub had conducted all of his research on foot, without translators or interpreters: "I found early that such independence was invaluable to the success of the project." This was before Transkei became diplomatically separated from the Republic, which probably made a difference, but his method of research also meant that he was able to avoid administration in the region (Scheub, *The Xhosa Ntsomi,* 4).

71. Jeff Opland, *The Dassie and the Hunter: A South African Meeting* (Scottsville, South Africa: University of KwaZulu-Natal Press, 2005), 192–93. Much of the information in this section on *iimbongi* and Transkei is from this valuable memoir by Opland describing the history of his relationship with David Yali-Manisi from the 1970s to the 1990s.

72. Opland, *The Dassie and the Hunter*, 141–43.

73. Opland, *The Dassie and the Hunter,* 145.

74. Opland, *The Dassie and the Hunter,* 149.

75. Opland, *The Dassie and the Hunter,* 158.

76. Mandela, *Long Walk to Freedom,* 441.

77. Opland, *The Dassie and the Hunter,* 157–61; 165.

78. *Sechaba*, vol. 13, No. 3 (March 1979), 2.

79. For more details on Transkei and Ciskei in the 1980s, see Jeff Peires, "The Implosion of Transkei and Ciskei," *African Affairs*, Vol. 91, No. 364 (July 1992), 365–87.

80. Luvuyo Dontsa, "Performing Arts and Politics in South Africa," paper presented at the International Library of African Music's 6th Symposium (1987).

81. A. T. Wainwright, "The Praises of Xhosa Mineworkers," M.A. Thesis (University of South Africa: 1979), 156–57.

82. Sweet Food and Allied Workers Union (SFAWU) AGM, Edendale Centre, 1984, in Ari Sitas, ed., *Black Mamba Rising: South African Worker Poets in Struggle* (Worker Resistance and Culture Publications, Durban: University of Natal, 1986), 9–12.

83. *Rixaka*, no. 1 (ANC: 1985), 16.

84. *Rixaka*, No. 1, 17–18.

85. "It should be said that the first successes of the group derived more from the excellence of their message and material than from their skill as performers . . . [but] passionate political commitment could often be more effective than the impersonal polish of professional performance." *Sechaba*, vol. 11, 3rd Quarter (1977), 43.

86. Shirli Gilbert, "Singing Against Apartheid: ANC Cultural Groups and the International Anti-Apartheid Struggle," *Journal of Southern African Studies*, Volume 33, No. 2 (June 2007).

87. Msila, *A Place to Live,* 219.

88. Msila, *A Place to Live,* 218.

89. Msila, *A Place to Live,* 251.

90. "Pebco Three: Bodies may have been found," *IOL* (Independent Online South Africa), July 16, 2007. https://www.iol.co.za/news/south-africa/pebco-three-bodies-may-have-been-found-362244, accessed 8/2/20.

91. Kimberly Lanegran, "Civic Associations in Transitional Local Government Structures in South Africa," *Critical Sociology* Vol. 22, 3 (October 1996), 120.

92. James Myburgh, "How the necklace was hung around Winnie's neck," *PoliticsWeb*, April 17, 2018. https://www.politicsweb.co.za/news-and-analysis/how-the-necklace-was-hung-around-winnies-neck, accessed 8/2/20.

93. "25 Years of Armed Struggle: Army Commissar Chris Hani Speaks," *Sechaba*, (December 1986), 16–18.

94. Msila, *A Place to Live,* 210–11.

95. Ansell, *Soweto Blues,* 197.

96. Ansell, *Soweto Blues,* 213.

97. Patricia Achieng Opondo, "African Music in Global Diasporic Discourse: Identity Explorations of South African Artist Johnny Mbizo Dyani," in *Music and Identity: Transformation and Negotiation*, eds. Eric Akrofi, Maria Smit, and Stig-Magnus Thorsén (Stellenbosch: Sun Press, 2007), 272.

98. Opondo, "African Music in Global Diasporic Discourse," 270.

99. Pallo Jordan, "Johnny Dyani: A Portrait," 8.

100. Ansell, *Soweto Blues,* 184.

101. Bob Mooki, "Popular Theatre and Struggle," *Rixaka*, No. 2 (1986), 7.

102. *Rixaka*, No. 3 (1986), 2.

103. Solberg, *Bra Gib*, 36–37.

104. Mooki, "Popular Theatre and Struggle," 6.

105. *Rixaka*, No. 1 (1985), 1.

106. Mookie, "Popular Theatre and Struggle," 6.

107. *Rixaka*, No. 3 (1986), 25; SABC Truth Commission Special Report, http://sabctrc.saha.org.za/victims/mini_nomkhosi_aka_mary.htm?tab=report, accessed 7-13-20; Deputy Minister of Human Settlements Honourable Zou

Kota-Fredericks memorial lecture of "Mary" Nomkhosi Mini speech, Port Elizabeth, 30 August, 2014, Republic of South Africa webpage, https://www.gov.za/deputy-minister-human-settlements-honourable-zou-kota-fredericks-memorial-lecture-%E2%80%9Cmary%E2%80%9D-nomkhosi, accessed 7-13-20.

108. *Daily Dispatch* (October 24, 1973), 3.

109. Sizwe Mayoli, "Inkululeko yase Sieskei," *Umgqala* 1: 18.

110. Jeff Opland and Pamela Maseko, editors and translators, *D. L. Yali-Manisi: Iimbali Zamanyange (Historical Poems), Opland Collection of Xhosa Literature, Volume 2* (Pietermaritzburg: University of KwaZulu-Natal Press, 2015), 181, 129.

111. Opland, *The Dassie and the Hunter*, 246.

112. Opland, *The Dassie and the Hunter*, 252.

113. *Rixaka*, No. 3 (1986), 3.

114. Opland, *The Dassie and the Hunter*, 254.

115. Opland, *The Dassie and the Hunter*, 302.

116. Opland, *The Dassie and the Hunter*, 303.

117. Magistrate, Xhalanga 242, N11/12/21, "Meeting of the Emigrant Thembuland Regional Authority,' 20 November 1969, cited in Timothy Gibbs, *Mandela's Kinsmen: Nationalist Elites & Apartheid's First Bantustan* (Rochester, NY: James Currey, 2014), 112.

118. *Daily Dispatch*, 5 October 1981; 9 December 1982, Truth and Reconciliation Commission Human Rights Violations Hearings, Kati, Eastern Cape, 1996—both cited in Gibbs, *Mandela's Kinsmen*, 117.

119. This was something I was told by a number of students and lecturers at UNITRA when I joined the faculty in 1989. It was confirmed later by former activists.

120. Truth and Reconciliation Commission Final Report, Volume 2, Chapter 5, Subsection 23, 443; Sonwabile Mancotywa, "A Revolutionary Life Cut Short: Bathandwa Ndondo Memorial Lecture," Walter Sisulu University, April 14, 2016.

121. Dr. Vangeli Gamede, Interview by author, July 20, 2020.

122. Gamede Interview.

123. Alton B. Pollard III, "Rhythms of Resistance: The Role of Freedom Song in South Africa," in *This Is How We Flow: Rhythm in Black Cultures*, ed. Angela M. S. Nelson (Columbia, SC: University of South Carolina Press, 1999), 98, 115–16. Translation by Paks Madikiza.

124. Gamede Interview.

Chapter 7

"Our Bull Has Escaped from the Pound"

1990s to the Present

In February 1990, the newly elected president of South Africa F. W. De Klerk announced the unbanning of the ANC, PAC, and SACP, and the forthcoming release of Nelson Mandela from prison. The streets in towns throughout the Eastern Cape filled with people celebrating, toyi-toyiing, and singing throughout the night. Returning to Mthatha from the celebrations in Butterworth where I was teaching for the University of Transkei (UNITRA—now Walter Sisulu University), I met with my friend and colleague Vangeli Gamede, who was at that time a graduate student at UNITRA and is now a professor at the University of KwaZulu-Natal. In our conversation about these changes, I voiced the sentiment of many white liberals that the country had finally taken a step forward. "It is not a step forward," replied Vangeli, "it is a correction of something that should never have happened in the first place."[1] In the eyes of activists in the Eastern Cape, the long period of resistance against colonialism and apartheid in the Eastern Cape and the music and *izibongo* that accompanied it could not be washed away through the public righting of a few wrongs by a regime that stayed in power. In the coming years, protest continued to apply pressure on moves towards not just correction but transformation, and were marked by violence, resistance on the part of white society to change, and songs and spoken word to fuel the final years of the anti-apartheid movement. The Eastern Cape remained at the forefront of many events that informed the narrative of apartheid's official demise, but the continued struggle with poverty and inequality also stayed particularly acute in that region and fundamental social problems remained. In the course of these developments, up through recent times, the amaXhosa maintained a strong sense of identity and worked to direct attention to their challenges.

As the violence and disruption in the Eastern Cape and throughout South Africa combined with outside pressure on the apartheid government and economy placed a tightening chokehold on the country in the late 1980s, businessmen and government officials such as De Klerk recognized that significant moves had to be made to introduce some element of calm in the situation. Nelson Mandela had already begun to negotiate with the government while still in prison in the 1980s regarding a transition away from apartheid, and one result of these discussions had been the release of Govan Mbeki in November 1987. On his release, Mbeki made clear his intention of remaining a member of the ANC and SACP and his continued support of MK as long as the ANC felt that its existence was necessary. Mbeki called on the youth to "continue with their struggle" and he came back to the Eastern Cape, settling in New Brighton in Port Elizabeth. On his return Mbeki was met by a mass of people singing *Babu uMbeki Yinkoledi* ("Father Mbeki is our leader"), and, according to the *Weekly Mail*, "all traffic laws were liberated. People hung out of the sides of fast-moving taxis, children and old women danced on the sidewalks and crowds of people toyi-toyied." The commotion accompanying Mbeki's release prompted official reaction, and led to the banning of a rally to be held for him in the Dan Qeqe Stadium, and a complaint from the Minister of Law and Order Adriaan Vlok that Mbeki would not "quietly retire." Mbeki was subsequently placed under house arrest in Port Elizabeth and prohibited from providing statements for publication.[2]

The pace of political change, however, was proceeding rapidly and repercussions were already in evidence throughout the Eastern Cape. The corruption rife among leaders in the homelands such as the Mathanzima brothers in Transkei and Charles Sebe in Ciskei fueled the existing opposition to apartheid and the Bantustan system in these regions, and the ANC, PAC, and MK operated with increased confidence among these populations. In September 1987 homeland leader George Mathanzima was overthrown by the Transkei Defence Force which proceeded to declare martial law and take control of the Transkei government. The Transkei military leader General Bantu Holomisa, who had always been sympathetic to anti-apartheid resistance and was already making contact with the ANC, went on to set up a benign dictatorship (after a brief period of control by Stella Sigcau) that created a stronger foothold for the ANC and UDF in Transkei. Holomisa first established his resistance credentials when he held a proper re-burial of fallen chief Sabatha Dalindyebo at Mbambane Great Place in October 1989. Tens of thousands came to the event and the ANC flag was flown for the first time in thirty years, while revolutionary songs and dances dominated the proceedings. Holomisa gave a speech in which he acknowledged that his government had not been democratically elected; however, he announced a potential referendum on Transkei's "independence" that would mean the region rejoining the

South African republic. Uncertain of this new leader's real intentions, the crowd's response was initially guarded, but ANC leaders encouraged those present to give Holomisa their support.[3]

After Thembu Chief Dalindyebo was deposed by K.D. Mathanzima in 1982, *imbongi* Bongani Sitole claimed that he "rolled up his blankets as there was no one worthy of praising." He remained largely silent during the next few years for fear of imprisonment, but then became excited over the leadership of Holomisa and the changes within Transkei. At Dalindyebo's re-burial Sitole spontaneously produced an *izibongo* for ANC Regional Representative and Dalindyebo family councilor A. S. Xobololo, just before Xobololo gave his speech, praising Xobololo for his efforts and connection to Dalindyebo:

> *Hamba ke Mhlekazi*
> *Sibulela ukuba sikubonile sizukulwana sikaDalindyebo*
>
> Go then, honorable one,
> We are thankful to see you, the great-grandchild of Dalindyebo,[4]

The event had apparently released Sitole from the psychological restrictions imposed by the fears of arrest by apartheid and Bantustan leaders, and Sitole began to perform praise poems that were particularly critical of K.D. Mathanzima, depicting him as an outsider who was responsible for the suffering of the ANC.[5]

People in Mthatha continued to celebrate throughout the weekend of the re-burial, and the following Monday brought one of the first tests of Holomisa's adherence to the ANC and resistance when protesters organized a march to the Transkei leader's house, demanding a change of sentence for two political prisoners facing execution for involvement in bombing casinos on the coast. In the pouring rain, masses gathered outside the gates of UNITRA as lecturers and students ran around the campus gathering supporters for the march. Two hours later a great shouting and roaring noise was heard from within the offices of the main university building and a massive crowd of people came singing and chanting up the steps of the great hall—students, schoolchildren, workers, cleaners and members of the clergy carrying banners supporting liberation and mercy for the prisoners. The gathering was marked by speeches, periodically interrupted by freedom songs and shouts of "Viva Mandela! Viva ANC! Forward Africa!" The crowd moved towards the city center continuing to sing and chant, and word came back later that the two prisoners, Ndibulele Ndzamela and Pumzile Mayapi, had been spared the death penalty through a moratorium on capital punishment.[6] It was clear that things were changing in the homeland of Transkei, and that it was moving out from under the thumb of the South African government, encouraged by the changes happening in the republic.

One of the first poems performed for Mandela after his release was *Inkunzi yakuthi eQunu iphumil'esikiti* (Our bull has escaped from the pound) by Xhosa poet L.W. M. Xozwa. The praise poem opened with a war cry—*wayekela*—which signified being in the midst of battle, and called on Mandela's people to wake up and greet the newly freed leader with open arms. Xozwa went on to name historical enemies of freedom: J. B. M. Hertzog, Jan Smuts, and the apartheid system. He also addressed women, Chief Dalindyebo, the whole South African nation, and resistance heroes Oliver Tambo and Steve Biko. The underlying message was that an "almighty" bull had been released from captivity and within the poem was a history of protest that recalled events such as the Sharpeville massacre, the Sasol bombing, violent attempts at suppression by the apartheid government, and international sanctions supported by key figures such as Archbishop Desmond Tutu. Even though Mandela technically had been freed from prison through a decision made by President De Klerk, the poem used the metaphor of a bull escaping from his compound, implying that it was the long history of resistance that had initiated this liberation, not the authority of the apartheid government.[7]

Xhosa Language Professor Peter Tshobisa Mtuze, from Middleburg in the Eastern Cape, also composed a praise poem for Mandela, *KuGqirha Nelson Rholihlahla Mandela* (To the Doctor Nelson Rholihlahla Mandela), that described the history of concerted opposition to apartheid and the release of Mandela:

> *Yalisonga layingqulana yalihamba layibholana,*
> *Isith' isemi inyaniso ayijikwa nayijele.*
>
> He then traversed the world as if it was a small ball,
> Holding on to his views which even jail could not alter.[8]

The ANC leader's release symbolized an increased momentum that was building throughout South Africa, and not long after this event Mandela came to Transkei to reunite with the region of his birth and childhood. At the tiny airport outside of Mthatha he was met by a crowd of over 3,000, and as soon as the plane was in sight, people began toyi-toyiing and ululating. Mandela emerged from the airport wearing a leopard skin and carrying a spear to reflect the importance of his heritage and connect with his people. He talked about his childhood in Transkei, becoming so moved by the moment that he paused, and the crowd responded by raising their fists. The mass rally the following day on the outskirts of Mthatha brought a crowd of over 100,000 and a resurgence of *izibongo* not seen since before the era of the Mathanzimas. People toyi-toyiied under ANC banners and all over the grounds anti-apartheid T-shirts and other regalia were on sale. Many *iimbongi* performed—mostly in English—not holding back on their expectations and expressions of their own and their people's reality. Their performances included criticism of leaders, especially U.K. Prime Minister Margaret Thatcher and U.S. President George Bush, both singled out due to their tepid responses to calls for joint action against apartheid and resistance to sanctions. Thatcher was called out as "a busy bitch" and Bush as "mafia" and the poems and chants connected these leaders with the imprisonment experienced by black people in South Africa:

> Moreover,
> I shall return,
> Behind the bars,
> Struggle inside,
> Solidarity outside,
> Margaret,
> Margaret.

The issue to these activists was maintaining solidarity on the question of sanctions outside the country while the struggle continued within South Africa.

At the rally *iimbongi* also praised the anti-apartheid leaders and celebrated their release, with special emphasis on Mandela's reunion with his people in Transkei:

> Welcome home, Walter
> Welcome home, Walter Sisulu,
> Welcome home . . .
> Welcome home, *bawo* Madiba, welcome home . . .
> The chief commander of MK
>
> *Yiza Mkhonto,*
> *Yiza Mkhonto,*
> *Amandla!*
> *Awethu*

In praising their leaders, the *iimbongi* also compared them to apartheid officials:

> He [Mandela] would see South Africa for what it could be,
> In justice and total equality . . . not power, money and personal interests.
> The world has never seen many leaders of the national party,
> More especially Verwoerd, P. W. Botha and Vorster, ever achieve such leadership,

> Instead, they drag the black struggle into the deep sea of Robben Island for life.

As Mandela came forward on the platform to speak, the crowd surged forward with more chanting and singing, and ANC "guards" dressed in brown fatigues carrying wooden replicas of guns acted as makeshift human barriers to keep people under control. Mandela spoke in both English and isiXhosa, echoing the praise of anti-apartheid resistance and ending his speech with the ANC power salute that brought a roar of response from his followers.[9]

The following months marked a tumultuous time in Transkei: there were strikes in Mthatha and Butterworth and schools were boycotted and burned. Holomisa began to distance himself from the South African government, releasing six MK leaders and unbanning the ANC and PAC during Transkei's annual "independence" celebrations. Recently freed ANC leaders such as Walter Sisulu praised the Transkei leader, as Holomisa's government initiated corruption charges against Sun International, the resort hotel chain that took advantage of the admission of gambling in the homelands to set up casinos in places like the Wild Coast in Transkei as playgrounds for wealthy whites.[10]

Gamede recalls the situation in Mthatha at that time, especially at UNITRA: "There was a lot of political activity from the side of the students and people from the outside." According to Gamede, any action demonstrating dissatisfaction with the apartheid government or officials running the university would be accompanied by songs: "Music was used to communicate oneness in fighting whatever students were fighting for." They might be focused on issues, or focused more specifically on particular officials, or even professors within the university. "Some didn't make sense at all, with just words like 'Ta-ta-ta,' but they were instilling that spirit of the toyi-toyi of the time—even if it doesn't carry any meaning and it was an energizer, and a way of intimidating those they are demonstrating against."[11]

If Nelson Mandela was regarded as the father of the ANC by the 1980s, the MK leader Chris Hani was viewed as the son, particularly in Transkei. As the MK gained a presence in Eastern Cape homeland, Hani became a prominent figure in that region, making the most of his good relationship with Holomisa and his popularity with the amaXhosa. Shawn Johnson, journalist for the *Saturday Star*, reported the near-cult status of Hani in Transkei in 1990: "On the streets of Umtata (and especially among younger men), the mention of Hani's name elicits a grin, a thumbs-up sign and, not infrequently, a loud impression of the sound of AK47 gunfire."[12] Holomisa's coup had marked the end of the personal enmity endured by Hani's family with the Transkei leadership that had existed under the Mathanzimas, and Holomisa had provided assistance for the MK training program in Uganda. Along with his revolutionary skills and agenda, Hani also brought to Transkei his love of music. He was an avid jazz fan, with a great liking for the bands Stimela, Bayate, and Sonkomoto, and his former bodyguard recalled that "he felt no shame in singing freedom songs out loud when they were all in the house 'and dancing.'"[13]

The South African government viewed Hani's presence in Transkei with alarm, since he was head of MK and had been refused indemnity from prosecution by apartheid authorities. Holomisa provided Hani access to government facilities and soon other MK fighters followed their leader to the homeland, returning to their families. Working with Holomisa, Hani used his presence in Transkei to organize pressure on the South African government yet maintain calm in the face of growing aspirations among his people. "The bantustans should not be used as a springboard to launch attacks against the apartheid regime," Hani warned, pointing out that armed resistance from the Transkei would be no match for the SADF.[14] To the South African government, however, Hani and his MK comrades' return to Transkei constituted a potential military threat, and government officials sanctioned and provided support for a coup against Holomisa. The coup was planned by the "Transkei Group" which included K.D. Mathanzima, and aimed to replace Holomisa with the former head of Transkei military intelligence Craig Duli. Holomisa undermined the attempted coup, however, by offering military protection to the South African embassy in Transkei in the event of potential disruption, to which the embassy was forced to reply that this was unnecessary. The Transkei leader went on to publicize the embassy's response, consequently denying South African forces a tangible reason to intervene. Without South African support, the coup failed and Duli was killed in the ensuing shoot-out with no chance of rescue from the SADF. De Klerk denied his government's involvement but proof emerged that all incriminating evidence had been removed by South African security forces from Duli's East London hotel.[15] The attempted coup increased Holomisa's popularity, with crowds of people pouring on to the streets to protect his regime against the rebels and against a feared invasion by South African forces. On the grounds of Mthatha Hospital, patients and staff came out of facilities to aid the Transkei Defence Force by pointing with fingers (and crutches) the direction Duli's army had taken.[16] The event fueled more singing and toyi-toyiing in Mthatha in its aftermath and highlighted the widespread support for Holomisa in Transkei, while also creating larger implications regarding the overall failure of apartheid's homeland policies.

The situation in the Eastern Cape homeland of Ciskei was very different during this time than that of Transkei. The prominent Ciskei leader Lennox Sebe attempted to create a form of local nationalism but was increasingly at odds with the rising power of trade union activists. Crowds in the town of Mdantsane singing and celebrating the release of Nelson Mandela were met with gunfire from Ciskei police with at least ten people killed, and Sebe was ousted in 1990 by Brigadier Oupa Gqozo. Gqozo initially promised reforms and an alliance with Nelson Mandela and the ANC, but moved towards dictatorship and greater connections to Inkatha Freedom Party leader Mangosuthu Buthelezi. As Gqozo lost credibility and hurt De Klerk's image through his links to South African military intelligence, the South African government began to take direct charge of Ciskei, reflecting the change in purpose of the homelands from sources of cheap labor to containment of large sections of the African population.

Hani and other anti-apartheid leaders recognized this development and organized their own resistance accordingly. In the late summer and early autumn of 1992, protesters demonstrated for several weeks in King William's Town in preparation for a rally followed by a mass march to the town of Bisho in Ciskei. Hani led the march, along with ANC executive member Ronnie Kasrils and UDF regional coordinator Steve Tshwete. The crowd swelled as it left King William's Town and marched towards the Ciskei border where, for over an hour, the demonstrators faced SADF troops and soldiers of the homeland. As they moved towards Bisho Stadium, the protestors found themselves trapped by a fence. Led by Kasrils, they crawled through a hole in the fence and toyi-toyied in front of Ciskei soldiers who responded by firing on the unarmed crowd, killing twenty-eight people and injuring 200. The demonstrators stayed put through the night while SADF soldiers arrived and attempted to break up the crowd. As anxiety grew among the protestors, Hani launched into a freedom song, and, according to fellow demonstrator Bususiwe Dingaan Stofile, "We all forgot about the SADF and chanted." The protestors sang through the night and at 5:00 a.m. they were awakened with a revolutionary song, reaching a state of calm by mid-morning.[17]

The Bisho massacre occurred during a period of breakdown of talks between the ANC and the South African government in the move towards a new dispensation and the event was instrumental in bringing the two sides back to the negotiating table. Twenty-six parties were now to be involved in the new set of agreements, including the PAC and SACP, and the following year a settlement was reached that scheduled nonracial elections for a five-year transitional government for April 27, 1994. This hopeful period of negotiations, however, was marred by a series of violent events, including the assassination of Hani on April 10, 1993. Hani had always believed that the key to political transformation was directly attacking the problem of poverty—a problem particularly severe in his own region—and the apartheid government, as viewed in retrospect, was clearly determined to maintain a great deal of economic control for the white minority even as it negotiated itself out of political power. Hani also knew that he was a particular target, informed by various sources that the South African security forces wanted his death to have a purpose and be unusual. "I think that they are calculating that if they kill me," said Hani, "the whole country might go up in flames."[18] The assassination by Janusz Waluś, an anti-communist with ties to the South African Conservative Party, took place in the driveway of Hani's home in the suburbs of Boksburg, and soon after, people gathered around his body, chanting and singing the MK song for fallen comrades, *Hamba Kahle Mkhonto, Mkonto, Mkonto we Sizwe* (Go well, Mkhonto we Sizwe). "We heard it," said Rachel Leruthla, who lived in Hani's neighborhood. "Everybody was running. Everybody was emotional. Everybody was crying. You could see it had struck everybody. . . . It was a spontaneous reaction."[19] Chris Hani's love of music and performance was honored in numerous ways after his death, including the establishment of Chris Hani Secondary School in Khayelitsha, which was designated one of ten "arts and culture" schools by the Western Cape Education department in 2006. In 2018, influenced by the hip hop style of the U.S. musical *Hamilton*, and adding its own South African flavor, the performance piece "Hani: The Legacy" celebrated the life and work of the MK leader and explored what would happen if his influences were put into practice now, ending with film footage of Hani's covered body being driven away in the immediate aftermath of his assassination.[20]

The period of transition in South Africa in the early 1990s was marked not only by a sense of urgency in protest songs as they were sung with increasing confidence and aggression at rallies and funerals, but also by the new direction of performances of *izibongo*. As noted earlier in Sitole's outburst of creativity at the Dalindyebo re-burial and the praise poems of Xozwa and Mtuze, *iimbongi* were readjusting their craft to the changing circumstances in South Africa. The Xhosa literature scholar Wandile Kuse made the point in 1988 that "we no longer live in tribal communes. The oral tradition of the old days does not fit—and can never fit—the situation of today. . . . We have in Xhosa *izibongo* an instance of a tradition undergoing the process of change."[21] As the political situation in the Eastern Cape and South Africa as a whole took on a new resolve, *iimbongi* performed oral poetry and praise songs that matched the aspirations of their public and at the same time called on their people and their leaders to address the challenges at hand. Author and community educator Astrid von Kotze noted in 1988 that workers were increasingly organizing to fight oppression through culture and putting their views into poems, plays, and songs: "They tell stories of their exploitation, they talk about their history of struggle against oppression and about their organizations and their leaders."[22] Just as they had always done, however, *iimbongi* combined historical truths and beliefs of their people and the craft of praising-singing with contemporary circumstances. Transkeian poet Alfred Qabula held on to childhood memories of the *imbongi* in his village praising the chief. He disapproved of the chiefs themselves because of what he viewed as their false position in Transkei, but he liked the poetic style of *izibongo* and adapted it to his purpose of enlightening workers and raising consciousness. At a May Day celebration in Durban in 1989, Qabula witnessed women workers singing labor songs and poets performing, and this experience moved him to come on stage to take the microphone. He began performing a rhythmic dance, dressed in old torn clothes to convey a message about poverty and the fight against capitalism. In his performance, he called out those who had not joined the struggle and criticized them for their apathy. His was a praise poem, but one focusing on anti-apartheid heroes and attacking chiefs, and his dance mirrored the toyi-toyi as he invited the audience to clap in rhythm.[23]

Imbongi David Yali-Manisi also moved away from focusing on chiefs, placing more emphasis on new leaders, unions, and power structures; for example, he reinforced the African philosophy of *ubuntu* espoused by Mandela when, in preparation for assuming power, the latter pushed for reconciliation as part of the healing process of transition:

> *Akukho mnt' ungumntu yedwa*
> *umntu ngumntu kubasebantwini*
> *ubuntu bubuntu kuba ngumntw' ebantwini.*

> No person's a person in isolation,
> A person's a person by being with people,
> Humanity's essence is being with people.[24]

Imbongi Sitole moved in the same direction as Manisi and continued to be a political and social voice in Transkei, focusing on current events. Performing at a rally at UNITRA in 1990, where Nelson Mandela had come to address the crowd, Sitole depicted the ANC leader as Christ-like, maintaining a truthful and dignified presence among his many followers:

> *Kuloko sinokungqina khona ke siv' amazw' akhe,*
> *Kuloko amazw' akhe siwaqinisekisile ukuba ayinyaniso*

> That's where we can witness and hear his words,
> That's where we have confirmed that his words are true.[25]

Similar to other contemporary *iimbongi*, Sitole incorporated history in his praise poetry, referring to Mandela as Dalibhunga (his initiation name), and recounting Mandela's experiences of disguise in the early days of his resistance in Johannesburg as he called on the ANC leader to maintain his strength:

> *Qina Madiba ooyihl' omkhulu bakujongile,*
> *Bafung' oonyokokhulu bathi soze ufele ejele . . .*

> Be strong, Madiba, your ancestors are guarding you,
> Your grannies swore that you won't die in jail.[26]

Sitole also stressed unity in his *izibongo* of the transitional period, while at the same time criticizing the division caused by leaders such as Buthelezi and his Inkatha Freedom Party—both unpopular in the ANC stronghold of the Eastern Cape:

> *Ncedani niyokuthatha uGatsha Buthelezi imfak' estoksini*
> *Ingxak' ilapho*
>
> Please go and fetch Gatsha Buthelezi and arrest him,
> The problem is there.[27]

While *iimbongi* recalibrated their craft to reflect the period of transition to democracy in South Africa, Eastern Cape jazz musicians carried on their pursuit of unique forms of creativity in response to the changing times, putting emphasis on cultural and social justice that mirrored concerns with political justice. The compositions of Big T of the Soul Jazzmen that reflected their lives of oppression under apartheid, "Tears for Sharpeville," *Unolali*, "Bastard," and "Teargas," continued to be played and to raise the consciousness of succeeding generations. These Eastern Cape jazz performances, however, still operated somewhat under the radar. Ulagh Williams writes of the genre in the 1990s: "I soon discovered that to see or hear any live jazz in Port Elizabeth, one had to visit the Northern areas or the Townships and with the exception of handful of high school band programmes incorporating Big Band Jazz, it was—unbelievably—very much an underground art form."[28]

Combining social consciousness with philosophy in performance and composition, the jazz pianist Erroll Eric Cuddumbey grew up in Korsten and Gelvandale in Port Elizabeth during the era of the Group Areas Act and forced removals. Influenced by the religious music played by his mother on the piano and the popular music he heard on records and the radio, he studied a book on big band harmony that belonged to his father, a jazz aficionado and saxophone player, and sneaked into jazz clubs as a young boy to hear the Soul Jazzmen and musicians such as Dudu Pukwana, Dollar Brand, and Winston "Mankunku" Ngozi. Cuddumbey became friends with Athol Fugard and later wrote essays on the relationship between jazz and Zen principles, developing a philosophy of music and life that put emphasis on artists as "curators of cultural values" and fulfillment through the truth exposed in art. To Cuddumbey, music was an intrinsic part of a person and the instrument that person played was just one way of expressing that part of himself or herself. The jazz pianist also wrote poems, which he referred to as "lyrics without tunes," which he would often later put to music. One such composition, "While the City Sleeps," he described as a tribute "to those who work through the dark nights, while we sleep." Written in 1993 with a style similar to that of African American gospel, the poem, set to music, reflected his experience as a youth of working the night shift in a factory and offering solace in the collective experience of those who may feel alone in their labor:

> For together we walk into the future . . .
> while the city sleeps.[29]

Cuddumbey never left Port Elizabeth, describing the jazz scene in that city as a family and preferring the encouragement of creativity in this region to the competitive atmosphere of cities such as Johannesburg and Cape Town. He worried that he might eventually give way to that competition if he moved to Cape Town, at the expense of his pursuit of truth in music. Claiming that he liked staying in the "Little Village" of Port Elizabeth, Cuddumbey became the first lecturer of Jazz Studies at the University of Port Elizabeth (now Nelson Mandela University) in 1999 and created the first jazz curriculum for the university.[30]

Jazz musicians of the Eastern Cape like Cuddembey continued through their work in the 1990s to search for meaning in a confusing world of racism and oppression, and used instrumentation to express what could not always be conveyed in words. Saxophone player Zimasile (later Zimology or "Zim") Ngqawana personified that pursuit to make sense of his life and his place in the world in his music. Born in New Brighton and starting out on the pennywhistle in his youth, Zim studied classical music at Rhodes University, but left to work with keyboardist Darius Brubeck (son of the American jazz musician Dave Brubeck) at the University of Natal, joining Brubeck's band the Jazzanians. After attracting the attention of jazz master drummer Max Roach, Zim was given a scholarship to study at the University of Massachusetts with Roach, and worked with American jazz saxophonists Archie Shepp and Yusef Latiff, as well as Wynton Marsalis. Eastern Cape activist Government Zini describes Zim as "the most imperative saxophonist in jazz," and recalls a remarkable performance at a memorial service for the jazz drummer Lulu Gontsana at the Centenary Great Hall in New Brighton where Zini witnessed "the profound humanity and disciplined economy of [Zim's] playing." Zini felt that the music he was hearing from Zim was an expression of Zim's youth in New Brighton through the incorporation of a child's song from that time: *khangel' aphaya, umlilo, galel' amanzi* ("the dwelling is burning, look yonder, fire, extinguish with water"). Zini felt the words rising and falling: "Zim tore into that rhyme aggressively, assertively, inspirationally, spiritually and turned it upside down with great gusto and nostalgia. There was immediate pandemonium in the venue caused by his short, sharp, staccato, furious bursts. That was a musical experience I was never ever to forget."[31]

The first free and democratic elections of 1994 in South Africa resulted in a resounding victory for the ANC, not least in the Eastern Cape where the ANC garnered 84% of the vote in both the national and provincial legislatures. The ANC had clearly maintained strong support in this area throughout the apartheid years and Mandela, elected as president, was hailed as the region's own. Music and *izibongo* dominated his inauguration. The African National Congress Choir sang *Usilethela Uxolo* (Nelson Mandela Brings Us Peace), and Zim directed 100 musicians in the "Drums for Peace Orchestra," led by an elite group of presidential drummers, and featured in the ceremony as a solo saxophonist. Zolani Mkiva, of Dutywa in Transkei, who had performed at Mandela's Welcome Home Rally in Mthatha in 1990, took the stage to give two praise poems for the new president and became Mandela's official poet laureate. Mkiva recited in several languages at the inauguration, laying emphasis on Mandela's promotion of a new "Rainbow Nation," and used a folktale of victims rescued through birdsong from a cannibal trying to cut down their tree, with the singing keeping the tree standing—a tale used to illustrate the steadfastness of Mandela and his people's resistance, not least in the form of music. In the tradition of *iimbongi* before him, the young poet called to the ancestors to protect those who had fought for their liberation, rephrasing the words of Martin Luther King, "We are free at last! / Thank God we are free!"[32]

Figuring out a new national identity was one of the first challenges of the post-apartheid years, with ambitious experiments such as the Truth and Reconciliation Commission attempting to address the trauma of the past yet also unite South Africans under a new multicultural umbrella. The celebration of more Afro-centric culture in music, art, and food in the post-apartheid years, however, was often contrasted with the severe challenges of continuing poverty and inequality which inevitably brought a rise in crime. Mandela's focus on reconciliation before the elections had initially come from the leverage imposed on the apartheid government through boycotts and sanctions, and he largely operated from a position of strength that would lead to apartheid leaders being forced to bargain themselves out of political power. Between 1990 and 1994, however, ANC leaders came to the fatal conclusion that ground support was not strong enough to introduce a policy of wealth redistribution. This conclusion led to government transformation and economic reform moving in two different directions. While political negotiations produced one of the most progressive constitutions in the world, economic discussions reinforced and even increased greater inequality, with the Eastern Cape suffering the consequences to a large degree. The original vision of land redistribution was stymied by a clause in the new constitution that protected all private property. Plans for job creation for the millions of unemployed were thwarted by the closing of factories due to the signing of the General Agreement on Tariffs and Trade, which made it illegal to subsidize car manufacturing and textile industries. The distribution of free drugs to combat the fast-growing problem of HIV/AIDS in the townships could not be carried out because of an intellectual property rights commitment with the World Trade Organization. The level of funds needed for building houses and providing electricity to the poor was inadequate because the ANC government found that it had inherited a huge debt left over from the apartheid era. Even attempts to raise the minimum wage found an obstacle through pressure from the International Monetary Fund (IMF) to impose wage restraints. Any moves to change these basic policies were met by a loss in market confidence and potential flight of capital. The new post-apartheid economic system was trapped by restrictions kept in place from the old apartheid system. As anti-apartheid activist Rassool Snyman observed, "They never freed us. They only took the chain from around our neck and put it on our ankles."[33]

The ANC leadership still worked hard at some form of redistribution, and 100,000 homes were built for the poor, with millions gaining access to running water, electricity, and phone lines. The burden of international debt, however, caused the government to have to raise prices and ten years later, millions were cut off from access to water and electricity because they could not afford to pay the bills. According to British activist and Frantz Fanon scholar Nigel Gibson, the system that replaced apartheid bore many of the hallmarks of neocolonialism: "Born during the high period of neoliberal globalization, the post-apartheid government silenced more radical alternatives by trading on its credentials as the 'party of liberation.' Successfully outmaneuvering its left critics, the trajectory in South Africa has been a succession of neoliberal restructurings."[34] Thabo Mbeki, who was elected president after Mandela's term, reinforced this free market direction due to his comfort with business leaders and education in England during the Thatcher years, increasing privatization and free trade, and cutting government spending. Mbeki also initially and disastrously denied the danger of the spread of HIV/AIDS in his country, setting the country back tragically in terms of addressing the grave damage done by this deadly infection. These multiple setbacks became particularly severe in the Eastern Cape, a region that had already fallen behind the rest of the South African republic through its unique experience of oppression and inequality from the colonial years up through the period of apartheid. The harsh tactics of rule that had been part of the apartheid system were gone, but the social and economic mess it created had still to be dealt with, and the Eastern Cape felt this burden particularly with the rise of deaths in that region due to HIV/AIDS and the deprivation caused by a lack of resources. The suicide rate also rose in that region, particularly in rural areas, with financial hardship being the primary cause, and calls for a comprehensive poverty alleviation program to address the dire situation began to be heard. One study pointed out that an underlying reason for the rise in suicide rates was the history of trauma caused by human rights violations during the apartheid years. The added expectations of the post-apartheid era combined with new Western influences and continuing deprivation had further exacerbated stress levels in the region.[35] A survey of the richest and poorest municipalities in South Africa conducted in 2016 demonstrated that, while the majority of regions reflected a growing positive outlook for the country, the poorest municipalities were largely in the Eastern Cape, where places such as Alfred Nzo municipality in Mount Ayliff, Amathole in East London, and sections of Mthatha, Queenstown, and Barkly East contained majority populations earning less than R1,600 ($105) per month.[36] The years of government under Jacob Zuma were marked by a rise in corruption scandals and further deprivation of resources for the Eastern Cape, but, whatever their opinions of Zuma, the people of this region stayed largely loyal to the ANC party, with that loyalty becoming more solid with the election of ANC leader and former activist Cyril Ramaphosa as president in 2018.

The creative culture in South Africa in the years since apartheid ended has worked to redefine its relationship to protest and to social and political consciousness. For more than two hundred years, music and spoken word in the Eastern Cape had directed a large degree of its energy towards challenging colonial oppression and bringing down apartheid. The end of direct white rule in the 1990s, however, brought a momentary lull in united protest expressed in song and poetry. Eastern Cape *imbongi* Mandise Tele described the change, and she notes that during the struggle against apartheid performance arts were thriving in Mdantsane, with Xhosa songs and poetry kept alive among ANC branches: "People were singing traditional songs, producing poetry, and so on. . . . Someone would produce poetry and then burst into songs—it was spontaneous." In the years just after apartheid ended, according to Tele, "the fire of the struggle was gone . . . after the elections these cultural groups became silent."[37]

This perceived silence reflected a wrestling with post-apartheid culture among artists, and after the unbanning of the ANC and other political organizations in 1990, anti-apartheid activist Albie Sachs made the controversial declaration that there should now be a five-year ban on the use of the phrase "culture is a weapon of struggle." The statement opened up a hot debate among cultural activists over the role of art in the new dispensation and Sachs clarified his opinion by arguing that artists had to move beyond the themes they embraced during the apartheid years and "reflect on the beauty and the ugliness . . . of the lives and loves of our people." He viewed the discussion over this matter as healthy and one that would continue to keep the creative community sharp: "The struggle is still out there waiting to be engaged, and we shall be losers if we assume that this era simply means that we should fold our hands and conclude that the best has been achieved." The Port Elizabeth playwright John Kani, who had worked with Athol Fugard on the plays *Sizwe Bantu is Dead* and *The Island*, also expressed this perceived moment of reckoning for artists. Acknowledging that "things are not stable yet, the landscape is shifting all the time," Kani believed that initially the aspirations of freedom meant just taking over the white spaces, but then there came a recognition: "We have a hell of a responsibility. As artists there is now even a greater challenge than before of educating and informing our people, of proving to the people that we are not that different, that we are one nation although we could be culturally slightly different here and there." This did not mean, in Kani's opinion, however, that his people's culture should be merged with others and with the predominantly Western culture into a sort of historical melting pot. Instead, as he expressed it, "We are also attempting to rewrite the history of our people so that each culture, each grouping finds and feels that they too have a place in this new democracy with respect and dignity." To Kani, this process had to come in the form of personal stories first, and he warned, "We will not be tied to the apron strings of any political party. We've got to remain the conscience of our community."[38] Playwright and author Zakes Mda defined the situation for artists in the post-apartheid era in straightforward terms: "Writers wrote about apartheid merely because they were responding to what was happening at the time in this country. Now, after apartheid, they will continue to respond to what is happening at a particular time."[39]

While initially rejecting the social and political messages of previous generations, music and spoken word in the Eastern Cape has, therefore, continued to evolve in the next three decades into forms with more complex and nuanced lyrics and styles that still address the severe challenges caused by the legacies of colonialism and apartheid, and continuing inequality, and even revive songs and chants from the struggle against apartheid, as in the "Fees Must Fall" campaigns among students, and the crusades to take down or replace colonial and apartheid monuments and change the names of towns and regions. As a form of "symbolic reparation" to address the injustices of the past, the Truth and Reconciliation Commission recommended that geographic features be renamed, and in the years since apartheid ended, throughout the Eastern Cape, cities and locations changed their names or spelling of names back to those that more accurately represent African roots and history; Alice is now iDikeni, King William's Town is eQonce, Bisho is Bhisho, East London is eMonti, Queenstown is Komani, Butterworth is Gcuwa, and Port Elizabeth and surrounding areas are eBhayi or Nelson Mandela Bay. In 2018, Grahamstown officially became Makhanda, discarding the name that represented Colonel John Graham, "the most brutal and the most vicious of the British commanders on that frontier," according to South Africa's Arts and Culture Minister Nathi Mthethwa, and "one that evokes unimaginable pain."[40] The name replacing Grahamstown is that of the Xhosa warrior and prophet, also known as Nxele (see Chapter 2). These symbolic changes are significant in the reclaiming of heritage, history, and culture among the people of the Eastern Cape, but the lack of commercial recognition this region has historically struggled with has left its mark. Government Zini remarks that the treatment Eastern Cape jazz musicians often encountered in large cities during the 1970s and 1980s can still be observed in the present: "Even today the attitude still remains despite the awesome rich talent we possess—if one comes from the Eastern Cape one is easily marginalized, despite having produced political icons, arts gurus, theatre greats such as Gibson Kente, and on and on."[41] Eastern Cape actor and director Julius Mtsaka made a similar complaint about performance art at the end of the 1990s:

> There is another thing . . . which has always sickened me, and that's the attention the Johannesburg art and theatre companies are getting from overseas theatre managements to the exclusion of what is going on in places such as ours. Yet over the years the Eastern Cape has always ferried to Johannesburg, not only material, but also actors and other artists of note. The next thing we hear is that there is a festival happening in Norway, or in Denmark, and no companies, no groups from the Eastern Cape have been invited. And I find that very frustrating.[42]

The social and economic problems faced by the Eastern Cape population were in many ways the same as those faced during colonial rule and apartheid, but now there was no clear target at which to direct their grievances. A large section of the youth turned away from the protest music of their parents and grandparents, and embraced styles such as kwaito, which combined electronic and pop influences with local sounds and lyrics, and which contained no straightforward political message. Kwaito grew up with post-apartheid South Africa, a soundtrack for the new democracy, with a heavy bass sound and connection to house music that brought back the *pantsula* dance style of the 1950s. In an article describing a more recent revival of this music, Rofhiwa Maneta claims, "Kwaito was there when the rainbow nation was born," but adds that it was also there "when the rainbow started falling apart" in the early 2000s. Arguably, this new form of music's message was indirectly political through an absence of resistance themes; the younger generation was, in a sense, making the statement that their music should now reflect not what they suffered but who they were; and who they were was not just one thing. With greater artistic freedom to explore different genres free from government restrictions, young musicians absorbed outside influences such as hip hop and house music, and added their own flavor—very much as South African jazz musicians had been doing all through the apartheid years.

This reinvention of art has been reflected in the post-apartheid era in the Eastern Cape, and is expressed in different art forms, such as the literary and theater work of Zakes Mda. In his novel *The Heart of Redness*, Mda describes the tension in a village on the Wild Coast of the Eastern Cape viewed by his main character Camagu that seems to be a modernized revival or residue of the tension between "red" and "school" people (see Chapter 3). At one point, Camagu witnesses a dance that seems to be traditional: "In a slow rhythm the elders begin to dance. It is a painful dance. . . . They are going into a trance that takes them back to the past. To the world of the ancestors. Not the Otherworld where the ancestors live today. . . . But to this world when it still belonged to them." When Camagu grows afraid of the sadness that fills him, he is told, "There is nothing to be afraid of. They are merely inducing sadness in their lives, so that they may have a greater appreciation of happiness." But what Camagu believes to be an old custom, he discovers is, in fact, a new one:

> When the sad times passed and the trial of the Middle Generations [colonialism and apartheid] were over, it became necessary to create something that would make them appreciate this new happiness of the new age. What better way than to lament the folly of belief of the era of the child prophetess [Nonqawuse—see Chapter 2] and the sufferings of the Middle Generations which were brought about by the same scourge of belief?[43]

Camagu is intellectually attracted to Xoliswa Ximiya, a schoolteacher who represents modernizing influences of the West and who is disdainful of Xhosa tradition. But Camagu is also increasingly emotionally and physically drawn to Qukezwa, who represents something intrinsic and historical about the amaXhosa of the Wild Coast. He is almost fearful of the response she awakens in him, similar to the fear he feels of feelings evoked by the elders dancing. This historical and cultural pull marks a form of resistance that connects to identity. In one scene in the novel, as Qukezwa rides bareback on her horse Gxagxa with Camagu sitting behind her, she bursts into song and plays an *umrhabhe*—the one-stringed musical instrument traditionally played by Xhosa women stroking with a bow or plucking with their mouth to create an acoustic sound like a box:

> She whistles and sings all at the same time. Many voices come from her mouth. Deep sounds that echo like the night. Sounds that have the heaviness of a steamy summer night. Flaming sounds that crackle like a veld fire. Light sounds that float like flakes of snow on top of the Amathole Mountains. Hollow sounds like laughing mountains. Coming out all at once. As if a whole choir lives in her mouth. Camagu has never heard such singing before. He once read of the

amaXhosa mountain women who were good at split-tone singing. He also heard that the only other people in the world who could do this were Tibetan monks. He did not expect that this girl could be the guardian of a dying tradition.[44]

Camagu denounces the culture of dependency he sees evolving among his people as they continue to suffer the lingering effects of apartheid, both economically and culturally. "The notions of delivery and upliftment," he declares, "have turned our people into passive recipients of programs conceived by so-called experts who know nothing about the lives of rural communities. People are denied the right to shape their own destiny."[45] In criticism of a scheme by local white man John Dalton to create a "cultural village" to attract tourists, Camagu challenges the idea: "When you excavate a buried precolonial identity of these people . . . a precolonial authenticity that is lost . . . are you suggesting that they currently have no culture . . . that they live in a cultural vacuum?" Echoing the motivations that can be observed in the artistic pursuit of contemporary *iimbongi* and musicians in the Eastern Cape, Camagu declares, "I am interested in the culture of the amaXhosa as they live it today, not yesterday. The amaXhosa people are not a museum piece. Like all cultures, their culture is dynamic."[46] Gamede echoes these sentiments in expressing the present situation for people in the Eastern Cape. "They are living in a dual world," he says. "They have got to think about their identity only in certain circumstances." When, for example, at the end of the month they perform a certain ceremony, according to Gamede, "they make the mistake of saying they are celebrating culture. This is not culture. Culture is what you are . . . not something that you remember on a certain day."[47]

These opinions are also expressed by Dumisa Mphupha, a contemporary *imbongi* committed to maintaining his craft through performance, workshops, and encouragement of youth to participate and carry on the art of praise-singing. At a workshop he led in Grahamstown in 2016, Dumisa asserted that, since culture is dynamic, poetry also has to be dynamic. The youth involved in *izibongo* in recent years have often incorporated new elements such as rap into the art form, fueling a debate among *iimbongi* over the degree to which they should stick to original styles as opposed to absorbing modern developments and characteristics. One of the young *iimbongi* I spoke to at the workshop informed me that he had started out as a rap artist but found praise-singing held more meaning for him.[48] To Dumisa, music has always been a part of the development of praise-singing, and he believes that *marabi* and *kwela* music of the twentieth century is "95% *izibongo*" using *istibili* ("the sounds"), which he describes as the rhythm that takes the *imbongi* to the place where he or she will "jump in and praise." Dumisa also asserts that there is no music to which *izibongo* cannot be linked. At the same time, he says of *iimbongi*, "We are singers but we are not singing; [we] are talking, but not giving speeches."[49] Their work continues to rely on spontaneity, and composition that comes simultaneously with performance, and also perpetuates the historical link between *iimbongi* and power. The focus of their art in the post-apartheid era is on social issues that affect the daily lives of their people: poverty, crime, domestic abuse and assault of women, health struggles, service delivery, xenophobia, corruption, tuition fees, and all the combined social pressures that put a strain on relationships. According to Gamede, *izibongo* are often front and center when it comes to moral campaigns.[50]

The contemporary Xhosa *imbongi* Bhodl'ingqaka (Akhona Mafani) carries on the tradition of praise poems, performing for notable figures that include Xhosa novelist Peter Tshobisa Mtuze and Xhosa King Zwelonke Sigcawu. He also embraces the subjects of social injustice, local community, and his life growing up in the township of Vukani in Grahamstown through works such as his album *Iintonga Zetyendyana* ("the sticks of a young boy") which combines poetry with music, and on subsequent recordings that address social and environmental issues. "Many people have died through the chains of silence," observes Bhodl'ingqaka, and he feels his work is produced to raise awareness of all issues, including, as the poet puts it, issues of love. Bhodl'ingqaka takes his role as an *imbongi* seriously. In 2017 he was banned by the Eastern Cape's Minister of Arts and Culture from participating in arts events because he performed a poem that criticized the corruption of President Zuma. Bhodl'ingqaka remained defiant about his performance and his role as an *imbongi*: "I was speaking directly to the president as a poet as I have the authority to say, to demand and command that this and that cannot happen because we were given a license as poets to speak about issues."[51]

These issues are also taken up in the more conscious music of the Eastern Cape, which often engages with the *izibongo* tradition in a constant search for expression that addresses modern struggles yet maintains authenticity. The question of identity remains a central topic of debate in a post-apartheid era that began with the idea of a "rainbow nation" of unity, but followed with a realization that the identities imposed on populations in the era of colonialism and oppression still needed to be addressed, corrected, re-defined, and reclaimed through various means of political, social, and cultural representation. *Intonjane* music of Xhosa women, for example, preserves the tradition of caretakers of the rite of initiation into womanhood, but in more recent years, it has incorporated issues of sexism. The song *Zadan'izibanda* ("Headmen are disappointed") is a song of defiance that criticizes headmen's treatment of women. The main phrase in the song *mna ndoyik' izibanda* ("I am afraid of headmen") expresses disgust felt by women towards headmen and a rejection of their abuse. The tone of the song is sad, but it also encourages unity among women to defy mistreatment by the men. A number of these songs also express disenchantment with the social conditions endured by women in rural areas and the domestic chores they are expected to carry out. The song *Masiy' eGoli*, about men leaving their women to go to Johannesburg, begins with an exaggerated sigh which is repeated throughout the song as an expression of severe frustration.[52]

Female *iimbongi* have also served as a conduit between tradition and contemporary issues, carrying on the historical role as tellers of folktales, while moving into the *izibongo* space to criticize social ills, including the oppression of a patriarchal society. Mandise Tele, an *imbongi* who began practicing in the late years of apartheid and continued into the post-apartheid era, believes that if women are accepted as diviners and prophets then they should also be respected as *iimbongi*, as they feel moved by the same forces as male *iimbongi*. "There is something which says speak!" she explains, ". . . it's like a charismatic power you get—I mean it's there. . . . You feel it in your veins, they are tight, you feel like stretching . . . it's your ancestors in you."[53]

Maskandi music, represented by one of its Xhosa founders, Mlendelwa Mrlalatya—known as Nkunz'emdaka—has further preserved old African sounds while absorbing contemporary styles. Performed by Zulu and Xhosa artists, Maskandi comes from the Afrikaans word *musikant* (musician) and means someone who plays traditional music on guitar. The style is very much drawn from *izibongo*, and Nkunz'emdaka first helped to popularize it in 1985 with his album *Ibhubesi Elehlule Amadoda* and continued for the next 35 years to perform and record this music. Nkunz'emdaka's main ambition in recent years is to be instrumental in maintaining the growth of Maskandi, especially among Xhosa singers whom he feels there are not enough of in the music industry. He also expresses concern over the effect of piracy that often preys on less affluent musicians: "This bleeds us poor, it just kills us, hence many musicians die paupers."[54]

The social and economic inequality that has continued since apartheid ended has played out in a music industry that still manages to leave out significant talent emanating from the Eastern Cape, and Eastern Cape artists are well aware of this. South African artists as a whole face uncertain entrée into a system that guarantee success but is still limited in many ways to those already possessing the power that comes with knowledge and familiarity with the music business. Jazz musicians and rappers in the Eastern Cape battle to compete with the recognition afforded to artists from more cosmopolitan regions such as Cape Town and Johannesburg; at the same time, they pride themselves on remaining connected to their communities and the struggles faced by their people, sharing their talents and ideology with underprivileged youth and putting emphasis on improving their environment.

Artists such as Dumza, Tobela, and Sebenzile were among the first of hip hop artists to promote their music in Port Elizabeth, focusing on the townships of Motherwell and Zwide. They used the *nkqubela* community radio station as a main tool for spreading the local rap sound and educating young people and their parents on the positive aspects of their movement. Crews such as Shades of Blackness and Abantu have incorporated the influences of South African jazz, anti-apartheid songs, and religious music and reviving themes of critical awareness and black consciousness. Hip hop in Port Elizabeth has also had strong connections to Rastafarianism. Many of the acts began playing in public spaces such as parking lots, with sound systems that feature large speakers and turntables, and lyrics primarily in isiXhosa. Performing in their own languages brings up the challenge of authenticity versus appealing to a broader market, and illustrates another way that Eastern Cape artists often feel marginalized.

Just as female *iimbongi* have worked to find their space in a male-dominated profession, female musicians from the Eastern Cape have also challenged the patriarchy of their craft and made a name for themselves. An increasing number of female rap and hip hop acts, such as the Alpha Phonetics of Port Elizabeth, address issues that affect the black female population such as rape and drug and alcohol abuse. Thulisa, a journalism student and emcee in Grahamstown, feels the challenge is one of building confidence. She believes women have often felt intimidated by the hip hop scene, but she thinks their participation is needed as a response to male rappers, and she often uses rap or a combination of rap and spoken word to express situations women find themselves in.[55] Eastern Cape female musicians from other genres have also made their mark. The highly successful pop artist Zahara (Bulelwa Mkutukana) started out busking in East London and then recorded an album that reached double-platinum status in 2011, winning numerous awards, performing privately for Nelson Mandela in his home, and recording the album *Mgodi* that went gold after six hours. Zahara and her fellow female Eastern Cape musicians often perform primarily in isiXhosa and hold on to many of the influences from their heritage. Artist Nombasa Maqoko also started out in East London, and describes her music as "modern Afro-soul with an ancient Xhosa sound," although she admits that she does not really like the idea of "boxing" her music.[56] Maqoko's music addresses social issues such as fatherlessness with often poignant songs that evoke the historical tones of her heritage and combine them with more contemporary influences.

Msaki (Asanda Mvana), another musician from East London, uses her music and art to illustrate multiple aspects of South African life, including the struggles her generation has inherited from the past. The song "Blood Guns and Revolutions," written in 2020 in collaboration with Cape Town musician Neo Muyanga, addresses the Marikana Massacre of 2012 in which South African police fired on a crowd of striking mine workers, killing 34 and injuring 78. Msaki believes that unanswered questions from that event still leave a mark: "It's questioning the violence that makes us violent against each other and against ourselves." The song conjures up chants from the anti-apartheid struggle and reinforces Msaki's belief in art holding many narratives and many feelings. "It's the thing that's able to trick us in terms of time and space," says Msaki. "In the first verse I'm actually writing about my parents' generation and the fact that I couldn't make sense of this freedom in the face of this insane inequality that we're living out every day as the youth. . . . What happened in '94 if this is our reality?" Msaki sees the elections of 1994 as "a kind of dress rehearsal that left us in the same place, in the most important ways." She acknowledges that there was a significant change from apartheid, but laments the fact that police violence continues in South Africa as in other parts of the world, such as the United States. "How are we still running from bullets?" she asks, stating the belief that the answers lie in small decisions made on a personal level. "You can ask those questions and somehow hope that in the asking, and in the petitioning and alongside the protesting, that we keep hoping for justice. That's the world where I can still hold that hope."[57]

The increased participation of female artists feeds the development of a unique Eastern Cape artistic culture as a whole. With artists such as Xolile Madinda ("X" or "X-Nasty") and Yahkeem Mavalukuvaliwe leading a movement to uplift their communities through performance, an older generation of rap artists continues to work with younger musicians in this region to form an underground movement that resists commercialization yet flourishes and provides its people with greater confidence and sense of self. In 2011 X became one of the primary organizers that launched the Fingo Festival, an annual independent celebration of Eastern Cape artists operating as an "intervention" in response to the Grahamstown National Arts Festival. Its original purpose was to create a more local and accessible cultural event for Fingo township and other locations on the edge of Grahamstown. The first festival featured a week-long program that included children's workshops, dialogues, and musical performances. X observed, "There's a lot of cry that the [Grahamstown Festival] is for the elite, that the art is expensive, and all these questions. So, as artists we figured out [that] there's a deeper question that is not being addressed right here." The deeper question was that black people were not being brought up with an emphasis on art, and the purpose of the Fingo Festival was to not just be an event (like the Grahamstown Festival) that gave them a job cleaning the streets, but for them "to go and enjoy the arts." The focus of the festival is also practical in helping people in the townships establish themselves as artists and uplift their culture. A session at the 2014 Festival, for example, featured a University of Cape Town representative explaining to aspiring musicians how to use an app to help "bedroom producers" gauge the quality of their recordings.[58] The problem, as always with innovation in the Eastern Cape, however, is funding, with the more privileged sections of society paying lip-service to these types of enterprises without backing it up with resources. According to X, "Lending muscle to ensure that [the Fingo Festival] continues to exist doesn't come as easy as the praises they're so quick to dish out."[59]

X originally performed with the crew DEFBOYZ out of Fingo township and eventually went solo, performing hip hop in isiXhosa that addressed issues of abuse against women and children and working as a community activist. In 2007, he was part of a group that met with the South African Department of Social Justice to discuss the use of hip hop to influence the youth, and in 2008 he helped found and became director of the Save Our Schools and Community project. SOSAC's aim was to help transform the public-school system and solve many of the daunting problems facing the education system in the Eastern Cape. X has also worked with the Rhodes University School of Languages and organized the annual Steve Bantu Biko creative writing competition for high school students of Makana municipality. In 2018 X came to the states as a Mellon artist in residence at the University of Virginia, providing a week of performances, workshops, and class visits. He discussed the contrast between the community he was trying to generate in South Africa through a creative hub called the Black Power Station versus the regimen of student life at Rhodes University, and the struggle between the individual and collective approach towards art and life itself, referencing the strong influence of Black Consciousness on his activities. In a recorded interview shared through his residency, X recalled a politically conscious uncle who caught him rapping and introduced him to books that became a form of awakening. X's uncle told him, "I don't want you to be Americanized," recommending instead that X be grounded in his own culture.[60] Like many of his fellow artists, the subject matter of X's work often focuses on contemporary social issues that still cause division in his society. A play he worked on, *Ndiyindoda*, for example, explores gender roles and definitions of masculinity in an attempt to address the barriers between men and women, an issue along with the "gangsta" image with all its complicated trappings that rap and hip hop performers still grapple with in their music and their message.

In recent years, as artists pursue recognition through social media, the performer Yahkeem has felt that musicians from the Eastern Cape have to battle the bad image and commercialized aspects evoked by certain strands of hip hop: "In 2020 Hip Hop is synonymous to misogyny, violence, crime and every vile thing a man can conceive. The pressure to move units, battle for spotlight in the dwindling industry have sent many great artists to the edge, some have lost themselves in their quests to evolve." Yahkeem is often wary of news that an artist became famous through social media and believes that economics often trumps the importance of strengthening an artist's image. He finds comfort in those artists who depict township life with humanity, paying attention to details in their daily life that illustrate their struggles and highlighting the dilemma of having to choose between chasing their passion and finding a secure job.[61] The challenge for many of these performers is how to not only depict the hardship and injustice in their lives but how to also confront on a larger scale a post-apartheid system that still carries the inequalities, cultural assumptions, and corrupt political practices that causes these hardships to continue. Another challenge, of course, is how to find backing and resources to help them continue to be creative and express themselves with sincere enthusiasm and energy.

A contemporary revival of kwaito that connects the freedom of this '90s style with more modern sounds and more conscious subjects has appeared in the last decade in the Eastern Cape. Guitarist and trumpeter Siphosenkosi Nkodlwane (Laliboi) began as a notable kwaito musician in his region, with his initial project Impande Core combining multiple influences that created a new sound known as carrot funk. During this time, Laliboi met with saxophonist Zim Ngqawana, who gave him the advice, "Do not be limited by standards and rules that music dictates for musicians because it kills the musicality in you." After exposure to artists in the East Rand Laliboi soon began to create his own rap sound, incorporating culture and jazz influences from his roots in eGcuwa (formerly Butterworth) and layering in effects from his experiences in the East Rand. "With this rap thing," says Laliboi, "I didn't want to sound anything like what the Americans and the new kids are doing. I wanted to sound like everything that I know, from ezilaleni eGciwa [in the Eastern Cape], to the dusty streets of VosloForus [in Gauteng]." Laliboi has seen his work as a means of honoring that of his grandfather, the isiXhosa author K. K. Thamsangqa who wrote the novel *Buzani Kubawo*. The artist's 2019 album *Siyangaphi*, a combination of jazz, hip hop, and traditional sounds, is a celebration of manhood and Xhosa language and identity, while also addressing history. Tracks reference Mandela, Biko, and Hani, and illustrate social ills such as alcoholism, while the video for the song *"Emonti"* displays an array of traditional and modern images. The title track of the album calls for the return of the head of the nineteenth-century chief Hintsa from England, implying a return to the great chief's state of mind. Laliboi has expressed the hope that his work would cause young people to revisit their heritage and make them proud of it. "People don't read anymore," he says. "[I want to] reshape the minds of young South Africans to reconnect with who they are and not forget to embrace diversity." Music journalist Tseliso Monaheng describes *Siyangaphi* as "a reckoning with the past in order to correct the future," and believes the album to be "a refreshingly honest, pure and earnest addition to the African storytelling tradition."[62]

This emphasis on regional roots combined with contemporary influences is reflected in the music of Eastern Cape performers Katt Daddy and Yoza and their group Darkie Fiction, which the two artists describe as a mix of art and kwaito sounds. "It's a merger of my upbringing in the rural Eastern Cape," says Katt Daddy, "while Yoza had more of a suburban upbringing in East London." Their music celebrates the common ground between the two, who are described as a modern musical Bonnie and Clyde, challenging the limits of mainstream music and expressing some nostalgia for a social-media-free youth. Their debut single *"Selula"* of 2018 is a play on words: a *selula* is a cellphone but a rough translation in isiXhosa also carries the meaning "when it was easy." According to Yoza, "the song's about how cellphones have messed up everything but we're also talking about the nostalgia of the past—how easy things were when we were kids and had nothing to worry about." The video depicts a young man seemingly texting nonstop on his cell phone only to reveal in a focused shot that he is helplessly punching a melting popsicle. Darkie Fiction's track *"Bhoza"* calls on listeners to "stick it to the man" and has crowds in the video raising their fists in a power salute, but the music is upbeat and the mood is happy.[63] The message seems to be one that invites people to stay conscious but still celebrate life.

The music of Darkie Fiction also represents a continuing search for real identity and dealing with the remnants of apartheid. Like Msaki, Katt Daddy and Yoza believe that their history has created trauma from which their people are still recovering. The year 2019 in South Africa witnessed marches and protests against gender-based violence, xenophobic attacks, and battles for the acceptance of natural hair in schools and the workplace, and Katt Daddy observes, "We are FRESH out of apartheid. Don't get it twisted, we are young. 100% fresh out of apartheid and that was our biggest worry for the longest time. We did not get a lot of time to deal with anything else. Now . . . we have to focus on how we better ourselves rather than looking elsewhere." He mentions the continuing inferiority complex among black people that Steve Biko fought to overturn, and comments that oftentimes inferiority expresses itself in violence and hate. Like many of his contemporaries, Katt Daddy also challenges the original notion of a unified country of the post-apartheid era and calls for a more realistic approach: "It is not this Rainbow Nation idea of all colors, all races, all nations. We can pretend as much as we want but it's not happening right now . . . we need to heal. We need to create a bond with other Africans." To Katt Daddy, there are connections Africans in South Africa need to recognize with Africans throughout the continent and he puts emphasis on drawing these groups together. Yoza adds, "South Africa is a constant conversation. . . . This whole 'West is the Best' thing is so boring. . . . And as much as we have a lot of healing to do, there has been a bit of healing that's taken place already, especially when it comes to music. . . . People are looking for something more profound and much closer to their very South African understanding of home."⁶⁴

For many of these contemporary artists, there exists no single issue, like ending apartheid, to unite them, but there are multiple issues that add up to overall oppression and a feeling of marginalization. Much of the message of their art focuses on change within the system as opposed to overturning the system, and there still remains the challenge of creating a modern identity. X describes it as a "psychic wound" that has continued to cause pain since the apartheid era. In an observation that echoes that of Steve Biko in the late 1960s, X states, "Parents in many poor townships have been told for so many years that they are 'nothing' that this sense of uselessness has been internalized," and can result in a form of nihilism. X also describes a destructive phenomenon called the "tall poppy syndrome" where hip hop songs rap about people dragging artists down, claiming these artists are acting superior if they perform hip hop, or stop drinking, or question criminal activity. Artists such as X view this attitude through the lens of Black Consciousness: "People here are broken and they don't realize how they are destroying each other. They suffer a feeling of constant judgment by the rest of society, and so they judge others." But X believes that hip hop in Grahamstown fights against these attitudes: it "refuses to judge and hangs onto hope."⁶⁵ There is a political slant to Eastern Cape hip hop that puts an emphasis on upholding humanity. The Eastern Cape rapper Azlan Makalima, for example, uses the image of gangsters returning to prison as subject matter and urges people to see these individuals as human beings. Artists revisit their ancestors' messages in isiXhosa, and bring that history and politics into their lyrics. These artists claim that they want to do more than merely help people survive in an oppressive environment, but want to transform the environment itself, invoking the ambitions of the Black Consciousness generation that began among their people. Bringing back and updating metaphors that uphold their traditions, "they reclaim a black intellectual culture," according to researcher Alette Schoon, finding creative ways to put their work out into their communities and inspiring innovation among their people that will break the cycle of crime and despair.⁶⁶

Incorporation of regional African music into the standard curriculum of education in the Eastern Cape has also been a challenge. The study of Xhosa music is offered as an option but there arises the problem of educators not necessarily having the training or background to support this option. Simply put, teachers teach what they know, so in rural areas pupils are more likely to learn Xhosa music—mostly in choral form—while schools in the cities are less likely to offer Xhosa music education in any substantial form. A push to speak indigenous languages in society has more recently emerged and isiXhosa is now taught as a second language option in the Eastern Cape

(Afrikaans was formerly the curriculum's compulsory second language). The change represents a shift, though, rather than a norm, and students are now given the choice of Afrikaans or is Xhosa as the second language requirement. The history syllabus has also changed dramatically since 1994 to include indigenous narratives, but the subject of history is an elective made by students in grade 10, and is, therefore, not required.[67]

Arguably, when students are taught indigenous music in schools and universities, they are also learning the history behind that music and there is a uniting effect, illustrating the essential cohesion it brings and the overall power of music in preserving identity and fighting oppression. According to Rhodes Lecturer and African Musical Arts (AMA) activist Boudina McConnachie, exposure of Africans to their own music can have an electric effect: "Sometimes they're learning about their music for the first time when they get to university [and] it's like an 'aha' moment because they haven't had the opportunity to think about their music this way before."[68] There is a process of re-evaluation as AmaXhosa, along with AmaZulu, AmaSotho, and other Southern African ethnicities learn the similarities and differences within their forms and styles of music which contributes to the continuing development of African nationalism. This uniting effect helps to contradict the lingering influences of the apartheid system's attempt to divide populations through false and superficial definitions of indigenous music. McConnachie has contributed to this restoring of emphasis on African music in Eastern Cape education as part of a larger push to "decolonize" education in South Africa that began in the 1980s and culminated in the Rhodes Must Fall/Fees Must Fall campaigns of 2015/16, by substituting indigenous performance practice for Western musical approaches. Through focusing on the objective of training teachers to engage with African approaches to music, *uhadi*, *endingidi*, and *nyanga* pipes have replaced pianos, violins and flutes, and enrollment in the program increased after these changes were made.[69]

The many forms of music that emerged in resistance and response to colonialism and apartheid in the Eastern Cape has still to be fully developed in schools and universities, however, and seems to be more evident in the community projects of musicians such as X and Yahkeem. South African jazz and its history is really only taught at the university level and, according to McConnachie, "Very few people are aware of how unique our situation is and how powerful this music has been in shaping other musics around the world."[70] There is also the challenge of how the amaXhosa collectively view their own music. Education in the Eastern Cape involves a three-tiered system in grade 10, where students have a choice of studying jazz, African, or Western music. The students must have their parents' permission for their choice, and that choice often reflects a harsh perspective on the relationship between indigenous education and opportunity. In one instance, for example, a questionnaire was sent out to 20 students on their choice between the three areas of music education; nineteen responded that their parents made them take the Western music option—all of them Xhosa students—the one remaining student who chose the African tier being the only white. The rationale behind the Xhosa parents not pushing for the African option was, "What's the value in that? They already get it at home." But, according to music educators, this assumption is misleading as the music at home is largely urbanized and does not reflect the rich history and traditions of Xhosa music. What McConnachie and music teachers and lecturers at the forefront of promoting Xhosa music want to convey is that the Eastern Cape is evolving and growing: "It is not a relic of the past [but] an important part of the greater story of South Africa."[71]

One recurring message regarding the art of music and spoken word in the Eastern Cape is the challenge of recognition. Lukae Concepts, who created a YouTube channel that showcases Eastern Cape artists, believes that the biggest problem for the region's hip hop scene is that there is no scene to start with: "The artists aren't interacting with fans or even trying to convert non-fans to be supporters." To Lukae, the pandemic of 2020 has given artists some time to re-examine themselves and their approach to music, but there needs to be more platforms for artists and they need to find a way to create an industry outside of the commercial one. "I have done the research," he says, "and EC has the numbers to stand alone and be a force to be reckoned with. Jozi [Johannesburg] looks after Jozi artists and it's hard for EC artists to penetrate that scene. So, I say 'fuck 'em'—let's make our own dough and bake our own pie."[72]

COVID-19 has also brought more hardship to artists, hitting the Eastern Cape particularly hard, just as the spread of HIV/AIDS did. The devastation of COVID-19 is, in fact, connected to the lingering damage of HIV/AIDS inflicted on that region which left the population more vulnerable to the new disease. Nkunz'emdaka put out a special plea for assistance: "COVID-19 came at a difficult time for me, a time when I was facing hard times and added to my problems." His concern is echoed by other Eastern Cape musicians: "We have been badly affected by the lockdown since we were unable to perform in front of people. We would like to ask the government to assist us artists to deal with the effects of the pandemic." The Sports, Arts, and Culture Department in South Africa created a relief fund of R150 million to specifically help artists unable to make a living because of the pandemic, but the situation in the Eastern Cape became severe in the later months of 2020, with Nelson Mandela Bay declared a "hot spot," and the stress caused by the virus has added to the overall challenges faced by that region.

Throughout its history of contact with the West a large part of resistance in the Eastern Cape has been about finding ways to slip from the grasp of the

European worldview and find its own way. Using music itself as a metaphor, one could say that the artistic culture of this region maintained bass notes and beats from history that reflected the essence of its people, but also over time incorporated lyrics, melodies, and instrumentation of contemporary experiences that acted as a response to changing circumstances. This evolution of creative process in the Eastern Cape has upheld the core of its identity through a combination of language and culture expressed by a multitude of voices. Music, spoken word, and performance consistently put a spotlight on those unable to speak because of their status in an inequal and racist society and their general lack of opportunity, and much of post-apartheid music for Africans and an increasing number of those of mixed heritage in the Eastern Cape has not only been about holding on to their identity, but also creating their own definition of identity, free from Western interpretation. This involves making it hard for commercial influences and critics to place their music in convenient categories, such as "jazz," "pop," "electronic," "folk," "hip hop," and "rap." Even when new categories are defined, such as kwaito, musicians still resist by upending or contradicting the requisite characteristics of that style. Spoken word and the historical position of *iimbongi* have also maneuvered a clear and progressive place in Eastern Cape culture in response to the circumstances that reflect a troubled yet heroic past, in ways that continue to challenge their audiences. According to Yali-Manisi, *Nto zinolwimi hay' imbongi* ("Everyone tells lies, but no one more than the poet"), and he goes on to say, *Kodwa iimbong' azixoki, Silawul' amathongo njengokw' evela* ("But poets don't really tell lies: they give voice to visions revealed by the ancestors").[73] The role of ancestors among Africans as part of their history is one that merges past events with present responses found in the creative culture of their lives and creates that circular pattern of interpreting events that is central to understanding the history of this region. Having already established a strong sense of identity in their own history before contact with the West, African people of the Eastern Cape absorbed the influences of the initial experience of European encroachment to create clear explanations, responses and calls to action, while early modern African intellectuals at the turn of the nineteenth century acted to bridge the gap between oral practices and modern Western narratives. Resistance language and symbolism that often originated in the Eastern Cape became embedded in music and spoken word during the rise of direct protest in South Africa in the first half of the twentieth century; and a resurgence of cultural and historical confidence has formed the thread of African nationalism running through Eastern Cape actions and experiences in the years leading up to the end of the apartheid and the post-apartheid era. All of these developments have been informed by the strong creative impulse so evident in this region. The relationship between music, spoken word, and resistance in the Eastern Cape is undeniably dynamic and ongoing, reflecting both the hardships its people have faced and the unique energy and imaginative impulses they have employed to construct their own vibrant society.

NOTES

1. Author's private diary, February 3, 1990.
2. Colin Bundy, *Govan Mbeki* (Athens: Ohio University Press, 2012), 141.
3. J. B. Peires, "The Implosion of Transkei and Ciskei," *African Affairs*, Vol. 91, no. 364 (July 1992), 371.
4. Russell H. Kaschula, *The Bones of the Ancestors Are Shaking* (Lansdowne: Juta, 2002), 140–42.
5. Kaschula, *The Bones of the Ancestors Are Shaking*, 142–43.
6. Author's private diary, October 3, 1989.
7. P. T. Mtuze, "Facing Mount Nelson: A critical analysis of five Xhosa poems on Nelson Rholihlahla Mandela," *South African Journal of African Languages*, 16:2 (1996), 65.
8. Mtuze, "Facing Mount Nelson," 65.
9. Kaschula, *The Bones of the Ancestors Are Shaking*, 198–204; Author's private diary, April 22, 1990.
10. Peires, "The Implosion of Transkei and Ciskei," 271–72.
11. Dr. Vangeli Gamede, Interview by author, July 20, 2020.
12. Janet Smith and Beauregard Tromp, *Hani: A Life Too Short* (Jeppestown: Jonathan Ball Publishers, 2009), 221.
13. Smith and Tromp, *Hani: A Life Too Short*, 206.
14. Smith and Tromp, *Hani: A Life Too Short*, 228.
15. Peires, "The Implosion of Transkei and Ciskei," 373–74.
16. Author's private diary, December 1, 1990.
17. Smith and Tromp, *Hani: A Life Too Short*, 229–30.
18. Smith and Tromp, *Hani: A Life Too Short*, 232, 234.
19. Smith and Tromp, *Hani: A Life Too Short*, 245.
20. Chris Hani The Legacy #Hectic PT1, https://www.youtube.com/watch?v=p5vxtrzEN7U; HANI The Legacy, https://www.youtube.com/watch?v=-hV792xTxQQ; Hani: The Legacy, https://www.youtube.com/watch?v=tdZOJz_1K5o.
21. Jeff Opland, *The Dassie and the Hunter: A South African Meeting* (Scottsville, South Africa: University of KwaZulu-Natal Press, 2005), 362.
22. Astrid von Kotze, *Organize and Act: The Natal Workers Theatre Movement, 1983–1987* (Durban: Culture and Working Life Publications, 1988), 8.
23. Kaschula, *The Bones of the Ancestors Are Shaking*, 151–52.
24. Opland, *The Dassie and the Hunter*, 386.
25. Kaschula, *The Bones of the Ancestors Are Shaking*, 143.
26. Mtuze, "Facing Mount Nelson," 66.
27. Kaschula, *The Bones of the Ancestors Are Shaking*, 145–46.

28. Ulagh Williams, "Erroll Eric Cuddumbey—Inspiring a Generation," in *Generations of Jazz—At the Red Location Museum*, ed. Diane Thram (Exhibition Catalogue, Grahamstown: International Library of African Music, 2013), 51.

29. Williams, "Erroll Eric Cuddumbey," 55.

30. Williams, "Erroll Eric Cuddumbey," 54.

31. Sandile Ngidi, "Zim Ngqawana obituary: Free-spirited South African saxophonist," *The Guardian* (July 6, 2011); Government Zini, "Zimology Ngqawana—Jazz Master," *Generations of Jazz*, 58.

32. Mtuze, "Facing Mount Nelson," 66.

33. Naomi Klein, "Democracy Born in Chains: South Africa's Constricted Freedom," in *The Shock Doctrine* (New York: Picador, 2007), 257.

34. Nigel Gibson, *Fanonian Practices in South Africa: From Steve Biko to Abahlali baseMjondolo* (New York: Palgrave Macmillan, 2011), xiii–xiv.

35. B. L. Meel, "Determinants of suicide in the Transkei sub-region of South Africa," *Journal of Clinical Forensic Medicine* (2003), 10, 71.

36. *Business Tech*, (19 June 2016), https://businesstech.co.za/news/wealth/127213/the-richest-and-poorest-municipalities-in-south-africa.

37. Kaschula, *The Bones of the Ancestors Are Shaking*, 186.

38. Rolf Solberg, *Alternative Theatre in South Africa: Talks with Prime Movers since the 1970s* (Pietermaritzburg: Hadeda Books, 1999), 235–36.

39. Solberg, *Alternative Theatre in South Africa*, 37.

40. Luke Daniel, "Breaking: Grahamstown officially renamed as Makhanda," *The SouthAfrican* (October 3, 2018), https://www.thesouthafrican.com/news/grahamstown-now-makhanda-eastern-cape-south-africa/; "Here's why Grahamstown has been renamed Makhanda," *IOL* (October 3, 2018), https://www.iol.co.za/news/south-africa/eastern-cape/heres-why-grahamstown-has-been-renamed-makhanda-17334278.

41. Government Zini, "New Brighton, Monde Sikhutshwa and the Soul Jazzmen—a Tribute," *Generations of Jazz*, 19.

42. Solberg, *Alternative Theatre in South Africa*, 148.

43. Zakes Mda, *The Heart of Redness* (New York: Picador, 2000), 73.

44. Mda, *The Heart of Redness*, 152.

45. Mda, *The Heart of Redness*, 180.

46. Mda, *The Heart of Redness*, 248.

47. Dr. Vangeli Gamede, Interview by author, July 20, 2020.

48. *Iimbongi* Workshop, Rhodes University Department of African Language Studies, Puku Story Festival, February 18, 2016, Grahamstown.

49. Dumisa Mpupha, Interview by author, February 12, 2016.

50. Gamede Interview.

51. Zikhona Nyumka, "Xhosa praise poet, Bhodl'ingqaka, continues to soar to greater heights," *Grocott's Mail* (March 29, 2019), https://www.grocotts.co.za/2019/03/29/xhosa-praise-poet-bhodlingqaka-continues-to-soar-to-greater-heights/.

52. Luvuyo Dontsa, "Intonjane Music: A Forum of Identity Formation for Xhosa Women," in *Music and Identity: Transformation and Negotiation*, eds. E. A. Akrofi, Maria Smit, and Stig-Magnus Thorsén (Stellenbosch: Sun Press, 2007), 389–91.

53. Kaschula, *The Bones of the Ancestors Are Shaking*, 181–84.

54. Lulamile Feni, "The gripping sounds of a man on the rise," *Daily Dispatch* (December 18, 2018), https://www.dispatchlive.co.za/lifestyle/daily-life/2018-12-18-the-gripping-sounds-of-a-man-on-the-rise/.

55. Eric Charry, *Hip Hop Africa: New African Music in a Globalizing World* (Bloomington: Indiana University Press, 2012), 65–67.

56. "Nombasa Mqoko: Eastern Cape born independent singer and songwriter," SAfm podcast (October 4, 2016), ionofm./e/342348.

57. Nadia Neophytou, "Interview: Exploring Msaki's Genre-Defying Voice," *OkayAfrica.com* (October 8, 2020), https://www.okayafrica.com/south-african-music-msaki-interview/.

58. Ts'eliso Monaheng, "The Fingo Festival Revolution in South Africa's Eastern Cape," *Africa is a Country* (September 30, 2014), www.africasacountry.com/2014/09/the-fingo-festival-revolution.

59. Monaheng, "The Fingo Festival Revolution in South Africa's Eastern Cape."

60. "Xolile Madinda in Residence," Mellon Indigenous Arts Program, UVA Arts and Sciences (November 5, 2018), https://indigenousarts.as.virginia.edu/xolile-madinda-residence.

61. Yahkeem, "Review: Ndlulamthi—Substance EP," *The Blacksmithed*, https://theblacksmithed.com/2020/10/11/review-ndlulamthi-substance-ep/.

62. Tseliso Monaheng, "Laliboi: from the Eastern Cape, with raps," *Pan-African Music* (November 8, 2019), https://pan-african-music.com/en/laliboi-from-the-eastern-cape-with-raps/; Themba Kriger, "Laliboi channels his heritage," *Mail & Guardian*, (March 12, 2020), https://mg.co.za/article/2020-03-12-laliboi-channels-his-heritage/.

63. Rofhiwa Maneta, "A New Generation of South Africans Are Reviving 90s Genre Kwaito," *Noisey—Music by Vice* (July 6, 2018), https://www.vice.com/en/article/vbj4ej/south-africa-new-kwaito-generation-scene-report-feature.

64. Shiba Melissa Mazaza, "Darkie Fiction return for the next phase of their 'true South Africa' alter-narrative with a new supporting character—along with their latest offering, Endaweni." *Redbull* (March 6, 2020), https://www.redbull.com/za-en/darkie-fiction-start-a-riveting-new-chapter-with-endaweni.

65. Alette Schoon, "The town where Hip Hop is healing South Africa's broken youth," *The Conversation AFRICA* (April 4, 2016), https://theconversation.com/the-town-where-hip-hop-is-healing-south-africas-broken-youth-56943.

66. Schoon, "The town where Hip Hop is healing South Africa's broken youth."

67. Interview with Dr. Boudina McConnachie, Lecturer and African Musical Arts (AMA) activist at Rhodes University and International Library of African Music, January 31, 2021.

68. McConnachie interview.

69. Mateboho Green, "Unsettling Paradigms in the Fault Lines of Change: Re-Imagining a Curriculum," Universities of South Africa Teaching and Learning Strategy Group, (October 12, 2020), https://www.newssite.co.za/usaf/indigenous-music.html; Primarshni Gower and Austin Pinkerton, "Decolonisation of the humanities—No easy answers," *University World News—Africa Edition* (17 September 2020), https://www.universityworldnews.com/post.php?story=20200916105531416.

70. McConnachie interview.

71. McConnachie interview.
72. "Lukae Concepts: A PE Hip Hop Thought Leader," *The Blacksmithed* (June 23, 2020), https://theblacksmithed.com/2020/06/23/lukae-concepts-pe-hip-hop-thought-leader/.
73. Opland, *The Dassie and the Hunter,* 385.

Bibliography

"25 Years of Armed Struggle: Army Commissar Chris Hani Speaks," *Sechaba*, (December 1986), 10–18.

"A Letter from South Africa: Black Laws in the Orange Free State of Africa." *Southern Workman*, Volume 19, No. 11 (November 1890), Hampton University Archives.

Affidavit of Richard Nortje, May 13, 1929; affidavit of Richard Welsh, May 13, 1929; Welsh, May 15, 1929; NTS 1681, file 2/276 Part 1, National Archives of South Africa.

Albert, Don, Gwen Ansell, Darius Brubeck, Pallo Jordan, and Hotep Idres Galeta. *Jazz, Blues & Swing: Six Decades of Music in South Africa*. Claremont, South Africa: David Philip, 2007.

Allen, Lara. "Pennywhistle Kwela: A Musical, Historical, and Socio-Political Analysis," M.A. Thesis. University of Natal, Durban, 1993.

Allen, Lara. "The Effect of Repressive State Policies on the Development and Demise of Kwela Music: South Africa: 1955–65." Paper presented at 10th Symposium on Ethnomusicology, Rhodes University. Grahamstown: International Library of African Music, 1991.

Amandla! Directed by Lee Hirsch, New York and Johannesburg: ATO Pictures/Kwela Productions, 2002.

Amandla! Soundtrack, CD. New York: ATO Records, 2003.

Ansell, Gwen. *Soweto Blues: Jazz, Popular Music, and Politics in South Africa*. New York: Continuum International Publishing Group, 2005.

Armstrong, M. F. and Helen Ludlow. *Hampton and Its Students*. New York: G. P. Putnam's Sons, 1874.

Arnold, Millard, ed. *Steve Biko: Black Consciousness in South Africa*. New York: Random House, 1978.

Ashforth, Adam. "The Xhosa Cattle Killing and the Politics of Memory." *Sociological Forum*, vol. 6, No. 3 (September 1991): 581–592.

Baines, Gary F. *A History of New Brighton 1903–1953: The Detroit of the Union.* Lewiston, NY: Edwin Mellen Press, 2002.

Ballantine, Christopher. "Fact, Ideology and Paradox: African Elements in Early Black South African Jazz and Vaudeville." *African Music,* Volume 7, No. 3, (1996): 44–51.

Ballantine, Christopher. "Music and Emancipation: The Social Role of Black Jazz and Vaudeville in South Africa between the 1920s and the early 1940s." *Journal of South African Studies,* Volume 17, no. 1 (March 1991): 129–152.

Ballantine, Christopher. "The Identities of Race, Class and Gender in the Repression of Early Black South African Jazz and Vaudeville (circa 1920–1944)." Paper presented at the 11th Symposium on Ethnomusicology, University of Natal, 1993. International Library of African Music (ILAM).

Bantu World, July 13, 1935; February 12, 1938; May 15, 1962; Library of Congress.

Beinart, William and Colin Bundy. *Hidden Struggles in Rural South Africa: Politics and Popular Movements in the Transkei and Eastern Cape 1890–1930.* Berkeley: University of California Press, 1987.

Beinart, William. "*Amafelandawonye* (The Diehards): Rural Popular Protest and Women's Movements in Herschel District, South Africa, in the 1920s." Paper presented at the University of the Witwatersrand History Workshop, January 31–February 4, 1984.

Bennie, William G. *Imibengo.* Lovedale: The Lovedale Press, 1935.

Benson, Mary. *South Africa: The Struggle for a Birthright.* International Defence and Aid Fund, 1985.

Berger, Iris. "An African American 'Mother of the Nation': Madie Hall Xuma in South Africa 1940–1963." *Journal of Southern African Studies,* volume 27, No. 3 (September 2001): 547–566.

Biko, Steve. "Black consciousness and the quest for true humanity," address given to a Black Theology seminar, Pietermaritzburg, August 28, 1971, *SASO Newsletter* (September 1971). Digital Innovation South Africa.

Biko, Steve. *I Write What I Like.* Johannesburg: Picador Africa, 2004; originally published 1978.

Bokwe, John Knox. "Ntsikana, the Story of an African Hymn," in *The World of South African Music: A Reader.* Edited by Christine Lucia, 21–25. Newcastle, UK: Cambridge Scholars Press, 2005.

Bokwe, John Knox. *Ntsikana: The Story of an African Convert.* Lovedale, 1914.

Bonner, Philip, Isabel Hofmeyr, Deborah James, and Tom Lodge. *Holding Their Ground: Class, Locality and Culture in 19th and 20th Century South Africa.* Johannesburg: Ravan Press, 2001.

Brown, Joshua, Patrick Manning, Karin Shapiro, and Jon Wiener, eds. *History from South Africa: Alternative Visions and Practices.* Philadelphia: Temple University Press, 1991.

Brownlee, Charles. *Kaffir Life and History.* Lovedale Mission Press, 1896.

Bundy, Colin. *Govan Mbeki.* Athens, OH: Ohio University Press, 2012.

Business Tech, (19 June 2016), https://businesstech.co.za/news/wealth/127213/the-richest-and-poorest-municipalities-in-south-africa.

Campbell, John. *Travels in South Africa*. Andover: Flagg and Gould, 1816.
Cancellotti, Claudia. "Music, Culture & Identity: Pasts, Presents & Futures of San Musical Tradition." Paper presented at 18th Symposium on Ethnomusicology, International Library of African Music, Rhodes University, 2004. ILAM.
Carter, D. "The Defiance Campaign—a comparative analysis of the organization, leadership, and participation in the Eastern Cape and the Transvaal," *University of London Institute of Commonwealth Studies, Collected Seminar Papers on the Societies of Southern Africa in the 19th and 20th Centuries*, volume II (October 1970–June 1971).
Chalmers, J. A. *Tiyo Soga: A Page of South African Mission Work*. London: Hodder & Stoughton, 1877.
Charry, Eric. *Hip Hop Africa: New African Music in a Globalizing World*. Bloomington: Indiana University Press, 2012.
Chikanga, Kenneth. "Theatrical tour de force," *Citizen*, (February 17, 2001).
Chris Hani The Legacy #Hectic PT1, https://www.youtube.com/watch?v=p5vxtrzEN7U; HANI The Legacy, https://www.youtube.com/watch?v=-hV792xTxQQ; Hani: The Legacy, https://www.youtube.com/watch?v=tdZOJz_1K5o.
Christian Express. Lovedale, (September 1891). University of Pretoria Archives.
Cockrell, Dale. "Of Gospel Hymns, Minstrel Shows, and Jubilee Singers: Toward Some Black South African Musics." *American Music*, Volume 5, No. 4 (Winter 1987): 417–432.
Coplan, David and Bennetta Jules-Rosette. "Nkosi Sikele' iAfrika and the Liberation of the Spirit of South Africa." *African Studies*, 64 (December 2, 2005): 343–367.
Coplan, David. "A Terrible Commitment," in *Perilous States: Conversations on Politics, Culture, and Nations*. George E. Marcus, ed., 298–324. Chicago: University of Chicago Press, 1994.
Coplan, David. *In Township Tonight! South Africa's Black City Music and Theatre*. Chicago: University of Chicago Press, 2008.
Council Minutes, 1959, Fort Hare Papers.
Crais, Clifton C. *White supremacy and black resistance in pre-industrial South Africa: The making of the colonial order in the Eastern Cape, 1770–1865*. Cambridge University Press: 1992.
Daily Dispatch (October 24, 1973). Library of Congress.
Daniel, Luke. "Breaking: Grahamstown officially renamed as Makhanda," *The South African* (October 3, 2018), https://www.thesouthafrican.com/news/grahamstown-now-makhanda-eastern-cape-south-africa/.
Dargie, David. "Xhosa Music Terminology: How Traditional Thembu Xhosa Musicians Speak and Think About Their Music." Fort Hare: University of Fort Hare Music Department, 2005.
Dargie, David. *Xhosa Music: Its techniques and instruments, with a collection of songs*. Claremont, South Africa: David Philip.
Davis, Lionel. Interview November 2, 2020.

"The Defiance Campaign—a Comparative Analysis of the Organization, Leadership, and Participation in the Eastern Cape and Transvaal." *University of London, Institute of Commonwealth Studies, Collected Seminar Papers,* 2 (1970).

Deputy Minister of Human Settlements Honourable Zou Kota-Fredericks memorial lecture of "Mary" Nomkhosi Mini speech, Port Elizabeth, 30 August, 2014, Republic of South Africa webpage, https://www.gov.za/deputy-minister-human-settlements-honourable-zou-kota-fredericks-memorial-lecture-%E2%80%9Cmary%E2%80%9D-nomkhosi.

Dike, Fatima. *The Sacrifice of Kreli*. Alexandria, VA: Alexander Street Press, 2002.

Dontsa, Luvuyo. "Intonjane Music: A Forum of Identity Formation for Xhosa Women." In *Music and Identity: Transformation and Negotiation,* eds. E. A. Akrofi, Maria Smit, and Stig-Magnus Thorsén, 383–407. Stellenbosch: Sun Press, 2007.

Dontsa, Luvuyo. "Performing arts and politics in South Africa." Paper presented at the 6th Symposium on Ethnomusicology, International Library of African Music, Rhodes University, 1987. ILAM.

Drew, Allison, ed. *South Africa's Radical Tradition: A documentary history, Volume 2 1943–1964*. Cape Town: UCT Press, 1997.

Edgar, Robert and Hilary Sapire. *African Apocalypse: The Story of Nontetha Nkwenkwe, a Twentieth-Century South African Prophet.* Athens: Ohio University Press, 2000.

Edgar, Robert. "The Prophet Motive: Enoch Mgijima, the Israelites, and the Background to the Bulhoek Massacre." *The International Journal of African Historical Studies* Volume 15, No. 3 (1982): 401–422.

Erlman, Veit. "'A Feeling of Prejudice.' Orpheus M. McAdoo and the Virginia Jubilee Singers in South Africa 1890–1898." *Journal of South African Studies* Volume 14, no. 3 (April 1988): 331–350.

Erlmann, Veit. *Music, Modernity and the Global Imagination*. New York: Oxford University Press, 1999.

Erlmann, Veit. *African Stars: Studies in Black South African Performance*. Chicago: University of Chicago Press, 1991.

Erlmann, Veit. *Nightsong: Performance, Power, and Practice in South Africa*. Chicago: University of Chicago Press, 1991.

Eve, Jeanette. *A Literary Guide to the Eastern Cape: Places and the Voices of Writers*. Cape Town: Double Storey Books, 2003.

"Expelled students deny leading Fort Hare demonstration," *Rand Daily Mail*, (March 13, 1969). Library of Congress.

Fanon, Frantz. *The Wretched of the Earth*. New York: Grove Press, 1963.

Fast, Hildegarde H. *The Journal and Selected Letters of Rev. William J. Shrewsbury 1826–1835, First Missionary to the Transkei*. Johannesburg: Witwatersrand University Press, 1994.

Federation of South African Women (FSAW). "Report of the First National Conference of Women," April 17, 1954. University of Witwatersrand Historical Papers.

Fehr, William, translator. *Ludwig Alberti's Account of the Tribal Life and Customs of the Xhosa in 1807*. Cape Town: A. A. Balkema, 1968.

Feni, Lulamile. "The gripping sounds of a man on the rise." *Daily Dispatch* (December 18, 2018). https://www.dispatchlive.co.za/lifestyle/daily-life/2018-12-18-the-gripping-sounds-of-a-man-on-the-rise/.

Fisk Jubilee Singers, fragment of biography, "Foreword," author unknown, n.d., Hampton University Archives.

Fredericks, Troy. Interview October 3, 2020; Email November 1, 2020.

Frederickson, George M. *Black Liberation: A Comparative History of Black Ideologies in the United States and South Africa*. New York: Oxford University Press, 1995.

Fugard, Athol, John Kani, and Winston Ntshona. *Sizwe Banzi is Dead*. New York: Viking, 1976.

Fugard, Athol. *Notebooks: 1960–1977*. New York: Theatre Communications Group, 1984.

Galane, Sello, ed. *Beyond Memory: Recording the History, Moments and Memories of South African Music—From the diary of Max Mojapelo*. Somerset West, South Africa: African Minds, 2008.

Gérard, Albert S. *Four African Literatures: Xhosa, Sotho, Zulu, Amharic*. Berkeley: University of California Press, 1971.

Gerhart, Gail, and Clive L. Glaser. *From Protest to Challenge: A Documentary History of African Politics in South Africa, 1882–1990, Volume 6: Challenge and Victory, 1980–1990*. Bloomington: University of Indiana Press, 2010.

Gibbs, Timothy. *Mandela's Kinsmen: Nationalist Elites & Apartheid's First Bantustan*. Rochester, NY: James Currey, 2014.

Gibson, Nigel. *Fanonian Practices in South Africa: From Steve Biko to Abahlali baseMjondolo*. New York: Palgrave Macmillan, 2011.

Gilbert, Shirli. "Singing Against Apartheid: ANC Cultural Groups and the International Anti-Apartheid Struggle." *Journal of Southern African Studies* Volume 33, No. 2 (June 2007): 424–441.

Gower, Primarshni and Austin Pinkerton. "Decolonisation of the humanities—No easy answers," *University World News—Africa Edition*, 17 September 2020, https://www.universityworldnews.com/post.php?story=20200916105531416.

Green, Mateboho. "Unsettling Paradigms in the Fault Lines of Change: Re-Imagining a Curriculum," Universities of South Africa Teaching and Learning Strategy Group, (October 12, 2020), https://www.newssite.co.za/usaf/indigenous-music.html

Gumbi, Johannes. "The Transkei Constitution—Changes Needed," *Bantu World*, May 15, 1962. Library of Congress.

Hansen, Deirdre. "Music of the Xhosa-Speaking People." Ph.D. Dissertation, University of Witwatersrand, 1981.

Haupt, Adam. *Static: Race and representation in post-apartheid music, media and film*. Cape Town: HSRC Press, 2012.

"Here's why Grahamstown has been renamed Makhanda." *IOL*, (October 3, 2018). https://www.iol.co.za/news/south-africa/eastern-cape/heres-why-grahamstown-has-been-renamed-makhanda-17334278.

Hill, Robert A., ed., *The Marcus Garvey and Universal Negro Improvement Association Papers,* Durham: Duke University Press, 2011.

Hodgson, Janet. *Ntsikana's Great Hymn.* Cape Town: Center for African Studies, UCT, 1980.

Hughes, Lestie. "The Social and Cultural Significance of Dudley Tito's Music: A Postmodern Investigation." M.A. Thesis, University of Port Elizabeth, 1999.

Huskisson, Y. "A Survey of Music in the Native Schools of the Transvaal." M.A. Thesis. University of Witwatersrand: 1955.

Iimbongi Workshop, Rhodes University Department of African Language Studies, Puku Story Festival, February 18, 2016, Grahamstown.

Imvo Zabantsundu, December 15, 1892; February 25, 1929. Library of Congress.

International Library of African Music. Catalog # ILAM TR026, Compiled, recorded, and edited by Hugh Tracey, (Grahamstown: 1957).

Jaji, Tsitis Ella. *Africa in Stereo: Modernism, Music and Pan-African Solidarity.* New York: Oxford University Press, 2014.

Jolaosho, Tayo. "Anti-Apartheid Freedom Songs: Then and Now." *Smithsonian Folkways Magazine* (Spring 2014). http://www.folkways.si.edu/magazine-spring-2014-anti-apartheid-freedom-songs-then-and-now/south-africa/music/article/smithsonian.

Jordan, A. C. *Towards an African Literature: The Emergence of Literary Form in Xhosa.* Berkeley: University of California Press, 1973.

Jordan, Pallo. "Johnny Dyani: A Portrait." *Rixaka: Cultural Journal of the African National Congress,* No. 4 (1988): 4–8.

Jubilee Singers at the Vaudeville," *The Cape Argus*, Cape Town, July 1, 1890. Library of Congress.

Karis, Thomas and Gail Gerhart. *From Protest to Challenge: A Documentary History of African Politics in South Africa 1882–1990, Volume 5: Nadir and Resurgence 1965–1979.* Bloomington: Indiana University Press, 1997.

Karis, Thomas, Gwendolyn Carter, and Sheridan Johns III. *From Protest to Challenge: A Documentary History of African Politics in South Africa 1882–1964, Volume 1: Protest and Hope 1882–1934.* Stanford, CA: Hoover Institution Press, 1972;

Kaschula, Russell H. *The Bones of the Ancestors Are Shaking.* Lansdowne: Juta, 2002.

Kaschula, Russell. Interview and email, July 2016; June 16, 2020.

Kavanagh, Robert Mshengu. *Theatre and Cultural Struggle Under Apartheid.* London: Zed Books, 1985.

"The Khoikhoi at the Cape of Good Hope," National Library of South Africa, Library of Congress, World Digital Library. https://www.wdl.org/en/search/?collection=the-khoikhoi-at-the-cape-of-good-hope.

King, Robert M. *Reports of Cases Decided in the Eastern District Court of the Colony of the Cape of Good Hope. Vol. X Part I–IV.* Cape Town: J. C. Juta & Co., 1896. Reprinted by Leopold Classic Library.

Kirsch, Beverley, Silvia Skorge, Sindiwe Magona and Theresa Soci. *Complete Xhosa.* New York: McGraw-Hill, 2010.

Klein, Naomi. "Democracy Born in Chains: South Africa's Constricted Freedom." In Klein, *The Shock Doctrine*, 245–274. New York: Picador, 2007.

Kotze, Astrid von. *Organize and Act: The Natal Workers Theatre Movement, 1983–1987.* Durban: Culture and Working Life Publications, 1988.

Kriger, Themba. "Laliboi channels his heritage." *Mail & Guardian* (March 12, 2020). https://mg.co.za/article/2020-03-12-laliboi-channels-his-heritage/.

La Housse, Paul. *Brewers, Beerhalls, and Boycotts.* Johannesburg: Ravan Press, 1988.

Lanegran, Kimberly. "Civic Associations in Transitional Local Government Structures in South Africa." *Critical Sociology* Vol. 22, 3 (October 1996): 113–134.

"Let the Living Remember," *Dawn*, Umkhonto We Sizwe, Volume 8, No. 6 (1984). Digital Innovation South Africa.

Levine, Laurie. *The Drumcafé's Traditional Music of South Africa.* Johannesburg: Jacana Media, 2005.

Lichtenstein, H. *Travels in Southern Africa in the Years 1803, 1804, 1805, translation by A. Plumptre, 2 volumes.* Cape Town: Henry Collburn, 1812. Internet Archive, https://archive.org/details/travelsinsouther02lich/page/106/mode/2up.

Lucia, Christie, ed. *The World of South African Music: A Reader.* Newcastle: Cambridge Scholars Press, 2005.

"Lukae Concepts: A PE Hip Hop Thought Leader." *The Blacksmithed* (June 23, 2020). https://theblacksmithed.com/2020/06/23/lukae-concepts-pe-hip-hop-thought-leader/.

Lukhele, Khehla. *Stokvels in South Africa.* Johannesburg: Amagi, 1990.

Mac, Heather. Interview July 15, 2013.

Mackay, E. A. "Antigone and Orestes in the Works of Athol Fugard." *Theoria: A Journal of Studies in the Arts, Humanities and Social Sciences*, vol. LXXIV (October 1989): 31–43.

Mafeje, Archie. "The Role of the Bard in a Contemporary African Community." *Journal of African Languages*, VI, 3 (1967): 193–223.

Makeba, Miriam and Nomsa Mwamuka. *Makeba: The Miriam Makeba Story.*, Pretoria: STE Publishers, 2004.

Makiwane, Ambrose. "SRC Statement re: Findings of a Commission of Enquiry," August 21, 1958, SRC and other committees, Fort Hare Papers.

Makiwane, Ambrose. Cala, March 4, 1999, Interview by Danny Massey, Digital Innovation South Africa.

Mancotywa, Sonwabile. "A Revolutionary Life Cut Short: Bathandwa Ndondo Memorial Lecture." Walter Sisulu University, April 14, 2016.

Mandela, Nelson. *Long Walk to Freedom.* New York: Little, Brown and Co., 1994.

Maneta, Rofhiwa. "A New Generation of South Africans Are Reviving 90s Genre Kwaito." *Noisey—Music by Vice* (July 6, 2018). https://www.vice.com/en/article/vbj4ej/south-africa-new-kwaito-generation-scene-report-feature.

Mangcu, Xolela. "Retracing Nelson Mandela through the Lineage of Black Political Thought," *Transition*, No. 112, Django Unpacked (2013): 101–116.

"Mass Support for Defiance Campaign," *The Clarion*, (July 31, 1952).

Massey, Daniel. *Under Protest: The Rise of Student Resistance at Fort Hare.* Pretoria: UNISA Press, 2010.

Mathe, Sam. "Pioneer jazzman 'Bra Pat,' the legend," *Sunday Independent*, January 4, 2015. https://www.iol.co.za/sundayindependent/pioneer-jazzman-bra-pat-the-legend-1801075.

Matthews, Z. K. *Social Relations in a Common South African Society.* Johannesburg: Anglo American Corporation, 1961.

Mayer, Philip. *Townsmen or Tribesmen: Conservatism and the Process of Urbanization in a South Africa City.* Cape Town: Oxford University Press, 1971.

Mayoli, Sizwe. "Inkululeko yase Sieskei," *Umgqala* 1: 18.

Mazaza, Shiba Melissa. "Darkie Fiction return for the next phase of their 'true South Africa' alter-narrative with a new supporting character—along with their latest offering, Endaweni." *Redbull* (March 6, 2020). https://www.redbull.com/za-en/darkie-fiction-start-a-riveting-new-chapter-with-endaweni.

Mbeki, Govan, *Learning from Robben Island.* Cape Town: David Philip, 1991.

Mbeki, Govan. *South Africa: The Peasants' Revolt.* Harmondsworth, UK: Penguin, 1964.

McAdoo, Eugene. Editorial. *Southern Workman* (January 1894), Hampton University Archives.

McConnachie, Boudina. Interview, January 31, 2021.

McConnachie, Jenny. Interviews and email, July 2016; July 2017.

McGiffin, Emily. *Of Land, Bones, and Money: Toward a South African Ecopoetics.* Charlottesville: University of Virginia, Press, 2019.

Mda, Zakes. *Sometimes There Is a Void: Memoirs of an Outsider.* Johannesburg: Penguin, 2011.

Meel, B. L. "Determinants of suicide in the Transkei sub-region of South Africa," *Journal of Clinical Forensic Medicine*, 10: 2 (2003): 71–76.

Mencia, Nick. "Biography of Mtutuzeli Dudu Pukwana." *South African History Online*. https://www.sahistory.org.za/article/biography-mtutuzeli-dudu-pukwana-nick-mencia.

Michie, L. Personal Diary and articles written for the *Daily Dispatch* and *The New Bern Sun Journal*, 1988–91.

Mkhize, Kwezi. "Empire Unbound: Imperial Liberalism, Race and Diaspora in the Making of South Africa." Ph.D. dissertation. University of Pennsylvania, 2015.

Modisane, Jerry. "Why I walked off Fort Hare in protest," *SASO Newsletter* (May 1972). Digital Innovation South Africa.

Molefe, Sono, ed. *Malibongwe: Poems from the Struggle by ANC Women.* Durban: uHlanga Press, 2020.

Monaheng, Ts'eliso. "The Fingo Festival Revolution in South Africa's Eastern Cape." *Africa is a Country.* (September 30, 2014). www.africasacountry.com/2014/09/the-fingo-festival-revolution.

Monaheng, Tseliso. "Laliboi: from the Eastern Cape, with raps." *Pan-African Music* (November 8, 2019). https://pan-african-music.com/en/laliboi-from-the-eastern-cape-with-raps/.

Mooki, Bob. "Popular Theatre and Struggle," *Rixaka*, No. 2 (1986). Digital Innovation South Africa.

Mostert, Noël. *Frontiers.* New York: Alfred A. Knopf, 1992.

Mpola, Mavis Noluthando. "An Analysis of Oral Literary Music Texts in IsiXhosa." Ph.D. Thesis. Rhodes University, 2007.
Mpupha, Dumisa. Interview, International Library of African Music, July 2, 2017.
Mqhayi, Samuel Edward Krune. *Abantu Besizwe.* Edited and translated by Jeff Opland. Johannesburg: Wits University Press, 2009.
Msila, Vuyisile. *A Place to Live: Red Location and Its history from 1903 to 2013.* Stellenbosch: Sun Press, 2014.
Msila, Vuyisile. *The Black Train Rising: The Life and Times of Welcome Duru.* Lynwood Ridge, South Africa: Siyomba Projects, 2010.
Mteteli wa Bantu, June 6, 1931. University of Johannesburg.
Mtuze, P. T. "Facing Mount Nelson: A critical analysis of five Xhosa poems on Nelson Rholihlahla Mandela." *South African Journal of African Languages* 16:2 (1996).
Myburgh, James. "How the necklace was hung around Winnie's neck," *PoliticsWeb,* April 17, 2018. https://www.politicsweb.co.za/news-and-analysis/how-the-necklace-was-hung-around-winnies-neck.
Mzamane, Mbulelo Vizikhungo. "The Impact of Black Consciousness on Culture." In *Bounds of possibility: The Legacy of Steve Biko and Black Consciousness.* Edited by N. Barney Pityana, Manphela Ramphele, Malusi Mpumlwana, and Lindy Wilson, 179–193. Cape Town: Zed Books, 1992.
Naidoo, Indres. *Prisoner 885/63, Island in Chains: As told by Indres Naidoo to Albie Sachs.* Hammondsworth, Middlesex: Penguin Books, 1982.
Ndletyana, Mcebisi. *African Intellectuals in 19th and Early 20th Century South Africa.* Cape Town: HSRC Press, 2008.
Negro World, July 30, 1927. Library of Congress.
Neophytou, Nadia. "Interview: Exploring Msaki's Genre-Defying Voice." *OkayAfrica.com* (October 8, 2020). https://www.okayafrica.com/south-african-music-msaki-interview/.
Ngidi, Sandile. "Zim Ngqawana obituary: Free-spirited South African saxophonist," *The Guardian* (July 6, 2011). https://www.theguardian.com/music/2011/jul/06/zim-ngqawana-obituary.
Ngubane, Jordan. *Inkundla ya Bantu,* July 17, 1944. University of Cape Town Special Collections.
Nkosi, Lewis. "Jazz in Exile." *Transition* 5(24) (1966): 34–37.
Nobanda, Thembeka. Interview June 1989.
"Nombasa Mqoko: Eastern Cape born independent singer and songwriter," SAfm podcast (October 4, 2016). https://iono.fm/e/342348.
Nyumka, Zikhona. "Xhosa praise poet, Bhodl'ingqaka, continues to soar to greater heights," *Grocott's Mail,* (March 29, 2019). https://www.grocotts.co.za/2019/03/29/xhosa-praise-poet-bhodlingqaka-continues-to-soar-to-greater-heights/.
Odendaal, André. *The Founders: The Origins of the ANC and the Struggle for Democracy in South Africa.* Lexington, KY: University Press of Kentucky, 2013.
Odendaal, André. "African Political Mobilization in the Eastern Cape 1890–1910," Ph.D. Dissertation. University of Cambridge, 1983.

Odendaal, André. *Black Protest Politics in South Africa to 1912.* Totawa, NJ: Barnes and Noble Books, 1984.

Olwage, Grant. "John Knox Bokwe, Colonial Composer: Tales about Race and Music." *Journal of the Royal Musical Association,* Volume 131, No. 1 (2006): 1–37.

Opland, Jeff and Peter T. Mtuze, eds. *John Solilo: Umoya wembongi, Collected poems (1922–1935).* Pietermaritzburg: University of KwaZulu-Natal, 2016.

Opland, Jeff. "Abantu-Batho and the Xhosa Poets," in *The People's Paper: A Centenary History and Anthology of Abantu-Batho,* edited by Peter Limb. Johannesburg: Wits University Press, 2012.

Opland, Jeff. "The Early Career of D. L. P. Manisi, Thembu Imbongi." *Research in African Literatures,* Vol. 33, No. 1 (Spring 2002): 1–26.

Opland, Jeff. *The Dassie and the Hunter: A South African Meeting.* Scottsville, South Africa: University of KwaZulu-Natal Press, 2005.

Opland, Jeff. *Xhosa Poets and Poetry,* 2nd ed. Pietermaritzburg: University of KwaZulu-Natal Press, 2017.

Opland, Jeff, ed. *The Nation's Bounty: The Xhosa Poetry of Nontsizi Mgqwetho.* Johannesburg: Wits University Press, 2007.

Opland, Jeff. "The image of the book in Xhosa oral poetry." In *Print, text & book cultures in South Africa.* Edited by Andrew van der Vlies, 286–305. Johannesburg: Wits University Press, 2012.

Opondo, Patricia Achieng. "African Music in Global Diasporic Discourse: Identity Explorations of South African Artists Johnny Mbizo Dyani." In *Music and Identity: Transformation and Negotiation,* eds. Eric Akrofi, Maria Smit, and Stig-Magnus Thorsén, 257–276. Stellenbosch: Sun Press, 2007.

Ord, J. W. Acting Magistrate, Middledrift, to Magistrate, King William's Town, 23 October 1923. Justice Department 268 2/950/19. State Archives Depot, Pretoria.

Orkin, Martin. *Drama and the South African state.* Johannesburg: Witwatersrand University Press, 1991.

"Pebco Three: Bodies may have been found," *IOL* (Independent Online South Africa), July 16, 2007. https://www.iol.co.za/news/south-africa/pebco-three-bodies-may-have-been-found-362244.

Peires, J. B. *The Dead Will Arise.* Johannesburg: Ravan Press, 1989.

Peires, J. B. *The House of Phalo.* Berkeley: University of California Press, 1981.

Peires, J. B. Conversations and emails, July 7, 2017; July 30, 2018.

Peires, Jeff. "The Implosion of Transkei and Ciskei." *African Affairs,* Vol. 91, No. 364 (July 1992): 365–387.

Pollard, Alton B., III. "Rhythms of Resistance: The Role of Freedom Songs in South Africa." In *"This Is How We Flow": Rhythm in Black Cultures,* edited by Angela M. S. Nelson, 98–124. Columbia: University of South Carolina Press, 1999.

"Port Elizabeth Disturbances," *Natal Witness,* October 21, 1952. Library of Congress.

Posel. Deborah. *The Making of Apartheid 1948–1961: Conflict and Compromise.* Oxford: Clarendon Press, 1991.

Queenstown Daily Representative, October 13, 1920. Queenstown and Frontier Museum.

Randall, Peter. "The banning of 'Confused Mhlaba,'" *Index on Censorship*, 5:4 (1976) DOI: 10.1080/03064227608532569.

Rasmussen, Lars, ed. *Mbizo—A Book About Johnny Dyani*. Copenhagen: The Booktrader, 2003.

Raven-Hart, Major R. *Before Van Riebeeck*. Cape Town: Struik, 1967.

Raven-Hart, Major R. *Cape of Good Hope, 1652–1702: The First Fifty Years*, 2 vols. Cape Town: Balkema, 1970.

Record of Evidence to the Natives Economic Commission, Tshangana, March 18–April 10, 1931, p. 5992, TA K26, Volume 7. Central Government Archives, Pretoria.

Red Location Museum Exhibit, 2013.

Rixaka, no. 1 (ANC: 1985); No. 3 (1986). Digital Innovation South Africa.

Robinson, Jennifer. *The Power of Apartheid: State, Power and Space in South African Cities*. Oxford: Butterworth-Heinemann, 1996.

Roux, Edward. *Time Longer Than Rope: The Black Man's Struggle for Freedom in South Africa*. Madison: University of Wisconsin Press, 1948.

Ruiters, Greg, ed. *The Fate of the Eastern Cape: History, Politics and Social Policy*. Scottsville: University of KwaZulu-Natal Press, 2011.

SABC Truth Commission Special Report, http://sabctrc.saha.org.za/victims/mini_nomkhosi_aka_mary.htm?tab=report.

Sampson, Anthony. *Drum: A Venture into the New Africa*. London: Collins, 1956.

Sampson, Anthony. *Nelson Mandela: The Authorized Biography*. New York: Knopf, 1999.

Sandilands, Alexander. *120 Negro Spirituals*. Lesotho: Maroija Sesuto Book Depot, 1951.

SASO Newsletter. June 1971; August 1971; September 1970. Digital Innovation South Africa.

Schadeberg, Jurgen, and Pallo Jordan, eds., *Jazz, Blues and Swing: Six Decades of Music in South Africa*, (Claremont, South Africa: David Philip, 2007).

Scheub, Harold. Review of *Towards an African Literature: The Emergence of Literary Form in Xhosa* by A.C. Jordan. *The Journal of American Folklore*, Vol. 90, No. 357. July–September 1977.

Scheub, Harold. *The Xhosa Ntsomi*. Oxford: Clarendon, 1975.

Schoon, Alette. "The town where Hip Hop is healing South Africa's broken youth." *The Conversation AFRICA*. (April 4, 2016). https://theconversation.com/the-town-where-Hip Hop-is-healing-south-africas-broken-youth-56943.

Scully, W. C. *By Veldt and Kopje*. London: T. Fisher Unwin, 1907.

Sechaba, vol. 11, 3rd Quarter (1977). Digital Innovation South Africa.

Shingler, John. "Crack heard around the world: Leave Fort Hare alone—away with indoctrination," *Student: The International Student Magazine* (1959). Cory Library, Alexander Kerr Collection. PR 43228.

Sitas, Ari, ed. *Black Mamba Rising: South African Worker Poets in Struggle*, Worker Resistance and Culture Publications. Durban: University of Natal, 1986.

Smith, Charles Spencer. *A History of the African Methodist Episcopal Church: Being a Volume Supplemental to A History of the African Methodist Episcopal Church.* Philadelphia: A.M.E. Book Concern, 1922.

Smith, Janet and Beauregard Tromp. *Hani: A Life Too Short.* Jeppestown: Jonathan Ball Publishers, 2009.

Soga, John Henderson. *The Ama-Xosa: Life and Customs.* Lovedale Press, 1932. Reprinted by Cambridge University Press.

Soga, John Henderson. *The South-Eastern Bantu: Abe-Nguni, Aba-Mbo, Ama-Lala.* Johannesburg: Witwatersrand University Press, 1930.

Solberg, Rolf. *Alternative Theater in South Africa: Talks with prime movers since the 1970s.* Pietermaritzburg: Hadeda Books, 1999.

Solberg, Rolf. *Bra Gib: Father of South Africa's Township Theatre.* Scottsville, South Africa: University of KwaZulu-Natal Press, 2011.

Sophiatown Soundtrack, CD. Johannesburg: Gallo Records, 2005.

Sophiatown. Directed by Pascale Lamche, Ireland and South Africa: Little Bird Productions, 2003.

Sound of Africa Series 32: South Africa (Xhosa/Mpondo), Album. Grahamstown: International Library of African Music, 2014.

South African Freedom Songs, CD. University of Western Cape: Mayibuye Center, 2000. 2 Discs.

Southern Workman, Volume 20, No. 1 (January 1891); No. 2 (February 1891). Hampton University Archives.

Steedman, A. *Wanderings and Adventures in the Interior of Southern Africa.* London: 1835. Reprinted by Nabu Press, Charleston, 2012, 224.

Steingo, Gavin. *Kwaito's Promise: Music and the Aesthetics of Freedom in South Africa.* Chicago: University of Chicago Press, 2016.

Steve Biko Memorial Lectures 2000–2008. Johannesburg: The Steve Biko Foundation and Macmillan, 2017.

Switzer, Les, ed. *South Africa's Alternative Press: Voices of Protest and Resistance, 1880s–1960s.* Cambridge: Cambridge University of Press, 1997.

Taylor, Dexter, ed. *Christianity and the Natives of South Africa: A Year Book of South African Missions,* (Lovedale, n.d.).

"The Richest and Poorest Municipalities in South Africa." *Business Tech* (19 June 2016). https://businesstech.co.za/news/wealth/127213/the-richest-and-poorest-municipalities-in-south-africa.

"The Theatre and Black South Africa," *SASO Newsletter,* (June 1971), Natal: SASO Publications. Digital Innovation South Africa.

Thram, Diane, ed. *Generations of Jazz—At the Red Location Museum,* Exhibition Catalogue Grahamstown: International Library of African Music, 2013.

Township Jive and Kwela Jazz (1940–1960), CD. Grahamstown: Soul Safari/Ubuntu Publishing, 2011.

Transvaal Local Government (Stallard) Commission, 1922. TAB 1217, National Archives of South Africa.

Truth and Reconciliation Commission Final Report, Volume 2, Chapter 5, Subsection 23. https://www.justice.gov.za/trc/report/finalreport/Volume%202.pdf.

Ukpanah, Ime. *The Long Road to Freedom: Inkundla Ya Bantu (Bantu Forum) and the African Nationalist Movement in South Africa: 1938–1951*. Trenton, NJ: Africa World Press, 2005.

Vail, Leroy and Landeg White. *Power and the Praise Poem*. Charlottesville: University Press of Virginia, 1991.

Van der Merwe, Hendrik, and David Walsh, eds. *Student Perspectives on South Africa*. Cape Town: David Philip, 1972.

"Verwoerd blames Port Elizabeth for Native Riots," *Eastern Province Herald*, October 21, 1952; "Port Elizabeth Warned by Minister," *The Star*, October 23, 1952. Library of Congress.

"Verwoerd's Crown Colony: The Transkeian Scheme and the Future of the Chiefs." *Fighting Talk*. Vol. 16, No. 2 (March 1962): 3–4.

Vinson, Robert Trent. *The Americans Are Coming! Dreams of African American Liberation in Segregationist South Africa*. Athens, OH: Ohio University Press, 2012.

Wainwright, A. T. "The Praises of Xhosa Mineworkers," M.A. Thesis. University of South Africa, 1979.

Walker, Cherryl. *Women and Resistance in South Africa*. New York: Monthly Review Press, 1982.

Watkins, Lee William. "Keeping It Real: AmaXhosa Limbongi Making Mimesis Do Its Thing in the Hip Hop and Rap Music of the Eastern Cape." *Journal of the International Library of African Music* Volume 8: Number 4. (2010): 26–35.

Wenzel, Jennifer. *Bulletproof: Afterlives of Anticolonial Prophecy in South Africa and Beyond*. Chicago: University of Chicago Press, 2009.

Williams, Donovan. "African Nationalism in South Africa: Origins and Problems." *Journal of African History*, XI, 3 (1970): 371–383.

Women Marching into the 21st Century: Wathint' Abafazi, Wathint' Imbokodo. Cape Town: Human Sciences Research Council Press, 2000.

Woods, Donald. *Biko*. New York: Holt, 1991.

The World (February 9, 1967). Library of Congress.

"Xolile Madinda in Residence." Mellon Indigenous Arts Program, UVA Arts and Sciences (November 5, 2018). https://indigenousarts.as.virginia.edu/xolile-madinda-residence.

Xuma, Alfred. Evidence to the Native Economic Commission, 1931, *Izwi Lase Township*, January 1984, No. 7. University of Witwatersrand Historical Papers.

Yahkeem. "Review: Ndlulamthi—Substance EP." *The Blacksmithed*, https://theblacksmithed.com/2020/10/11/review-ndlulamthi-substance-ep/.

Yali-Manisi, D. L. P. *Iimbali Zamanyange—Historical Poems*. Edited and translated by Jeff Opland and Pamela Maseko. Pietermaritzburg: University of KwaZulu-Natal Press.

Index

abantu ababomvu. *See* red people
abantu basisikoweni. *See* school people
Abe-Nguni. *See* Xhosa people
Achebe, Chinua, 200
activism: for African nationalism, 104, 107, 126–27; for ANC, 27–28, 80, 110–11, 119–20, 129–30; against apartheid, 8, 140–41, 157–58; boycotts, 120, 127, 154, 178–80, 209; choirs in, 117–19; against Christianity, 48, 77–78; in Ciskei, 104, 111; against colonialism, 71; for community consciousness, 186–87; for culture, 2; with Defiance Campaign, 125, 129–30; against discrimination, 54; in education, 10–11, 159–60; for employment, 181; against Europe, 130–31; at Fort Hare, 109–10, 131, 177–80; freedom songs in, 183; guerrilla armies for, 9; for hymns, 73–74; for identity, 75–76; for *imbongi*, 206–7; with *izibongo*, 2; with jazz, 147–48; *kwela* as, 134–35; by Mandela, 91, 194–95; for Yali-Manisi, 31–32; by Mbeki, G., 125, 132, 145; Pan Africanist Congress in, 140–41, 180–82; performance and, 248–49; poetry for, 80–85; for police, 103–4, 142–43; politics of, 45, 132, 134–35, 210–13; against racism, 57–58; for school people, 178, 182; Sharpeville Massacre 1960 as, 222; South African Defense Force against, 226; with Soweto Uprising 1976, 9, 183–84; stayaways, 179, 201; in Transkei, 104, 111; at UNITRA, 210–11, 219, 221, 224, 228; by Virginia Jubilee Singers, 58–60; for women, 106–7, 117–18, 132–33; by Xhosa people, 7–8
Africa: All Africa Convention for, 109, 116; Black consciousness in, 8–9; culture in, 3–4, 21; education in, 47–48; Europe and, 27, 40, 111–12, 126–27; for Grey, 49; hip hop in, 13, 236, 240; jazz for, 3–4, 6–7, 93–94, 112, 184; middle class in, 97–98; for Mqhayi, 102–3; oppression in, 51; rap in, 240–43; sexism in, 238–39; World War I for, 75–76; World War II for, 116
African nationalism: activism for, 104, 107, 126–27; Christianity for, 29; education for, 38, 58–59, 110; history of, 15, 71, 75–76, 84–85, 157; identity from, 49, 65, 91, 248–49; *imbongi* for, 101–2; for Mandela,

115; for Yali-Manisi, 38–39; for Mqhayi, 49; music for, 246; in performance, 101; politics of, 7, 120, 127, 147
African Rhythm Crotchets (group), 128
afrobeat, 9
"Ah' Zanzolo: Bunjalo Ubomi" (Ngxokolo), 128
Alexander, Ray, 133
All Africa Convention, 109, 116
Allen, Lara, 134–35
amagqoboka, 46
Amandla! (documentary), 129
Amandla Cultural Ensemble, 9–10, 199
Amato, Rob, 174–75
amaXhosa. *See* Xhosa people
American Methodist Episcopal Church, 65–66, 69
American Negro Review (Xuma, M. H.), 117–18
ANC: activism for, 27–28, 80, 110–11, 119–20, 129–30; All Africa Convention for, 109; apartheid for, 140, 198; "Color Bar" bill for, 103–4; cultural workers for, 204–5; for culture, 120–21; exile of, 173, 195–96; extremism against, 13; history of, 6–7, 201–2; human rights for, 232–33; laws against, 155, 158; leadership for, 99, 102, 116; for Yali-Manisi, 136; membership in, 131; music for, 128–29; with Pan Africanist Congress, 141, 146, 180; performance for, 117–18, 205–6; in Transkei, 210–13; women in, 107. *See also specific topics*
Angola, 170
Ansell, Gwen, 160–61
Anti-Pass Hymn, 120
apartheid: activism against, 8, 140–41, 157–58; for ANC, 140, 198; art during, 190; for Black consciousness, 150, 168–71; Black Theater related to, 189–90; choirs during, 127; in Ciskei, 220–21, 225–26; culture after, 234–35; for education, 167–68, 234–35, 242; history of, 1, 130–31, 167–68, 233–34; identity during, 6; ideology of, 7–8; *imbongi* after, 228–29, 237–38; *izibongo* during, 66, 138–39, 227–28; jazz related to, 9–10, 229–30; Mandela during, 138–39; for Mbutuma, 195; oppression during, 4–5, 125–26, 152; politics of, 156–57, 231; Sharpeville Massacre 1960 for, 140–41; sports during, 181–82; in Transkei, 220–21, 223–24; Truth and Reconciliation Commission after, 183, 231, 234; violence with, 12–13, 132, 142–43, 201; for women, 188
Armstrong, S. C., 61
art, 160–61, 172–75, 183, 189–90, 205–9
Atwell, Count, 150–51
Azanian People's Liberation Army, 141–42
Azanian People's Organization, 200–201

Baard, Frances, 133
"Bahleli Bonke," 8
Ballantine, Christopher, 92, 111
Bantu Authorities Act, 136, 192
Bantu Education Act, 7
Bantu National Music, 97
Bantu people, 15–16, 76
Bantu songs, 4
Bantustans, 10; for culture, 145, 196, 211, 225; politics of, 157, 160, 167, 190–91. *See also* homelands
Baqwa, Jeff, 168, 179
Baqwa, Selby, 168, 177, 180

The Basin Blues (group), 119
"The Battle of Amalinde 1818" (Yali-Manisi), 31–32
Beckett, Samuel, 154
Beinart, William, 104
Belafonte, Harry, 128
Benson, Mary, 130

Bhodl'ingqaka (Akhona Mafani), 238
Biko, Stephen, 8–9, 156–60, 168–70, 182–87, 190–91, 222
Birkett, Christopher, 67
Bisho massacre, 225–27
Bisset, John Jarvis, 113
Blackburn, Molly, 187
Black consciousness, 8–9, 160; apartheid for, 150, 168–71; in art, 172–75, 183, 189–90, 205–9; for culture, 202–4; in education, 190–91; history of, 33, 158–59, 242; hymns for, 56–57; identity from, 167–68; ideology of, 177–79, 182, 184, 186; jazz for, 161, 239–40; movement, 156, 162; oppression of, 198–200
Black Local Authorities, 201–2
Black Panthers, 158
Black people: culture of, 92, 148, 154, 169–70; discrimination against, 70; education for, 96, 116, 145–46; Gallery of African Heroes for, 110; heritage of, 102–3; identity of, 162; jazz for, 153–54; for Yali-Manisi, 193–95; oppression of, 6–7, 135, 150; performance by, 147–48; police for, 99; politics for, 111–12, 161; racism against, 84; in U.S., 62–63, 74–75; white paternalism for, 84–85; in World War I, 115
Black People's Convention, 168–69, 182
Black Peril election, 102–3
Black Theater, 170–77, 189–90
"Blood Guns and Revolutions" (Msaki and Muyanga), 240–41
Blood Knot (Fugard), 154
blues music, 93–94
Bokwe, John Knox, 49, 55–56, 96, 112, 114–15
Bookholane, Fats, 154
Botha, P. W., 11, 212, 223–24
Botha, Thozamile, 182
Boweni, M., 68
boycotts, 120, 127, 154, 178–80, 209

Brand, Dollar, 229
British empire, 20, 69–70, 76, 101–2; colonialism for, 25, 27, 29–33; for Xhosa people, 1, 3, 5
Brownlee, Charles, 50, 113
Brubeck, Darius, 230
Bughwan, Devi, 109–10
Bundy, Colin, 104, 132
Burns-Ncamashe, S. M. See, 194–95
Bush, George H. W., 223
Buthelezi, Mangosuthu, 226, 229
Buthelezi, Wellington Elias, 74, 104–5
Buya, Ace, 112

Calata, Fort, 211–12
Calata, James A., 110, 116
Calderwood, Henry, 50
Caluza, Reuben, 68
Campbell, John, 27
Can You Take It? (play), 205
carrot funk, 243
censorship, 2, 5–8, 57, 60, 197, 202–3
Cherry, Don, 186
chiefs, 34–37, 46–47, 50–51. See also *specific chiefs*
choirs, 67–68, 117–19, 127
choral music, 55–56, 110–11, 128, 198
Christian, Albert, 73
Christianity, 26, 61, 65–66, 75, 137; activism against, 48, 77–78; with colonialism, 30, 47–48, 56; education with, 52–53; in Europe, 20, 28–29, 50; *imbongi* for, 80–81; Wars of Dispossession compared to, 51–52; for Xhosa people, 2–3, 7, 28–29
Churchill, Winston, 116
Church of God and Saints of Christ, 72–73
Ciskei, 104, 111, 183, 206–7; apartheid in, 220–21, 225–26; history of, 5, 10, 13; leadership for, 101, 192, 212, 220; Transkei compared to, 196–97, 225–26. See also homelands
Civil Rights Movement, U.S., 28
Clegg, Johnny, 23–24

Cockrell, Dale, 59–60
Colenso, John William, 68
colonialism, 5–6, 16–17, 39, 51–54, 71; for British empire, 25, 27, 29–33; Christianity with, 30, 47–48, 56; discrimination in, 160; by Europe, 1, 25, 42n46; Frontier Wars during, 4; for *izibongo*, 15, 50–51, 219; politics of, 3, 36–37, 48; psychology of, 46, 49–50, 111–12; in U.S., 64–65; for Xhosa people, 17–18, 26–27, 40
"Color Bar" bill, 103–4, 119–20
communism, 120, 144, 146–47
community consciousness, 186–87
Concepts, Lukae, 247
"coon," 121n7
Coplan, David B., 5, 69, 94, 134–35, 175–76
COVID-19, 247
Cradock, John, 27
Cronin, Jeremy, 140
Crowdy, William Saunders, 73
Crutze, Soloman, 108
Cuddumbey, Errol Eric, 229–30
culture, 1–2; in Africa, 3–4, 21; ANC for, 120–21; after apartheid, 234–35; Bantustans for, 145, 196, 211, 225; Black consciousness for, 202–4; of Black people, 92, 148, 154, 169–70; of Christianity, 26; Cultural Ensembles, 199; cultural identity, 133–34; cultural revolutions, 171; cultural workers, 204–5; for Defiance Campaign, 132–33; of Europe, 28, 54; festivals for, 97–98; hip hop for, 245, 247–48; of homelands, 5, 7, 10, 220, 224; *kwela* in, 5–7, 237; *marabi* in, 93–94, 93–99, 103, 134–35, 156; Marxism in, 110; Mkhonto We Sizwe for, 8–10, 158, 161, 183–84; for Mqhayi, 162; Native Reserve Location Act for, 100–101; during oppression, 13–14; Pan Africanist Congress in, 196, 210–11, 213; peace for, 29–30; for police, 202–3; rap for, 237, 245; Rubusana for, 53–54; of San, 15–16; of school people, 62, 119; Soweto Uprising 1976 for, 173, 193–94; township, 98–101; of Transkei, 11, 192; urban, 91–98; of Xhosa people, 7, 71
The Cure (play), 154–55
curfews, 131–32, 150, 200–201

Daddy, Katt, 244–45
Dalindyebo, Sabatha, 136–40, 146–47, 195, 206–7, 220–21
dance, 22, 65–66, 112, 235
Dargie, David, 21, 24–25
Darkie Fiction (band), 244–45
Davashe, Mackay, 187
Defiance Campaign, 125, 129–36, 178
De Klerk, F. W., 219–20, 222, 225–26
De Pitch Black Follies (group), 112
De Wet, J. M., 177, 179–80
De Wet Nel, Daniel, 145, 159
Dhlamini, Ezekiel, 148
Dike, Fatima, 175–76
Dinca, Walter, 72–73
discrimination, 42n46, 46, 54–60, 70, 91, 160
Dlula, Nomaniso, 119
dock workers strike, 127
Dontsa, Luvuyo, 20
Du Bois, W.E.B., 46, 60, 64
Dukwana, 32
Duli, Craig, 225
Duru, Kenneth, 118–19
Duru, Welcome, 99, 118–19, 128, 154–56
Dutch East India Company, 1
Dwane, James Mata, 65–67
Dwane, Ntombi, 146, 180
Dyani, Johnny Mbizo, 152–54, 185–86, 203–4
Dywili, Nofinish, 188

Eastern Cape. *See specific topics*
Edgar, Robert, 73

education: activism in, 10–11, 159–60; in Africa, 47–48; for African nationalism, 38, 58–59, 110; apartheid for, 167–68, 234–35, 242; Black consciousness in, 190–91; for Black people, 96, 116, 145–46; censorship in, 60; with Christianity, 52–53; in Ciskei, 183; Defiance Campaign in, 131; in Europe, 49–50; Extension of University Education Act, 145; at Fort Hare, 91–92; history of, 46–47; in homelands, 160; identity from, 15–16; literacy from, 48–49; by missionaries, 33, 45–46; racism in, 60, 62–63; for school people, 126, 137, 205, 227; Separate Education Bill, 145; Sharpeville Massacre 1960 for, 146; South African Student Organization, 159, 168–69, 181; after Soweto Uprising 1976, 190; at UNITRA, 11–12, 196; for Xhosa people, 246–47
Ellington, Duke, 152
employment, 98, 111, 127–29, 181, 197–99; Independent Industrial and Commercial Workers' Union for, 103–4, 106–8; Industrial and Commercial Workers' Union for, 72, 93, 103–4
England. *See* British empire
Ethiopia, 116–17
Ethiopianism, 57–58, 65–66
Europe, 4, 25, 31–34, 154, 158; activism against, 130–31; Africa and, 27, 40, 111–12, 126–27; for chiefs, 46–47; Christianity in, 20, 28–29, 50; colonialism by, 1, 25, 42n46; culture of, 28, 54; education in, 49–50; freedom songs in, 199; jazz in, 95–96; racism in, 59, 73–74
Extension of University Education Act, 145

Fanon, Frantz, 169–70

Federation of South African Women, 133
festivals, 97–98
Feza, KiJo, 186
Feza, Mongezi, 153, 186
Fingo Revolution Movement, 13
Fischer, Bram, 116
folk literature, 148–49
Fordyce, John, 114
Fort Hare, 126, 145–46; activism at, 109–10, 131, 177–80; education at, 91–92; police at, 159–60
FOSATU (praise poem), 198–99
Franchise and Ballot Act, 54
Frederickson, George, 75
freedom songs, 7–8, 133–34, 183, 184–85, 199
Frontier Wars. *See specific topics*
Fugard, Athol, 7, 154–55, 170–74, 205, 229, 234

Gaba, Ntsikana, 3
Galela, Champion, 201
Gamede, Vangeli, 211, 219, 224, 237
Garvey, Marcus, 72, 74, 104–5, 107
Gashe, Boet, 6, 94–95, 99
Gcalekas, 23, 50–51
General Agreement on Tariffs and Trade, 232
General Workers Strike, 103–4
Gerhart, Gail, 168
Glen Grey Act, 5, 69–71
Godolozi, Qaqawuli, 201
Goniwe, Matthew, 211–12
Gontsana, Lulu, 6, 187–88
Govender, V. R., 126
Gqoba, W. W., 35–36, 47, 52–53, 77
Gqozo, Oupa, 226
Great Cattle Killing, 3, 35–40, 45–46, 114
Great Depression, 111
Grey, George, 36, 39, 49
Group Areas Act, 7, 229
Gwashu, Enoch Fikile, 128

Hale, Edward Everette, 87n55
Hamba Kahle mKhonto (Mkhonto We Sizwe anthem), 212–13
"Hamba Kahle Mkhonto, Mkonto, Mkhonto we Sizwe (Go well, Mkhonto we Sizwe)," 227
"Hambani Madoda" (song), 149
Hani, Chris, 13, 202, 210, 224–27
Hansen, Deidre, 192–93
Hashe, Sipho, 201
The Heart of Redness (Mda, Z.), 35, 236–37
Hertzog, James, 74–75, 102–4, 108–9, 222
hip hop, 13, 227, 236, 240–48
HIV/AIDS epidemic, 232–33, 247
Hodgson, Janet, 29
Holomisa, Bantu, 11, 213, 220–21, 225
"Holy Ntsikana (on events that occurred c. 1800–21)" (Yali-Manisi), 31
homelands, 13, 160, 190–91; culture of, 5, 7, 10, 220, 224; politics of, 136, 157, 167, 192, 195–96, 226
How Long? (play), 173, 190
Huddleston, Trevor, 150
human rights, 231–33
Huskison, Yvonne, 160
hymns, 75, 112, 120; activism for, 73–74; for Black consciousness, 56–57; jazz related to, 93; for Xhosa people, 105–6

ibali, 20
Ibali laMamfengu (Kawa), 24
I Believe (play), 173, 190
Ibhubesi Elehlule Amadoda (Nkunz'emdaka), 239
Ibrahim, Abdullah, 203
"Idabi lama Linde (The Battle of Amalinde)" (Mqhayi), 102
"Idabi laseCacadu (The Battle of Cacadu)," 24
identity, 6, 18, 20, 40, 112; activism for, 75–76; from African nationalism, 49, 65, 91, 248–49; from Black consciousness, 167–68; of Black people, 162; in colonialism, 52–53; cultural, 133–34; from education, 15–16; in homelands, 190–91; from performance, 22, 93; from white paternalism, 126; for Xhosa people, 13–14, 32–33, 56–57, 115–16
ideology, 7–9, 52–53, 177–79, 182, 184, 186
iDoyili parties, 99
"igwatyu (national song)," 23
ihlombe, 21–22
"The Image of the Book in Xhosa Oral Poetry" (Opland), 34–35
imbongi: activism for, 206–7; for African nationalism, 101–2; after apartheid, 228–29, 237–38; in Black Theater, 175; censorship of, 57, 197; for Christianity, 80–81; culture of, 4; history in, 30–31, 136; for identity, 18; with *izibongo*, 19–20; leadership for, 139, 223–24; magistrates for, 50; Yali-Manisi as, 144; memory in, 37; for Mqhayi, 55; nature in, 77; poetry for, 12, 18–19; politics for, 4–5, 125; rap by, 13; Sharpeville Massacre 1960 for, 229; spoken word, 129; style, 76; war for, 26–27; women as, 239–40
Imihobe Nemobongo (Mqhayi), 68
impundulu, 27
Independent Industrial and Commercial Workers' Union, 103–4, 106–8
Industrial and Commercial Workers' Union, 72, 93, 103–4
"Ingoma yaba-ntwana base Africa (Song of the children of Africa)" (Solilo), 83–84
"Ingxoxo (Inyembezi ezingenamsuli)" (Solilo), 81–83
Inkululeko yase Sieskei (Mayoli), 206–7
"Inkunziyakuthi eQunu iphumil' esikiti (Our bull has escaped from the pound)" (Xozwa), 222
In Township Tonight! (Coplan), 5

intsomi, 76, 188, 216n70
"Inyameko (Perseverance)" (Matshikiza, P.), 153
"Iqilika" (Motsieloa), 96–97
The Island (play), 234
"I Tye lesiseko se Tiyopiya! (Foundation stone of Ethiopia!)" (Mqhayi), 115–16
izibongo: activism with, 2; apartheid during, 66, 138–39, 227–28; colonialism for, 15, 50–51, 219; in employment, 197; for Europe, 33–34; *imbongi* with, 19–20; in *marabi*, 237–38; for Mathanzima, K., 207; paronomasia in, 88n77; performance of, 101–2; for religion, 84; Wars of Dispossession in, 53–54; for women, 238–39
"Izwe Lethu (This Land is Ours)," 8

Jabavu, D. D. T., 106–7
Jabavu, John Tengo, 49, 54–55, 60, 115
Jabavu, Mac, 104
Jacobs, Lumkile, 128
jazz: activism with, 147–48; for Africa, 3–4, 6–7, 93–95, 112, 184; apartheid related to, 9–10, 229–30; for Black consciousness, 161, 239–40; for Black people, 153–54; culture of, 5–6; in Europe, 95–96; hymns related to, 93; ideology in, 8–9; with *mbaqanga*, 112, 189; performance of, 7; reputation of, 151; for Union of Southern African Artists, 149–50; in U.S., 128–29, 152; after World War II, 127–28; for Xhosa people, 204
Johnson, Shawn, 224
Jones, Peter, 182–83
Jonguhlahoga. *See* Dalindyebo
Jordan, A. C., 47–48, 50, 52, 109
Jordan, Pallo, 153–54, 186, 204
Jules-Rosette, Bennetta, 69

Kadalie, Clements, 103–8
Kaffir Express, 33, 42n46

Kani, John, 171–72, 234
Kasrils, Ronnie, 161, 226
Kati, Tata James "Castro," 210
Kavanagh, Robert Mshengu, 147
Kawa, R. T., 24
Kente, Gibson, 7, 155–56, 170–74, 190, 205, 235
"Khawuleza (Hurry, Mama)" (song), 185
Khayinga, Wilson, 142–44
Khoi/Khoi-Khoi, 1–2, 6, 15–18, 21, 28
King, Martin Luther, Jr., 28
King Cole Basses (group), 128
King Kong (musical), 148–49, 155
Korsten Village, 100
Kota-Fredericks, Zou, 206
Kruger, Jimmy, 191
Kulman, Whitey, 151
Kuti, Fela, 9
Kwaito, 235, 243–44, 248
Kwatsha, Gogi, 128
kwela, 5–7, 134–35, 136, 150–52, 204, 237
Kwela, Allen, 185

Laduma (It Thundered) (play), 205
Laliboi, 243
Lebakeng, Shirley Lineo, 188–89
Leballo, Potlako. *See* Poqo
Lembede, Anton, 7, 126
Leruthla, Rachel, 227
Lichenstein, H., 22
literacy, 48–49
Long Walk to Freedom (Mandela), 19
Loubère, Limon de la, 16–17
Louden, Frederick, 58–59
Lovedale, 48–49, 56, 61–62, 179
Lucky Stars (group), 112
Luthuli, Albert, 129–30
Luzipho, Vuyelwa Qwesha, 188–89

Mabunu, Nelson, 139–40
Machiavelli, Niccola, 154
Maclennan, Don, 174
Madikane (chief), 23

Madinda, Xolile (X), 13, 241–42, 245
Maduba, Robert, 119
Mafani, Akhona, 238
Mafu, Dumisani, 211
Magada, Mabel, 154
Magade, Joel, 105–6
magistrates, 50
Mahabane, Z. R., 76, 109–11
Makalima, Azlan, 245
Makeba, Miriam, 2, 128, 129, 134; reputation of, 18; singing by, 8; Xhosa style for, 185
Makinana, Silimela, 101
Makiwane, Elijah, 49, 114–15, 145–46
Makwezela, Bulelo ("Bully"), 119
Malan, D. F., 108
Malcolm X, 28, 158
Mandela, Nelson, 4, 6–7, 13, 19, 240; activism by, 91, 194–95; African nationalism for, 115; during apartheid, 138–39; in debates, 136; imprisonment of, 8, 142; leadership of, 119, 183, 224; legacy of, 141–42, 231; for Yali-Manisi, 228; oppression of, 141; release of, 12, 219, 225–26; reputation of, 221–23, 228–29; at Robben Island, 191, 195; trial of, 152; violence for, 158
La Mandragola (Machiavelli), 154
Maneta, Rofhiwa, 235
Mangcu, Xolela, 121
Manisi, D. L. P., 125–26
Manisi, David, 11, 19, 136–37, 144, 248; activism for, 31–32; for African liberation, 65–67; African nationalism for, 38–39; Black people for, 193–95; Mandela for, 228; missionaries for, 39–40; for Opland, 216n70; poetry by, 138–40, 207–9; royal family for, 193
Manye, Charlotte. *See* Maxeke, Charlotte
Maqoma, 51

marabi, 5–7, 111–12, 150, 237–38; in culture, 93–99, 103, 134–35, 156; performance of, 118, 128
Marikana Massacre, 240–41
Marxism, 110
Masabalala, Samuel Makana, 103–4
Masekela, Hugh, 185
Masiza, Hamilton, 97
Maskandi music, 239
Masondo, Andrew, 145
Mathanzima, George, 220
Mathanzima, Kaiser, 10–11, 20–221, 34, 206–7, 225; criticism of, 156–58, 191, 193–97; leadership of, 136–40, 146–47, 210–11
Matji, Robert Mkxotho, 125
Matomela, Florence, 133
Matshikiza, Meekly "Fingertips," 153
Matshikiza, Pat, 152–54, 185, 203
Matshikiza, Todd, 94–95, 148–49, 153
Matthews, Frieda Bokwe, 96, 126
Matthews, Joe, 126
Matthews, Z. K., 96–98, 116, 126
Matyu, Jimmy, 118
Mavimebela, John, 111
Maxeke, Charlotte (neé Manye), 63–65, 76, 80, 109, 115–16
Maxeke, Marshal, 64, 80
"Maxhegwana (Little Old Man)" (Matshikiza, P.), 153
Mayibuye Cultural Ensemble, 9–10, 199
Mayoli, Sizwe, 206–7
Mazwi, B. S., 76
Mbambisa, Fats, 152
Mbambisa, Ida, 152
Mbambisa, Tete, 152–53, 187
mbaqanga, 6–7, 151, 184–86, 204; jazz with, 112, 189; U.S., for, 128, 156
mbayizelo dance songs, 22
Mbeki, Govan, 91, 93, 109–10; activism by, 125, 132, 145; communism for, 144
Mbeki, Thabo, 187
Mbutuma, Melikhaya, 11, 125–26, 136; apartheid for, 195; for Dalindyebo,

140; with Yali-Manisi, 137; politics of, 157–58
McAdoo, Eugene, 61–62
McAdoo, Orpheus, 58–65
McConnachie, Boudina, 246–47
McGregor, Chris, 7, 152–53, 161–62, 186–88
McGregor, Tony, 161–62
McLaren, Rob, 174–75
Mda, Ashby, 7
Mda, Zakes, 35, 170–71, 189, 234, 236–37
Mdalidiphu, 30
Mdlalose, Frank, 131
Merklein, Johann Jakob, 17
Mfecane, 46
Mfengu, 37, 50–51, 54
Mfengu people, 46
Mgcina, Sophie, 13
Mgijima, Enoch, 72–73
Mgqwetho, Nontsizi, 4, 76–81, 88n77
Mhlaba, Raymond, 130–31
Mhlauli, Sicelo, 211–12
middle class, 97–98
"Mind in Chains" (Yahkeem), 13
Mines and Works Amendment Act, 103
Mini, Nomokhosi, 205–6
Mini, Vuyisile, 129–30, 140, 142–44
minstrelsy, 59, 121n7
missionaries, 4, 20, 28–29, 96–97, 109; education by, 33, 45–46; Lovedale for, 48–49; for Yali-Manisi, 39–40
Mjo, Sergeant, 128
Mkaba, Zinakile, 142–44
Mkhonto, Sparrow, 211–12
Mkhonto We Sizwe: for culture, 8–10, 158, 161, 183–84; leadership for, 202, 210–13, 220, 223, 225; reputation of, 8, 141, 199, 213, 224, 227. *See also* ANC
Mkiva, Zolani, 231
Mkutukana, Bulelwa (Zahara), 240
Mkuzo, Nomzamo, 189
Mkwayi, Wilton, 143
Mlanjeni, 28

Mnika, Alfred, 105–6
Modisane, Jerry, 179
Moholo, Louis, 185–86
Mokone, Mangena, 65–67
"Molweni nonke," 22
Momvete, Eric, 161
Monaheng, Tseliso, 243
Monk, Thelonius, 152
Moroka, James, 109, 130
Motsieloa, Griffiths, 96–97
Moyake, Nick, 152–53
Mozambique, 170
Mpumlwana, Malusi, 182
Mpupha, Dumisa, 5, 27, 237–38
Mqhayi, Samuel Edward Drune, 4, 18–20, 30–31, 55, 121; Africa for, 102–3; African nationalism for, 49; British empire for, 101–2; culture for, 162; history for, 110, 112–16; influence of, 137; Nongqawuse for, 37–39; Nqangomhlaba for, 106; poetry by, 68–69, 76; reputation of, 80–81; World War II for, 117
Mqhayisa, Khayalethu, 176–77
Mqoko, Nombasa, 240
Mralatya, Mlendelwa (Nkunz'emdaka), 239
Msaki, 240–41
Msikinya, John, 73
Msila, Vuyisile, 125, 127, 180–81, 183, 200, 202
Mthethwa, Nathi, 235
Mtintso, Thenijwe, 180, 182
Mtsaka, Julius, 174
Mtuze, Peter Tshobisa, 222, 238
music. *See specific topics*
Muyanga, Neo, 240–41
Mvana, Asanda (Msaki), 240–41
Mzamane, Mbulelelo Vizikhungo, 169, 189–90
Mzimba, Pambani, 49–50, 114–15

Namibia, 184
"nansi 'ndondemnyama we Verwoerd" (song), 143–44

Native Administration Act, 103
Native Affairs Department, 111
Native Reserve Location Act, 100–101
native reserves. *See*
  Bantustans; homelands
Natives Land Act, 5, 10, 72, 75–76, 92
Natives' Representative Council, 108–9
Natives Urban Areas Act, 75–76, 92–93
Ncamashe, S. M. *See* Burns-Ncamashe, S. M.
Ndela, Stokwe (chief), 24
Ndlazilwana, Victor, 112
Ndondo, Bathandwa, 211
New Brighton township, 100–101
Ngozi, Winston Mankunku, 184, 229
Ngqawana, Zim, 187, 230–31
Ngquika, 18
Ngubane, Jordan, 119–20
Nguni people, 1–2
Ngxokolo, Mike, 128
Nhalpo, Walter, 112, 121
Njongwe, Lowell Zwelinzima, 125
Njongwe, "Nompie," 131
Nkodlwane, Siphosenkosi (Laliboi), 243
Nkosi, Lewis, 6, 150, 155
"Nkosi Sikilel' iAfrika" (Sontonga), 10, 56, 68–69
Nkunz'emdaka, 239
Nkwenkwe, Nontheta, 73–74
Nobanda, Thembeka, 159
Nobaza, Dorrington, 138
No-Good Friday (Fugard), 155
Nomvete, Eric, 153
Nongqawuse, 37–39
"No talili," 22
Nqangomhlaba (chief), 106
Nteyi, Tyala, 113–14
Ntola, Jansen Jongilizwe (chief), 157
Ntsele, "Big T," 151
Ntshinga, James, 118–19
Ntshinga, Norman, 128
Ntshona, Winston, 171–72
Ntsikana, 26–33, 40
Ntsikana kaGaba music, 26–35
Ntsiko, Jonas, 47

Nxele, Makhanda, 26–33, 40

Opland, Jeff, 18, 34–35, 80, 137; Mandela for, 139; Yali-Manisi for, 216n70; Mathanzima, K., for, 193; Mbutuma with, 207
oppression: in Africa, 51; during apartheid, 4–5, 125–26, 152; of Black consciousness, 198–200; of Black people, 6–7, 135, 150; culture during, 13–14; of curfews, 200–201; of Mandela, 141; of Pan Africanist Congress, 146, 167, 191; poetry against, 7–8; by police, 132; politics of, 47; psychological, 39; with segregation, 5–6; after Sharpeville Massacre 1960, 8; from State Security Council, 200; from Transkeian Territorial Authority, 146–47; in U.S., 58

"Paint Riot," 131–32
Pan Africanist Congress: in activism, 140–41, 180–82; ANC with, 141, 146, 180; in culture, 196, 210–11, 213; history of, 8, 10; oppression of, 146, 167, 191; politics for, 219–20, 224, 226
pantsula dance, 235
Parliamentary Voters Registration Act, 54
paronomasia, 88n77
Pasha, Beauty, 151
Pasha, Patrick, 7, 128, 151–52, 187
"Pasopa nansi 'ndondemnyama we Verwoerd (Look out, Verwoerd, here are the Black people)" (Mini, V.), 129
peace, 29–32, 40, 51–52
performance: activism and, 248–49; African nationalism in, 101; for ANC, 117–18, 205–6; by Black people, 147–48; boycotts in, 209; censorship of, 7–8, 202–3; Defiance Campaign in, 135–36; of hip hop,

242–43; identity from, 22, 93; ihlombe in, 21–22; of *izibongo*, 101–2; of jazz, 7; of *marabi*, 118, 128; of *mbaqanga*, 151; of poetry, 18–19; politics of, 11–12, 217n85; at T. C. White Hall, 118; in Transkei, 216n70; in U.S., 58–59
Pityana, Barney, 159, 169, 177–78
Plaatje, Solomon, 68'
"Plea for Africa" (Bokwe), 56
poetry: for activism, 80–85; colonialism for, 5; Great Cattle Killing in, 114; history in, 222; for *imbongi*, 12, 18–19; by Yali-Manisi, 138–40, 207–9; by Mqhayi, 68–69, 76; against oppression, 7–8; performance of, 18–19; politics in, 50; praise, 197; by Qabula, 197–98; rap compared to, 13; Robben Island in, 223–24; women in, 79–80
police: activism for, 103–4, 142–43; for Black people, 99; boycotts for, 178–79; culture for, 202–3; at Fort Hare, 159–60; Marikana Massacre by, 240–41; for Msila, 200; oppression by, 132; reputation of, 176–77; Security Police, 187; theater groups for, 155; violence by, 131, 181–83, 200, 225–26
politics: of activism, 45, 132, 134–35, 210–13; of African nationalism, 7, 120, 127, 147; of apartheid, 156–57, 231; of Bantustans, 157, 160, 167, 190–91; for Black people, 111–12, 161; of Black Peril election, 102–3; of Black Theater, 170–77; of British empire, 69–70; of Christianity, 61; of colonialism, 3, 36–37, 48; in employment, 198–99; of homelands, 136, 157, 167, 192, 195–96, 226; for *imbongi*, 4–5, 125; of *marabi*, 111–12; of *mbaqanga*, 184–85; of Mbutuma, 157–58; of oppression, 47; for Pan Africanist Congress, 219–20, 224, 226; of performance, 11–12, 217n85; in poetry, 50; South African Communist Party in, 120; of "total strategy," 199–200; in Transkei, 196; of voting, 108–9; women in, 205–6
Poqo, 8, 141–42
Port Elizabeth Black Civic Organization, 182, 201–2
Posel, Deborah, 129
praise poetry, 197
praise singers. *See* imbongi
praise songs. *See* izibongo
Present-world (Gqoba), 52–53, 57, 77–78
propaganda, 160–61
protest. *See* activism
psychological oppression, 39
psychology, 46, 49–50, 57–58, 91, 111–12, 212–13
Pukwana, Dudu, 152–53, 186, 229

Qabula, Alfred Temba, 11, 197–98, 227–28
Qangule, Mncedisi, 206
"Quongqothwane (The Click Song)," 18

racism, 57–63, 70, 73–76, 84, 127, 160
Radebe, Mark, 97
Radio Bantu, 160
Rally. *See* Mini, Nomokhosi
Ramphele, Mamphela, 182
rap, 13, 237, 240–43, 245, 248
Rathebe, Dolly, 129
Reagan, Ronald, 209
red people, 3, 36, 45–47, 93, 192; Red Location for, 99, 119, 127, 131, 156, 200–201; school people compared to, 63, 77–78, 236
religion, 28–29, 58–60, 65–66, 65–67, 110–11, 121n7, 198; biblical characters, 118; hymns, 56–57, 73–75, 93, 105–6, 120; *izibongo* for, 84. *See also specific topics*
religious separatism, 57, 69–70, 72, 103–5, 107–8

resistance. *See specific topics*
Rhodes, Cecil, 54, 70
Rhodesia, 158. *See also* Zimbabwe
Rivonia Trial, 142
Roach, Max, 230
Robben Island, 223–24; Mandela at, 191, 195; prison on, 36–37, 155, 172, 176, 182–83
Robeson, Paul, 111–12
Roosevelt, Franklin, 116
Ross, Johannes Jurgens, 145
Rubusana, Walter, 49, 53–54, 115, 162

Sabata (chief). *See* Dalindyebo
Sachs, Albie, 233–34
Sampson, Anthony, 148–49
San, 15–18, 21
Sandile (chief), 34, 50, 76, 113
San people, 1–2
Sarhili (chief), 37, 50–51
Saul, Pinise, 152
Scheub, Harold, 216n70
school people, 3, 45–46, 52, 192; activism for, 178, 182; culture of, 62, 119; education for, 126, 137, 205, 227; leadership for, 242; red people compared to, 63, 77–78, 236; reputation of, 93
Scott, Ronnie, 186
Scully, William Charles, 23
Sebe, Charles, 196, 220, 225–26
Sebe, Lennox, 225–26
Sebenzile, Zalabe, 13
Security Police, 187
Selula (Daddy and Yoza), 244
Seme, Pixley, 110
"Senzeni Na?" ("*Senzenina*"), 8–9
Separate Amenities Act, 7, 135
Separate Education Bill, 145
separatist churches, 66–67
Serpent Players, 154–55, 170–72, 205
settler policies, 45
sexism, 238–39
Sharpeville Massacre, 8, 140–41, 146, 200, 222, 229

shebeen queens, 98–99
Sigcau, Botha (chief), 191–92
Sigcawu, Zwelonke, 238
Sihlali, Simon, 49
Sikalo (Kente), 156
Silgee, Wilson "King Force," 94, 98–99
Sililo, Edward, 93
Singana, Margaret, 188–89
Sisulu, Albert, 119
Sisulu, Walter, 7, 56, 126, 142
Sitole, Bongani, 11, 227–29
Siyiyo, Annie, 107
Sizwe Bantu is Dead (*Sizwe*) (play), 171–72, 234
Skweyana, Jamani, 189
Smith, Harry, 50–51, 112–13
Smuts, Jan, 74–75, 102–3, 108, 222
Sobukwe, Robert, 140
Social Darwinism, 40
Soga, John Henderson, 20, 50, 115
Soga, Tiyo, 32–33, 48–50, 52, 112
Solilo, John, 4, 23, 80–84, 94
Sontonga, Enoch, 68
Sotho music, 93
South Africa. *See specific topics*
South African Bantu Board of Music, 97
South African Broadcasting Company, 149–50
South African Communist Party, 120
South African Congress of Trades Unions, 129
South African Defense Force, 201, 226
South African Student Organization, 159, 168–69, 177–79, 181
Soweto Uprising, 9, 173, 183–84, 190, 193–94, 199–200
sports, 181–82
Stallard, Charles, 92
Stallard Doctrine, 92–93
State Security Council, 200
stayaways, 179, 201
Steedman, A., 29
Stewart, James, 62
Stofile, Makhenkesi, 178
strategic violence, 141–42

Suthu (queen), 114

Tambo, Oliver, 7, 91, 119, 126, 222
T. C. White Hall, 118
Tebetjana (musician), 94
Tele, Mandise, 239
Temiz, Okay, 186
Thabethe, Mary. *See* Mini, Nomokhosi
Thamsangqa, K. K., 243
Thatcher, Margaret, 223
theater groups, 154–56
Thembu, 23
"Thina Sizwe," 8
Thixo, 30
Thoroughgood, Sallie Davis, 87n55
tickey draai, 94
Tile, Nehemiah, 65
Tiny Tots (group), 118–19
Tiro, Onkgopotse Ramothibi, 178–79
Tito, Dudley, 7, 151–52, 156
"To Arms!" (Ntsiko), 47
tone, 67–68
tonic solfa, 67–68
Too Late (play), 173–74, 190
torture, 200
"total strategy," 199–200
township culture, 98–101
township music, 7–8
toyi-toyi, 11, 199, 222–23, 226, 228
Tracey, Hugh, 22
Transkei, 5, 8, 10–13, 191–92, 216n70; activism in, 104, 111; ANC in, 210–13; apartheid in, 220–21, 223–24; Black Theater in, 175–76; Ciskei compared to, 196–97, 225–26; colonialism for, 46; politics in, 196; taxes in, 70; Transkeian Territorial Authority, 146–47; Transkei Voters Association, 120. *See also* homelands
Truth and Reconciliation Commission, 183, 231, 234
tsaba tsaba music, 112, 134
Tsewu, Edward, 65–66
Tshangana, Gilpin William, 118–19
Tshinga, Norman, 154
Tshona! (song), 184–85
tula ndivile, 94
Turner, Henry, 65
Turok, Ben, 143–44
Tutu, Desmond, 222
Twala, Dan, 94
Tyamzashe, Benjamin ("B ka T"), 108

ukubongo, 20
umdudo, 22
umgidi, 22
"Umhala wasetywaleni (Umhala the Beer Song)," 22
Union of Southern African Artists, 147–50, 154
United Democratic Front, 200–201
United Kingdom, 223
United Nations, 12
United Negro Improvement Association, 72, 75, 105
United States (U.S.): Black consciousness in, 169; Black people in, 62–63, 74–75; blues music in, 93–94; boycotts in, 154; Civil Rights Movement, 28; colonialism in, 64–65; discrimination in, 57; Europe and, 158; hip hop in, 227; jazz in, 128–29, 152; for *mbaqanga*, 128, 156; missionaries from, 96–97; music in, 87n55; oppression in, 58; performance in, 58–59; religion in, 59–60; United Kingdom and, 223; for Xhosa people, 5–6
University of Transkei (UNITRA). *See* Walter Sisulu University
urban culture, 91–98
U.S. *See* United States
"Usilethela Uxolo (Nelson Mandela Brings Us Peace)," 231
"Utebetjana ufanaNe'mfene (Tebetjana resembles a Baboon)" (Tebetjana), 94

vandalism, 145–46, 159

Verwoerd, Hendrik, 129, 132, 134, 144, 191
Vikiva, Dilesa, 119
violence: with apartheid, 12–13, 132, 142–43, 201; at Bisho massacre, 225–27; by gangs, 119; for Mandela, 158; at Marikana Massacre, 240–41; by police, 131, 181–83, 200, 225–26; psychology of, 212–13, 220; from racism, 127; at Sharpeville Massacre, 8, 140–41, 146, 200, 222, 229; strategic, 141–42; torture, 200; from xenophobia, 244–45
Virginia Jubilee Singers, 58–65
Vlok, Adriaan, 220
Vorster, B. J., 160, 181, 223–24
Voters Registration Act (1887), 70
voting, 108–9, 120

Waiting for Godot (Beckett), 154
Walklett, Albert, 63–64
Walter Sisulu University: activism at, 210–11, 219, 221, 224, 228; education at, 11–12, 196
Waluś, Janusz, 227
War of Mlanjeni, 51
War of the Axe, 24, 72
Wars of Dispossession, 51–54
war songs, 22–25
Washington, Booker T., 58, 60
Wauchope, William, 114–15
"Wenyuk'umbombela (The Train Song)" (Duru, W.), 128
We Shall Sing for the Fatherland (play), 189
"While the City Sleeps" (Cuddumbey), 230
white paternalism, 57–58, 84–85, 95, 108–9, 126
Wilberforce University, 64
Williams, Ulagh, 229
women, 79–80, 98–101, 114, 205–6, 238–40; activism for, 106–7, 117–18, 132–33; in music, 188–89
The Woody Woodpeckers (group), 112

World Festival of African Arts and Culture, 186
World-to-come (Gqoba), 52–53, 77–78
World War I, 75–76, 91, 115
World War II, 116–17, 127–28

X (Madinda), 241–42, 245
Xaba, Nkiho, 161
Xapa Goes to Town (variety show), 153
xenophobia, 244–45
Xhosa people, 245–46; British empire for, 1, 3, 5; chiefs for, 34–35; Christianity for, 2–3, 7, 28–29; Ciskei for, 196–97; colonialism for, 17–18, 26–27, 40; communism for, 146–47; culture of, 7, 71; discrimination against, 42n46; education for, 246–47; folk literature of, 148–49; Great Cattle Killing for, 35–40, 45–46; history of, 1–2, 5–6, 21, 29–30, 53–54, 114; hymns for, 105–6; identity for, 13–14, 32–33, 56–57, 115–16; *imbongi* for, 4; jazz for, 204; leadership for, 30–31; missionaries for, 20; music of, 93; Ntsikana kaGaba music for, 26–35; U.S., for, 5–6; war songs for, 22–25. *See also* Bantu people
Xinwa, Skhala Leslie, 174–75
Xobololo, A. S., 221
Xozwa, L. W. M., 222
Xuma, Alfred, 99, 109, 116, 121
Xuma, Madie Hall, 117–19
xylophones, 204

Yahkeem, 13, 242–43, 246
Yali-Manisi, David. *See* Manisi, David
"Yeha! Watshonona! Afrika! ELundini (Alas! Africa, you fade into the horizon!)" (Mgqwetho), 78–79
Yoza, 244–45

Zahara, 240
Zanengxaki. *See* Mathanzima, Kaiser
Zibi, Edward, 105

Zimbabwe, 184
Zokufa, Lami, 151
Zulu music, 93
Zyl, G. Brand van, 126

About the Author

Lindsay Michie is associate professor of history and co-chair of the Africana Studies Department at the University of Lynchburg. She is the author of *The End of Apartheid in South Africa* and co-editor with Dr. Eunice Rojas of *Sounds of Resistance: The Role of Music in Multicultural Activism*. Michie has a doctorate in modern history from St. Andrew's University and taught at the University of Transkei (now Walter Sisulu University) while also working as a freelance photojournalist in the Eastern Cape during the late 1980s and early 1990s.

www.ingramcontent.com/pod-product-compliance
Lightning Source LLC
Chambersburg PA
CBHW061707300426
44115CB00014B/2590